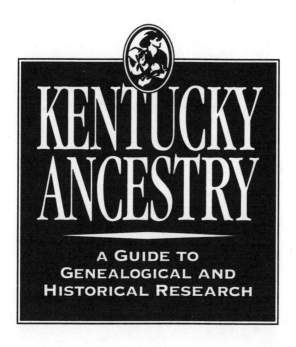

KENTUCKY ANCESTRY

A GUIDE TO GENEALOGICAL AND HISTORICAL RESEARCH

BY

ROSEANN REINEMUTH HOGAN, PH.D.

D1594223

P.O. Box 476
Salt Lake City, UT 84110

Library of Congress
Catalog Card Number 92-28193

ISBN Number 0-916489-49-3

First Printing 1992
10 9 8 7 6 5 4 3 2 1

To the women who inspired my interest in my family history—my sisters Janet and Linda, my mother, Meta Reinemuth Hogan, my aunts, my grandmothers, and my great-grandmothers.

CONTENTS

ACKNOWLEDGMENTS

A reference as detailed as this one can only be accomplished with the help and cooperation of many others. This book is no exception. This reference relied heavily on articles and books published by the many interested and energetic Kentucky historians and genealogists in the state. However, there are a number of people to whom I owe special thanks.

The entire staff of the Kentucky Research Room in the archives is to be commended for their unfailing assistance. Mr. Tim Tingle, an archivist at the Kentucky archives research room, was always there for me when I was on the trail of some obscure discrepancy between what is and what is supposed to be. Ms. Dianne Matzke also provided expertise and cheerful assistance. Finally, Mr. James M. Prichard, also an archivist at the Kentucky archives research room, helped with questions on holdings as well as with updating the county and record destruction listing. Their help was invaluable in making this work accurate.

Likewise, at the University of Kentucky special collections, Ms. Terry Wurth and Ms. Clare McCann were consistently willing and able to help with questions. Ms. Shirley Martin at the Kentucky Department of Vital Statistics was helpful and generous with her time and knowledge.

The inventory of federal records would not have been possible without the unfailing help of two people: Ms. Mona Odle, records deputy, U.S. District Court, western district in Louisville, who provided me with the original transmittal records for the western district, and Mr. David E. Hilkert, archivist at the National Archives-Southeast Region, who continued to answer my letters until the bitter end. With his help, we even uncovered previously undescribed materials from Kentucky's early court history.

Also instrumental to obtaining a complete inventory from the National Archives and Federal Records Centers were Mr. Leslie G. Whitmer, clerk of the U.S. District Court, Eastern District of Kentucky; Mr. Tom Steinichen, chief, Appraisal and Depository Branch of the Federal Records Center; and Mr. Charles Reeves, assistant director, National Archives-Southeast Region.

The courthouse disaster chapter could not have been completed without the help, advice, and previous work of several Kentucky genealogists. Ms. Clifford Wonn of Owingsville provided courthouse information for Bath County, and Ms.

Elizabeth Garr Lawrence made Kentucky's first attempt at bringing order to the history of Kentucky courthouses.

Ms. Linda Anderson at the Kentucky Historical Society provided unpublished lists of courthouse disasters and other information from her files that was critical. Her help and advice throughout this project was always on the mark. Her review of the final draft of this book was especially appreciated and helpful. Mr. Ron Bryant, also of the Kentucky Historical Society staff, helped with finding materials; he answered my numerous questions with humor, enthusiasm, accuracy, and a depth that was appreciated. Ms. Kandie Adkinson of the Land Office of the Secretary of State reviewed the chapter on land grants to ensure its accuracy and currency. Her comments were greatly appreciated.

Other people who also helped along the way: Mr. Donald L. Armstrong, manager, Military Records and Research Branch, Division of Veterans Affairs; Mr. J. Richard Abel, head, History Department, Public Library of Cincinnati and Hamilton County; and Mike Averdick, Kenton County Public Library. I would also like to thank my editor at Ancestry, Ms. Cinde Smith, for her helpfulness, cooperation, patience, and good sense of humor.

Finally, special thanks go to my family. To my son, Derek Haggard: his wit and iconoclastic attitude prevented me from losing perspective. His advice, help in obtaining materials, and readings of earlier drafts helped ensure the book's validity and readability. To my husband, Dennis Haggard: his continuing support of all my various projects, including this one, is greatly appreciated yet rarely communicated. His attentiveness, advice, and readings of early drafts improved the work and sharpened the focus.

INTRODUCTION

While research in each of our fifty states shares common logic, strategy, and problems, each state poses special challenges. Kentucky is no exception; it has a unique history that influenced its people and the records they left behind. Its geography dictated that it would play a key role in the development of the early American frontier, and as a result, Kentucky is a key to many early American family genealogies. A guide to Kentucky resources will enhance the effectiveness of many researchers exploring the history of the commonwealth and its people.

This book on Kentucky resources brings together, in a single, practical reference, up-to-date information on Kentucky's genealogical and historical sources. The holdings of the commonwealth's major statewide archives and libraries are outlined along with information on its courthouses, local libraries, and regional historical societies for each of Kentucky's 120 counties.

ORGANIZATION OF THE CHAPTERS

The most important genealogical archives in Kentucky are the Kentucky Department for Libraries and Archives, the Kentucky Historical Society, the University of Kentucky special collections library, and the Filson Club. Each of these archives, along with other regional libraries with significant historical and genealogical collections, is discussed in chapter 2. The development and functioning of Kentucky's courts and judicial system is traced from their Virginia roots to the fourth Kentucky constitution in chapter 3.

Chapter 4 addresses Kentucky's vital records, their availability, and their interpretation. Chapter 5 continues the discussion of Kentucky primary records and includes information on early Kentucky land acquisition along with tax, census, military, and naturalization records. For each record, factors affecting content, accuracy, and availability are discussed. Chapter 6 is devoted to the special problems and resources available in searching for Kentucky's women and African-American families.

The scope and diversity of Kentucky's secondary sources is impressive. Printed materials as well as other secondary research works are covered in chapter 7. Uses of unique resources such as the Kentucky Newspaper Project, and various manuscript collections such as the Draper manuscripts and oral history projects, are discussed.

An inventory of microfilmed local court historical records in the three major Kentucky archives and libraries has been compiled for chapter 8. The repositories surveyed and included in this book are the Kentucky Department for Libraries and Archives, the Kentucky Historical Society Library, and the University of Kentucky special collections library. A comprehensive inventory of each county's microfilmed records including the years of the documents is provided.

Six appendices round out this book. The first is a bibliography of important statewide historical and genealogical published materials. The second is a collection of maps marking county boundary changes throughout Kentucky's history. Appendix 3 lists Kentucky journals and publication sources specializing in Kentucky material. The fourth appendix is a bibliography of sources of African-American genealogy for Kentucky. An annotated bibliography of social history references and novels makes up appendix 5. Appendix 6 is a compilation of all known county and state historic site surveys.

CHAPTER 1

EARLY KENTUCKY SETTLEMENT

While Kentucky was formed in 1792 from Virginia, the first land companies and surveyors explored the state as early as 1750. After the revolution was over and settlement of Kentucky was safe, its population grew rapidly. The number of Kentuckians nearly tripled in the ten years from 1790 when there were 61,133 residents to 179,873 by 1800 (Purvis 1982, 261).

Several factors encouraged such rapid growth. An expanding population in the eastern states was a major factor. In addition, the influx of Revolutionary War soldiers contributed to the rise in Kentucky's population as they and their families joined the migration into Kentucky to claim service bounty lands.

Another important factor contributing to Kentucky's early settlement was the rapid exhaustion of the tidewater's tillable land due to Virginia's exploitative agricultural practices. Without rotation of crops or artificial fertilizers, new land had to be cleared for cultivation about every seven years (Clark 1960, 61). Farmers boasted about the number of farms they depleted during their lives. As a result, there was strong pressure for new land, not only because of a rapidly expanding population, but also because of the deteriorating value of land for agricultural uses.

The promise that drew many of these early frontier families to Kentucky was one of plentiful, cheap, fertile land. But the promise of rich land was not the only reason, and in some cases it may not have even been a major reason. Kentucky was not simply an early frontier settlement, but a promised land. Rumor had transformed Kentucky into a rich and strange legend over a century before the first white settlements in the state. Kentucky had become the romantic, nearly mythical, paradise of the eighteenth century fueled by extravagant reports from Indian and white explorers. One minister called heaven "a Kentucky kind of place" (Moore 1957, 11–43). Land speculators naturally used these stories to their advantage in advertisements in the hopes of driving up the prices of their cheaply bought land.

Faced with less productive agricultural lands and the promise of new lands in Kentucky, thousands of Virginians and North Carolinians set out over the Blue Ridge Mountains into the rich farming areas of the Bluegrass, the Ohio River Basin, and the western regions of the state.

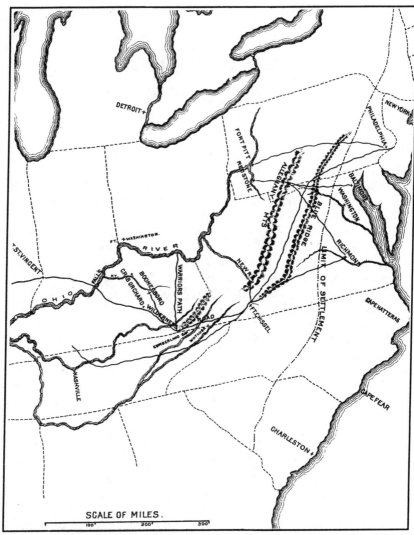

FIG. 1.1 Travel routes of early Kentucky settlers. (*The Wilderness Road*, Speed 1886)

PIONEER ROUTES

These early settlers to Kentucky generally took one of two major routes. One route followed the Ohio River into Kentucky. Many early settlers who arrived by this route came from Maryland and Pennsylvania. They left Pittsburgh and floated down the Ohio River to Kentucky. One of the early stopping points for this route was Limestone, now Maysville, Kentucky.

A majority of pioneers, however, came to Kentucky through the Cumberland Gap along the famous Wilderness Trail from Virginia through the Appalachian Mountains. The Gap was of critical importance in the settlement of the West, because it was the only natural route through the Appalachian Mountains. As a result, the Wilderness Trail continued to be an important route for westbound settlers until the Civil War. Of the approximately 400,000 pioneers who came west before 1800, it is estimated that three-quarters used the Cumberland Gap route (Dietz 1976, 114; Kincaid 1973).

The settlers who used the Wilderness Trail originated from as far north as Pennsylvania, but the majority came from Virginia and North Carolina. From the southeast corner of Kentucky, where the Gap is located, they proceeded north and westward along the Warrior's Path to the Bluegrass region, to the Ohio River Basin and northern Kentucky, and to the falls of the Ohio, now Louisville. Even today, Lexington, Louisville, and the cities in northern Kentucky on the Ohio River opposite Cincinnati, have the largest populations and dominate the state economically.

EARLY KENTUCKY POPULATION AND MIGRATIONS

The composition of the Kentucky population in 1790, based on recently completed analyses, was primarily English (Hammon 1986; Purvis 1982; Sanderlin 1987). Table 1.1 is reproduced from one of the latest studies (Purvis 1982, 259).

Analysis of the surnames of the surrounding states of North Carolina, Virginia, Maryland, Pennsylvania, and Tennessee indicate that Kentucky probably drew its earliest settlers from North Carolina and Virginia, possibly in equal proportions. The low percentage of Germans among the 1790 taxpayers may indicate that relatively fewer settlers from Pennsylvania and Maryland moved to Kentucky by 1790 (Purvis 1982, 260-61).

TABLE 1.1	Distribution of White Population of Kentucky by National Descent, 1790–1820	
Surname Origin Head of Household	1790 Estimate (%)	1820 Estimate (%)
English	51.6	56.6
Scotch-Irish	24.8	18.2
Irish	9.0	8.2
Welsh	6.7	8.7
German	4.9	5.6
French	1.6	1.5
Dutch	1.2	1.0
Swedish	.2	.2

Source: Purvis 1982, 259-63.

After 1790, there was an increase in the proportion of Germans in Kentucky indicating that there may have been an increase of settlers from Pennsylvania and Maryland during the years 1790 to 1820 (Purvis 1982, 263). By 1820, Kentucky's population more closely resembled that of Virginia than that of North Carolina, substantiating the popular view that there was a large migration of pioneers from Virginia during these early years. After 1820, Kentucky ceased to attract large numbers of settlers into its borders, and thus began the great net migration loss of surplus population that lasted for the next 150 years until the 1970s (Purvis 1982, 266).

These surname studies, of course, underestimate the non-English speaking population for several reasons. First, many surnames are changed, adopted from English names, or simply anglicized. As a result, names such as Carpenter, Miller, Smith, etc., which would naturally be counted as English, may actually be German families originally named Zimmerman, Mueller, or Schmitt. Second, these studies can only count the ethnic origin of male heads of households. The ethnic origin of the total population, such as married women and their families is not considered in these studies. Nevertheless, this analysis gives us the best estimate possible of the ethnic composition of early Kentucky.

The ethnic composition of Kentucky may also be investigated by examining the origins of Revolutionary veterans. Analysis of the veterans on Kentucky pension rolls, whose military service could be identified, shows that ninety percent of the Revolutionary pensioners came from four states. A majority, sixty-one percent, were from Virginia. Since Virginia was authorized to grant lands in Kentucky, this should not be particularly surprising. An additional fourteen percent were from North Carolina; nine percent served with Pennsylvania units; and six percent were with Maryland units (Purvis 1982, 263-64).

By 1880, eighty percent of Kentucky residents who had been born outside of the state came from just five states: Tennessee, Virginia, Ohio, Indiana, and

North Carolina. Of the 454,000 who had moved to other states by 1880, nearly seventy-five percent had moved to Missouri, Indiana, Illinois, Texas, Kansas, and Ohio (Ford 1982, 12).

HISTORY OF KENTUCKY'S COUNTY BOUNDARIES

Because the Kentucky General Assembly has authorized 120 counties, knowledge of the formation of Kentucky counties and development of current county borders is a challenge to all Kentucky genealogists. Small tracts of land were exchanged among neighboring counties, and new counties formed as late as 1912. The tables contained in this chapter are a preliminary effort to bring some order to the mass of conflicting information on the development of Kentucky county boundaries. Courthouse construction and disaster dates have also been compiled and are included here in table 1.4. Maps showing Kentucky's county boundary changes through the years can be found in appendix 2.

KENTUCKY COUNTIES PRIOR TO STATEHOOD

Kentucky County was formed in 1776 from Virginia. Prior to that time, from 1 December 1772 to 31 December 1776, the area was Fincastle County, Virginia. It was during the four years of Fincastle's existence that many pioneers and land companies made their way to Kentucky. The three original Kentucky counties of Fayette, Jefferson, and Lincoln were formed in 1780. Together they encompassed all of current-day Kentucky.

By 1792, when Kentucky was made a state, there were six counties in addition to the original three: Nelson, Woodford, Mason, Madison, Bourbon, and Mercer. Lincoln still covered most of the southern part of the state except for a large area that was taken in 1786 to form Madison County. Jefferson's area had been substantially reduced with the creation of Nelson County; and Fayette's area had been divided to form Mason, Woodford, and Bourbon.

From these nine original counties (together with the Chickasaw Indian Hunting Grounds, or the Jackson Purchase, as it is now known) Kentucky eventually formed 120 counties. Kentucky's county boundaries continued to shift until 1912 with the formation of McCreary County.

County Formation and Final Boundary Dates

Because of the sheer number of counties, the need to have easily accessible information is important in Kentucky genealogical research. Two excellent sources for early Kentucky are Dollarhide's census maps of Kentucky and Rone's *Historical Atlas of Kentucky and Her Counties* (Rone 1965). Table 1.2 gives the effective dates of the counties, parent and progeny counties, and date the county assumed its present boundary.

Interpreting Dates and Boundary Information

Because of the abbreviated format of table 1.2, some explanation is needed to interpret the numbers and dates. The first two columns of the table give the effective date of the county's formation (not the date of the legislation) and the year in which the county assumed its present boundary.

The column labeled "Parent Counties and Gained Areas From" shows those counties from which land was acquired at the time of the county's formation, and subsequent land acquisitions after its formation. Note that only the first generation of parent counties is given. It is necessary to refer to information on these parent counties to completely trace a county's origins.

The "Progeny Counties and Lost Areas To" column includes whole counties or parts of counties that were taken to form new counties. Again, only the first generation of partitioned land is listed. NOT included are counties that were subsequently formed from these offspring counties, or the county's second generation descendants.

For example, the offspring counties of Fayette are listed as Bourbon, Clark, Jessamine, and Woodford. Mason County was encompassed in the original bounds of Fayette. However, it is not listed in this table since it was second generation offspring county formed directly from Bourbon.

The manner in which parentheses are used in this table is important in interpreting the information. First, parenthesis enclosing both the county and the year, such as "(County Year)," indicates that the county acquired or lost land to another county during that year. This does not mean that it was a parent or progeny county, only that land was transferred between the two counties.

> *Example:* "(Pulaski 1826)" listed under Whitley County means that Whitley County acquired a small tract of land from Pulaski in 1826.

The use of the parenthesis to enclose only a year following a county name also has a special meaning. The format "County (and Date)" indicates that the county was formed from, or parent to, another county at the time of the county's formation. In addition, on the date shown in the parenthesis, an additional piece of land was acquired from or lost to that county.

> *Example:* Pulaski (and 1818) listed under Wayne County means that Pulaski was a parent county to Wayne County when it was formed in 1801, and that an additional piece of land was acquired by Wayne from Pulaski's area in 1818.

TABLE 1.2   Parent and Progeny Areas of Kentucky Counties

County	Effective Date Formed	Assumed Current Boundary	Parent Counties and Areas Gained From	Progeny Counties and Lost Areas to
Adair	1802	1860	Green, (Cumberland 1805)	Metcalfe, Russell, (Wayne 1804), (Casey 1844)
Allen	1815	1825	Barren, Warren, (Monroe 1825)	Simpson, (and 1819)
Anderson	1827	1827	Franklin, Mercer, Washington	
Ballard	1842	1886	Hickman, McCracken	Carlisle
Barren	1799	1860	Green, Warren, (and 1827)	Allen, (and 1825), Hart, Metcalfe, Monroe
Bath	1811	1869	Montgomery (Floyd 1818)	Menifee, Morgan
Bell	1867	1867	Harlan, Knox	
Boone	1799	1870	Campbell, (Gallatin 1821)	(Gallatin 1837), (Grant 1870)
Bourbon	1786	1817	Fayette	Clark, (and 1793, 1798), Harrison, Mason, Nicholas, (and 1817)
Boyd	1860	1860	Carter, Greenup, Lawrence	
Boyle	1842	1842	Lincoln, Mercer	
Bracken	1797	1867	Campbell, Mason	Pendleton, Robertson, (Harrison 1820, 1834)
Breathitt	1839	1884	Clay, Estill, Perry	Knott, Lee, Owsley, Wolfe
Breckinridge	1800	1831	Hardin, (Ohio 1831)	Hancock, Meade
Bullitt	1797	1824	Jefferson, (and 1811), Nelson	Spencer
Butler	1810	1890	Logan, (and 1813), Ohio	(Muhlenberg 1890)
Caldwell	1809	1854	Livingston, (Christian 1819)	Hickman, Lyon, Trigg, (and 1825, 1826, 1827)
Calloway	1821	1842	Hickman	Marshall
Campbell	1795	1840	Harrison, Mason, Scott	Boone, Bracken, Kenton, Pendleton
Carlisle	1886	1886	Ballard	
Carroll	1838	1838	Gallatin, Henry, Trimble	
Carter	1838	1869	Greenup, Lawrence	Boyd, Elliott
Casey	1807	1844	Lincoln, (Adair 1844)	(Mercer 1820)

County	Effective Date Formed	Assumed Current Boundary	Parent Counties and Areas Gained From	Progeny Counties and Lost Areas to
Christian	1797	1820	Logan	Henderson, Livingston, Muhlenberg, (Caldwell 1819), (Hopkins 1820), Todd, Trigg
Clark	1793	1852	Bourbon, (and 1798), Fayette	Estill, Montgomery, Powell
Clay	1807	1878	Floyd, Knox, Madison	Breathitt, Jackson, Laurel, Owsley, Perry, (and 1843), (Estill 1815), Leslie
Clinton	1836	1836	Cumberland, Wayne	
Crittenden	1842	1842	Livingston	
Cumberland	1799	1876	Green	Clinton, Metcalfe, Monroe, (and 1830), Russell, (and 1876), Wayne, (Adair 1805)
Daviess	1815	1860	Ohio, (and 1830), (Henderson 1860)	Hancock, McLean
Edmonson	1825	1825	Grayson, Hart, Warren	
Elliott	1869	1869	Carter, Lawrence, Morgan	
Estill	1808	1870	Clark, Madison, (Clay 1815), (Montgomery 1816)	Breathitt, Jackson, Lee, Owsley, Powell
Fayette	1780	1799	Kentucky, Virginia	Bourbon, Clark, Jessamine, Woodford
Fleming	1798	1856	Mason	Floyd, Rowan, (Nicholas 1824, 1816)
Floyd	1800	1884	Fleming, Mason, Montgomery, (and 1818)	Clay, Johnson, Knott, Lawrence, Magoffin, Martin, Morgan, Perry, Pike, (Bath 1818)
Franklin	1795	1827	Mercer, Shelby, (and 1820), Woodford, (Henry 1827), (Owen 1827)	Anderson, Gallatin, Owen
Fulton	1845	1845	Hickman	
Gallatin	1799	1838	Franklin, Shelby, (Boone 1837)	(Boone 1821), Carroll, Owen, (and 1821), Trimble
Garrard	1797	1801	Lincoln, (and 1801), Madison (and 1800), Mercer	
Grant	1820	1870	Pendleton, (Harrison 1827), (Boone 1870)	
Graves	1824	1824	Hickman	
Grayson	1810	1825	Hardin, Ohio	Edmonson
Green	1793	1860	Lincoln, Nelson, (Hardin 1804)	Adair, Barren, Cumberland, Metcalfe, Pulaski, Taylor
Greenup	1804	1860	Mason	Boyd, Carter, Lawrence

County	Effective Date Formed	Assumed Current Boundary	Parent Counties and Areas Gained From	Progeny Counties and Lost Areas to
Hancock	1829	1829	Breckinridge, Daviess, Ohio	
Hardin	1793	1843	Nelson	Breckinridge, Grayson, Hart, Ohio, Larue, Meade, (Green 1804)
Harlan	1819	1878	Knox, (and 1820)	Bell, Leslie, Letcher
Harrison	1794	1867	Bourbon, Scott, (Nicholas 1817), (Bracken 1820, 1834)	Campbell, Robertson, (Grant 1827)
Hart	1819	1825	Hardin, Barren	Edmonson
Henderson	1799	1860	Christian, (Ohio 1810)	Hopkins, Union, Webster, (Daviess 1860)
Henry	1799	1838	Shelby	Carroll, Oldham, Trimble, (Franklin 1827)
Hickman	1821	1845	Caldwell, Livingston	Ballard, Calloway, Fulton, McCracken, Graves
Hopkins	1807	1860	Henderson (Christian 1820)	Webster
Jackson	1858	1858	Clay, Estill, Owsley, Madison, Rockcastle, Laurel	
Jefferson	1780	1824	Kentucky, Virginia	Bullitt, (and 1811), Nelson, Oldham, Shelby
Jessamine	1799	1799	Fayette	
Johnson	1843	1870	Floyd, Lawrence, Morgan	Magoffin, Martin
Kenton	1840	1840	Campbell	
Knott	1884	1884	Breathitt, Floyd, Letcher, Perry	
Knox	1800	1867	Lincoln, (Madison 1805)	Bell, Clay, Harlan, (and 1820), Laurel, (and 1834), Rockcastle, Whitley
Larue	1843	1843	Hardin	
Laurel	1826	1858	Clay, Knox, (and 1834), Rockcastle, Whitley	Jackson
Lawrence	1822	1870	Floyd, Greenup	Boyd, Carter, Elliott, Johnson, Martin, (Morgan 1854)
Lee	1870	1870	Breathitt, Estill, Owsley, Wolfe	
Leslie	1878	1878	Clay, Harlan, Perry	
Letcher	1842	1884	Perry, Harlan	Knott
Lewis	1807	1807	Mason	
Lincoln	1780	1842	Kentucky, Virginia	Boyle, Casey, Garrard, (and 1801), Logan, Madison, Mercer, (and 1810), Pulaski, Rockcastle, Knox, Green
Livingston	1798	1842	Christian	Caldwell, Crittenden, Hickman

County	Effective Date Formed	Assumed Current Boundary	Parent Counties and Areas Gained From	Progeny Counties and Lost Areas to
Logan	1792	1869	Lincoln	Butler, (and 1813), Christian, Muhlenberg, Simpson, (and 1869), Todd, Warren
Lyon	1854	1854	Caldwell	
Madison	1786	1858	Lincoln	Clay, Estill, Garrard, (and 1800), Jackson, (Knox 1805), Rockcastle (and 1821)
Magoffin	1860	1860	Floyd, Johnson, Morgan	
Marion	1834	1834	Washington	
Marshall	1842	1842	Calloway	
Martin	1870	1870	Floyd, Johnson, Lawrence, Pike	
Mason	1789	1867	Bourbon	Bracken, Campbell, Fleming, Greenup, Lewis, Nicholas, Robertson, Floyd
McCracken	1825	1842	Hickman	Ballard
McCreary	1912	1912	Pulaski, Wayne, Whitley	
McLean	1854	1854	Daviess, Muhlenberg, Ohio	
Meade	1824	1824	Breckinridge, Hardin	
Menifee	1869	1869	Bath, Montgomery, Morgan, Powell, Wolfe	
Mercer	1786	1842	Lincoln, (and 1810), (Casey 1820)	Anderson, Boyle, Franklin, Garrard
Metcalfe	1860	1860	Adair, Barren, Cumberland, Green, Monroe	
Monroe	1820	1860	Barren, Cumberland, (and 1830)	(Allen 1825), Metcalfe
Montgomery	1797	1869	Clark	Bath, Floyd, (and 1818), Menifee, Powell, (Estill 1816)
Morgan	1823	1869	Bath, Floyd, (Lawrence 1854)	Elliott, Johnson, Magoffin, Menifee, Rowan, Wolfe
Muhlenberg	1799	1890	Christian, Logan, (Butler 1890)	McLean
Nelson	1785	1824	Jefferson	Bullitt, Green, Hardin, Spencer, Washington
Nicholas	1800	1867	Bourbon, (and 1817), Mason	Robertson, (Fleming 1816, 1824), (Harrison 1817)
Ohio	1799	1854	Hardin	Butler, Daviess, (and 1830), Grayson, McLean, (Henderson 1810), (Breckinridge 1831), Hancock

County	Effective Date Formed	Assumed Current Boundary	Parent Counties and Areas Gained From	Progeny Counties and Lost Areas to
Oldham	1824	1856	Henry, Jefferson, Shelby, (and 1856)	Trimble
Owen	1819	1827	Franklin, Gallatin, (and 1821), Scott, Pendleton	(Franklin 1827)
Owsley	1843	1870	Breathitt, Clay, Estill	Jackson, Lee, Wolfe
Pendleton	1799	1820	Bracken, Campbell	Grant, Owen
Perry	1821	1884	Clay, (and 1843), Floyd	Breathitt, Knott, Leslie, Letcher
Pike	1822	1870	Floyd	Martin
Powell	1852	1869	Clark, Estill, Montgomery	Menifee, Wolfe
Pulaski	1799	1912	Green, Lincoln, (Wayne 1818)	McCreary, Rockcastle, Wayne, (and 1818), (Whitley 1826), (Russell 1839)
Robertson	1867	1867	Bracken, Harrison, Mason, Nicholas	
Rockcastle	1810	1858	Knox, Lincoln, Madison, (and 1821), Pulaski	Jackson, Laurel
Rowan	1856	1856	Fleming, Morgan	
Russell	1826	1876	Adair, Cumberland, (and 1876), Wayne, (Pulaski 1839)	
Scott	1792	1819	Woodford	Campbell, Harrison, Owen
Shelby	1792	1856	Jefferson	Franklin, (and 1820), Gallatin, Henry, Oldham, (and 1856), Spencer
Simpson	1819	1869	Allen, Logan, (and 1869), Warren	(Allen and returned in 1822)
Spencer	1824	1824	Bullitt, Nelson, Shelby	
Taylor	1848	1848	Green	
Todd	1820	1820	Christian, Logan	
Trigg	1820	1827	Caldwell, (and 1825–27), Christian	
Trimble	1837	1838	Gallatin, Henry, Oldham	Carroll
Union	1811	1860	Henderson	Webster
Warren	1797	1827	Logan	Allen, Barren, (and 1827), Edmonson, Simpson
Washington	1792	1834	Nelson	Anderson, Marion
Wayne	1801	1912	Cumberland, Pulaski, (and 1818), (Adair 1804)	Clinton, McCreary, Russell, (Pulaski 1818)
Webster	1860	1860	Henderson, Hopkins, Union	
Whitley	1818	1912	Knox, (Pulaski 1826)	Laurel, McCreary
Wolfe	1860	1870	Breathitt, Morgan, Owsley, Powell	Lee, Menifee
Woodford	1789	1795	Fayette	Franklin, Scott

Current Boundary = date that the county assumed its present boundary

Parent Counties = only direct parent counties are given

Progeny Counties = includes whole and parts of counties directly taken from the county

(County Name) = land was lost or gained from this county other than at the time of formation

Minor boundary shifts are listed individually in table 1.3.

TABLE 1.3	Chronological List of Territory Changes by County	
Date of Change	County from Which Land Was Transferred	County to Which Land Was Transferred
1794	Bourbon	Harrison (see 1795)
1795	Harrison	Campbell (see 1794)
1798	Bourbon	Clark
1800	Madison	Garrard
1801	Lincoln	Garrard
1804	Hardin	Green
	Adair	Wayne
1805	Madison	Knox
	Cumberland	Adair
1810	Lincoln	Mercer
	Ohio	Henderson
1811	Jefferson	Bullitt
1813	Logan	Butler
1815	Clay	Estill
1816	Montgomery	Estill
	Nicholas	Fleming
1817	Bourbon	Nicholas
	Nicholas	Harrison
1818	Montgomery	Floyd
	Pulaski	Wayne
	Wayne	Pulaski
	Floyd	Bath
1819	Allen	Simpson (returned in 1822)
	Christian	Caldwell
1820	Bracken	Harrison
	Christian	Hopkins
	Casey	Mercer
	Knox	Harlan
	Shelby	Franklin
1821	Gallatin	Owen
	Gallatin	Boone
	Madison	Rockcastle

Date of Change	County from Which Land Was Transferred	County to Which Land Was Transferred
1824	Fleming	Nicholas
1825	Caldwell	Trigg
	Barren	Allen
	Monroe	Allen
1826	Caldwell	Trigg
	Pulaski	Whitley
1827	Caldwell	Trigg
	Warren	Barren
	Owen	Franklin
	Henry	Franklin
	Harrison	Grant
1830	Ohio	Daviess
	Cumberland	Monroe
1831	Ohio	Breckinridge
	Pulaski	Wayne (Clarifying Act)
1834	Knox	Laurel
	Bracken	Harrison
1837	Boone	Gallatin
1839	Pulaski	Russell
1843	Clay	Perry
1844	Adair	Casey
1854	Lawrence	Morgan
1856	Shelby	Oldham
1860	Henderson	Daviess
1869	Logan	Simpson
1870	Boone	Grant
1876	Cumberland	Russell
1890	Butler	Muhlenberg

Source: Rone 1965, 34–39.

COURTHOUSE CONSTRUCTION AND DISASTER DATES

Construction and disaster dates for all Kentucky county courthouses are given in table 1.4. A number of sources have been used to compile this data including information from the Kentucky Historical Society (Hearn 1973) and the Kentucky archives (Pritchard 1989).

Four additional published sources were also used: (1) Garr's *History of Kentucky Courthouses* (Garr 1972); (2) *Kentucky Courthouses* (Carpenter 1988); (3) *Kentucky Treasure Trails* (Henderson 1977); and (4) *History of Kentucky* (Collins

1976). County histories were also consulted to resolve conflicting dates. Nevertheless, in some cases, consistent data is simply unavailable.

Conflicting courthouse construction and disaster dates are sometimes due to lack of clear definitions rather than inaccuracies. For example, some authors inconsistently report the date construction began or was authorized by the court; others report when the building was completed. Completion dates are also inconsistently reported as the date a building was accepted or when it was formally dedicated.

Similar confusion exists for the disaster dates. Some reports of "courthouse" fires were actually burnings of other buildings such as the jails, court clerk's offices, or even private homes that housed important records. Since early Kentucky records were not always kept in the courthouse, dates regarding "courthouse" fires are often confused. In some counties, courthouses were used solely to hold court and not necessarily to store records. As a result, the extent of record destruction is even more inconsistently reported by these various sources.

Dates given for the courthouses in table 1.4 are the dates the courthouses were completed, not authorized by the court, or when construction was begun. Dates shown for the disasters are dates of courthouse disasters, unless otherwise indicated in the footnotes. The letter "R" after a date indicates a major renovation. A dash (–) indicates that the first structure used as a courthouse was a converted structure, and the dates of construction are unknown.

TABLE 1.4	County Courthouse Construction and Disaster Dates

County	Courthouse Completed						Courthouse Disasters		
	1st	2nd	3rd	4th	5th	6th	1st	2nd	3rd
Adair	1806	1884							
Allen	1816	1903	1969				1902		
Anderson	1830	1860	1916R				1859	1915	
Ballard	1844	1883	1905				1880		
Barren	1800	1802	1806	1839	1896	1965			
Bath	1816	1831	1868				1864		
Bell	1871	1888	1914	1920	1944R		1914	1918	1944
Boone	1801	1817	1889				1880s		
Bourbon	1787	1799	1874	1905			1872	1901	
Boyd	1861	1912							
Boyle	1842	1862					1860		
Bracken	1797	1839	1864	1915			1848		
Breathitt	1840	1866	1877	1965			1866	1873	
Breckinridge	1800?	1869	1960				1864	1958	
Bullitt	1804	1901							
Butler	1811	1873	1975				1872		
Caldwell	1820	1840	1866	1941			1864		
Calloway	1823	1831	1843	1913			1906		

County	Courthouse Completed						Courthouse Disasters		
	1st	2nd	3rd	4th	5th	6th	1st	2nd	3rd
Campbell									
Newport	1795	1805	1815	1884					
Alexandria	1842								
Carlisle	1887	1982					1980		
Carroll	1841	1884							
Carter	1840	1907							
Casey	1808	1844	1889						
Christian	1800	1810	1838	1869			1864		
Clark	1794	1797	1821	1855					
Clay	?	?	1889	1939			1936		
Clinton	1836	1873	1895	1980			1864	1980	
Crittenden	1842	1860	1865	1871	1961		1865	1870	
Cumberland	1800	1858	1868	1934			1865	1933	
Daviess	?	1819	1858	1868	1964		1865		
Edmonson	–	1873							
Elliott	1869	1937	1968				1957		
Estill	1808	1867	1941				1864		
Fayette	1782	1788	1806	1885	1900		1803*	1897	
Fleming	1799	1830	1952						
Floyd	1807	1815	1821	1891	1964		1808		
Franklin	1806	1835							
Fulton	1848	1903							
Gallatin	1800	1810	1838						
Garrard	1799	1813	1868						
Grant	1821	1856	1939						
Graves	1824	1834	1866	1889			1864	1887	
Grayson	1810	1865?	1890s	1938			1864	1896	1936
Green	1796	1804	1931						
Greenup	1806	1816	1940						
Hancock	1829?	1868	1978R						
Hardin	1795	1806	1874	1934			1864	1932	
Harlan	1820	1838	1870	1888	1922		1863**		
Harrison	1794	1816	1853				1851		
Hart	1821	1893	1928				1928		
Henderson	–	1814	1843	1965					
Henry	1799	1804	1875				1804		
Hickman	1823	1830	1832	1885					
Hopkins	1808	1820s	1840s	?	1892	1937	1829	1864	
Jackson	1859?	1872	1924	1951			1949		
Jefferson	1785	1790	1818	1860					
Jessamine	1823	1878							
Johnson	1846	1892	1958						
Kenton									
Independence	1843	1911							
Covington	1843	1899	1970						
Knott	1884	1890s	1936				1929		
Knox	1802	1812	1829	1875	1964				
Larue	1844	1866	1964				1865		
Laurel	1827	1885	1961				1958		

County	Courthouse Completed						Courthouse Disasters		
	1st	2nd	3rd	4th	5th	6th	1st	2nd	3rd
Lawrence	1823	1870s	1964						
Lee	1873	1977							
Leslie	1878	1954							
Letcher	1843	1899	1965						
Lewis	1807	1810	1865	1940					
Lincoln	1785	1787	1832	1909					
Livingston	1801	1809	1845						
Logan	1793	1822	1904						
Lyon	1854	?	1961						
Madison	1786	1799	1850						
Magoffin	1862	1893	1959				1957		
Marion	1835	1935					1863		
Marshall	1844	1847	1888	1915			1888	1914	
Martin	1873	1882	1893				1892		
Mason	1790	1794	1848						
McCracken	1832	1861	1942						
McCreary	1914	1929	1953				1927	1951	
McLean	1854	1870	1908				1908		
Meade	1825	1851	1873	1976			1974		
Menifee	1872	1928							
Mercer	1789	1820	1913	1928R			1928		
Metcalfe	1860	1869	1968R				1865	1868?	
Monroe	1823	1865	1888	1976			1863	1888	
Montgomery	1798	1853	1868	1891	1960		1851	1863	
Morgan	1826	1840s	?	1907			1862	1925	
Muhlenberg	1800	1814	1836	1907					
Nelson	1785	1787	1892						
Nicholas	1805	1818	1844	1894					
Ohio	1800	1815	1867	1943			1864		
Oldham	1828	1875					1873		
Owen	1823	1858							
Owsley	1844	1930	1970s				1929	1967	
Pendleton	1800	1848							
Perry	1823?	1836	1866	1871	1912	1965	1885	1911	
Pike	1834	1889	1932				1977		
Powell	1852?	1865?	1890	1978			1863	1864+	
Pulaski	1801	1808	1840	1874	1975		1838	1871	
Robertson	1872								
Rockcastle	1811	1873	1965				1871		
Rowan	1856?	1865?	1899	1981			1864	1890s	
Russell	1826	1878	1978				1976		
Scott	1793	1816	1846	1877			1837	1876	
Shelby	1793	1796	1814	1847	1912				
Simpson	1822	1860	1883				1882		
Spencer	1825	1828	1866	1915			1865	1914	
Taylor	1848	1866	1966				1864		
Todd	1822	1836	1976						
Trigg	1821	1831	1843	1865	1895	1923	1864	1892	1920

County	Courthouse Completed						Courthouse Disasters		
	1st	2nd	3rd	4th	5th	6th	1st	2nd	3rd
Trimble	1837	1884	1953R				1952		
Union	1812	1819	1872						
Warren	1798	1805	1811	1868	1958R		1864		
Washington	1794	1797	1816				1795	1814	
Wayne	1801	1816	1825	1878	1899	1950	1898		
Webster	1860	1940							
Whitley	1818	1880s	1931	1970s			1930		
Wolfe	1860	1885	1917				1886	1913	
Woodford	1790	1793	1809	1970			1965		

* Clerk's office burned.

** Records were in clerk's office.

+ Jail burned, destroying all records.

CHAPTER 2

RESOURCES IN KENTUCKY LIBRARIES AND ARCHIVES

Kentuckians take pride in their heritage as evidenced by the variety and scope of the genealogical and historical holdings in libraries throughout the state. In this chapter, the latest available information on important libraries and archives in Kentucky is summarized by area of the state.

The libraries that are included in this reference do not undertake genealogical research. Many of these organizations depend largely on volunteers and have limited resources to respond to detailed inquiries. When corresponding, please send a stamped, self-addressed envelope for a reply. In order to ensure a response, it is wise to limit your request to one or two questions and to include a small fee for payment of the work requested or copies to be made.

FRANKFORT AREA RESOURCES

Kentucky Historical Society and Library
P.O. Box H
Lewis and Broadway Streets
Frankfort 40602-2108
502-564-3016

Kentucky Historical Society membership is $25 annually and $300 for a lifetime membership. Membership includes a subscription to the *Kentucky Historical Register*, *Kentucky Ancestors*, and their newsletter, *The Bulletin*. The society's genealogical quarterly, *Kentucky Ancestors*, prints original family history records, queries, and book reviews. The Kentucky Historical Society library is open Monday through Saturday with the exception of New Year's Day, Easter, Thanksgiving, and Christmas.

An arm of the Kentucky Historical Society is the Kentucky Historical Confederation, which publishes an excellent newsletter called *The Circuit Rider*. Cost is $9.50 for nonmembers and $7.50 for Kentucky Historical Society members. To obtain a subscription to *The Circuit Rider*, write to the confederation at Box H, Frankfort, Kentucky 40602-2108.

The Kentucky Historical Society library is a good place to begin a Kentucky genealogy. The library is easy to use, and the helpful and knowledgeable staff are always pleased to help a newcomer. Send a stamped, self-addressed business envelope and receive a beginner's packet, free of charge. The packet includes sample forms, historical maps of Kentucky, and other useful information.

The library's 50,000-volume genealogical collection contains thousands of family histories and privately printed genealogies. The library has a large family surname file collection, query card file, church records, family Bible records, regional genealogical materials, newspapers, manuscripts, maps, and many other primary and secondary sources. The library also subscribes to many historical and genealogical journals.

The library also has an extensive collection of published county records. A computerized list of these records, plus microfilms, vertical files, and maps in the library's holdings, has been completed and may be purchased from the society. Each county bibliography is sold separately. Prices vary depending on the size of the bibliography. Write the society for details.

Special collections within the society's library include the photographic archives, a rare book room, and a map collection. Materials from these special collections are available only on weekdays.

The society library has a number of valuable tools and unique resources. For example, the library has records of cemetery inscriptions collected through the society's statewide Cemetery Records Project, a vital statistics card index for the years 1852 to 1861, an index of divorces granted by the Kentucky legislature from 1792 to 1849, indexes of vital statistics since 1911, and the state's delayed birth certificates, dating from 1890 to 1911, together with its index.

Primary records available at the Kentucky Historical Society include all available Kentucky censuses and indexes, surviving tax lists for each county from formation through 1875, and the 1890 tax lists for all counties except Fayette and Jefferson. The society has the recently published 1860 and 1870 census indexes. The soundex/miracode for 1880, 1900 through 1920 are available at the society. The microfilm holdings of the society are listed in chapter 8. The society also provides filming services to the public at low cost. Discounts are available to members wishing to purchase microfilms from the micrographics department, and printed materials and maps from the gift shop.

Kentucky State Archives
P.O. Box 537
300 Coffee Tree Road
Frankfort 40601-0537
502-875-7000

The Kentucky Department for Libraries and Archives Public Records Division is the central repository for the state's permanent public records. The archives houses original and microfilmed public records including city, county, state, and judicial records. These primary sources are supplemented by a collection of federal records pertaining to Kentucky. The holdings currently consist of approximately 86,000 cubic feet of original materials and 22,000 rolls of microfilm.

Although the archives does not actively collect or solicit private materials such as family records, church, or Bible records, its holdings include a small collection of nongovernmental materials including the Draper manuscripts, some genealogical collections, as well as some early newspapers and historic maps.

Because of the extensive scope of its holdings, the help that its excellent and helpful staff provides, and the fact that it is a repository for original early records, the archives has become the most important source of primary Kentucky historical and genealogical data in the state.

The archives has a vast collection of county court records. For example, it has all county court records microfilmed in the 1960s by the Church of Jesus Christ of Latter-day Saints. Because of its archival and preservation functions, the archives also serves as a repository for Kentucky's old documents. As a result, the archives receives from the counties original documents that the counties no longer maintain. In addition to county records, the archives has city and other important historical statewide records.

All available federal censuses for Kentucky are available at the archives along with indexes to the census. The archives has printed census indexes for the state to 1870 plus the 1880 to 1920 soundex or miracode. In addition, many census and census indexes are available for Kentucky's border states at the archives.

The archives maintains a collection of military records. The Revolutionary War service records for military and naval personnel are available for all states. The index to pension applications for all states, and the 1840 census of Revolutionary War pensioners can also be used at the archives.

Kentucky military records at the archives include the Adjutant General's reports for the War of 1812, the Mexican War, and the Spanish American War. The library also has the Compiled Service Records for Confederates and Union Soldiers along with an index. Amnesty papers and other Confederate records are also available.

All microfilmed county records, whether federal, city, county, or state, of the archives are listed in chapter 8 by county. Statewide records are listed under the Kentucky section in chapter 8.

The research room is open Tuesday through Saturday but is closed on all state holidays and on Saturdays immediately preceding and following state holidays. It is wise to call ahead to check if the library will be open prior to a visit.

Researchers help to support the archives' preservation projects by joining Friends of Kentucky Public Archives. The address is Box 4224, Frankfort, Kentucky 40604. Individual membership is $10. Benefits include a quarterly newsletter, invitations to workshops, special events, the Kentucky Archives Institute, and the annual meeting. Gifts to the Friends are tax deductible.

Kentucky Genealogical Society
P.O. Box 153
300 Coffee Tree Road
Frankfort 40602
502-875-7000

The Kentucky Genealogical Society was formed in 1973. The society's quarterly, *Bluegrass Roots*, publishes genealogical records and queries. Society membership is $15 annually.

The society's holdings are housed adjacent to the Archives Research Room at the Department for Libraries and Archives Public Records Division (known herein simply as the archives) in Frankfort. Kentucky Genealogical Society members often serve as volunteers to help staff the research room of the Kentucky State Archives. The room provided by Kentucky State Archives contains the genealogical society's family files, the groups sheets from the Kentucky Family Archives Group Sheet Project, the Cemetery Records Project, as well as other genealogical journals and publications. The Kentucky Oral History Project houses its interviews here. As a result, there are several hundred taped oral history interviews from counties around the state.

Military Records and Research Branch
1121 Louisville Avenue
Pine Hill Plaza
Frankfort 40602
502-564-4883
FAX 502-564-4437

The Military Records and Research Branch has a large collection of manuscripts and records relating to Kentucky soldiers. Historical records on file in the library date from the beginning of statehood in 1792 through the present. This branch is an official State Departmental Library, and holdings are varied.

Table 2.1 is a partial list of this branch's holdings. All materials are reserved for use on the premises only.

TABLE 2.1	Military Records and Research Branch Library Partial List of Holdings

REVOLUTIONARY WAR AND FRONTIER PERIOD

Grave Registrations of Veterans
Officers Roster, Corn Stalk Militia 1792–1811
Pension Roll of 1835

WAR OF 1812

Adjutant General's Report
Muster Rolls
Roster of Known Military Dead During War of 1812
Roster of Deserters, War of 1812

MEXICAN WAR

Adjutant General's Report, War with Mexico 1846–48
Index to Mexican War Pensions

CIVIL WAR

Adjutant General's Report
Discharges not shown in Adjutant General's Report
Muster Rolls, Kentucky State Guard
Muster Rolls, Union and Confederate Armies
Residents of Peewee Valley Home for Confederate Veterans

SPANISH AMERICAN WAR

Adjutant General's Report, Spanish American War 1898–99
Muster Rolls
Kentucky State Guard in Spanish American War, Vols. I and II

WORLD WAR I

Casualty Rosters
Inductees Lists (for only twenty counties)
Veterans Service Statements

KENTUCKY NATIONAL GUARD

Active Militia Officers and Enlistment Records (1941–45)
KNG Personnel Files (late 1800s to present)
Kentucky State Guard Payrolls Prior to Spanish American War
History of KNG Units (1865 to present)

OTHER RECORDS

Air National Guard Records (1948 to present)

Army Registers of Officers (1936-72 except 1842-46,1950,1967)

Army National Guard Records (generally from 1922 to present)

Casualty lists from WWI through Vietnam

Grave Registration Records (Indian Wars to 1940)

Medal of Honor Recipients files, all conflicts 1861 to present for those with Kentucky connections, including USA and CSA

Muster Rolls, Kentucky National Guard in the Mexican Border Incident (1916-17)

Officers and Soldiers from Kentucky (1846-47)

U.S. Military Academy, Register of Graduates and Former Cadets (1802-60)

Veterans Bonus Records from Spanish American War through Vietnam Conflict

---

Source: Department of Military Affairs, Military Records and Research Branch, 1121 Louisville Road, Frankfort, Kentucky 40601-6169.

These records generally contain the veteran's name, rank, enrollment dates, muster, and separation dates. Records dating from 1792 to 1918 are available to the public for genealogical research. Records from 1918 to the present are considered personal, and they are protected by the Privacy Act. As a result, post-1918 records are only available to authorized governmental agencies, the veterans themselves, or, if deceased, the veteran's next of kin.

It is wise to know as much as possible about the unit in which your ancestor served prior to visiting the library. Not all military records are housed at this library, and not all sources in this library can be searched by the patron. For many sources, the very helpful staff will assist your search or search the indexes and locate the material.

Kentucky Department of Human Resources
Office of Vital Statistics
275 E. Main Street
Frankfort 40621
502-564-4212

Uniform civil registration of births and deaths began in Kentucky in 1911. The Office of Vital Statistics maintains these original certificates, as well as an index to them for the commonwealth from 1911 to the present. The office is also responsible for filing delayed birth certificates for those people born prior to 1911.

A separate index to these delayed certificates is maintained. Marriage and divorce records have been filed with this office since 1958.

The manner in which the indexes have been kept is easy to follow. In the microfilm version of the index, births and deaths are often included in the same volume. Some volumes contain a number of years, each indexed separately. Births are indicated by the presence of a mother's name. Deaths are printed in bold and have no mother's name. The name, date of the event, and the volume and certificate number are needed in order to complete the request slip to obtain the record.

There is a microfiche version of the index that includes all births from 1911 to 1983 and deaths from 1911 to 1986. There is also an index of births for this period arranged by the mother's maiden name.

The indexes to vital records can be searched at this location. Unfortunately, recent administration changes no longer allow researchers to view these records unless the record is purchased.

Official copies of birth certificates cost $6; death, marriage, and divorce records cost $5. Unofficial copies of the certificates can no longer be made. Birth and death certificates can be ordered over the telephone using a credit card; there is a $5 surcharge for this service.

Kentucky Secretary of State
Land Office
Capitol Building
Frankfort 40601-3493
502-564-3490

This office has the complete set of original documents for the Kentucky land grant records. Warrants and miscellaneous papers such as caveats and wills are included in their records and are not available elsewhere. These documents may be inspected anytime during regular office hours. For a complete description of the Kentucky land grant system and its records, consult the section on the Kentucky land grant system in chapter 5.

LEXINGTON AREA RESOURCES

University of Kentucky
Division of Special Collections and Archives
Lexington 40506
606-257-8611

The University of Kentucky special collections library and the University of Kentucky Margaret I. King Library (see below) house a wealth of genealogical and historical research materials.

The special collections library has a rich accumulation of primary research materials including manuscripts, family papers, political papers, photographic archives, rare books, and maps. The library houses over 11,000 microfilm reels of Kentucky court records and over 200 reels of microfilm of early Virginia court records. The 1790 and 1800 tax lists and 1810 to 1920 censuses for Kentucky are available as well as indexes to 1870. The census records for the Appalachian counties in the states of Ohio, Tennessee, Virginia, West Virginia, and North Carolina were recently acquired and date from 1790, where available, to 1900. The library also owns many standard Kentucky and Virginia genealogical references.

The manuscript collection contains many nineteenth-century manuscripts, unpublished family papers, several hundred Henry Clay letters, business and church records, and historical materials relating to Kentucky, the Ohio Valley, and the university. The university's modern political collections date from the 1870s to modern times. These collections contain newspaper articles, correspondence, speeches, and other materials collected during the office tenure and lives of Kentucky political figures.

The photographic archives collects visual Kentuckiana with emphasis on family portraits, scenes, and subjects such as agriculture and railroads. A variety of photographic processes, including daguerreotypes, ambrotypes, tintypes, and glass plate negatives, are represented. A total of 300,000 photographic images are included in this collection. Approximately 2,100 oral history interviews have also been collected. The Appalachia Collection contains books, pamphlets, journals, manuscripts, records, and tapes that deal with the eastern Kentucky region.

The special collections library owns a complete set of the Draper manuscripts, including the Kentucky Papers. The library has the state's early city directories as well as telephone books for Louisville and Lexington. A number of genealogical collections, including those of Mrs. William B. Ardery of Paris and E. E. Barton of Pendleton County, have been donated to the university. The university also has a card index for the Barton Collection files. Church records including correspondence, minutes, and record books from various churches are also held by the university library. Of special interest is the biographical file that indexes approximately twenty of Kentucky's standard biographical sources printed in the late 1800s.

The microfilm holdings of the special collections library of the University of Kentucky are listed in chapter 8. Most microfilm holdings are listed in a handy set of notebooks near the microfilm area. However, not all manuscripts or county records are included in these books. Three other indexes in the special collections library, which are maintained separately from the main card catalog, should be consulted: the card catalog of manuscripts; the chronological manuscript index, which covers the years 1840 to 1950; and the inventory notebooks of manuscripts. These inventories list family papers, church records, the Virginia county courthouse holdings, and other valuable private sources. A printed index, *Guide to Selected Manuscripts Housed in the Division of Special Collections and Archives*, is also available.

Hours vary based on the school term, so it is wise to call ahead to ensure the library is open. Some materials may not be accessible during Wednesday evening and Sunday.

University of Kentucky
Margaret I. King Library
Lexington 40506

While the major genealogical and rare holdings are in the special collections library, the main library also has a great deal of material that is useful to genealogists and historians. A large collection of family genealogies and local histories are available in the Margaret I. King main library stacks.

The library's journal collection contains historical and genealogical journals from many states including the standard Virginia genealogical and historical publications indexed by Swem.

The University of Kentucky holds the most extensive collection of Kentucky newspapers in the state. These are listed in the card catalog; however, there is also a chronological card index of newspapers held. Using this index, all newspapers available for a specific date can be identified. This index is kept behind the reference desk in the newspaper room.

The Kentucky Newspaper Project is housed at the university. When this project is completed, the university will have microfilm copies of all surviving Kentucky newspapers as well as all newspapers held by Kentucky libraries in the state. Some of these films will be available for interlibrary loan. (See chapter 7 for a complete discussion of the Kentucky Newspaper Project.)

The university's map department is well organized and extensive; it includes detailed maps of the United States and Europe. Microfilmed historical maps are also available in the newspaper room in the main library and are cataloged. (See chapter 7 for a complete discussion of Kentucky historical maps.)

The University of Kentucky Independent Study Program offers an award winning genealogy course by correspondence entitled "Searching for Ancestors." The course was developed by Dr. David McMurtry and is designed for those beginning in genealogy. Tuition is $40 plus $10 for the text. Information may be obtained by writing the university's Independent Study Program, 1 Frazee Hall, Lexington, Kentucky 40506-0031.

One interesting collection on microcard is the Kentucky Culture Series, a collection of religious, social, economic, and educational studies of Kentucky materials. Consult the *Guide to Microtext* at the service desk in the newspaper room for a description and the location of these resources.

The University's Margaret I. King Library has nearly completed computerizing their card catalog. However, some old manuscripts and other publications may not be in the on-line catalog. In addition, the Periodicals/Newspapers/Microtext Department houses approximately 75,000 microcards that provide primary source materials in a variety of subject areas. These are not included in the card catalog. To search for these references, check the index and checklists at the department's service desk.

Lexington Public Library
140 E. Main Street
Lexington 40507
606-231-5520
606-231-5523 (Kentucky Room)

The Lexington Public Library downtown facility has a Kentucky Room with a growing number of genealogical materials. However, none of the volumes in its Kentucky collection circulates. Primary records include the 1790 and 1800 tax list indexes, and census indexes for the years 1810 to 1850 for the state. All Fayette County censuses are available from 1800 to 1880, and 1900 to 1920 on microfilm. The 1920 Fayette County census will be acquired. The library has a number of standard genealogical references including military indexes, bibliographies, and genealogical periodicals. There are also county histories and family genealogies.

Because Lexington was a center of early Kentucky life and commerce, its newspapers can be an important source of information. Old Lexington newspapers available on microfilm at the library are shown in table 7.1 in chapter 7. They also have the index to the *Louisville Courier-Journal* for 1917 to 1977. The *Lexington Leader and Herald* index to its photographic archives from 1944 to 1974 is also available.

Some microfilmed Fayette County records at the Lexington library include the following: deeds (1794-1901), marriages (scattered) (1785-1898), order books (1803-53), tax lists (1787-1875), will books (1793-1905), and Lexington city directories (1806 to present).

Some of the unique aids in this library include the index of funeral notices for Lexington for the period 1806 to 1887 and a local history index that dates from the late 1700s to the present.

LOUISVILLE AREA RESOURCES

The Filson Club
1310 S. Third Street
Louisville 40208
502-635-5083

The purpose of the Filson Club is to collect and preserve historic matter and encourage historic inquiry and study. As a result, the Filson Club emphasizes historical materials. Their manuscript department is the best in Kentucky for pioneer, antebellum, and Civil War periods.

The Filson Club's library contains approximately 50,000 research books including county histories and secondary sources. In addition, the library has the Kentucky census from 1810 to 1920 on microfilm along with all available printed indexes or soundex. The following materials are also available for research in this library: early taxpayer lists for most counties to 1850; abstracts of Revolutionary and War of 1812 pensions for sixty-nine of ninety-five counties formed by 1842; correspondence folders on 3,000 surnames; Louisville city directories, 1832 to present; the Draper manuscripts; various nineteenth- and twentieth-century Kentucky newspapers; historical periodicals and other materials concerning adjoining and nearby states with special emphasis on Virginia; and an extensive collection of Kentucky maps.

The Filson Club library has one of the largest old newspaper collections in the state. The manuscript collection contains more than one million items including personal and family papers, diaries, records of organizations and business firms, and some genealogical collections. The photographs and prints department has approximately 50,000 photographs and several thousand historical prints. The Filson collection includes maps, sheet music, microfilm, and other items. The club also has a museum that has an extensive collection of portraits, textiles, silver, and weapons.

Membership is $35 annually for an individual membership, which entitles the member to a subscription to *The Filson Club Quarterly*, newsletters, and printed notes.

Louisville Public Library

Fourth and York Streets
Louisville 40203
502-561-8600
502-561-8616 (Kentucky Room)

The Kentucky Room of the Louisville Library includes materials on Kentucky, books by Kentucky authors, and an index to the *Courier Journal*. The library has 692 shelves of printed genealogy and Kentucky books. The Louisville city directories are on microfilm and are available beginning with 1832.

The library has copies of the Kentucky federal census for 1810 to 1920 along with indexes. They also have some Virginia censuses. Their Louisville newspaper collection dates from 1815. A copy of the Kentucky Civil War Service records is available as are about half of the Draper manuscripts. Vital statistics held by this library for Jefferson County and Louisville include the statewide vital statistics records covering the years from 1851 to the 1880s, and the city of Louisville vital records to 1910.

Sons of American Revolution Genealogy Library

1000 S. Fourth Street
Louisville 40203
502-589-1776

The National Headquarters of the National Society of the Sons of the American Revolution was founded in 1889 and moved to Louisville in 1978. The library's total collection, excluding society archives, was 23,000 items in January of 1991.

The collection contains census (or tax substitute) indexes of 44 states from 1790 to 1880, and complete census information for the years 1790 to 1840. There are 300 indexes to the various U.S. census records. The library also has the *Index to Genealogical Periodicals*.

Other important library materials include approximately 4,000 family genealogies, and 6,700 state, county, and local histories. The library's largest state sections are New York (925 volumes), Massachusetts (690), Virginia (560), Pennsylvania (520), Kentucky (450), and Ohio (430). The library also has the LDS Family History Library's International Genealogical Index (IGI) on microfiche.

There is also an historical section specializing in the Revolutionary era. The Revolutionary War histories, pension records, rosters of soldiers and patriots include 1,400 books and 1,600 reels of microfilm. The microfilm collection contains 898 reels of Revolutionary War pension and bounty land warrant application files.

Special holdings include the following collections: Leach Collection—genealogy of the signers of the Declaration of Independence; George Washington Collection—including the Morristown Manuscript Collection and the George Washington Papers on microfilm; Barbour Collection—colonial period vital records for Connecticut.

There is a $1 daily admission fee for non-SAR or non-DAR members.

NORTHERN KENTUCKY/CINCINNATI AREA RESOURCES

Kenton County Public Library
5th and Scott Streets
Covington 41011
606-491-7610

The Kenton County Library, under the leadership of Mr. Mike Averdick, has become a leader in preserving the heritage of the area and serves as a model for other libraries in Kentucky.

In 1977, an index was begun for all existing nineteenth-century Covington and Newport newspapers held by the library. There is an every-name index as well as an index to events and places. The index is completed from 1835 to 1925, and 1984 to 1990 and is ongoing. The index currently contains approximately 340,000 citations. The *Kentucky Post* indexing begins with 1892.

The library's microfilm collection stands at well over 4,500 reels of Kentucky material. There are over 600 family files covering about 1,200 family surnames. Local history files number approximately 1,000. The photography collection now stands at approximately 2,000 pre-1940 photographs and in excess of 6,000 post-1960 photographs. A majority of the post-1960 photographs are from the collection of the *Kentucky Post*.

In addition to the newspaper index and the microfilm collection, the library has a number of standard genealogical references and many Kentucky family genealogies. City directories from 1834 to the present are available for Covington, Newport, and vicinity. Extensive published holdings are available for Kenton County and, to a lesser extent, Campbell County. The library also has a good collection of Kentucky historical and genealogical works.

The library has the Kentucky census from 1810 to 1920 on microfilm along with available indexes and soundex for 1880 and 1900 through 1920. Tax lists for the northern Kentucky counties date from 1785 to 1875. Early health department vital statistics for Covington and Newport are available.

The collection is growing rapidly and includes many genealogical references and family histories. For example, by 1992 a complete set of the Lost Cause Press microfiche, *The Kentucky Thousand* and *The Kentucky Culture Series*, adding over 3,000 titles to the Kentucky Collection, will be available for public use. Mr. Charles D. King is the local history librarian in charge.

Northern Kentucky State University
Kentucky Archives
Highland Heights 41076
606-572-6312

The new university in northern Kentucky has developed an impressive collection of historical resources including a collection of family files for the northern counties, court records dating from 1799 to the 1820s, census materials, and over 6,000 books related to Kentucky history and life.

The Public Library of Cincinnati and Hamilton County
Union 800 Vine Street
Cincinnati, Ohio
513-369-6900

By far the strongest of these resources is the Cincinnati and Hamilton County library. Their collection of Kentucky materials exceeds in size and scope the collections of most of the genealogical libraries in Kentucky. In addition, they have a complete set of census records for the United States and a very strong periodical collection.

The Cincinnati library has all available U.S. census microfilm for 1810 to 1910. It also has all available soundex for 1880 for all forty-seven states as well as most U.S. census indexes. The library also has the 1910 soundex/miracode for all states. The 1790 to 1800 tax lists are available for all states. With their latest acquisition of the 1910 census, the Cincinnati library joins the Allen County Library in Ft. Wayne, Indiana, as the only other public library in the country to have the complete U.S. census population schedules for 1810 to 1910. The library has also plans to purchase the complete 1920 census and soundex, again making it one of only two public libraries in the country with a complete set of census materials.

The library also has a strong collection of local genealogy resources. There is a large collection of printed family genealogies, reference books, military records, and periodicals. City directories for Cincinnati date from 1819. These directories are particularly important for searching urban immigrant ancestors. Many area church records have been filmed and are available at the library through a special joint project between the Hamilton County Genealogical Society, the Genealogical Society of Utah, and Wright State University.

The Public Library of Cincinnati and Hamilton County has a genealogical periodical collection that is international in scope and ranks among the top five in size in the country (only behind such giants as the LDS Family History Library in Salt Lake City, the Library of Congress, and the New York Public Library).

While a newspaper index of obituaries, not death notices, was begun in the nineteenth century, it was only maintained on a systematic basis since 1940. There are earlier notices, but usually only for prominent people. However, since August of 1988, death notices have been indexed systematically. The large newspaper collection at the Cincinnati Library includes the *Daily Gazette* (1828-81) and the *Enquirer* (1818 to present). Cincinnati's large German population was responsible for an active German press, and the *Freie Presse* from 1874 to 1964 and the *Volksfreund* dating from 1850 to 1908 are available on microfilm.

Cincinnati Historical Society
Museum at Cincinnati Union Terminal
1301 Western Avenue
Cincinnati, Ohio 45203
513-287-7030

The Cincinnati Historical Society library has 70,000 historical and genealogical volumes. City directories from 1819 to present, church records, business and personal papers, maps, and vital statistics files from local newspapers are some of the resources available in this library.

American Jewish Archives
Hebrew Union College Campus
3101 Clifton Avenue
Cincinnati, Ohio 45220-2488
513-221-1875

The Hebrew Union College in Cincinnati has two sources that are valuable sources of Jewish-American genealogy. The Jewish Institute of Religion—Klau Library and the American Jewish Archives. The American Jewish Archives has collected many records of Jews in America for the period before 1900 including synagogue records, personal letters, diaries, wills, family files, and vital statistics records. The archives has an indexed manuscript of their holdings as of 1971. You may research the records yourself or engage a student researcher to do research for you in the library.

CHAPTER 3

KENTUCKY'S CONSTITUTIONS, COURTS, AND CLERKS

"Mr. Haggard said, 'Charley is nothing but a liar and thief and a son of a b___.' And Charley took his hand and went after his pistol and I went on back behind the house. . . . Three or four shots were fired. . . . I heard the horses' feet. Seemed like he was riding away fast. . . .

"Haggard had on . . . striped pants and a work apron . . . it was made out of bed ticking . . . and a blue shirt . . . he [Mr.Haggard] would weigh about 125, I guess, and was about 56 years old I think. . . ."

The above excerpt was taken from the case files of the trial of Charles T. Forkner for the murder of Tandy Quissenberry Haggard of Clark County (Madison County Circuit Court, *Commonwealth of Kentucky v. Charles T. Forkner*, October 1910).

"I [John Frelinger] have been blacksmithing since 1851; it was prosperous in 1871 but for the last two years it has not been prosperous. . . . I was husband to Catherine and father of the codefendents. . . . I married his [Michael Scanlon's] sister in the year 1861 and he came to live with me immediately after my marriage. . . ."

The Frelinger deposition above is taken from case file materials filed with a suit to settle the estate of Catherine Frelinger, deceased (Campbell County Chancery Court Records, *Michael Scanlon v. John Frelinger and children*, 23 October 1888).

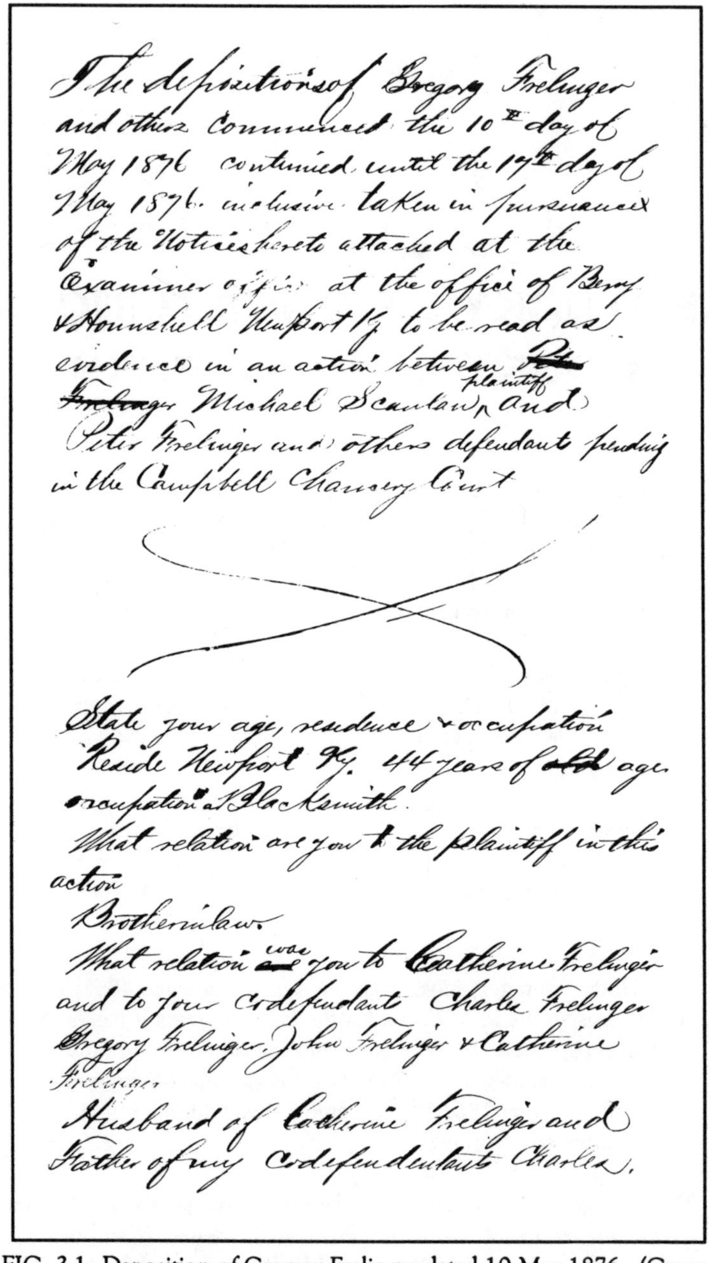

The depositions of Gregory Frelinger and others commenced the 10th day of May 1876 continued until the 17th day of May 1876 inclusive taken in pursuance of the Notices hereto attached at the Examiner office at the office of Berry & Hounshell Newport Ky to be read as evidence in an action between Michael Scanlan plaintiff and Peter Frelinger and others defendants pending in the Campbell Chancery Court

State your age, residence & occupation
Reside Newport Ky. 44 years of age.
occupation a Blacksmith.
What relation are you to the plaintiff in this action
Brotherinlaw.
What relation was you to Catherine Frelinger and to your Codefendant Charles Frelinger
Gregory Frelinger, John Frelinger & Catherine Frelinger
Husband of Catherine Frelinger and Father of my codefendants Charles.

FIG. 3.1 Deposition of Gregory Frelinger dated 10 May 1876. (Campbell County Chancery Court Case Papers, Kentucky State Archives)

Stories told in the words of our ancestors still exist in our courthouses. Quotes like the ones above bring to life a long dead ancestor and give us what we so desperately seek: understanding, a common humanity, and a bond with an ancestor we cannot know in any other way.

Neglecting these records, and the stories they reveal, may mean overlooking an exciting piece of personal history. A single circuit court case file can include hundreds of pages of eyewitness accounts, depositions, examinations of witnesses, and testimony of neighbors, friends, and relatives. Within these pages, a researcher can piece together an unbelievably rich account of important events, as well as the everyday life, of a Kentucky ancestor.

Because of its importance, the Kentucky court system and the dry details of its organization will be discussed in this chapter with the hope it will promote wider use of these records. The information provided here is summarized from a variety of publications including the documents of the WPA project surveys (Kentucky Historical Records Surveys 1937), federal court publications, unpublished manuscripts of the Kentucky Department of Libraries and Archives, and Administrative Reports of the Courts (Kentucky Court of Justice 1986). Following the overview of Kentucky's constitutions, each of the old court records will be discussed in detail.

HISTORICAL OVERVIEW OF KENTUCKY'S CONSTITUTIONS

THE FIRST CONSTITUTION

In 1792, the state's first constitution was adopted in Danville when Congress granted statehood to Kentucky. At that time, judicial power of the commonwealth was vested in one supreme court, known as the court of appeals, and inferior courts as deemed necessary by the legislature. This court had original and final jurisdiction in land titles and, as a court of record, recorded deeds. In all other cases, the court of appeals had appellate jurisdiction only. The court of appeals met twice a year at Lexington.

In addition to the court of appeals, civil courts were established by this constitution. First, a "competent number" of justices of the peace were mandated to be appointed in each county. The legislature appointed 125 justices of the peace who were to serve as judicial officers. In the thirteen counties that existed at the time, a court of quarter sessions was established whose power was primarily civil. However, it did have power to award writs and injunctions. The county court was also created and presided over by three of the justices in the county. Its jurisdiction was, then as now, largely administrative.

Criminal jurisdiction was vested in a court of oyer and terminer, which was presided over by three judges with statewide jurisdiction. This court was eliminated three years later in 1795 under a reorganization. It was replaced with a system of district courts of general, civil, and criminal jurisdiction. All criminal cases were heard by the Franklin District Court. Order books from the old court of oyer and terminer survive and are available in the Kentucky archives research room.

A general court was established to decide cases for and on behalf of the commonwealth. The general court, also known as the district court of general sessions, was created as the coordinating body for all district courts. Records of the old general court, as well as those of the district courts, were transferred to the custody of the clerk of the newly organized general court. The general court was abolished in 1850 under the third constitution. Fifteen volumes of records of this general court, dating from 1797 to 1851, are available for research at the Kentucky Libraries and Archives research room.

THE SECOND CONSTITUTION

By 1799, a new constitution was adopted that retained most of the provisions of the previous system. The court of appeals, however, now had only appellate jurisdiction. County courts were composed of the justices of the peace presiding in each county.

The courts were reorganized again in 1802 to handle an increasing work load on the district courts. A nine-district circuit court system was established at that time, and the old district courts were abolished.

In 1824, the legislature attempted to abolish the court of appeals and replace it with an appellate court. This new appellate court was more sympathetic to legislative and governors' views regarding repayments on what had become rapidly depreciating bank notes issued by the Old Bank of Kentucky and the Bank of the Commonwealth. The old court, however, refused to recognize the new court. As a result, for a period of about two years from 1824 to 1826, both courts existed. For a time, both heard and decided cases. However, it appears that the new court did not decide any cases after October of 1825. By 1826, a new legislature was elected, and it repealed the new court (Hilliard 1960, 229–35).

THE THIRD CONSTITUTION

The third Kentucky constitution was established in 1850, and with it came total reorganization of the judicial department.

The court of appeals was again granted appellate jurisdiction only. Circuit courts were established and were to be held in each county.

The general court was abolished, and, in its place, a system of circuit courts with no centralized coordination was established in each county. Commonwealth cases, however, continued to be heard in Franklin Circuit Court.

In 1882, the legislature created an intermediate appellate court known as the superior court to reduce an accumulation of 1,300 cases. This court was abolished in 1890 under the fourth constitution, but only after bitter controversy surrounding the two courts, which came to be known as the rich man's appellate court and the poor man's appellate court.

THE FOURTH CONSTITUTION

The 1890 Constitutional Convention created the judicial system that more closely resembles Kentucky's modern system. The court of appeals had seven elected judges from each of the seven appellate districts.

This fourth constitution established a circuit court in each county and divided the state into circuit court districts. The number of districts increased from thirty to fifty-six. The circuit courts had original jurisdiction over all cases not vested exclusively in some other court and appellate jurisdiction to try de novo appeals from inferior courts.

In each county, a group of lower courts was created consisting of justice of the peace courts, a county court, a fiscal court, a quarterly court, and city police court. All were given overlapping or concurrent jurisdiction, both civil and criminal, by the general assembly. As a result, by 1975, there were over 1,000 part-time courts.

MODERN CONCEPTS:
THE UNIFIED COURT OF JUSTICE

Three important reorganizations helped to bring Kentucky's old judicial system into line with a modern structure. First, in 1901 the state was divided into two federal districts, an eastern and western district. In 1911, the circuit courts were abolished and district courts assumed their jurisdictions. From these beginnings, the modern courts, known as federal courts, were established. (See Eakle and Cerny 1984, 153–55, for a discussion of the development of the American federal courts.)

Finally, the current Kentucky court structure, as revised by the Judicial Article of 1975, provided for a unified court system. There are currently four levels of courts: the supreme court, the court of appeals, the circuit courts, and the district courts.

KENTUCKY'S OLD JUDICIAL SYSTEM

Kentucky's old judicial system had consisted of a single appellate court, the court of appeals, two levels of trial courts, the circuit courts, and the local courts. These local courts consisted of the county, quarterly, magisterial, and police courts.

In this section, relevant aspects of Kentucky's old courts in order of their power will be discussed. The court of appeals, of course, had the highest authority. The circuit court had greatest power and was the next highest court; the quarterly courts operated as intermediate courts; and the county courts were the lowest courts. Availability and content of the records are also outlined for each of these courts.

KENTUCKY COURT OF APPEALS

The court of appeals was established by the first state constitution of 1792 and was given original and final jurisdiction over all land title cases. "Original jurisdiction" means a court can begin a case. "Final jurisdiction" means its decisions cannot be appealed. The initial jurisdiction of the court included the power to review all final judgments and decrees of the court of quarter sessions in civil cases where the amount involved twenty or more pounds and cases related to franchise or freehold of any amount. It also had jurisdiction to review all judgments of the Virginia Supreme Court for the District of Kentucky.

By 1891, the constitution had established this court as the state's supreme court, consisting of between five and seven judges. In 1895 the number of judges was set at seven and the jurisdiction of the court was to include review of all final orders and judgments of Kentucky courts except (1) those granting a divorce or punishing contempt; (2) those of a quarterly, police, fiscal, or justice's court; (3) those of a county court unless the action was for division of dower; and (4) bonds having the force of judgments. The court operated under basically similar statutes until 1976 when a new court of appeals was created.

CONTENT OF COURT OF APPEAL RECORDS

The Kentucky Court of Appeals was vested with both appellate jurisdiction and jurisdiction as a court of record. Court of appeals records contain case files, materials relating to administrative matters, and other documents such as wills, inventories, powers of attorney, and other probate documents. Each case file may include trial transcripts and other legal documents generated in the lower courts. Among the documents included are briefs for the appellant and appellee, petitions for rehearing, supplemental briefs, opinions of the court, court orders, circuit court transcripts, supplemental transcripts, and exhibits. As a court of record, deeds were

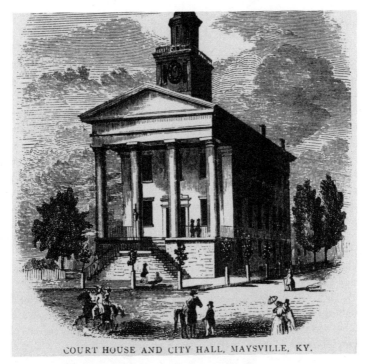

COURT HOUSE AND CITY HALL, MAYSVILLE, KY.

FIG. 3.2 Courthouse and City Hall, Maysville, Kentucky. (*History of Kentucky*, Collins 1874)

recorded with the court beginning in 1796 and continuing to 1835. Cook has abstracted and indexed these records of the court of appeals (Cook 1985).

AVAILABILITY OF RECORDS

The Kentucky archives has court of appeals records dating from 1780 to 1976. These records, except for case files, are unprocessed and difficult to access. The case files date from 1854 to 1976 and consist of 413 volumes and 908 rolls of microfilm. Arrangement is by case number.

Cook has abstracted and published court of appeals deeds and other records in four volumes for the period 1796 to 1835 (Cook 1985). Some of these records date as early as 1775.

The new court of appeals records date from 1976 to 1980 and consist of 320 rolls of microfilm. The materials contained in each case file is the same as the old court of appeals and arrangement is also by case number. These materials are available at the Kentucky archives.

KENTUCKY CIRCUIT COURT

The jurisdiction now exercised by the circuit court was originally held by the Quarterly Court of Virginia. In 1782, a district court was established in all existent counties. This court had jurisdiction that was previously held by the general court and the high court of chancery. In 1792, when Kentucky became a state, three courts were established that exercised jurisdiction in the circuit court: the court of oyer and terminer, the quarterly court, and the court of appeals.

While the court of oyer and terminer was responsible for criminal cases, the quarterly court was the civil court. The quarterly court was established with jurisdiction over (1) common law cases and (2) chancery except cases involving less than five pounds currency or 1,000 pounds of tobacco. Common law is based on custom and precedent and is not written statute or code. Chancery courts had jurisdiction over equity cases, hence, the terms "chancery" and "equity" courts are synonymous. Equity or chancery cases are concerned with property and rights, and they include challenges to wills, adoptions, disputes over payments or land, divorce, and estate divisions.

By 1802, district and quarterly courts were abolished and the circuit courts were established with the powers that were formerly held by these courts. The circuit courts now had power previously held by the district and quarterly session courts. For example, circuit courts now had power

- over all common law and chancery cases, except criminal suits involving less than five pounds;
- to award injunctions, in other words, to make orders;
- to award writs of certiorari; "Writs of certiorari" are writs that allow the circuit court to order an inferior court to certify and submit the record of a particular case;
- of habeas corpus; "Habeas corpus" means one has the power to order a person with custody of a detained person to produce him/her to appear before court;
- to appeal ferry and road cases;
- to naturalize foreigners;
- to appoint commissioners to convey title to lands by deed in chancery cases;
- to arrest and imprison fugitives from other states;
- over all matters relating to persons of unsound mind.

From 1802 to 1849, the circuit court of the county ruled on divorce petitions and forwarded those they approved to the state legislature. The state legislature was required to act on each divorce as a separate act. After the third constitution, in 1850, the circuit court had the sole responsibility to grant or deny divorce petitions. After 1894, the court's appellate jurisdiction, the power to review decisions and actions of other courts, included the following:

- all orders and judgments of fiscal or quarterly courts in civil cases involving more than $15;
- actions of tax supervisors;
- actions concerning ferries, passways, mills, water works, and dams;
- all judgments of county courts over $50;
- all judgments and orders of county court in bastardy cases, probate matters, and guardian actions;
- all county orders refusing to grant licenses;
- judgments in proceedings to condemn land;
- judgment against defendants in criminal actions;
- judgments of justices' courts in forcible entry and detainer proceedings (Historical Records Survey 1937).

CONTENT OF CIRCUIT COURT RECORDS

The circuit court clerk was authorized to draw up and record the orders of court, keep records of appeal cases, forward papers when a change of venue had been granted, keep equity and common law dockets, keep a rule docket of names of parties in the cases, and keep other miscellaneous records.

An act of 1833 provided that the circuit court clerk should certify the claims of Revolutionary War soldiers without charge. Early duties of the circuit court also included certifying to the state auditor the number of slaves condemned and executed. This duty was held until the abolition of slavery in 1863.

Other recording duties of the circuit court clerk included maintenance of the following lists: idiots, lunatics, and their committees; pauper idiots; suits to settle insolvent estates; witnesses attendance; a general index of names of parties in each suit; as well as civil and criminal index judgment books.

Circuit court records thus contain a wide variety of cases including criminal cases and trials, civil matters, coroners' inquests, adoptions, divorce recommendations, and orders.

AVAILABILITY OF RECORDS

The circuit court records that are on microfilm have been inventoried and are listed in chapter 8. The Kentucky State Archives has the largest collection in the state of microfilmed and original circuit court records including case files, docket books, indexes, and other types of miscellaneous records. The archives does hold some original circuit court records no longer held at the county level.

KENTUCKY COURT
OF QUARTER SESSIONS

Kentucky's quarterly courts grew out of the quarterly courts of Virginia. The quarterly court was an intermediate court between the circuit court and the county courts and operated between 1785 and 1802. The judge of the quarter sessions held four sessions yearly in the courthouse at the county seat.

When this system was created in 1785, the quarterly courts had jurisdiction over criminal cases, common law suits, and chancery suits in cases where the amount of dispute was in excess of five pounds currency or 800 pounds of tobacco. The quarterly courts were abolished in 1802 with the circuit courts taking over its duties. In 1850, the quarterly courts were reestablished with new jurisdictions; and, in 1891, the quarterly court was made a constitutional court, but this time with no change in its jurisdiction, which still included authority over both criminal and civil cases.

CRIMINAL JURISDICTION

In penal and criminal proceedings, the quarterly court was given all the powers of a justice of a court of inquiry. It also had concurrent jurisdiction with justices' courts in cases of riots. The quarterly court was a court of record with power to administer oaths and punish all contempts of its authority.

The quarterly court also played a role in the regulation of slaves and legal matters of free blacks. For example, it had jurisdiction for trials of slaves charged with capital offenses. Slaves were usually tried in separate courts presided over by one or two justices of the peace. Free blacks may also have been similarly tried in this court.

CIVIL JURISDICTION

When Kentucky became a state in 1792, the quarterly court system was authorized with jurisdiction over common law, chancery, escheats, and forfeiture cases. It was given concurrent original jurisdiction, both in law and equity, with justices of the peace in all civil cases. In all civil cases where the amount in controversy did not exceed $100, it had concurrent jurisdiction with the circuit court.

The quarterly court also had power to award writs of ne exeat, injunctions, and habeas corpus. "Writs of ne exeat" were writs that restrained a person from leaving the district or from taking property out of the district. The quarterly court originally had been given power to impanel a jury.

In 1850, the quarterly courts were reestablished with new jurisdiction in a number of areas. These courts now had concurrent jurisdiction with the circuit court in cases between $50 and $100, in all actions of trespass, and writs of replevin ("replevin" involves recovering possession of goods or property) except where title or land boundaries may be at issue. It had no jurisdiction in real estate.

They granted injunctions and attachments. These courts held inquests for idiots and lunatics. Finally, the quarterly court is where the county's fiscal affairs were conducted.

In summary, the jurisdiction of the quarterly court fell between, and overlapped to a large extent, the jurisdiction of the justices of the peace court below it and the circuit court above it. The court also served as an appellate court for all judgments and orders of justices, fiscal, and police courts (Kentucky Historical Records Survey 1937, 24).

CONTENT OF QUARTERLY COURT RECORDS

Civil records of the quarterly court may include case papers, judgments filed and off docket, surety bonds including civil replevin bonds, attachment bonds, appeal and supersedeas bonds, orders, and default judgments. Criminal records may include commonwealth cases off docket, bail and replevin bonds, case papers, orders, and criminal judgments.

AVAILABILITY OF RECORDS

Although many of the quarter session court records are not microfilmed, some microfilmed records date from as early as 1793. Microfilmed records of the court of quarter sessions are listed in chapter 8 of this book. Consult the listings under Orders as well as Minute Books. The best collection of quarter session records is held by the Kentucky archives. While access to some of these records is hampered by lack of good indexes, many of these records do have indexes by defendant and plaintiff, which give the date or location of the case papers. Other indexes are listed simply by case number.

JUSTICE OF PEACE COURTS

The role of the justice of peace courts in early Kentucky was quite different from its current image of marrying justices today. The justice of peace courts were modeled after the Virginia courts and had jurisdiction in small claims cases, minor criminal cases, warrants, some slave matters, and cases involving free blacks. They were also, as their name implies, charged with preserving the peace of the county.

PRESERVING THE PEACE

In 1802, the justices kept the peace through their responsibility for executing tavern regulation laws and punishing violations of the laws of taverns and tippling houses. Theirs was the power to suppress riots, routs, and breaches of the peace. They could try persons for disorderly conduct, and place such persons under bond to keep the peace. These courts were also authorized to suppress gaming and lotteries.

The justices also heard cases concerning anything or anyone who posed a threat to the town's peace, such as strays, strangers, vagrants, stray boats, stray animals, or escapees from jail. Mad dogs and even rewards for killing wolves also fell under the justices' authority.

CIVIL AND SMALL CLAIMS JURISDICTION

In 1792, the jurisdiction of the justice of peace courts included cases where the value of the dispute was less than five pounds currency or 1,000 pounds of tobacco. However, only those cases where executions would be against goods and chattels, and not the body of the defendant, fell into their jurisdiction.

By late in 1792, their jurisdiction was final in cases under twenty-five shillings, but appeals could be taken to the court of quarter sessions in larger cases. By an act of 1810, the legislature gave the justice courts jurisdiction in cases of bonds, bills, notes, or open accounts when the original amount was five pounds current money or more. By 1812, the jurisdiction was increased to all debts and accounts not exceeding $50, subject to appeal to the circuit court.

In more recent times, the justices had jurisdiction concurrent with the circuit court in all actions for recovery of money and property that did not exceed $100. They also had jurisdiction concurrent with the quarterly and circuit courts in personal civil actions when the amount in question was not above $100. In other words, they were yesterday's small claims courts.

CRIMINAL JURISDICTION

The justice court also had some jurisdiction in petty and minor criminal cases. In 1809, justices were empowered to conduct examining trials for criminal charges. Their jurisdiction included forcible entry, detainer proceedings, and distress warrants. They issued warrants for arrest of traitors, felons, other criminals, and in bastardy cases. In 1851, they had power to hold inquests in the absence of the coroner.

SLAVES AND FREE BLACKS JURISDICTION

The justice of the peace court has historically had a role in the regulation of slaves and free blacks. For example, an act of 1798 gave the justices authority to examine charges against slaves and to recover and return run away slaves. They also investigated cases of free black immigrants entering the state in contravention of law. In 1827, they had authority for licensing Indians and free blacks to keep firearms.

PERFORMING MARRIAGES

The modern function of performing marriage ceremonies was only one of the early functions of the court. Statutes in force in 1827 gave justices of the peace the ability to perform marriages when there were insufficient ordained ministers.

Since 1891, justices have been permitted to perform marriages when authorized by the county court or the governor.

CONTENT OF RECORDS

Early legislation required the justices to report to the county court clerk all fines assessed by them and the constables.

They also kept a record of all court proceedings. On the first day of each circuit court session, the justices reported the amount of money due and collected, all unsatisfied judgments, and all persons against whom such judgments were rendered. Typical justice of the peace records will include docket books, execution books, and order books.

AVAILABILITY OF RECORDS

Few justice of the peace records have been microfilmed in Kentucky. There are a number of original records from these courts, however, in the Kentucky archives. These unmicrofilmed records are listed in the inventory sheets of the archives, but will not be reflected in this reference. Microfilmed records, where they do exist, are listed in chapter 8.

OFFICE OF THE CONSTABLE

The county constables acted as ministerial officers of the justice of the peace in their district. Constables executed warrants in bastardy and other cases, summoned witnesses, served and made returns of notices of injunctions, and gave notice of ejectment. An old Virginia law authorized the constable to execute warrants to search for deer skins in order to detect violations of hunting laws. Later statutes required him to enforce game and bird laws.

From the beginning of the office, the constable also had a responsibility to maintain order and had the right to carry concealed weapons. The constable could destroy gambling devices without warrant and call upon bystanders for assistance if needed. He could arrest people engaged in riots, routs, and breaches of the peace, conduct prisoners to jail, arrest persons charged with bribery, arrest fugitives from justice, and whip slaves by order of a justice of the peace.

The duties of the constables were so curtailed after the justices no longer held court, that the need for the office is nearly nonexistent. However, the office still exists in Kentucky today. These officers kept no records since record keeping was the justice's function. Therefore, record of any actions taken by constables will be in the justice's records.

THE COUNTY COURTS AND OFFICES

The county courts in Kentucky were based on those in Virginia which were in turn modeled after the English court system.

The county courts in Virginia were composed of two separate sessions: (1) a quarter session with jurisdiction in all common law or chancery matters over $20 or 800 pounds of tobacco, except those involving loss of life or outlawry, and (2) a monthly session with jurisdiction over small debts, trover and conversion or detention, and of any matter not exceeding $20 or 800 pounds of tobacco. These two sessions together were called the county court. The jurisdiction separating them was the amount of money involved.

When Kentucky became a state, however, important changes were made to the county courts. The Kentucky judicial system consisted of two distinct courts: the monthly or county courts, and circuit or district courts. This monthly county court lost its role as an intermediary judicial body and became essentially a court of administration, supervision, and regulation of county affairs with limited civil or criminal jurisdiction.

The major functions of the county courts included processing land claims and surveys, issues relating to the public good including child welfare, and administration of public works.

LAND TITLES AND PROCESSIONER'S BOOKS

The county court appointed commissioners for processing land claims and disputed land causes. It was authorized to lay off the county into districts for processing land, to appoint commissioners to resurvey old boundary lines of applicant's lands, and to certify alterations in boundary marks to the county clerk. These commissioners worked with the county surveyor. Information in processioners books typically includes the names of the processioner(s), plaintiff and defendant, amount, location and description of original survey, description of boundaries established by processioners, and date of survey.

THE PUBLIC GOOD

County court responsibilities included superintending public inspections, bastardy proceedings, and providing for the poor in the county. The county court also appointed inspectors, collectors, highway surveyors, jailers, and other inferior officers including inspectors for flour, hemp, and tobacco.

CHILD WELFARE

In 1799, the county court was extended the power to appoint guardians for nonresident infants with property in the county. The court's child welfare duties included authorization to bind out poor orphan children, including free blacks, as apprentices. Complaints of apprentices or hired servants against their masters were heard in this court. The court could also commit a child to a house of reform. Since its beginning, the county court has heard and determined bastardy cases.

ROADS AND OTHER PUBLIC WORKS

The jurisdiction of the county court has always extended over road matters. The court could build and maintain county roads and toll gates by 1833. It also had authority to establish and regulate ferries. The court has always had authority over all matters pertaining to mills, mill dams, and obstructions in such dams.

PUBLIC HOUSES

The county courts were empowered to grant tavern licenses and to regulate tippling houses. Surety bonds were furnished by tavern and coffeehouse keepers as covenant that they would keep an orderly house, would neither sell or give any spirituous or vinous liquors to any person who was intoxicated, nor sell or give such liquor to any minor. The records show the name of the principal and surety, amount of bond, and date of execution.

CONTENT OF COUNTY COURT RECORDS

In addition to the matters recorded in the county order books maintained by the county clerk on issues discussed above, the recording of deeds and other documents into the court record was the responsibility of the county courts. As a result, by far the most extensive sources for Kentucky history are the records of the clerk of the county court. In these records are the essentials for Kentucky researchers: deeds, marriages, probate records, depositions, licenses, tax lists, widow and soldiers' pension claims, life estates regarding slaves, and naturalization records.

AVAILABILITY OF RECORDS

A majority of the early county court records were microfilmed in Kentucky over twenty years ago by the Church of Jesus Christ of Latter-day Saints. Some counties did not participate in the project for various reasons. However, the Kentucky State Department of Libraries and Archives has filmed or refilmed most of these early records. Chapter 8 details the holdings of these microfilmed records for each Kentucky county. The archives is also a repository for additional original county court records that the county clerk no longer wishes to maintain or that have not yet been microfilmed.

OFFICE OF THE SHERIFF

The 1792 and 1799 constitutions provided for the office of sheriff in every Kentucky county. Functions of the sheriff's office have varied since its creation in 1792 from one that emphasized law enforcement, to one that today focuses on tax collection.

LAW ENFORCEMENT FUNCTIONS

Sheriff's responsibilities included enforcing peddlers licensure, suppressing gambling, executing writs, making arrests, enforcing game and fish laws, impounding unlicensed dogs running at large, pursuing escaped convicts, arresting persons engaged in riots, routs, unlawful assemblies or breaches of the peace, impaneling a jury for their trial, and arresting persons disturbing public worship.

The sheriff had the duty to report on accidents and take statements when a person was wounded or killed, and to investigate any public house, camp, restaurant or place where liquors were sold or furnished to the public, and places that provided rooms or lodging for the public. It was long the duty of the sheriff to summon grand and petit juries.

It was also the sherriff's duty to convey persons sentenced to prison, execute persons condemned to be hanged in the county, and execute the sentence of the court in other criminal or penal cases.

TAX COLLECTION

Collection of revenue has always been a major duty of the sheriff's office. The sheriff can hold the property of insolvent debtors for creditors and sell it to settle estates and collect taxes due. One of the initial duties of the sheriff was to make a report to the state auditor of public accounts. On 1 October of each year, and every sixty days thereafter, the sheriff reports the amount of taxes collected for the state.

SUMMONING THE JURORS

The common law required the sheriff at each term of court to summon "between thirteen and twenty-three gentlemen of estate, intelligence, and character from the different neighborhoods of the county," who should compose the grand jury. One of the earliest Kentucky laws required the sheriff to summon twenty-four freeholders, qualified as the law required, for grand jurors to appear at the court of oyer and terminer. These early laws have undergone several changes as to the number of grand jurymen; today a grand jury consists of twelve persons, nine of whom concurring, may find an indictment (Kentucky Historical Records Survey 1937, 50).

JAILING THE JAILER

Political corruption being what it evidently always has been in Kentucky, the general assembly, in a brief flash of brilliance, authorized sheriffs to serve as jailer if the jailer himself was incarcerated.

CONTENT OF SHERIFF'S RECORDS

From the beginning of the office, the sheriff made an annual report and paid to the state treasurer the state taxes levied in the county. Records kept by the sheriff include assessor's books, tax lists, tax reports, whiskey tax reports, sheriff's land sold for taxes, and animal records including licenses, claim books, and estray or stray books. A law passed in 1799 required the sheriff to make lists of insolvent taxpayers, persons who had moved out of the county, and delinquent taxpayers. The delinquent list sometimes listed an explanation for the delinquency—such as moved out of the county, deceased, etc. The "persons removed" lists often include valuable information such as the state, county, or city to which the person moved.

Records of lands sold for taxes were maintained by the sheriff's office. These records typically show the date and place of sale, name of delinquent taxpayers, years delinquent, amount, location and description of property, assessed value, amount of tax, name of purchaser, and associated costs.

The sheriff also kept records of warrants showing the name of defendant, offense, trial, and bond information. Notices to tenants to vacate property from the justice courts showed the names and addresses of property owners and tenants, location, and description of property to be vacated. Sheriff's books will thus include execution books, warrant books, witness and rule books, and writ books.

AVAILABILITY OF RECORDS

The bulk of sheriff's records that survive today exist in the form of microfilmed tax records and sheriff's deed books. The best collection of microfilmed records are at the Kentucky State Archives. The archives also holds scattered original sheriff's records for some counties.

MASTER COMMISSIONER'S OFFICE

In Kentucky, according to laws enacted in 1811 and 1839, the master commissioner has authority to sell land and estates in which (1) there is insufficient money to pay the debts for settlement of an estate, or (2) where there is no living person to execute a deed transferring property, or (3) where heirs are unwilling or unable to settle the estate.

It was not until the 1839 law that the name of "master commissioner" was used. At that time, appointments of the commissioners were to be made by the several chancery courts.

In 1852, the act created the office of master commissioner in each county and appointments were made by the circuit court.

AVAILABILITY OF RECORDS

Master commissioner deed books in Kentucky are often separated into their own volumes, and many have been microfilmed. Microfilmed records are listed in chapter 8 by county. These records are variously called sheriff's deeds or commissioner's deeds. In some counties, this distinction is not made; all deeds, including the commissioner's deeds, are filed in the same volumes. Where these records are filed together, the records may be filed under various filing schemes (check under the "H" pages for heirs, "C" for commissioner, and under "S" for settlement and sheriff). These deeds are sometimes filed under the surname of the commissioner or sheriff who took the action.

FISCAL COURT

The fiscal court in Kentucky was patterned after the Virginia system and was originally administered by various tribunals. In 1892, the fiscal court was created as a distinct entity, although the composition and function was about the same as its predecessor, the court of claims and levy.

The fiscal court had jurisdiction over fiscal matters of the county including public works such as roads, mills, and ferries. Transportation matters, such as appointing surveyors of the highways, appointing patrollers, and establishing ferries, was the responsibility of this court. The fiscal court partitioned the county into districts and appointed constables for each district. This court also levied taxes and sold unappropriated lands to pay for county needs such as roads, providing for widows, and building poor houses.

KENTUCKY PUBLIC ROAD SYSTEM

Early county dirt roads, or "pikes," were built and maintained at county expense. As a result, during the first century of Kentucky's statehood, the county courts exercised supervision of county roads and bridges. The Basic Road Act of 1797 gave the county court the power to divide all the public roads in the county into precincts and to appoint a road surveyor to oversee the roads in the precinct. In 1893, the fiscal court became a separate entity replacing the county court of claims and levy. At this time, the county and fiscal courts had joint control of the county's roads and bridges.

Since 1912, the Kentucky State Department of Public Roads and the federal government have cooperated with counties in construction and maintenance of roads and federal highways. Today, the counties continue to be responsible for roads that are not an integral part of the state and national highway system.

THE ROAD SURVEYOR SYSTEM

A description of the duties of the road surveyor, or overseer, gives an excellent picture of the development of the road system in the county. An account of his functions shows the evolution from a simple system of communal road labor, to the use of road fines and slave labor, to a modern system.

In 1799, the road surveyor was appointed by the court and continued indefinitely in office until the county court replaced him. The typical term was at least two years. One law stated he could not resign within two years without the consent of the court, unless he moved from the precinct. An 1894 law specified that the appointment be for two years.

The duty of the early road surveyor was to superintend the road in his precinct and to see that it was cleared and in good repair. These duties meant he was responsible for calling out all eligible men to help repair the road at appropriate times.

The surveyors were also responsible for providing road markers and keeping them in repair. When bridges or causeways were needed, they were to be built at least twelve feet wide.

If the job was too difficult, the county could, and did, contract to have them built by construction companies.

All male laborers over the age of fifteen, white and black, were appointed by the county court to work on some public road. Within ten days after the appointment of a road surveyor, the sheriff delivered a copy of the order to the new appointee, a description of the bounds of the road precinct, and a list of eligible men in the neighborhood over whom the road surveyor was placed.

There were exemptions to the road duty: masters of two or more slaves were exempted, as were ministers of the gospel and all free male inhabitants of the county who were fifty years or older. Evidently, men over fifty with two or more slaves made these laws.

Men who failed to appear at the workplace, as well as those who appeared without proper tools, were fined. A man could provide a worker to substitute for himself and thereby escape the fine. There were some restrictions to this call for road duty: the surveyor had to give two days' notice and could not call out road hands on militia muster days. However, he could call out one or more hands at any time to remove road obstructions.

By 1893, the law was changed to allow the fiscal court to require all able-bodied citizens of the county between the ages of eighteen and fifty to work on the roads. There were again restrictions. The work was not to exceed six days a year. Ministers and citizens of incorporated towns and cities were exempt. A day's work was eight hours; delinquent road workers were fined $2.50. In some counties, the overseers were responsible for reporting the number of road workers and the time worked to the fiscal court and furnishing each worker with a certificate of time spent.

ESTABLISHING A NEW ROAD

Establishing a new road involved a number of legal steps. A person, or group of people, who wanted to open a new road or change the route of an existing road, made application to the county court. Three or more road viewers were appointed. These viewers examined the existing road or proposed route and reported back to the court the advantages or disadvantages of the proposal.

If the project was approved, the court issued summonses to landowners whose property the new road would impact to show cause why the work should not be done. The parties would agree to a price, and then the court ordered the work to be done.

If no price could be agreed upon, the clerk issued a writ of ad quod damnum to the sheriff directing him to impanel a jury of twelve freeholders. This jury would view the ground and assess costs for the use of the land and additional fencing, if necessary. This recommendation was considered by the court in determining whether the project should proceed.

If it was decided to go ahead with the project, the county levied the costs in the next county levy. If the court decided not to do the work, the jury costs were charged against the applicants.

This procedure was only applicable for rural property. It was not legal for the court to order a road opened through any lot of land in any town without the consent of the owner or tenant. A different procedure was used for roads when the road crossed county boundaries or terminated in a different county. This basic method was continued until 1912 when the State Department of Public Roads was created and took over the duty of building and maintaining state roads and bridges.

CONTENT AND AVAILABILITY OF RECORDS

Road order books include the orders issued by the court appointing road surveyors and often give not only the name of the surveyor, but also the precinct and name of the road along with the boundaries of the precinct. Orders in the county clerk's books will also list the names of the other men responsible for maintaining or building the road. These orders can be used to document residence in a county when tax lists are unavailable.

Road books still exist for some counties. The archives has a number of original road books that have not been microfilmed. Chapter 8 lists the microfilmed records available for each county.

LAW ENFORCEMENT RECORDS AND POLICE COURTS

Availability of early police court records is limited statewide. This is, of course, due to the fact that a less formal approach to security was taken in early, rural Kentucky.

However, Lexington established as early as 1796 a system of night watches. These watchmen were appointed by the city trustees to protect city dwellers from the hazards of criminals, teenagers, and fires (Wade 1959, 88-90). These types of activities would, of course, be recorded in the city records or perhaps in the county order books.

The content of the police court records consists of dockets and a record of disposition of cases brought before it. Police court records are not limited to criminal records, but will contain records of any problems requiring immediate attention that were brought before the court during its hours of operation.

For example, because they were open at night and were courts of record, urban workers often filed their naturalization papers in the Jefferson County Police Court. Jefferson County Police Records have been microfilmed; a copy of these is held by the archives in Frankfort.

The Kentucky State Archives has scattered municipal and other city and town record books that may be helpful in a genealogical search. However, city records are inventoried separately, and these "city" notebooks must be consulted in addition to the county records. Where such records have been microfilmed, they appear under the city name in the appropriate county in chapter 8.

OFFICE OF THE CORONER

The major function of the coroner was, and has always been, to hold an inquisition, with the aid of a jury, over the body of any person whose death may have resulted from violence, including suicide. In the case of a violent death, the coroner ordered the sheriff or constable to summon a jury to the place where the death or crime occurred to determine the cause or the culprit. The coroner also had the right to search and investigate any deaths in the county that were not attended by a qualified physician.

The coroner also had peace officer functions and could execute process in all criminal, penal, and civil cases. The coroner was the highest peace officer in the county and had power of arrest.

Coroner records will describe the circumstances of a death and conclude, if possible, the cause of death. However, the Kentucky coroner was not required to keep records, but did make reports to the circuit court. As a result, Kentucky coroner

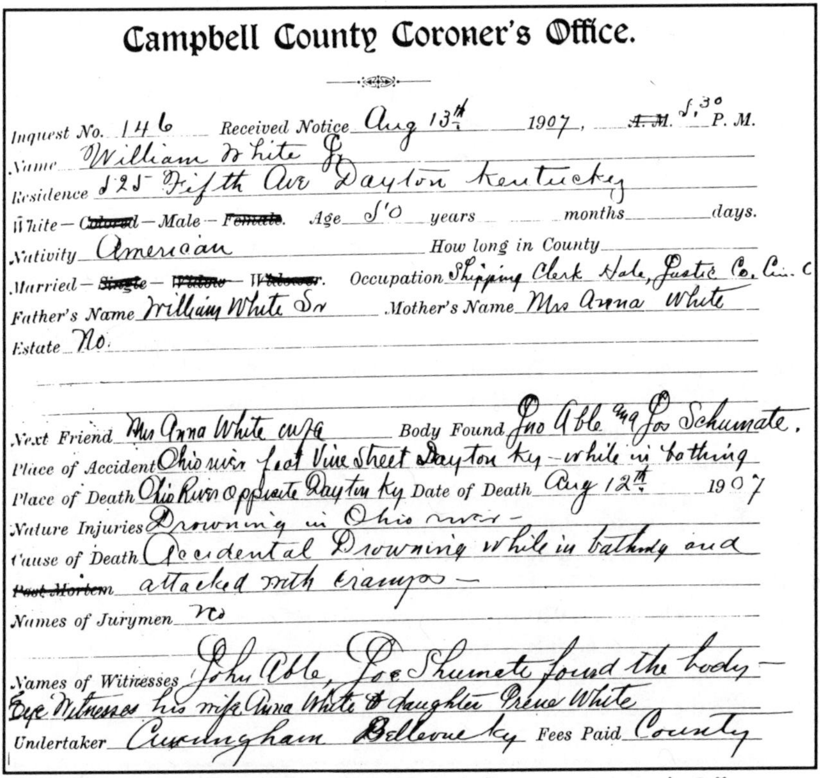

Campbell County Coroner's Office.

Inquest No. _146_ Received Notice _Aug 13th_ 1907, _A.M._ _5.30_ P. M.
Name _William White Jr_
Residence _825 Fifth Ave Dayton Kentucky_
White – Colored – Male – Female. Age _50_ years _____ months _____ days.
Nativity _American_ _____ How long in County _____
Married – Single – Widow – Widower. Occupation _Shipping Clerk Hale, Justis Co. Cin. O_
Father's Name _William White Sr_ Mother's Name _Mrs Anna White_
Estate _No._

Next Friend _Mrs Anna White wife_ Body Found _Jno Able Mq Jos Schumate._
Place of Accident _Ohio river foot Vine Street Dayton Ky – while in bathing_
Place of Death _Ohio River opposite Dayton Ky_ Date of Death _Aug 12th_ 19 0 7
Nature Injuries _Drowning in Ohio river –_
Cause of Death _Accidental Drowning while in bathing and_
Post Mortem _attacked with cramps –_
Names of Jurymen _no_
Names of Witnesses _John Able, Joe Shumate found the body –_
Eye Witnesses _his wife Anna White & daughter Irene White_
Undertaker _Cunningham Bellevue Ky_ Fees Paid _County_

FIG. 3.3 Coroner's report , 1907. (Campbell County Coroner's Office
records, Kentucky State Archives)

records are inconsistent or minimal at the county level. Where they do exist, they are usually maintained with the health department in the larger cities. The existence of modern coroner records can sometimes be identified by the presence of the coroner's signature or note of an inquest on the death certificate.

FEDERAL COURT RECORDS

HISTORICAL OVERVIEW

While Kentucky did not become a state until 1792, it became its own judicial district earlier. Kentucky was partitioned from the Middle Federal Circuit, of which Virginia was a part, in 1789. At that time, there were four other federal circuits: the Eastern and Southern districts, a Western Territories Circuit, and Maine.

The first Kentucky district court was held on 15 December 1790 at Harrodsburg by Henry Innes. The sessions of this court continued until 9 June 1794 when the court was moved to Frankfort (Hathaway 1974, 99). District and circuit court sessions for all Kentucky were held at Frankfort until 1860 when legislation was passed that determined sessions of both courts would be held at Louisville, Covington, and Paducah. Owensboro was added in 1888.

In 1901, Kentucky was divided into two federal districts: an eastern and western district. The eastern district originally included sessions at Frankfort, Richmond, London, and Covington. The western district held sessions at Louisville, Bowling Green, Owensboro, and Paducah. Beginning in 1902, sessions were also held in the eastern district at Catlettsburg.

The circuit courts were abolished in 1911 and their jurisdiction was passed to the district courts. This 1911 act also extended the Eastern District to hold sessions in Jackson. In 1920 and 1936, the Eastern District was again expanded to include sessions at Lexington and Pikeville (Hathaway 1974, 99).

At the present time, Kentucky has two of the ninety-four federal judicial districts in the United States. Table 3.1 lists the courts of the two districts.

TABLE 3.1	District Courts of the United States in Kentucky
Jurisdiction	Court Location
Eastern District	
Ashland	1405 Greenup Avenue, Room 336 41101
Catlettsburg	Closed; replaced by Ashland
Covington	P.O. Box 1012 41012
Frankfort	330 W. Broadway 40602-1041
Jackson	*
Kentucky	**
Lexington	206 Federal Building 40586
London	Box 689, U.S. Courthouse 40741
Pikeville	203 Federal Building 41501
Richmond	*

Western District	
Bowling Green	213 Federal Building 42101
Louisville	230 U.S. Courthouse 40202
Owensboro	210 Federal Building 42302
Paducah	322 Federal Building 42001

* The Richmond and Jackson offices were closed in the 1960s; their order books are held by the Lexington office.

** Early records for the years 1789 to 1798 had been on display in Lexington; they have recently been moved to the Kentucky archives in Frankfort.

Sources: 16 October 1989 personal correspondence from the Clerk of the United States District Court, Eastern District of Kentucky. 11 April 1990 personal correspondence from the Federal Records Center—Atlanta.

CONTENT OF FEDERAL COURT RECORDS

The functions of the federal district courts and appeals courts are limited compared to those of the state courts.

Nevertheless, the court's jurisdiction is quite broad. Cases heard by the federal courts include those where the parties involved are the U.S. government, citizens of different states, or foreign diplomats. Violations of constitutional law, federal law, regulatory statutes, and orders of governmental administrative agencies are heard in federal court. The courts also hear admiralty cases and cases dealing with patents and copyrights. In recent years, half of the federal district court cases were bankruptcy cases, and another ten percent were minor criminal cases. In summary, most of its cases are civil rather than criminal.

LOCATION OF KENTUCKY FEDERAL COURT RECORDS

The federal court records of Kentucky are in three major locations: the federal courts themselves, the National Archives—Atlanta Branch, and the Federal Records Center—Atlanta.

The federal court clerks in Kentucky typically have only the order books for cases heard in their courts, not the original case papers. The older records and original case papers are usually transferred to either the archives or the records center in Atlanta. As a result, the National Archives and the Federal Records Center in Atlanta possess a variety of early and modern records generated by the Kentucky federal courts. The National Archives has the original Kentucky federal court records listed in tables 3.3, 3.5, and 3.6. No microfilm copies are available, and, thus, records are not available for loan. The Federal Records Center in Atlanta holds the records listed in table 3.4.

SEARCHING KENTUCKY RECORDS AT THE NATIONAL ARCHIVES—ATLANTA

Kentucky's federal court records were originally held in the Chicago Branch of the National Archives. Early references to Kentucky federal court records in the Chicago Archives Center are out of date; these records have been transferred to the National Archives located in an Atlanta suburb at East Point, Georgia.

The National Archives—Atlanta Branch in East Point allows researchers access to both microfilmed records, original case files, and other documents. However, original records listed in this chapter are not typically available during evening and Saturday hours unless prior arrangements have been made during normal operating hours.

SEARCHING KENTUCKY RECORDS AT THE FEDERAL RECORDS CENTER IN ATLANTA

The Federal Records Center—Atlanta, although located in the same building with the archives, is a separate entity. The Federal Records Center serves as a "halfway house" for older records. The center typically holds records until they are twenty-five years old and then transfers them to the National Archives—Atlanta Branch. However, in Kentucky's case, some older records are still at the records center. As a result, the Federal Records Center has older Kentucky records as well as more recent ones.

Access to records in the Federal Records Center is by appointment only. This means that researchers must call ahead and make an appointment. Walk-ins are generally not permitted. When arranging for the appointment, it is necessary to provide the file location information obtained from the court of record. Requests should be made twenty-four hours in advance to ensure that records will be available.

TABLE 3.2	National Archives and Federal Records Center Information

---

The National Archives	The Federal Records Center
1557 St. Joseph Avenue	1557 St. Joseph Avenue
East Point, Georgia 30344	East Point, Georgia 30344
Telephone: 404-763-7477/7650	Telephone: 404-763-7474

AVAILABILITY OF KENTUCKY'S FEDERAL COURT RECORDS

EARLY KENTUCKY RECORDS

Frankfort was the sole site of district and circuit court sessions until 1860. Many of these Kentucky court records have been moved to the National Archives in Atlanta. Those records that could be located for early Kentucky are shown in table 3.3.

TABLE 3.3	Early Statewide and Frankfort Circuit and District Court Records in the National Archives—Atlanta Branch and in the Federal Records Center—Atlanta

---

NATIONAL ARCHIVES—ATLANTA BRANCH

Circuit Court

1807–35	Executions
1804–60	Judgments and Decrees
1880–90	Cases Dismissed by U.S. Commissioner
1836,1845	Chancery Cases

District Court

1805–1901	Executions
1800–57	Judgments and Decrees
1842–83	Bankruptcy Cases
1878–80	Bankruptcy Cases
1842–83	Bankruptcy Discharges

Miscellaneous Materials

1789–1889	Judgments—James Morrison, Ancient Causes; Warrants and Subpoenas, Ignored Indictments
1799–1860	Bankruptcy Records*

FEDERAL RECORDS CENTER—ATLANTA

1879–1978	Civil Case Files
1885–1964	Criminal Case Files and Records
1898–1964	Bankruptcy Files

---

* These records are not yet described and archived, but comprise 110 cubic feet (per Archivist David E. Hilkert, 22 January 1990 correspondence).

Sources: Personal correspondence from David E. Hilkert, archivist, National Archives—Southeast Region, 19 March 1990. Personal correspondence from Tom W. Steinichen, chief, Appraisal and Disposition Branch, Federal Records Center—Atlanta, 11 April 1990.

EASTERN DISTRICT RECORDS

Eastern district Kentucky federal court records begin in 1860 when courts outside Frankfort could begin to hear cases.

Recent eastern district order books are maintained in the six district court offices at Ashland, Covington, Frankfort, Lexington, London, and Pikeville. These local court offices generally maintain copies of their order books only and send to Atlanta the case files and other records for older cases.

Kentucky's eastern district federal court records are still in both the federal courts in Kentucky as well as the Federal Records Center–Atlanta. The older case files, which date from the early 1800s up to 1980, were sent to the Federal Records Center in East Point, Georgia in November of 1986.

WESTERN DISTRICT RECORDS

The western district court order books are also still in courts in Louisville, Bowling Green, Owensboro, and Paducah.

A substantial number of records have been transferred to the Archives and Records Center in East Point. Many of these older records were transferred to the archives in 1956. These old records are listed in the detail report (table 3.6) at the end of this chapter.

SCOPE OF KENTUCKY RECORDS IN THE NATIONAL ARCHIVES

Kentucky records held by the Federal Records Center–Atlanta are summarized in table 3.4 below.

| TABLE 3.4 | Kentucky Federal Court Records in the Federal Records Center–Atlanta |

ASHLAND

1976–85	Civil Cases
1975–85	Criminal Cases

BOWLING GREEN

1905–87	Bankruptcy Records
1954–74	Civil Records
1956–77	Criminal Records

CATLETTSBURG

1957–66	Admiralty
1903–79	Bankruptcy Records
1909–83	Civil Records
1902–80	Criminal Records

COVINGTON

1867–1979	Bankruptcy Records
1866–1978	Civil Records
1929–32	Commissioner Docket
1860–84	Criminal Records
1915–78	Criminal Records

FRANKFORT

1898–1964	Bankruptcy Records
1879–1978	Civil Records
1885–1964	Criminal Records

JACKSON

1909–64	Bankruptcy Records
1909–64	Civil Records
1909–64	Criminal Records

LEXINGTON

1920–85	Bankruptcy Records
1920–80	Civil Records
1935–41	Commissioner's Docket
1918–83	Criminal Records

LONDON

1902–79	Bankruptcy Records
1902–83	Criminal Records
1940–83	Civil Records

LOUISVILLE

1899–1987	Bankruptcy Records
1945–84	Civil Records
1892–92	Criminal Records Cases
1954–86	Criminal Records
1936–78	Naturalization Petitions (in 3 series)
1946–81	Miscellaneous Cases

OWENSBORO

1875–1987	Bankruptcy
1955–84	Civil Records
1955–84	Criminal Records
1974	Admiralty Records

PADUCAH

1902–86	Bankruptcy Records
1955–83	Civil Records
1955–83	Criminal Records

PIKEVILLE

1937–79	Bankruptcy Records
1936–82	Criminal Records
1936–82	Civil Records

RICHMOND

1900–49	Bankruptcy Records
1905–64	Civil Records
1900–64	Criminal Records

Source: National Archives (NARS–5 Database) as of 11 April 1990.

Table 3.5 gives the summary listing of Kentucky federal court records in the National Archives–Atlanta Branch. The information for this inventory was obtained from the National Archives–Atlanta Branch and represents the most current information available.

TABLE 3.5   Kentucky Federal Court Records
in National Archives–Atlanta Branch (Summary)

BOWLING GREEN

1938–56	Civil Action Case Files (by case number)
1915–38	Equity Case Files (by case number)
1907–38	Law Case Files (by case number)
1902–55	Criminal Case Files (by case number)
1915–35	Commissioners' Books
1957–62	Order Books

LONDON

No Dates	Bankruptcy Cases (six feet)

LOUISVILLE

Naturalization Records

1920–21	Naturalization Fee Abstracts (chronological)
1906–57	Petitions for Naturalizations
1906–51	Declarations of Intention
1918–21	Military Naturalizations (World War I)
1920–21	Naturalization Records

Bankruptcy Records

1867–71	Bankruptcy Cases Register (by surname)
1867–1943	Bankruptcy Docket Books (by case number)
1867–1911	Bankruptcy Order Books (chronological)
1876–78	Orders of Reference to Register in Bankruptcy
1876–83	Orders for Bankruptcy Discharges (chronological)

1872–75	Bankruptcy Assignees (alphabetical)
1867–78	Bankruptcy Case Files (by case number)
1867–84	Bankruptcy Records, Clerk's Miscellaneous (unarranged)
1899–1916	Bankruptcy Minute Books (chronological)
1925–44	Bankruptcy Record Books, Referees' Summaries of Proceedings (by case number)
1869–79	Bankruptcy Appeal and Order Docket Book (chronological)
1870–87	Bankruptcy Appeals Case Files (by case number)
No Dates	Register of Cases in Execution Dockets (by surname)

Civil, Law and Equity Records

No Dates	Unidentified Registers (by surname**)
1912–34	Registers of Criminal, Law and Equity Cases (by surname—to be used as index to other case files)
1866–69	Criminal and Civil Cases Docket Book
1860–1911	Mixed Cases Order Books—Criminal, Civil, and Admiralty (by plaintiff or defendant surname)
1879–88	Mixed Cases Minute Book—Admiralty, Bankruptcy, Civil, and Criminal
1863–69	Appeals and Writs of Error (by surname and chronological)
1860–1916	Final Record Book of Mixed Cases—Civil, Criminal, and Admiralty (most with registers by surname)
1860–1911	Mixed Case Files (consecutive arrangement)
1860–1928	Miscellaneous Case Papers (chronological***)
1939–56	Admiralty Case Files (by case number)
1912–48	Civil Judgment Docket Books (by surname)
1861–63	Execution of Judgments Record Book (chronological)
1938–47	Civil Order Book (chronological+)
1938–54	Civil Action Case Files (by case number)
1929–38	Equity Journals (chronological)
1920–29	Equity Order Books (chronological)
1913–38	Equity Case Files (by case number)
1930–31	Law and Equity Calendars (by term of court)
1868–80	Suits by Assignees (by case number)
1909–38	Law Order Books (chronological+)
1907–38	Law Case Files (by case number)

Criminal Records

1903–07	Criminal Docket Book (by case number)
1902–16	Complete Record Books of Criminal Cases (chronological)
1907–48	Criminal Judgment Docket Books (by defendant surname)
1912–45	Criminal Order Books
1862–65	Bonds for Good Behavior
1906–54	Criminal Case Files (by case number)

1924–32	Registers to Criminal Calendars (by term of court and surname)
1927–32	Criminal Calendars (by term of court and case number)
1931–38	Parole and Probation Records (by surname)
1863–92	Criminal Recognizances (chronological and most with register by surname)
1861–63	Treason Case Files (Civil War)
1879–1904	Oaths of Poor Convicts (chronological)
1893	Reports of Prosecutions for Violations of IRS Laws (chronological)
1882–1901	U.S. Commissioners' Criminal Record Books (chronological and register by surname)

Witness and Jury Records

1891–1916	Witness Docket Books, U.S. Attorney (by court term and surname)
1924–33	Grand Juries, Praecipes and Subpoenas (by court term)
1894–1933	Grand and Petit Juries, Venires (chronological)

U.S. Marshall Records

1878–95	Witness Compensation, U.S. Marshall's Records (chronological)
1895–97	Criminal Process Book, U.S. Marshall (chronological)
1889–99	Execution Docket Books, U.S. Marshall (rough chronological)
1882–1901	U.S. Marshall's Letter Press Books (chronological and partial register by surname)
1885–96	Vouchers for Support of Prisoners (chronological)

Clerks and Other Miscellaneous Case Records

1865–1911	Minute Book, Clerk's (chronological)
1855–65	Fee Books, Clerk's (chronological and by surname)
1875–92	Fee Book, Criminal Cases, Clerk's (chronological and by surname)
1919–32	Witness Certificates, Clerk's (by case number)
1919–21	Witness Discharge Slips (chronological)
1914–20	Subpoenas, Clerk's Records (chronological)
1921–27	Clerk's Correspondence Files (by correspondent)
1920–21	Whiskey Bonds Reports (chronological)
1925–49	U.S. Commissioners' Transcript Dockets (chronological)
1862–68	U.S. Commissioners' Docket Book (chronological)
1897–1936	U.S. Commissioners' Criminal Record Books (most with register by defendant's surname ++)
1889–96	Warrants, U.S. Commissioners (chronological and by surname)
1863–1911	Minute Books, Mixed Cases (chronological)
1860–1909	Order Books, Mixed Cases (chronological and partial register by surname)

1860-1911	Complete Record Books (final), Mixed Cases (chronological and partial register by surname)
1860-1917	Mixed Case Files (by case number)
1893-94	Docket Book of Claims for Debt, against Railroad Employees (chronological)
1860-69	Record Book of the Execution of Judgments (chronological)
1860-62	Judgment Case Files (by case number)
1866-1903	Habeas Corpus Case Files (chronological)
1860-61	Administrative Order Book (chronological)
1882-94	Rules of Courts for Eastern and Western District of Kentucky (chronological)
1894-1902	Calendar of Cases (by case number)
1876-91	Clerk's Correspondence
1880-1906	Clerk's Jury List (alphabetical)
1863-83	Clerk's Cash Books (chronological)
1893-96	Clerk's Records of Fees (chronological)
1893-95	Vouchers of Fees Paid to Witnesses (by voucher number)

OWENSBORO

1890-1924	Docket Book of Mixed Cases (chronological and case number+)
1889-1924	Minute Books (chronological)
1898-1900	Bankruptcy Docket Book (by case number)
1899-1922	Bankruptcy Minute Books (chronological)
1895-1916	Civil Complete (final) Record Books (chronological)
1938-54	Civil Case Files (by case number)
1913-38	Equity Case Files (by case number)
1908-38	Law Case Files (by case number)
1905-16	Criminal Record Books, Complete (final) (chronological and some by surname)
1894-1954	Criminal Case Files (by case number)
1900-05	Commissioners' Case Files (chronological)
1889-1912	Complete (final) Record Books of Circuit and District Court Cases (chronological and some registers by surname)
1889-1912	Law and Equity Docket Books (chronological and by case type and number)
1889-1912	Law and Equity Minute Books (chronological)
1890-1912	Law and Equity Journal Rule Book (chronological)
1888-1911	Equity Case Files (by case number)

PADUCAH

1912-38	Law/Admiralty Case Files (by case number)
1867-78	Bankruptcy Case Files (by case number)
1938-57	Civil Case Files (by case number)
1912-38	Equity Case Files (by case number)
1912-54	Criminal Case Files (by case number)

1936–48	Grand Jury Votes Records (chronological)
1869–1911	Mixed Case Files (by case number)
1926–27	Clerk's Correspondence

**   By Surname—indicates that there is a register or index arranged by the initial letter of the surname.

***   These records contain papers related to the Hatfield-McCoy feud, Freedmen's bureau, and loyalty oaths filed during the Civil War.

+   Contains naturalization records.

++   Contains records from Louisville, Paducah, Bowling Green, Tompkinsville, Albany, Bardstown, Hodgenville, Leitchfield, and Williamsburg.

Sources: Listings provided by National Archives—Atlanta Branch by Mr. David Hilkert, archivist, 7 December 1989, and supplemental list by Mr. Charles Reeves, assistant director, National Archives—Southeast Region, 19 October 1989.

The inventory of material accessioned to the Federal Archives is detailed in table 3.6. This information was taken directly from the accession sheets prepared by the Louisville court during the accession process and was provided by the Louisville District Court clerk office.

This inventory will show records that are not listed in the National Archives Records Center's computerized database, which is summarized in table 3.4. This is because the records at the Federal Records Center are compiled by accession number and, therefore, are reported by date of acquisition. Their inventory, as a result, is not always completely descriptive of all the materials contained in the transfer. The list below, on the other hand, breaks out each shipment of records and does not group them by accession number; it reflects more precisely all types of records contained in each shipment.

TABLE 3.6	Western District Court Records Accessioned to Federal Archives Detail Report
1863	Appeals of Judgment
1863–68	Appeals, Circuit Court
1895–1903	Appearance Cases
1900–28	Bankruptcy
1899–1941	Bankruptcy Case Files (nos. 1,000–14,701)
	Bankruptcy Case Files, Act of 1867 (nos. 1–6,097)
1866–1929+	Bankruptcy Dockets and Order Books (vols. 1–18)
	Bankruptcy Dockets Referees
1927–27	Bankruptcy Minute Book
1926–41	Bankruptcy Order Books
1867–81	Bankruptcy Records
1868–72	Bankruptcy, Equity Bonds for Good Behavior
1860–65	Circuit Cases Civil and Criminal (nos. 1–7,316)

1864–66	Circuit Court Cases
1861–1917	Circuit Court Dockets (37 books)
	Circuit Court Recognizances (books 1–7)
1867–1916	Civil and Bankruptcy Records
1830–1910	Civil and Criminal Cases
	Civil Case Files, District Court (nos. 391–540)
?–1872	Civil Dockets (books 1–10)
1938–42	Civil Order Books (vol. 11)
post-1912	Civil Records
1830–1910	Civil, Criminal, and Admiralty Cases, Circuit Clerk Records
1931	Commissioners' Accounts
	Commissioners' Criminal Records (Owensboro)
	Commissioners' Criminal Records (Paducah)
	Commissioners' Transcripts
1880–1910	Commissioners' Reports
1862	Commissioners' Docket
1902–24	Commissioners' Transcripts
	Commissioners' Vouchers
1898–1901	Complete Records (vol. 3)
1860–1904	Complete Records, Circuit Court (vols. A–GG)
1890–94	Complete Records, District Court (vols. AA–Z)
	Court Calendars
	Court Order Book (vol. 22)
1900	Criminal Cases
1876–94	Criminal and Bankruptcy
1906–44	Criminal Cases (nos. 7,200–21,745)
?–?	Criminal Cases (nos. 9,300–12,000)
1904–44	Criminal Docket of District Court (vols. 1–29)
1891	Criminal Process Book
1895	Criminal Process Book
1871–91	Criminal, Admiralty, Equity Cases
1877–1901	Criminal, Equity, Law
	D. A. Criminal Docket
	D. A. Grand Jury Dockets
1892–93	Depositions, Bonds and Bankruptcy, Criminal Cases
1929	Discharge Journal
1861–99+	District Court Civil Dockets
post-1911	District Court Equity Cases
	District Court Files (nos. 78–7992)
1864	Docket
1886–90	Docket and Index, District Court
1901–09	Docket, District Court
1925–49	Dockets, Commissioner's Transcript
1899–1906	Dockets, District Court
1877	Equity
1897–1905	Equity and Law

1913–1935	Equity Case Files (nos. 1–2,335)
post-1911	Equity Cases (nos. 26, 54, 74, 86, 88, 1046)
1920–29	Equity Journal (vols. 2–3)
1913–20	Equity Order Book (vols. 9–11)
1913	Equity Volumes (vols. 1–4)
1938	Equity Volumes (vols. 5–6)
1833	Equity, Civil
1879	Equity, Criminal
1870	Equity, Criminal
1916–21	Equity, District Court
1892–96	Equity, District Court
1860–91	Execution Books (with gaps)
1860–?	Execution Dockets
	Exhibit Material
1862–64	Fifas (nos. 1–279)
	Final Court Records (vols. 1–8)
1867–67	Freedmen's Bureau
1922–29	Grand Jury Assignments
1895–1905	Grand Jury Lists
	Grand Jury Praecipes and Subpoenas
	Grand and Petit Jury Venires
	Habeas Corpus Case Files
1920s	Habeas Corpus Cases
1837	Immigration and Naturalization
	Index Book, Circuit and District Courts
1903	Indictments File
	Judgment and Index Dockets
1868–76?	Judgment Dockets
1863–1925	Jury Lists, Clerks
	Jury Praecipes and Subpoenas
	Louisville Law (no. 42)
1862–63	Loyalty Oaths
1878–85	Marshalls' Accounts
1880–96	Marshalls' Vouchers
	Marshalls' Vouchers
1899–1900	Marshalls' Letters
1895–1916	Marshalls' Ledger
1912	Minute Books, District Court
1863	Minute Books, Circuit Court (vols. 1–10)
	Miscellaneous Law and Equity
	Miscellaneous Case Papers
1921	Naturalization Reports
	Oaths of Poor Convicts
1907–38	Old Law Case Files
1857–75	Old Law, Equity, Criminal Cases
1868–1911	Order Book, District Court (vols. C–R)
1860	Order Books

ca. 1909	Order Books (nos. 1-7)
1860-1909	Order Books, Circuit Court (vols. A-Z)
	Paducah Equity (nos. 2, 129)
1878-98	Petitions for Discharge in Banks
1916	Petitions for Discharge in Banks
	Prisoner Register, U.S. Marshall
1938-42	Record Book
1927-29	Record Book, District Court
1928-31	Record Book, District Court
	Referee Bankruptcy Records
1881-85	Referee Book
	Referee Claim Registers
1936-46	Referee Diary
1899	Referee Report in Banks
1926-47	Referee Bankruptcy Records
	Referee Bankruptcy Reports to Clerks
	Register Complaints
	Rules of Practice, Circuit Court and District
	Rules of Various Courts
1870-1913	Rules, District Court
1893	Tax Commissioner's Reports on IRS violations
	Unnumbered Case Papers
1875-1910	Unnumbered Cases
	Western Union vs. L & N Railroad
	Witness Certificates
	Witness Discharge Slips
	Witness Dockets, U.S. Attorneys
1891-93	Witness List
1862-99	Witness and Jurors Compensation Lists

Sources: Shelf Lists for District and Circuit Court Case files of the Western District of Kentucky, which were accessioned by the archives (Chicago) with an original accession number of 56A47 and listed as of 6 March 1981. Peter Bunce, chief, Archives Branch of the Chicago General Services Administration, Region 5 correspondence dated 6 March 1981. Materials from Accession 56A47 were sent from Chicago to East Point in 1986.

Shelf Lists for District Court of the Western District of Kentucky as of 22 June 1979 listed in correspondence of R. L. Hutchinson, director of General Services Administration, Federal Archives and Records Center, Chicago, Illinois.

Note: This information was the most recent compilation available from the courts and the archives as of June 1990.

CHAPTER 4

Marking Life's Stages: Kentucky's Birth, Marriage, and Death Records

Birth and Death Records

Kentucky was the first state west of the Alleghenies to require registration of births, marriages, and deaths. This first vital statistics law, known as the Sutton Law, was approved in January of 1852 by the Kentucky General Assembly. It required tax assessors in the auditor's office to register all vital events. In 1862, it was repealed under the pressure of the Civil War and the need for funds for other purposes. In 1874, another law was passed that required birth and death records be sent to the state auditor.

Despite the early legislative efforts, however, during the period from 1852 to 1910 birth, death, and marriage records were irregularly maintained in Kentucky. It was not until 1910, after Kentucky reenacted a second registration statute, that consistent statewide registration began. However, more uniform registration began in the state's larger cities almost twenty years earlier. Lexington, Louisville, Newport, and Covington have substantial numbers of birth and death records from as early as the 1890s. Marriage certificates have been maintained statewide in Frankfort since 1958.

Early Vital Records In Kentucky

Vital Records From 1852 to 1862

The earliest vital records for Kentucky began in 1852 after passage of the Sutton Law. This was not a popular law, and, as a result, compliance was inconsistent. Tax assessors were given the job since they were the only officers of the court required to visit every Kentucky house in the course of their duties.

The 1852 legislation directed all clergy, physicians, and other attending individuals to deposit their registers of births, deaths, and marriages (for the year ending 31 December) with the county clerk where the event occurred no later than 10 January of the following year. The assessors were directed to interview heads of families to confirm these registers and return them 1 May annually with the tax lists. The county clerks were, in turn, required to copy the lists and send copies to the state auditor of public accounts by 1 July annually.

Because of problems with administration and lack of support for the law, there are many problems with these records. The assessors resented the extra work; other officials did not see the value of keeping the records. Dates may be inaccurate. There may be significant omissions of vital events occurring during the year. The lists frequently include events that actually occurred in other counties. From 1861 to the end of the Civil War, reporting was lax or nonexistent among the counties. This law was repealed in 1862.

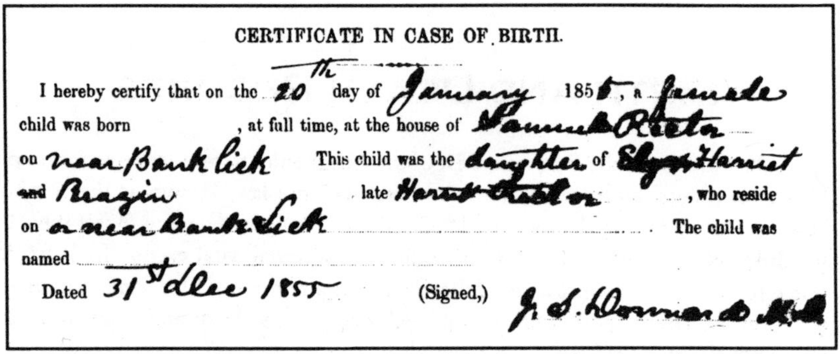

FIG. 4.1 Birth certificate from Kentucky's first vital statistics law, 1855. (Kentucky State Archives)

VITAL RECORDS FROM 1863 TO 1910

From 1863 until 1911, when the current Office of Vital Statistics was established, scattered attempts were made to require vital records. In 1874, a second law required birth and death records be sent to the state auditor.

As a result of the 1874 law, some returns for the period 1874 to 1878 exist. However, it was again poorly administered and results are irregular. Many counties did not participate or dropped the program after a few years. In 1878, clergy were no longer required to report their activities. As a result, returns exist but are scattered for these years. There are also vital records for some counties for the period 1893 to 1894 and again for 1900 to 1904 or 1905.

Fortunately, the exceptions are the larger cities. Lexington, Louisville, Covington, and Newport maintained early vital statistics records beginning in the late 1890s. These records are significant because these areas cover the most populous regions in the state and thus provide a means to track mobile urban ancestors. In addition, these areas serve the medical needs of surrounding rural counties. Some rural Kentuckians, especially eastern Kentuckians, come to Lexington to have illnesses treated. As a result, death records may be found for people who lived hundreds of miles away in these urban records.

Table 4.1 indicates cities maintaining early vital statistics records prior to the 1911 legislation. (See figure 4.3 for sample record.)

TABLE 4.1 — Local Vital Statistics for Kentucky Cities

City	Births	Deaths
Covington	1896–1910	1880–1910
Lexington	1906–1910	1898–1910
Louisville	1898–1910	1866–1910
Newport	1890–1910	1884–1910

Source: Cabinet for Human Resources, Vital Statistics Department.

The microfilms listed in table 4.2 may be purchased from the Kentucky Historical Society Micrographics department.

TABLE 4.2 — Dates of Microfilmed Records

City	Births	Deaths
Covington	1896–1910 and index	1881–1910 and index to 1915
Lexington	1888–1926 and index 1906–1910	1894–1912 1894–1910
Newport	1905–1911	1884–1928

Source: *Kentucky Ancestors* 1983, 19:108; and Kentucky Historical Society Micrographics Department.

CONTENT OF EARLY VITAL RECORDS

The *Inventory of Kentucky Birth, Marriage, and Death Records 1852 to 1910* has been published by the Department of Library and Archives and compiled by Jeffrey M. Duff (Duff 1980). A brief overview of the contents of the records is summarized below based on Duff's compilation. The records are arranged by county and then by year of the event.

Birth Records. The vital statistics inventoried by Duff include assessors' lists of births from 1852 to 1910. Beginning with 1874, separate lists of African-American births exist. Information includes date of birth, child's name, sex, race, condition (born dead or alive), place of birth, name of father or owner, mother's

RETURN OF A DEATH.

1. Name of deceased, - -	*James Marshall*
2. Color, - - - -	*White*
3. Age, - - - -	*about* *25* years months days.
4. Sex, - - - -	*Male*
5. Condition, - - -	*Free*
6. Occupation, - - -	*Farmer*
7. Residence, - - -	*Horse Branch*
8. Where born, - - -	
9. Name of parents or owner, -	*Thomas Marshall*
10. Place of Death, - -	*Horse Branch*
11. Time of Death, - -	*January*
12. Cause of Death, - -	*Diabetes*
13. Remarks, - - -	
N. B. At No. 5, say whether Single, Married, or Widowed.	*Married*

FIG. 4.2 Sample death return dated 1859 from Kentucky's first vital statistics law. (Kentucky State Archives)

maiden name, parents' residence, and remarks. There is no information for the years 1863 to 1873, 1880 to 1892, and 1895 to 1899.

Birth returns were kept during the periods 1856 to 1861 and 1874 to 1877 based on records of physicians or midwives who attended the birth and then reported the event to the county clerk.

Marriage Records. Assessors' lists of marriages date from 1851 to 1910 but do not include 1863 to 1873, 1880 to 1891, or 1895 to 1897. Not all counties have these lists. The record includes date of marriage, groom's name, residence, age, marital status, and birthplace. Information on the bride includes her name, residence, age, marital status, birthplace. Remarks are sometimes included. In 1874, separate lists were kept for black marriages.

Marriage returns are available for the years 1856 to 1858 and 1874 to 1876. Information includes marriage date, groom's name, residence, age, number of marriages, and birthplace. Bride information includes her name, residence, age, number of marriages, birthplace, and remarks.

Death Records. Information from assessors' lists of deaths dates from 1852 to 1914 and includes name, age, sex, marital status, occupation, residence, birthplace, parents' names or names of owners (if a slave), the place, time, cause of death, and remarks. Beginning with the 1874 lists, additional information also includes the deceased's race and parents' names and birthplaces. No records exist for the years 1863 to 1873, 1880 to 1892, and 1895 to 1899.

Death returns exist for 1856 to 1861 and 1874 to 1878. Information includes the deceased's name, race, age, sex, marital status, occupation, residence, birthplace, parents' or owners' names, the place, time, cause of death, and remarks.

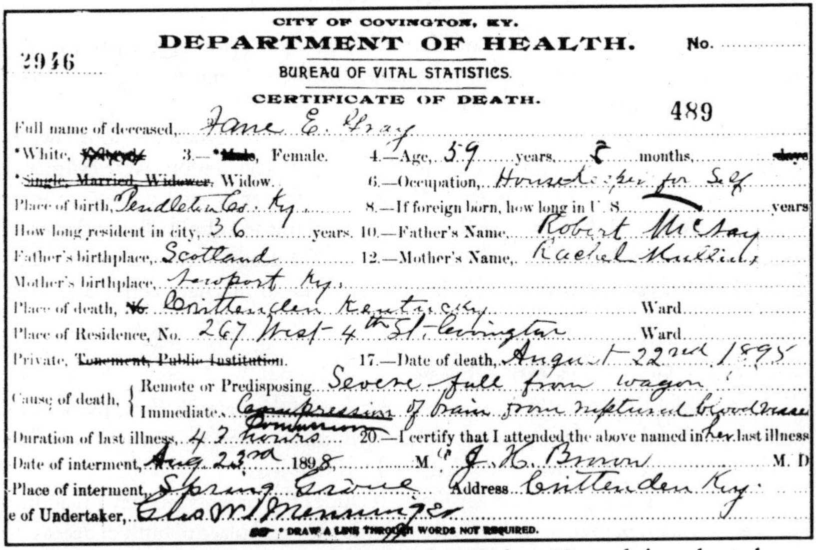
CITY OF COVINGTON, KY.
DEPARTMENT OF HEALTH. No.
2946
BUREAU OF VITAL STATISTICS.
CERTIFICATE OF DEATH.
489
Full name of deceased, Jane E. Gray
White, ~~Colored~~ 3.—~~Male~~, Female. 4.—Age, 59 years, 5 months, ~~days~~
*~~Single, Married, Widower,~~ Widow. 6.—Occupation, Housekeeper for Self
Place of birth, Pendleton Co. Ky 8.—If foreign born, how long in U. S. years
How long resident in city, 36 years. 10.—Father's Name, Robert McCay
Father's birthplace, Scotland 12.—Mother's Name, Rachel
Mother's birthplace, Newport Ky.
Place of death, ~~No.~~ Crittenden Kentucky Ward
Place of Residence, No. 267 West 4th St. Covington Ward
Private, ~~Tenement, Public Institution.~~ 17.—Date of death, August 22nd 1898
Cause of death, Remote or Predisposing Severe fall from wagon
Immediate ~~Compression~~ Concussion of brain from ruptured blood vessel
Duration of last illness, 47 hours 20.—I certify that I attended the above named in her last illness
Date of interment, Aug 23rd 1898, M.D J. H. Brown M. D
Place of interment, Spring Grove Address Crittenden Ky.
e of Undertaker, Chas W. Menninger
* DRAW A LINE THROUGH WORDS NOT REQUIRED.

FIG. 4.3 Sample death certificate dated 1898 from Kentucky's early vital statistics records. (Kentucky Historical Society)

Availability of Early Vital Records

It is possible that scattered volumes of early assessors' lists, and returns of births, marriages, and deaths for 1851 to 1910 may still be found with the county clerk. However, all known early vital statistics records that survive have been microfilmed and are available in the state archives, the historical society, and the University of Kentucky's special collections library.

Thanks to the efforts of the Kentucky Historical Society, records generated from the 1874 law were saved and are available for research. In 1920, the Kentucky Historical Society began to salvage the remnants of the records kept during the

1852–62 period. It now has an alphabetical card index to the vital statistics for the years 1852 to 1862. This index is known to have inaccuracies but may be consulted prior to reviewing the original records.

The microfilm holdings for vital statistics are shown in chapter 8 under the county where the event took place. The "vital statistics" heading indicates that the records may contain births, deaths, as well as marriages. Records that were filed separately by type of event (birth, marriage or death) will be listed under the specific heading of birth or death records. Some additional scattered records exist and are included in chapter 8 in the section with other statewide Kentucky material.

VITAL RECORDS: 1911 TO PRESENT

The Vital Statistics Law of Kentucky, providing for and legalizing the registration of births and deaths, was enacted by the General Assembly of 1910 and became effective 1 January 1911.

While this new law achieved much better compliance than previous laws, it is still not without biases and omissions. By 1917, the registrations were estimated to be only ninety percent complete. The former registrar of vital statistics, Omar Greeman, estimated that due to failure of county clerks to submit all certificates as required, three in 10,000 births and one in 10,000 deaths were not recorded in 1981. He also estimated that only eighty percent of all marriage certificates were received in 1981.

CONTENT OF VITAL RECORDS

An original birth certificate gives the name of the parents, date, place, time of birth, and address of the parents. Other birth information may include whether it was a single or twin birth, and whether the infant lived.

Information in the death certificate includes the parents' names (including mother's maiden name), parents' places of birth, date and place of birth of deceased, marital status, occupation, the date, time and place of the death, and the address of the deceased. Medical information concerning nature and onset of the fatal illness and contributory illnesses is provided by the physician, if known. The date and place of burial, cemetery of burial, and the funeral home are also provided at the bottom of the certificate. Signatures of the attending physician and sometimes the coroner are present. Later certificates may also include the person's social security number and whether they served in the military. The name and address of the informant who provided the information is also given and should be noted since informants are typically relatives.

AVAILABILITY OF VITAL RECORDS

The Department of Human Resources, Office of Vital Statistics, 275 Main Street, Frankfort, Kentucky 40601, is the official repository of vital statistics from the period 1911 to the present. Official copies can be obtained from that office through the mail for $5 for death certificates and $6 for birth certificates or by telephone with a credit card number. There is a $5 surcharge for credit card orders. Marriage certificates, beginning in June of 1958, are available from this office for $5. The fee for searching for a certificate is the same as the fee for a copy.

The vital records indexes can be searched at the office on Main Street. Genealogists may consult these indexes, which begin with 1911 and continue to the present. In addition, records may be viewed, but unfortunately, a record must now be purchased prior to viewing it. At the present time, unofficial copies can no longer be made.

The Kentucky Historical Society also has microfiche copies of the index from 1911 to 1986. This index will give the name of the individual, the date and county of the event, and the volume and page number of the certificate. If the event was a birth, the name of the mother is also shown in the index.

DELAYED FILED BIRTH CERTIFICATES

Persons born prior to the 1911 registration can register their birth dates through a "delayed filed" birth certificate. These are filed with proper proof of age and identification. Several means of establishing the age of the person can be used including the oath of a relative or other long-time acquaintance, a federal or school census, a family Bible or family physician's record, a marriage record, a dated voter registration record, a military record, or a church baptismal. These privately maintained records must be of a certain age, usually fifteen years, in order to be accepted.

Kentuckians have filed over a half-million of these delayed certificates, which are typically completed in order to obtain social security benefits. Social Security, for a time, accepted completed certificates that were not filed with the Department of Vital Statistics in Frankfort. Therefore, it is possible, that even if no official certificate can be found in Frankfort, a certificate may have been filed with Social Security or other government agencies.

CONTENT AND AVAILABILITY OF DELAYED CERTIFICATES

Information contained on the certificates include the following: gender, legitimacy of the birth, date, and place of birth. Parental information includes full name and race of the father and mother, place of residence and age at the time of the birth, and mother's maiden name. The nature of the supporting documentation will be listed. An affidavit of an attending physician, midwife, parent, or nearest relative who was an adult at the time of the birth may be given, along with the relationship to the applicant.

These delayed certificates are indexed separately from other birth and death certificates and are available in the Office of Vital Statistics on Main Street in Frankfort. The index of these delayed birth certificates is also available at the Kentucky Historical Society along with the certificates themselves. These microfilms

Registrar of Vital Statistics
Certified Copy

THE FACE OF THIS DOCUMENT HAS A COLORED BACKGROUND · NOT A WHITE BACKGROUND

1 PLACE OF BIRTH		NOTE: All facts must be given as of the Date of the Birth being recorded.
County **Boone**	RECEIVED MAR 2 1943 BUREAU OF VITAL STATISTICS	**COMMONWEALTH OF KENTUCKY**
City of **Near Hebron**		STATE BOARD OF HEALTH
No.		Bureau of Vital Statistics
		Special Certificate of Birth and Affidavits
		(For Use in Recording Births Occurring Prior to 1911)
		File No. **203870**

2 FULL NAME OF CHILD Grace Beemon

3 Sex of Child **Female**	4 Legitimate? **Yes**	5 Twin, Triplet or other To be answered in case of plural births only	6 Number in order of birth **4**	7 Date of Birth **Sep't. 20 1887** Month Day Year

8 FULL NAME FATHER **Barry Andrew Beemon**	14 FULL MAIDEN NAME MOTHER **Mabel Stephens**
9 POST OFFICE AT TIME OF THIS BIRTH **Hebron Ky**	15 POST OFFICE AT TIME OF THIS BIRTH **Hebron Ky**
10 COLOR OR RACE **W**	11 AGE AT TIME OF THIS BIRTH **29** (Years)	16 COLOR OR RACE **White**	17 AGE AT TIME OF THIS BIRTH **23** (Years)
12 BIRTHPLACE **Kentucky**	18 BIRTHPLACE **Kentucky**

Affidavit: I hereby declare upon oath that the above statements are true. (To be signed by registrant, if possible.)

Signature _____ Pfe   Address 345 Wood Ave (Ftown) Cov (?)

Subscribed and sworn before me 11th of Feb. 19 43   J. Blaine Robinson

[SEAL] KENTON COUNTY, KY.   (Applicant—Do not write below this line.)   Notary Public

Abstract of Supporting Evidence
Name and Kind of Document	Date Original Document Was Made
1 Affidavit Hattie L Adams, aunt, age 73	2-24-43
2 " Mrs Hattie D Clore, non-relative, 80	2-11-43
3	
4	

Information Concerning Registrant As Stated in Documents
Birth Date or Age	Birthplace	Name of Father	Maiden Name of Mother
1	✓	✓	✓
2	✓		✓
3			
4			

Additional Information:

Signature J. F. Blackerby   Date Filed March 10 1943
J. F. Blackerby, State Registrar, Reviewing Official

THE BACK OF THIS DOCUMENT CONTAINS AN ARTIFICIAL WATERMARK · HOLD AT AN ANGLE TO VIEW

I, Robert N. Hurst III, Registrar of Vital Statistics, hereby certify this to be a true and correct copy of the certificate of birth/death of the person therein named, and that the original certificate is registered under the file number shown. In testimony thereof I have hereunto subscribed my name and caused the official seal of the Office of Vital Statistics to be affixed at Frankfort, Kentucky this _____ day of June, 19 90 ____ C

Robert N. Hurst

Robert N. Hurst III, State Registrar

FIG. 4.4 Delayed filed birth certificate, 1943. (Kentucky Office of Vital Statistics, Frankfort)

(forty-four rolls) can be purchased from the historical society Micrographics Department.

MARRIAGE RECORDS

In early Kentucky, civil and ecclesiastical laws and rules regarding marriage records in the English colonies were not only contradictory, but confusing. In frontier Kentucky, regulations may have been unknown or disregarded. The earliest Kentucky marriage records naturally fall under the jurisdiction of Virginia, and so its laws applied until Kentucky became a state. *(Bluegrass Roots* 1987, 54)

MARRIAGE LAWS OF VIRGINIA

Before the Revolution, only ministers of the Church of England were permitted to celebrate marriage rites. Other marriages were not legal. A marriage license was issued by the governor or a justice of the peace, and banns had to be published for three Sundays or Holy Days. A marriage bond was required from 1660 to 1849.

After the revolution, under the law passed in May of 1783, courts on the "western waters," including Kentucky, could license laymen to perform marriages when there were insufficient clergy. The act also confirmed the legality of former marriages performed by magistrates and others not authorized at that time (Conrad 1988, 104–05). Recording of marriages by the county clerks became more uniform after this law despite the fact that it had been required previously (*Bluegrass Roots* 1987, 54).

Under this 1783 law, laymen could perform the ceremony and produce a marriage license certifying that the intention of marriage had been published three times. The publication of banns of matrimony had to be made on three days and over a period of not less than two weeks in an open and public assembly. This assembly could be either military or religious in nature, but it was required to be within the bounds of the respective congregations or militia companies in which the parties to be married resided (Conrad 1988, 104–05).

An act effective 1 July 1785 required a certificate be filed of all marriages by the minister or clerk. The certificate was to be transmitted to the clerk of the county where the marriage was performed within twelve months of the ceremony (Conrad 1988, 105).

KENTUCKY MARRIAGE RECORDS

Marriage records in Kentucky include bonds, consents, licenses, certificates, marriage registers or ministers' returns, and marriage contracts. In the narrative below, laws governing each of these records are discussed along with information regarding the legal status of the parties involved and the content of the records.

MARRIAGE BONDS

In Kentucky, a bond is posted when applying for a marriage license. This document is a performance bond that assures the court that there is no lawful cause

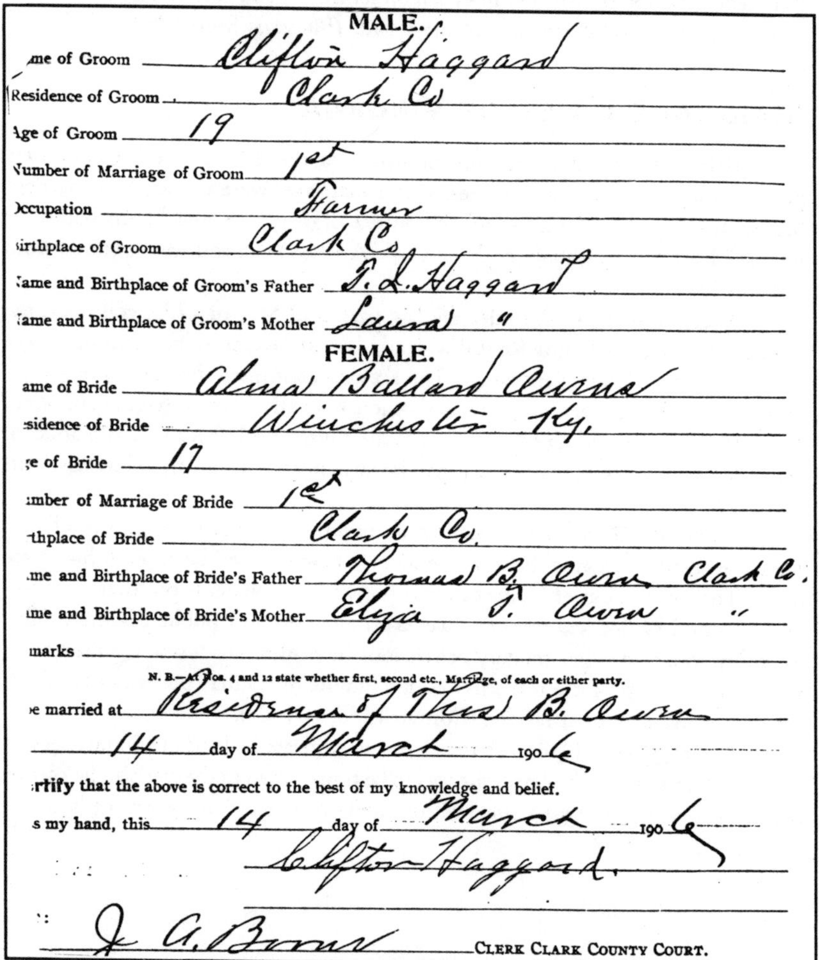

MALE.

Name of Groom _Clifton Haggard_
Residence of Groom _Clark Co_
Age of Groom _19_
Number of Marriage of Groom _1st_
Occupation _Farmer_
Birthplace of Groom _Clark Co_
Name and Birthplace of Groom's Father _F. L. Haggard_
Name and Birthplace of Groom's Mother _Laura_ "

FEMALE.

Name of Bride _Alma Ballard Owens_
Residence of Bride _Winchester Ky._
Age of Bride _17_
Number of Marriage of Bride _1st_
Birthplace of Bride _Clark Co._
Name and Birthplace of Bride's Father _Thomas B. Owens Clark Co._
Name and Birthplace of Bride's Mother _Elizja J. Owens_ "
Remarks _____

N. B.—At Nos. 4 and 12 state whether first, second etc., Marriage, of each or either party.

Be married at _Residence of Thos B. Owens_
_14_ day of _March_ 190_6_

I certify that the above is correct to the best of my knowledge and belief.

Witness my hand, this _14_ day of _March_ 190_6_

Clifton Haggard.

J. A. Brown _____ CLERK CLARK COUNTY COURT.

FIG. 4.5 Information supplied to obtain a marriage bond in 1906. (Clark County Marriage Bonds, Kentucky State Archives)

to obstruct the marriage. The bond amount would be paid if this was not the case. A bond does not guarantee that the marriage took place. In rural counties where the clerk knew the parties, a bond might not be required (Conrad 1988, 111).

Since women had no contractual rights under Virginia or early Kentucky law, this contract of marriage could not be arranged by the bride (Conrad 1988, 104). As a result, two parties were necessary to obtain the marriage license based on the bond executed: a male relative or guardian of the bride and the groom himself. The bondsman was usually the bride-to-be's father or brother; but a close friend or guardian of either the bride or the groom often served as bondsmen as well.

Bonds beginning circa 1860s to 1900 included the ages of the bride and groom and places of birth of both the marrying parties and their parents. Beginning in 1902, the names of parents are also given. By 1900, the marriage bond fell into disuse by some county clerks (Conrad 1988, 109-10).

CONSENTS

Beginning in 1799, the Kentucky General Assembly amended its 1798 act so that both parties had to have the consent of the parent or guardian prior to a marriage if either the bride or the groom was less than twenty-one years old. Thus, the consent of a parent or guardian was required for the first time (Conrad 1988, 107-08)

The consent was usually filed as loose papers along with the bond and a copy of the license. The consent listed the signer's relationship to the future bride or groom. If the parent is not the signer of the consent, the consent will often m ention that the bride or groom is the "infant son or daughter of" the deceased. If the consent is signed by the mother, it can often be assumed that the father was deceased at the time of the proposed marriage.

LICENSES

Upon completion of the bond, the court clerk would issue a marriage license. The license gave permission for a marriage ceremony to be performed. Thus, once a license was issued, it was presented to the minister or other person who performed the marriage ceremony.

The licenses were written on any small piece of paper available. The clerk did not always keep a copy. After 1799, it was usually addressed "to any minister of the Gospel or magistrate authorized to perform marriages" (Conrad 1988, 107). A copy of the license is usually filed with the bond and consent.

CERTIFICATES

The fact that a bond or a license was issued does not necessarily mean that the marriage actually took place. The marriage certificate, however, does. The certificate was completed by the minister or judge and given to the couple. In some counties, certificates are filed in their own books.

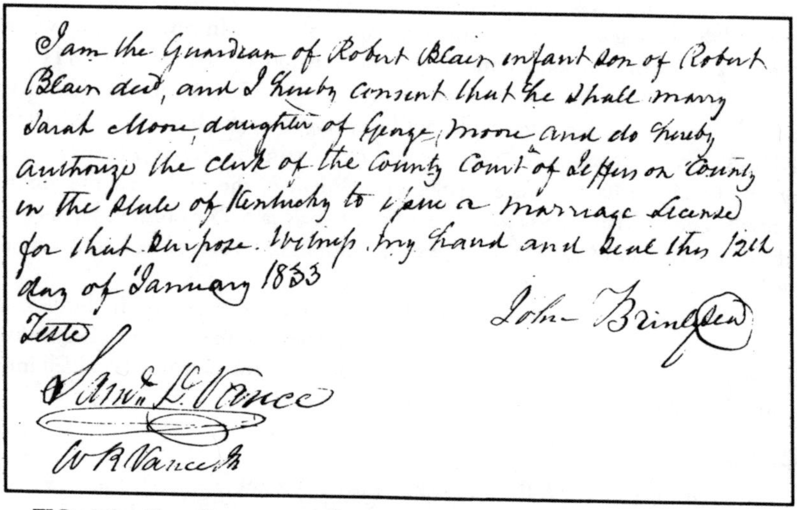

I am the Guardian of Robert Blair infant son of Robert Blair dec'd, and I hereby consent that he shall marry Sarah Moore daughter of George Moore and do hereby authorize the clerk of the County Court of Jefferson County in the State of Kentucky to issue a marriage License for that purpose. Witness my hand and seal this 12th day of January 1833

John Brinley (seal)

Teste

Saml. L. McVance

W R Vance

FIG. 4.6a Guardian consent for 1833 marriage license. (Jefferson County Marriage Records, Kentucky State Archives)

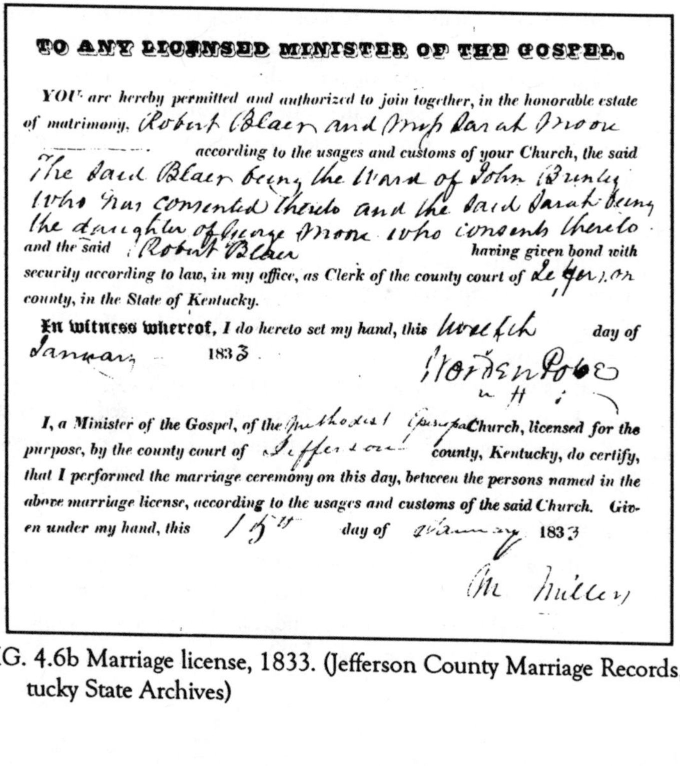

TO ANY LICENSED MINISTER OF THE GOSPEL.

YOU are hereby permitted and authorized to join together, in the honorable estate of matrimony, Robert Blaer and Miss Sarah Moore according to the usages and customs of your Church, the said The said Blaer being the Ward of John Brinly who has consented thereto and the said Sarah being the daughter of George Moore who consents thereto and the said Robert Blaer having given bond with security according to law, in my office, as Clerk of the county court of Jefferson county, in the State of Kentucky.

In witness whereof, I do hereto set my hand, this twelfth day of January 1833.

Worden Pope

I, a Minister of the Gospel, of the Methodist Episcopal Church, licensed for the purpose, by the county court of Jefferson county, Kentucky, do certify, that I performed the marriage ceremony on this day, between the persons named in the above marriage license, according to the usages and customs of the said Church. Given under my hand, this 15th day of January 1833

M Miller

FIG. 4.6b Marriage license, 1833. (Jefferson County Marriage Records, Kentucky State Archives)

The marriage certificate typically includes the following information: names of the bride and groom, place of the marriage, witnesses, and minister performing the ceremony. The marriage typically took place in the county in which the bride resided.

MARRIAGE REGISTER OR MINISTER'S RETURN

After the ceremony, the person performing the marriage was required by law to register, or "return" the marriage to the county clerk's office. This book is called the Marriage Register or Minister's Return Book. These return books usually do not contain much information beyond the names of the bride and groom, date of marriage, and name of minister performing the ceremony.

Since many marriages were performed in rural communities miles from the courthouse, the pastor or justice of the peace usually registered the marriages en masse once or twice each year. If the person performing the marriage died or moved away, the marriage might not be registered.

As a result, ministers' returns should be viewed with caution, since they may have been recorded as long as a year after the event. The given names shown in these records are often wrong, and witnesses may be confused with grooms and vice versa.

MARRIAGE CONTRACTS

While not a marriage record per se, researchers should be alert to the existence of marriage contracts in early Kentucky records. While they are not great in number, they do exist. Marriage contracts were used by widows or widowers to protect the property of children by previous marriages. These agreements can be filed in the deed books or in county order books since they deal with property rather than matrimonial matters.

EVALUATING KENTUCKY MARRIAGE RECORDS

Kentucky marriage records are often difficult to use. They are not always indexed, complete, or accurate. The greatest problem, however, is under-reporting. Many frontier marriages simply were not recorded (Felty 1987, 54).

There were a number of reasons for failure to report a marriage. First, there was probably a lack of understanding among the citizenry regarding the laws. And it was often difficult to travel to the courthouse to file the necessary papers, especially in eastern Kentucky during the winter months.

Shortcomings of the officials were also responsible for under-reporting. Ministers typically maintained lists of marriages performed with the hope and promise of recording them in bulk. Since months, or even a year, may have passed between filings, some marriages may simply have been forgotten.

During the period 1852 to 1862, all vital records, including marriages, were inconsistently kept because of lack of support of the vital statistics registration law.

However, even as late as 1980, the registrar of vital statistics estimated that twenty percent of all marriages recorded in the counties were not reported to Frankfort. It seems reasonable to assume that earlier records, particularly frontier records, were even less complete.

CONTENT AND AVAILABILITY OF MARRIAGE RECORDS

STATE REGISTERED MARRIAGE RECORDS

Between 1852 and 1861, marriage records listed bride and groom names, date of marriage, place of marriage, the number of the marriage (whether first, second, etc.), age, residence, and birthplace. In 1878 until 1910, some counties filed marriage records with the state. Marriages have been recorded uniformly in the Kentucky Office of Vital Statistics since July of 1958.

From the period 1866 to the early 1900s, some background information on the bride and groom was given. Information might include the age, occupation, birthplace of parties, place of the ceremony, and whether they had been previously married. Some records also give the birthplaces and names of the parents. After 1902, the parents' names are more consistently recorded.

COUNTY MARRIAGE RECORDS

Whatever weaknesses existed in the state system of filing marriages, the county clerk nevertheless continued to record and maintain marriages at the county level. Most of these records are indexed; however, some are only arranged chronologically and are thus difficult to search.

Available county marriage records, along with the dates of the records, are listed under the county in which the event occurred in chapter 8. If the records are known to be indexed, or not indexed, an indication is made; otherwise, no notation is given.

DIVORCE RECORDS

In early Kentucky, from early statehood until the enactment of new legislation, the only way to obtain a divorce was by an act of the General Assembly. In 1809, a law authorized the circuit courts to grant divorces (Littell and Swigert 1822, 442-43; Morehead and Brown 1834, 122-24). However, divorces were still granted by legislative acts until 1849 when the state's third constitution prohibited such special legislation (*Bluegrass Roots* 1981, 103).

While an act of the legislature may seem to have made divorce all but impossible, recent analysis of divorce laws and practices in the antebellum South indicate that divorce may not have been as difficult to attain as previously thought (Censer 1981, 24-25).

Kentucky's divorce laws reflected the general attitude toward divorce that existed in the larger society. By a statute passed in 1809 by the Kentucky General Assembly, a man could obtain a divorce if the wife voluntarily left his "bed and board" for three years, if she lived with another man, or committed a felony. Determining the spouse at fault for the divorce was important since this had implications for remarriage and for division of any property the couple owned jointly or that was brought to the marriage.

By 1894, Kentucky statute provided for divorce to the wife in cases of (1) abandonment for one year; (2) habitual drunkenness for not less than one year; or (3) cruel beating or injury, attempt at injury, or probable danger to her life. Husbands were granted divorces in cases of (1) abandonment for one year; (2) habitual drunkenness for not less than one year; or (3) adultery by the wife or such lewd, lascivious behavior on her part as proves her to be unchaste without actual proof of an act of adultery (Barbour and Carroll 1894, 768-70).

Under the early statutes, the offending party could not remarry as long as the former spouse lived. The earliest law stated that the offended party could not be released from "the pains and penalties which the law prescribes against a marriage whilst a former husband or wife is living" (Littell and Swigert 1822, 443). By 1873, divorced parties could remarry, but only one divorce was permitted to any person, except in those cases when the person was found not at fault for the divorce (Bullock and Johnson 1873, 524).

See chapter 6 for a more complete discussion of divorce as it related to women in Kentucky.

AVAILABILITY OF DIVORCE RECORDS

Early divorces could be recorded in the Acts of Kentucky until as late as 1850. These early records are indexed in the Kentucky Historical Society for the period 1792 to 1849 in a card catalog file drawer. The bills themselves, and the names of the parties, will also be indexed by Hening's Statutes (Hening 1823).

Later divorce records may be found in the circuit court records in the county of residence, which will show a divorce as a chancery or equity case. Since July of 1958, divorces have been recorded in the Kentucky Office of Vital Statistics in Frankfort; copies of divorce decrees dating from 1958 can be obtained from that office.

PROBATE RECORDS

VIRGINIA AND EARLY KENTUCKY INHERITANCE PRACTICES

According to contemporary sources, American inheritance laws were among the biggest surprises for immigrants from Europe. Early colonial laws were largely based on English, rather than European, inheritance law. As a result, many immigrants were unfamiliar with the laws (Shammas 1987a, 161).

For example, prior to 1776, inheritance of land could be limited to a specific line of heirs. This process was called entail. Entailing land meant that the deceased had determined the line of heirship for generations to come. Entailed land inherited in this manner could not be sold, only passed on to a specific person, usually a direct descendent of the heir so long as any existed. The land was normally passed to the eldest son, but might be entailed to another descendent. The entail might or might not have a restriction as to gender of the heir. In 1705, Virginia passed a statute making it impossible to break an entail without obtaining a special act of the assembly (Shammas 1987a, 157).

Before 1786, Virginia law stipulated that inheritance of an estate was to be divided into thirds. One-third of the property went to the widow. This was called her dower. Two-thirds went to the eldest son unless specified otherwise in a will. Upon the death of the widow, the eldest son received the dower. If there was no will, the eldest son received the entire estate. This tradition of inheritance to the eldest son was called primogeniture. By 1811, all former colonies had revoked the primogeniture law by statute (Eakle and Cerny 1984, 183). If the eldest son was dead, the eldest grandson became the heir. If a man was single, his heir was his eldest brother. If married but childless, his widow kept the estate for her lifetime (Shammas 1987a, 160–63).

In Kentucky, these Virginia traditions continued for a time. There was a tendency to leave the widow a life estate of one-third of the total estate with the balance being divided among the children or an eldest son. As late as 1872, the widow had only a dower right of one-third of the real estate of her husband. This dower was insufficient to force partition or sale of the property.

An 1898 act provided that after the death of either husband or wife, the survivor would have an absolute estate in one-half of the surplus personally left by the decedent. This 1898 act repealed one that provided that the husband should have the whole of the surplus of the deceased wife's personal estate.

KENTUCKY PROBATE RECORDS

Kentucky probate records are filed in the county court. Wills were usually probated at the first term of the county court following the death. However, if a death occurred close to a court session, it was sometimes necessary to file the probate papers at the next term. Occasionally, wills were not filed until years after the death, so searches must be made for some time after the death was known or suspected to have occurred. In Kentucky, recordation of wills often followed customs similar to recording of marriages and burial of the dead: Wait until a convenient time.

The types of probate records that will be filed at the time of the death include wills, appraisements, inventories, and settlements. In Kentucky, various types of documents associated with probating a will or settling an estate will sometimes be maintained in several distinct volumes. Each of these is discussed below.

ORDER BOOKS

The county court order books may contain a great deal of information about the activities of the estate. Order books record when a will was recorded or entered, the date the probate was accepted, the names of the people appearing in court who presented the will, and witnesses to the will. Settlements and statements of accounts by the executor, administrator, or guardian of children will also be recorded in the order books.

ADMINISTRATOR AND EXECUTOR BONDS

After the will was filed, an executor may be accepted or an administrator appointed. These were usually appointed by the deceased, if he left a will, and then the relationship with the deceased is usually mentioned. Eldest sons and sons-in-law were common choices. If not appointed by a will, the court would appoint an administrator.

If minor children are involved, a guardian would be appointed to represent their interests. The guardian may not be the mother. Since women could not always act for themselves legally, such an appointment does not necessarily mean that the mother was dead, unfit, or unable to care for her children.

APPRAISALS AND INVENTORIES

A committee of two or three appraisers would be appointed if a settlement was necessary. These men were often neighbors or trusted citizens. They were responsible for submitting the inventory to the county court with the estimated value of each item in the estate. These documents may be recorded in the will books or may be recorded in separate volumes called inventories and settlements or inventories and appraisements.

These inventories provide a unique and detailed glimpse into the daily lives of ancestors. The inventories were usually taken by room. By observing the order in which the possessions are listed, a complete picture of the household and its activities can be obtained.

SALES AND SETTLEMENTS

Following the recording of the appraisement and inventory, there may be a sale of the estate. The sale will record each item sold, its price, and the name of the purchaser. Relatives and neighbors were typically purchasers, so attention to the sale record can result in clues about relatives and the husbands of married daughters.

Once the sale is complete, the estate will be settled. It is here that all heirs will be listed together with their spouses. If land is partitioned in settling the estate, those records would be recorded in the deeds. These divisions-of-land records may be the only probate record entered into the county annals.

INTESTATE SETTLEMENTS

Even if a person died intestate, or without a will, there may be records of the estate. For example, an administrator will still have to be appointed. And a settlement would still be made if the deceased had property.

After a settlement, heirs would often exchange or buy out another heir to consolidate land holdings, and, as a result, deeds are important records to consult especially when the deceased died without a will. In any case, if the deceased held property, the deeds should be checked to see how land was disposed of after the death. Check in the deed index under the surname of the deceased, under "H" for heirs and sometimes under "S" for settlement. It is not necessary to file a new deed if land remained in the family after the death.

Another source that can document the death of an intestate ancestor is the commissioner's or sheriff's deeds. Sheriffs and master commissioners had the power to settle an estate if the heirs were unable or unwilling to come to an agreement. These transactions are often maintained in separate volumes in Kentucky. These special deeds are recorded in the deed books or in special commissioners' or sheriffs' deed books. If they are recorded in the deed books, they may be indexed under the sheriff's personal name. Some Kentucky county clerks also filed these records under "S" for sheriff, or "C" for commissioner.

CONTESTING A WILL

If the settlement was contested by the heirs, the suit would be filed in circuit court. Depositions would be taken, relationships would have to be established, and supporting documents presented to the court. All of this material would be filed in the case files. After the settlement of the suit by the court, these case files would be filed in the circuit court clerk's office, and the location of the papers would be listed in an off-docket index. Suits filed for the settlement of an estate were commonplace and should always be checked. If there was a suit, all probate papers relative to the case may be with these case files.

CONTENT AND AVAILABILITY OF PROBATE RECORDS

The forms of wills have not changed substantially in the many years people have desired to stipulate their legacies to the next generation. The heirs along with their relationships will be cited. Each of the documents discussed in this section is critical in building the total picture of the ancestor.

There are many ways to document a death in addition to the formally filed will in the county clerk's office. For example, cemetery records, church and funeral home records, the federal mortality schedules, and newspaper notices of deaths or settlements of estates are only a few sources.

In addition to these sources, there are also numerous documents that must or could be filed at the courthouse in addition to the will: deeds, widow pension applications, appraisements, inventories, appointments of executors or administrators, county or circuit court orders, estate sales, guardian settlements and accountings, and final settlements.

A particularly valuable reference for early Kentucky wills is a compilation of testators in all Kentucky counties prior to 1850 (Jackson et al. 1977). This remarkable reference includes only Kentuckians who probated a will, not all probate documents. Thus, if no formal will was made, the deceased will not be included.

Probate records that have been microfilmed, along with the dates of the records, are listed in chapter 8. Most will books in Kentucky are indexed. If the original records are not, county historians have often undertaken to compile every-name indexes of the early documents. Many of these indexes are available at the Kentucky Historical Society.

CHAPTER 5

KENTUCKY SETTLES IN: HOMESTEADERS, TAXPAYERS, AND SOLDIERS

In this chapter, the basic records of genealogical and historical research are discussed. The Kentucky land grant system, deeds, taxes, census, military, and naturalization records are discussed. The last section is devoted to records of the early banks of the commonwealth.

EARLY KENTUCKY LAND RECORDS

To the early frontier family, Kentucky was the promise of land ownership. As a result of pressing economic and social factors that attracted large numbers of settlers in search of land, the influx into Kentucky was large and rapid. Unfortunately, the mother colony, Virginia, was too involved in the Revolution to effectively regulate distribution of its western lands. As a result, when the large migration began, problems already existed in the land distribution and tenure system. Chaos in land purchase and tenure resulted. Many early settlers, even as famous as Daniel Boone, lost their land claims and moved to other areas of Kentucky or left the state entirely.

VIRGINIA REGULATION OF KENTUCKY LANDS

In 1763, the British government declared that land, rather than cash, would be used to pay veterans of the French and Indian War. Land grants authorized by these military warrants can be found in the Virginia and Old Kentucky Land

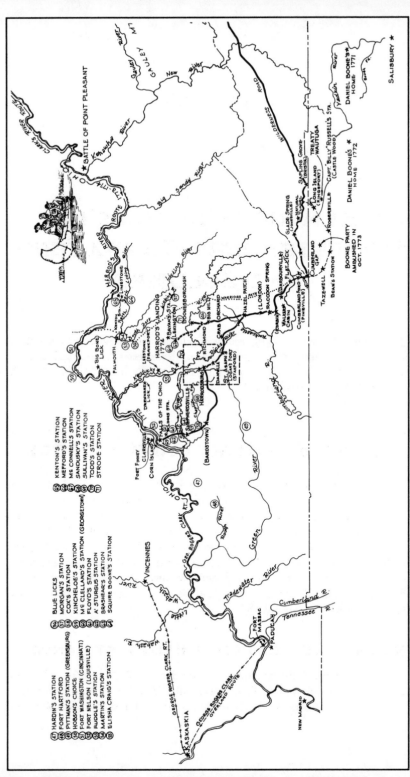

FIG. 5.1 Kentucky Settlement and Statehood Map, 1750–1800. (Brookes-Smith Master Index)

Grants. The names of the soldiers receiving such warrants can also be found in the *Calendar of Warrants for Land in Kentucky* (see Taylor 1967).

In 1773 and 1777, there had been agreements not to extend English settlements further west into Kentucky. During this time, frontier land in Kentucky was supposed to be entered only on military warrants issued to veterans of the French and Indian Wars. There was, nevertheless, continual surging against the established line limiting westward expansion. Settlers disregarded these lines and proceeded into Kentucky to stake claims on the most desirable land (Clark 1960, 62). In 1773, claims totaling 13,000 acres were already entered in Fincastle County records for Kentucky land. An additional 173,050 more acres were entered on military warrants in 1774; 37,850 acres were added in 1775; and an additional 27,090 in 1776. A total of 318,990 acres of Kentucky land had been entered prior to 1777. Of this amount, 190,850 acres had been entered on military warrants before Fincastle County was abolished in 1776 (Hammon 1986, 84, 242).

By the time that Virginia could legally act to settle land claims on 4 July 1776, Kentucky land claims were already entangled. Virginia had to recognize the claims of squatters, French and Indian War veterans, and the grant of the Transylvania Company at Boonesboro. By 1776, there were more than 900 claims of 560,000 acres registered under the terms of the Transylvania grant (Clark 1960, 63).

In order to bring some order to the situation, the Virginia General Assembly passed a law in May of 1779 that allowed additional claims. Settlers under this law were entitled to 400 acres at $2.25 per hundred and preemption rights to an additional 1,000 acres adjacent to his original settlement for $40 per hundred acres. Settlers arriving after 1 January 1778 could still purchase a 400-acre preemption warrant, but did not receive a certificate of settlement. In either case, the preemption could be issued only if it did not interfere with another homesteader's settlement certificate.

In order to qualify as a settler, a person had to have lived in Kentucky for one year prior to 1778, built a cabin, and grown a crop of corn on the claim prior to 1 January 1778. People who lived in forts for protection and had raised corn collectively were defined as villagers and were given the same rights as settlers. These people were allowed to claim vacant land convenient to the fort or village (Hammon 1986, 84, 245–46).

This new law further required claimants to register their surveys with the land court. A person who marked off a tract of land and made their cabin improvements had three years in which to legally survey the land, enter the survey, and pay the requisite fees in order to obtain a patent (Hammon 1986, 84, 242).

However, many earlier settlers failed to properly register their claims. Some early settlers believed that simply settling on the land, building a cabin, and planting a crop of corn was sufficient to establish ownership. Others delayed in registering their claims until it was claimed by others. As a result, both delinquent and rightful claimants became the victims of speculators who claimed all unregistered plots (Brookes-Smith 1976, ii).

Early Kentucky settlers also found their land claims were hopelessly confused by the manner in which claims were made and the lack of professional surveys. Settlers moving to Kentucky chose tracts that fit their tastes (Clark 1960, 63). To complicate matters further, early surveys were not always conducted by officials. Use of trees, stones, bends in a river or creek, a house, or a fence were all used as reference points for the surveys.

As a result of pioneers neglecting to register surveys and registering the surveys improperly, the disputes and overlapping claims continued. Settlers continued to "shingle over" the very early claims of the large land warrants obtained in the names of wealthy Virginians. As a result, actual settlers sometimes bought their land several times over as different claimants made their appearance. Others abandoned their farms and moved to other states where they could get a good title to their land (Brookes-Smith 1976, i).

The 1779 land law helped to alleviate some of these problems. For example, a land commission with jurisdiction over land claims was established. This commission sat first at Harrodsburg and then moved from community to community to adjudicate claims. The commission passed upon claims and issued 400-acre certificates of settlement and 1,000-acre preemption warrants by the hundreds, worked on settling 'shingle' claims, but failed to prevent complete duplication of surveys (Clark 1960, 61-63). The first land court of Kentucky dealt exclusively with lands in Fincastle County for the period 1772 to 1780. These commissioners were appointed by Governor Thomas Jefferson.

The law also declared certain surveys null and void unless they were made by commissioned surveyors. Surveyors were to be certified by the president and professors of William and Mary College.

Finally, surveys were directed by law to use bounds as marked trees or water courses. As a result, some surveys had to be remade. Some uniformity of the shape of the claims was attempted by the stipulation that the breadth of each land parcel was supposed to be one third of its length, unless restrained by a geographical feature such as rivers, mountains, or other bordering grants. As a result, most early surveys were rectangular. But some early claims could follow the personal tastes of the settler (Clark 1960, 63).

Important dates relating to the Kentucky land grant system are listed chronologically in table 5.1.

TABLE 5.1	Important Dates in Land Grant History
1763	King George III's Proclamation of 1763 for French and Indian War soldiers to be paid in land warrants instead of cash.
1779	Land Law of 1779 established a land office and commission to settle claims and provided for claims of existing settlers.
1779	First treasury warrants were sold.
1780	George Rogers Clark was issued 300 Virginia Treasury Warrants for his soldiers engaged in the 1777–1808 northwestern offensive at Corn Island. These warrants were located across from Louisville in Indiana.
1782	The first warrant for Revolutionary War service was issued. Acreage was determined by rank.
1784	Virginia signed a deed of cession to western claims. A reserve of 3.8 million acres was authorized north of the Ohio River between Scioto and Miami rivers. These tracts were in addition to the acreage allotted in Ohio in 1796 known as the U.S. Military District.
1795	Act approved allowing land grants for settlers in the South of Green River area of Kentucky. Settlers over the age of twenty-one and heads of families who had improved the land by building a cabin or planting a crop were eligible for up to 200 acres. These were known as South of Green River Grants or headright claims.
1805	Lands were ceded to the United States by Cherokee Indians at Tellico, Tennessee, in the southeastern region of Kentucky. These lands form the basis of the Tellico grants.
1810	An act appropriating land grants for the Tellico lands entitled residents of at least six months to 100 to 200 acres at $40 per 100 acres.
1812	War of 1812 soldiers received bounty land warrants in Michigan, Illinois, Arkansas (Louisiana Territory), and Missouri as an incentive to enlist.

1815   Act authorized the sale of vacant land in Kentucky at the rate of $20 per 100 acres.

1818   The Jackson Purchase (lands west of the Tennessee River) was ceded to the United States by Chickasaw Indians. These lands would be listed under the West of Tennessee River Military Claims and West of Tennessee River Land Grants.

1820   Act authorized poor widows with children to receive warrants for 100 acres of land, with no fee. Widows had to file an affidavit in the county or circuit court. Lands in the regions known as West of Tennessee River and South of Walker's Line were excluded.

1826   Deadline for surveyor to file West of Tennessee River Military Claims, entries made before 1 May 1792.

1829   West of Tennessee River patenting process established for settlers at twenty-five cents per acre. Preemption rights had been given to settlers in the West of Tennessee River region for a one year period in 1828.

1830   Congress authorized the exchange of Virginia Warrants for scrip for purchase of lands in Ohio, Illinois, and Indiana.

1835   Kentucky General Assembly allowed all vacant lands to be sold at not less than $5 per 100 acres by the counties. These sales are found in the County Court Order Grants.

1842   Congress declared warrants for Revolutionary War and War of 1812 service could be honored in any public domain lands.

1850   Federal Bounty Land Act gave land to all veterans (or their beneficiaries) of the War of 1812 or any Indian war since 1790, and to each commissioned officer of the War with Mexico. The amount of land was based on the term of the service.

1855   Federal Bounty Land Act extended benefits to wagon masters, teamsters, volunteers at Battle of King's Mountain, Battle of Nickijack, and Lewiston, Delaware in War of 1812, and chaplains in all wars. The only requirement was fourteen days service in one battle.

1856   Federal Bounty extended to officers, seamen, and marines in naval service during the Revolutionary War.

| 1862 | Homestead Act gave only minor privileges to Civil War veterans. Because nearly three-quarters of the bounty land warrants issued in the bounty land acts of the 1850s were reassigned, there was reluctance to encourage further land speculation. |

Source: Kentucky Genealogical Society Manuscript, January 1991.

RECIPIENTS OF KENTUCKY LAND GRANT SYSTEM

A person could be entitled to a Kentucky land grant based upon settlement in Kentucky, purchase, headright, or military service. Land granted for nonmilitary reasons could have been authorized through settlement, preemption claims, purchase, importation, village rights, and special acts of the general assembly. The general assembly also acted directly to grant land to persons for surveying, for relief of poor persons, and for seminary funding. (Adkinson 1990, i).

Warrants for military service were in the minority. Only eleven percent of the Virginia and the old Kentucky patents were awarded for military service (Adkinson 1990, i). These military warrants for Revolutionary War service were generally used in Kentucky's military district located south of the Green River. Only veterans of the French and Indian War and the Revolutionary War were awarded Kentucky land grants. No military warrants were used in the War of 1812 or any later wars (Adkinson 1990, iv).

STAKING A CLAIM IN EARLY KENTUCKY

Most of the nation's states are public domain states where the federal government appropriates the state's land. However, Kentucky, the original colonies, and a handful of other states including Maine, Tennessee, Texas, Vermont, and West Virginia, are "state-land" states. In a state-land state, the state government is responsible for appropriating all land within its borders. As a result, the process of obtaining a patent for land in Kentucky involved four legal steps, each recorded at the state level. Each of these steps must be accomplished before a title can be granted.

The settler would scout the area for what was deemed a desirable location, perhaps armed with a warrant or certificate saying he was entitled to a certain amount of land. The boundaries of the land would then be walked or marked off. Next, the settler entered his claim (the petition or entry) and then obtained authorization for a survey or plat of the tract. Once the survey was completed, the government could then award the title by issuing a grant. The entire process is called the patenting process and each of these four steps are detailed below.

Step 1. The Land Warrant or Certificate

A person who was entitled to land due to military service, settlement in Kentucky, purchase, or headright received a warrant. A warrant is also known as a certificate or an order. A warrant authorizes a survey to be made. Warrants do

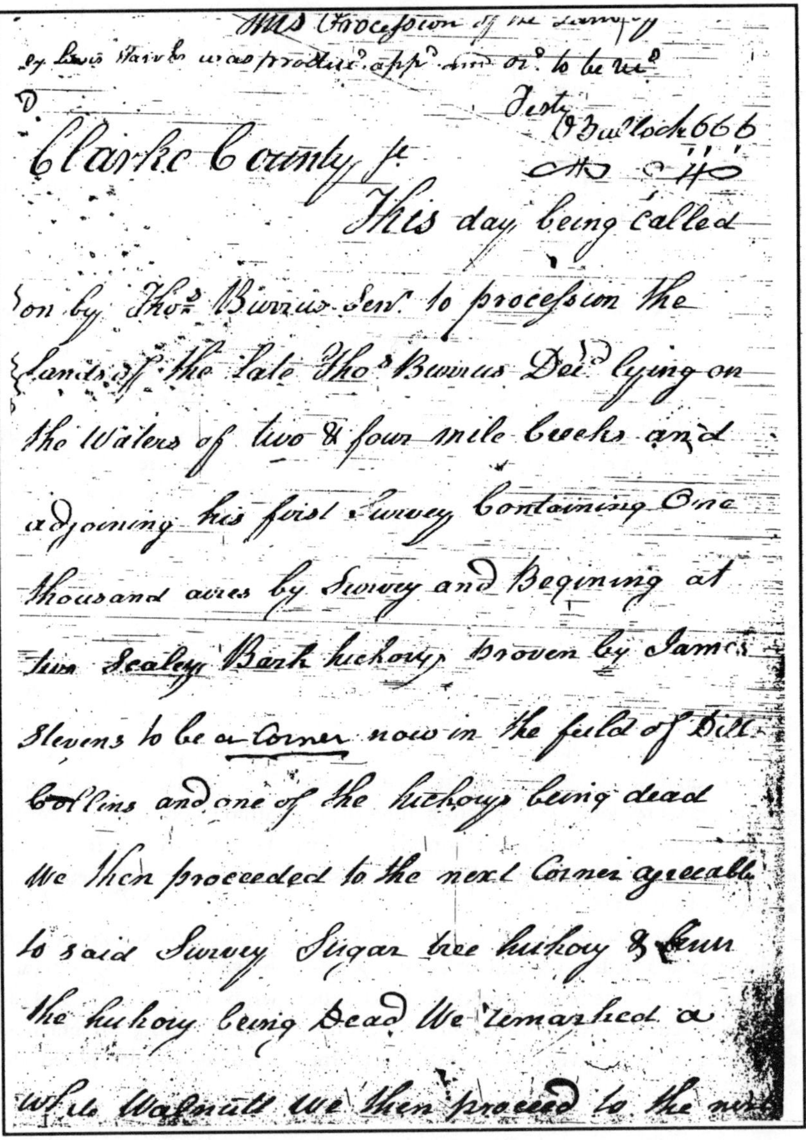
The Procession of the Survey
by Lewis Harris was produced app.d and or.d to be rec.d
Teste
D Bullock 666
Clarke County Sc.
This day being called
on by Thos Burris Senr to procession the
lands of the late Thos Burris Decd lying on
the Waters of two & four mile Creeks and
adjoining his first Survey Containing One
Thousand acres by Survey and Begining at
two Sealey Bark hickorys proven by James
Stevens to be a Corner now in the field of Bill
Collins and one of the hickorys being dead
We then proceeded to the next Corner agreeable
to said Survey Sugar tree hickory & Gum
the hickory being Dead We remarked a
white Walnutt we then proceed to the next

FIG. 5.2 1805 Processioner's Survey. (Kentucky Land Survey for Thomas Burris in Clark County)

not indicate where the land is to be located, only the site of the tract allocated. Warrants could be traded, sold or assigned in whole or in part. Therefore, it is advisable to examine the back of the warrants to determine if the warrant was assigned (Adkinson 1990, ii). There were four basic types of warrants:

(1) Military warrants were issued by the land office on the basis of a military certificate. The military warrant was given to soldiers as payment for military service. It authorized patenting of unappropriated land. The amount of land depended upon the soldier's rank. If a soldier chose not to take the land, he could assign the warrant to another party for money or goods. The warrant directed the surveyor of lands to lay off land in the amount specified. In Kentucky, these lands were in the southern and western regions of the state.

(2) Certificates of settlement and preemption warrants were issued by the land office for actual settlement on the land or raising a crop. Certificates of settlement were given to settlers who occupied the land prior to 1 January 1778. These certificates of settlement entitled the settler to 400 acres of land at $2.25 per 100 acres.

Settlers after 1 January 1778 could also purchase a 400-acre preemption warrant. Virginia preemption rights required a purchase price unless a settler could prove to the satisfaction of the county court that he/she could not pay the stated price. The preemption warrant is, thus, similar in nature and function to a treasury warrant.

(3) Treasury warrants were printed documents that were issued for land purchased. Treasury warrants could also be authorized by an act of the Kentucky General Assembly. These vouchers were prepared by the auditor of the commonwealth showing the quantity of land the person had bought. It authorized a qualified surveyor to lay off and survey the desired land. A voucher is a certificate from the auditor showing how much land a person was entitled to based on the receipt from the treasurer who had received payment.

(4) Exchange warrants were issued when it became necessary to exchange an original military, preemption, or treasury warrant.

STEP 2. THE ENTRY

Once a warrant was obtained, it was presented to the surveyor who listed the name of the warrant holder and the date of entry in the surveyor's record book. This was the entry. Thus, the entry into the county surveyor's record indicated an applicant's intention to file for a patent. The type of warrant being used, the acreage, and the approximate location of the land to be appropriated is included in an entry. See table 5.2 for an explanation of the measurements used in Kentucky surveys.

The entry date was very important in cases of conflicting claims. The entry was filed by the surveyor in his entry book under the name of the person wishing to reserve a patent for a particular piece of land. The surveyor also recorded in this entry book the type of warrant authorizing the survey and the date the intention was declared. Entries could be changed or withdrawn; therefore, an entry is not synonymous with a patent. It is an intention to file a patent.

Jillson's *Old Kentucky Entries and Deeds* contains entries in early Jefferson, Lincoln, and Fayette counties along with the military district. The original entry books are in the land office in Frankfort. Jefferson County entry books are housed at the Jefferson County archives. The original Fayette and Lincoln County entries are housed in the Secretary of State Land Office. Newer entries were recorded and housed at the county court (Adkinson 1990, ii).

TABLE 5.2	Measurements Used in Kentucky Surveys

A pole or rod is 16.5 feet.
A chain made of 100 links is sixty-six feet or four rods.
A mile is 320 rods, eighty chains or 5,280 feet.
A square rod is 272.25 square feet.
An acre contains 43,560 square feet.
An acre contains 160 square rods.
An acre is about 208.75 feet square.

---

* = a square that measured 208.75' on each of its sides would equal an acre

Source: City of Lexington, *Water Works and Sewerage*, vol. 91, no. 6, June 1944.

STEP 3. THE SURVEY OR PLAT

Once the entry was recorded, the survey was prepared that outlined the tract in metes and bounds. The survey could be referred to variously as a plat or survey certificate. A plat is the surveyor's drawing of the tract to be patented. Plats are usually included with the survey certificate.

The surveyor prepared a statement giving the name of the person for whom the survey was made, the type of warrant authorizing the survey, and, in most instances, the closest watercourse. The county surveyor was responsible for keeping accurate records to prevent duplication of surveys. However, because of poor markings and the large tracts of land surveyed in the early years, many duplicate and overlapping surveys were made. Surveys could also be sold or assigned to another party before the grant was issued.

STEP 4. THE GRANT

While a deed transfers ownership from one individual to another, the grant transfers ownership from the government to a private individual. Because owner-ship of land was first held in the colonies by the sovereign, the first transfer of ownership of unappropriated land is via a grant. In Virginia, the governor passed title to individuals. After the Revolution, Virginia gave up its claims to the Northwest Territory to the federal government. These federal land grants were signed by the president for many years.

Kentucky's grants are easily recognized by the governor's name in the heading. The grant typically includes the date of the survey, type of warrant, the metes and bounds description, the date the grant was issued, and the governor's signature. The original was mailed to the owner; the copy is entered in the land office grant book. Transfer of ownership, after the grants are registered in the land office, is the responsibility of the county clerk in the county in which the land is situated.

For the Kentucky settler, this meant that once the survey was completed, a copy was sent to the governor's office who issued a grant. Prior to June 1792, this was the governor of Virginia. The grant is also sometimes erroneously called a patent or patent deed. The patenting process transfers land from the colonial governor, or modern day government, to an individual. Grants convey unappropriated land by the governor to an individual. Grants cannot be assigned. However, once the grant has passed from the governor to a private citizen, the recipient may sell or will the property. These transactions are recorded through deeds. Thus, deeds transfer title from one private citizen to another.

Some early landowners recorded land transactions on the back of grants by simply writing the name of the person buying the land. The settler would then simply give the buyer the grant and the deed would be recorded with the court. As a result of this practice, it is wise to examine both sides of the owner's grants and to follow the patenting process completely through the four-step process.

BOUNTY LAND

During the Revolutionary War, free land was promised to the soldiers instead of money. As a result, many Virginia soldiers came to Kentucky to protect the frontier and for their promised bounty land in the western part of the state.

In 1830, holders of warrants that had not been used to patent land in the reserved land areas could be surrendered for scrip certificates. This scrip could be used for land anywhere in the public domain. Virginia warrants for service in the Virginia State Line and for the Virginia Continental Line could both be surrendered for this scrip.

The last major bounty land act for public domain states was passed in 1855 and provided 160 acres to anyone who fought in any battle or served at least fourteen days in any war, not just the Revolution. However, no bounty land warrants for military service were issued in Kentucky after 1796. As a result, if a Kentuckian was due land from one of the later acts, he would have had to use it in a public domain state.

CONTENT OF KENTUCKY GRANT RECORDS

Kentucky granted land under several different acts during its early history. The discussion below outlines each of the major programs and discusses the terms of the grants as well as who was eligible for the land. There are a number of relevant indexes for searching these records including Jillson's *Kentucky Land Grants* (1971) and *Old Kentucky Entries and Deeds* (1978). For a complete listing of references for Kentucky land grant research, see table 5.4.

VIRGINIA GRANTS 1782–92.

These grants were issued for service in the French and Indian and the Revolutionary Wars. Grants of Kentucky land prior to statehood are housed in the land office in Frankfort, even if the grant was issued by the Virginia government. There are approximately 10,000 patents in this series.

To locate these records, two references must be used. First, consult the *Master Index to Virginia Surveys and Grants, 1774–91,* (Brookes-Smith 1976) to obtain the patent number. Next, consult Jillson to obtain the actual grant book and page number.

OLD KENTUCKY GRANTS 1793–1856

These 7,600 grants were made by Kentucky under a plan similar to Virginia's grants. These grants include military, seminary, academic, treasury warrants, and preemption grants. Some of the grants in this series were based on warrants and surveys originally issued by Virginia. Searching these records involves finding the grant book reference in Jillson's *Index to Kentucky Land Grants* (1971), then obtaining the patent number in the left margin of the grant. The Kentucky Historical Society has a cross index for grant name and survey name that should be used in case of errors in Jillson (Adkinson 1990, iii).

GRANTS SOUTH OF THE GREEN RIVER 1797–1866

Virginia had designated these lands for distribution to Revolutionary War soldiers prior to 1797. Settlers arriving after 1797 were required to be twenty-one years of age, a resident on the property for at least a year, and have planted a crop or built a cabin.

These grants were also known as headright claims because after 1797, anyone over twenty-one years old could claim 200 acres of headright land. The terms of the purchase were attractive since families did not have to pay the purchase price at once. The provisions of purchasing this land were $30 per 100 acres, with a maximum of 200 acres per householder. Once the land was paid for, the title passed to the landholder.

There are over 16,600 patents filed in this series on land generally bounded by the Green River on the north. Many of these claims, however, were located outside the northern boundary of the Green River military district; some as far north as Pendleton County.

Due to repeated time extensions granted by the General Assembly to pay filing fees, many of these patents span decades from the time of the warrant until the grant was made (Adkinson 1990, iii).

Tellico Grants 1805–53

The Tellico Grants were for lands ceded to the United States by the Cherokee Indians under an 1805 treaty. In 1810, the Kentucky General Assembly passed an act appropriating the land under the patent system. The nearly 600 patents in this series are primarily in the Big Sandy Valley and in eastern Kentucky. These grants were issued on a treasury warrant.

Residents who had lived in the area at least six months were entitled to warrants of 100 to 200 acres of land at $40 per 100 acres. The money generated from this fund was used to produce weapons for the state militia. In 1831, the cost was reduced to $5 per 100 acres.

Kentucky Land Warrants 1816–73

In 1815, Kentucky passed an act that offered for sale all vacant lands within the state. This act consolidated the three existing series of land patents (Old Kentucky, south of Green River, and Tellico) into one land warrant system. All land west of the Tennessee River (with the exception of land in the Jackson Purchase) was eligible for patenting through the purchase of a treasury warrant from the Kentucky Land Office. The original price was $20 per 100 acres.

There are over 26,000 patents in this series issued under various types of warrants: warrants purchased from the land office, warrants issued to poor widows under the 1820 Act, and warrants issued by the general assembly to trustees and commissioners overseeing educational institutions, building roads, or constructing bridges (Adkinson 1990, iii).

Grants West of the Tennessee River 1822–58

In 1818, the United States obtained from the Chickasaw Indians all lands between the Tennessee and Mississippi rivers in what is now Tennessee and Kentucky. This area, known as the Jackson Purchase, includes land in the present counties of Calloway, Graves, Fulton, Hickman, McCracken, Carlisle, Ballard, and Marshall.

At that time, there were settlements of Revolutionary War soldiers in the area who had come to protect the western frontier. These soldiers had to register their entries with the Military Land Office prior to 1 May 1792. In 1820, the land was officially opened up for settlement and veterans were advised to apply for warrants on their land as soon as possible. Four thousand acres were donated by the state to establish a town near the Iron Banks for "the benefit of the soldiers." There were 242 patents issued for Revolutionary soldiers in the West of Tennessee River Military Series (Hathaway 1974, 26-27; Adkinson 1990, iii).

In 1821, lands that were not patented by the veterans were ordered sold at public auction if a minimum price was met. As a result, there were also nonmilitary patents in this area. These patents were issued on a receiver's office receipt. Sales were held at Princeton and Waidsborough. The 9,308 patents in this west of Tennessee River series show the receipt including the amount of money paid for the land (Adkinson 1990, iii).

GRANTS SOUTH OF THE WALKER LINE 1825–1923

Due to a surveying error, the Kentucky Land Office became responsible for patenting lands in a small area of northern Tennessee located between the present state line (Walker's line) and the thirty-sixth degree parallel. These 4,327 grants were originally issued on a treasury warrant.

COUNTY COURT ORDERS 1836+

An act of the Kentucky Legislature passed on 28 February 1835 gave all unappropriated lands to the county courts in the county where the land lay. The money generated from the sales of the land was used to fund roads and bridges. The price was set at not less than $5 for 100 acres. Later legislation set the maximum acreage at 200 acres per warrant.

The warrant, survey, and affidavit declaring the land to be unappropriated were sent to Frankfort where the grant was issued. This series of over 70,000 land patents is currently being microfilmed by the Kentucky Historical Society and a computerized index is being generated to facilitate access (Adkinson 1990, iv).

Common abbreviations used in the Kentucky land patent documents can be found in table 5.3.

TABLE 5.3	Abbreviations Used in Land Patent Documents
D.D.	Deed Delivered
Mk	Marker for Surveying Party
CC	Chain Carrier for Surveying Party
HK	Housekeeper for Surveying Party
S_C	Surveyor for _____ County (Example: SFC would mean the surveyor for Fayette County)
ch	chain (one chain equals 100 links or sixty-six feet)
L.O.	Land Office
Reg.	Register
Aud.	Auditor

po.   Pole (one pole equals one rod or 16.5 feet)

Source: Kentucky Genealogical Society Manuscript.

AVAILABILITY OF LAND RECORDS

Kentucky's early land grants are well indexed. Most Kentucky libraries have copies of these indexes. However, the Kentucky Historical Society and the Secretary of State's Land Office are the only Frankfort agencies with the complete documentation for all the Kentucky land grant records. The original records are held by the Secretary of State's Kentucky Land Office, the Capitol, Frankfort, Kentucky 40601.

The records listed below are filed with the land office in the secretary of state's office and are available in the archives research room:

- Resident lands forfeited to the state, 1854–1913
- Reports of payments made by Green River settlers, 1799–1814
- Resident lands sold for taxes, 1833–68
- Land office records (actual settlers), 1796–1806
- Land office records (sales of nonresident lands), 1806–19

See chapter 8 for specific listings under Kentucky's statewide records.

In *Kentucky Land Grants* by Jillson, all records were prepared using the recorded grants. However, many surveys south of Green River do not appear in this book since some plats were surveyed and recorded, but not paid for. As a result, no grant was issued. The Kentucky Historical Society has compiled an additional list of these plats through meticulous research using the original documents. A copy of this list can be purchased from the society.

Listed in table 5.4 are the most important publications for use in researching Kentucky land grants in addition to those cited in this chapter.

TABLE 5.4   Resources For Land Grant Research

Cook, Michael L. 1985. *Kentucky Court of Appeals Deed Books*. Volumes 1–4. Evansville, Ky.: Cook Publications.

Fowler, Ila. 1935. "Revolutionary Soldiers and Their Land Grants in the Tradewater River Country of Western Kentucky." *Register of the Kentucky Historical Society* 33:160–64.

Kentucky Historical Society. 1923. "Certificate Book of the Virginia Land Commission, 1779-1780." *Register of the Kentucky Historical Society* 21.

——. 1975. *Index for Old Kentucky Surveys & Grants.* Frankfort: Kentucky Historical Society. This also included Tellico surveys and grants. A cross-index for old Kentucky and Tellico series grants is available separately.

——. 1980. *Warrants Used in Virginia and Old Kentucky Surveys.* Frankfort: Kentucky Historical Society. Includes references to those warrants actually located and appropriate survey numbers.

Virginia Land Commission. 1981. *Certificate Book of the Virginia Land Commission of 1779-1780.* Easley, S.C.: Southern Historical Press. (See also "Locations and Water Courses," *Register of the Historical Society* (1921) 19:314-21, for locations and water courses mentioned in this book.)

Wilson, Samuel Mackay. 1953. *Catalogue of Revolutionary Soldiers and Sailors of the Commonwealth of Kentucky to Whom Bounty Land Warrants were Granted by Virginia for Military Service in the War for Independence.* Baltimore, Md.: Southern Book Company.

Source: Kentucky Genealogical Society List, January 1991.

In summary, the steps to a complete search of old Kentucky land grants are as follows:

1. Determine the military warrant number by consulting Jillson's *Old Kentucky Entries and Deeds* (Jillson 1978).

2. Check the military surveys list in Jillson's *Old Kentucky Entries and Deeds* (Jillson 1978).

3. Search the *Master Index* (Brookes-Smith 1976).

4. Examine the microfilm for the warrant, survey, grant, and any other miscellaneous papers.

5. Plat the patent. Topographical maps are available from the Kentucky Department of Commerce in Frankfort, Kentucky, or the University of Kentucky Geological Survey in Lexington, Kentucky.

6. Order related documents such as military service records and pension records from the National Archives in Washington, D. C.

If no warrant records are found, there are still a number of resources to research before giving up. Write the land office in Frankfort to determine if it was assigned. Contact the National Archives to see if pension records or military service records exist. Virginia also awarded land in southern Ohio, so contact the Ohio State Auditor's Office, Broad Street, Columbus, Ohio, for information. Some soldiers did not claim their land because they died, or because they felt it was a patriotic duty and so the state owed them nothing.

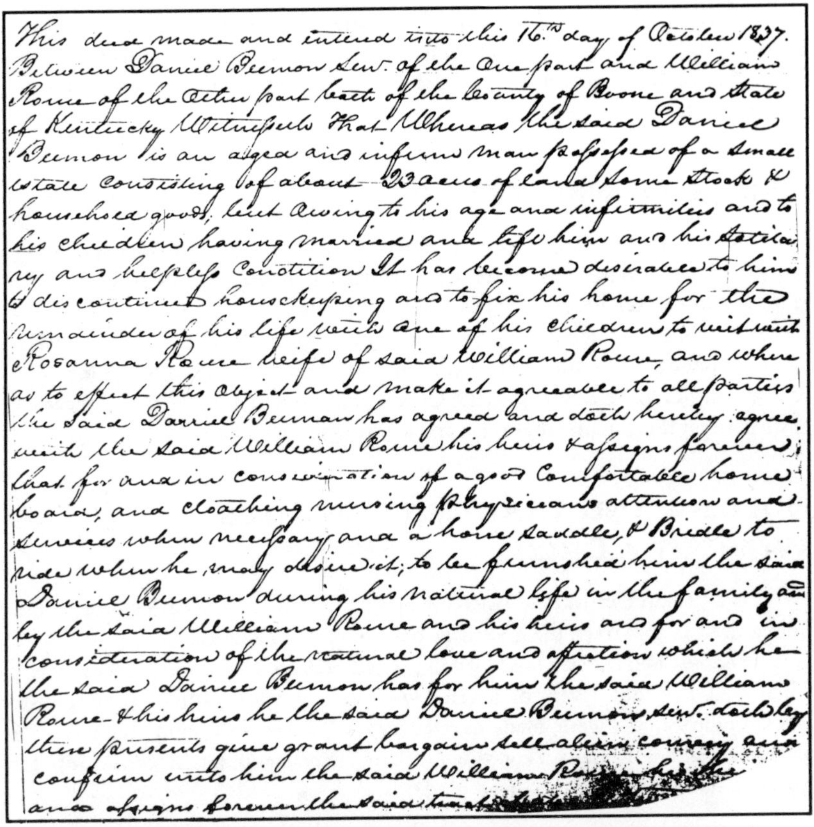

FIG. 5.3 Deed transferring land to heirs, 1837. (Boone County Deed Book L:28-29)

KENTUCKY DEED RECORDS

Deeds are a mainstay of the genealogical record. Deeds can be used to document residence, migrations, heirs, neighbors, and financial status of our ancestors. Deeds can sometimes be the only way to document a relationship or a marriage, particularly in early Kentucky when marriages were not uniformly recorded. It is, therefore, critical that these valuable records be completely exploited for the clues they can yield. In Kentucky records, there are situations where it is known that land was held, but a deed can not be located. Below are some tips on searching Kentucky deed records that may help to solve the problem.

COURTS OF RECORD

Deeds could be filed in Kentucky in any court of record. These courts of record include the Supreme Court of the District of Kentucky (prior to 1792), the court of appeals, courts of quarter session, district courts, circuit courts, and the county courts.

UNIQUE FILING SYSTEMS

Kentucky clerks were quite ingenious in developing their own systems of filing land transactions. Therefore, when searching indexes for deeds, check both grantor and grantee indexes. Some filing techniques observed in more than one Kentucky county include the following: filing deeds under the H pages for "Heirs of . . ."; under S for "Settlement of . . ." and for "Sheriff"; even under W for "Will of . . ."; and C for "Commissioner." Check under the first name of the ancestor, particularly if it is a name that might be a surname.

HOLDING AND TRANSMITTING TITLE WITHOUT A DEED

If a person owned land by virtue of a land grant, it is not necessary to also hold a deed to that tract; the grant was held in place of a deed.

People often devised land by will instead of deed. Deeds were not necessary when land was sold, given, or devised via a will, to a son, daughter, or spouse. Deeds could be, and were, made to relatives for "love and affection" but were not always recorded. If heirs kept the property, they could retain ownership for generations without having a deed made.

DEEDS OF PARTITION AND COMMISSIONERS' DEEDS

If an estate had to be settled or partitioned among heirs, however, these transactions would be recorded in the deed books. Some Kentucky counties have maintained separate deeds of partition books. In order to track land ownership under these circumstances, the tax rolls can be consulted to determine whether land was given to a descendent.

Commissioners appointed by the court made deeds to fulfill the orders of the courts. These records may be in separate books called the commissioners' books or commissioners' deeds. Check under the C section of the book if the surname check does not list the records.

UNRECORDED DEEDS

Some counties have files or books of "unrecorded" deeds. This means that there were original deeds transferring title to property from one party to another in the county clerk's office, but were unrecorded because the recording fee was not paid. There are also unrecorded deeds of partition, mortgages, powers of attorney, etc.

AVAILABILITY OF COUNTY DEEDS

Deeds for each of Kentucky's counties are listed in chapter 8. Almost without exception, these deeds are indexed by both grantee and grantor. It is exceptionally rare to find a deed book without some type of index, either an internal one appearing in the book itself or an external index appearing in a separate book. Most internal deed indexes appear within the first few or last few pages of each book. If an index appears on pages within the deed, a note is usually made on the first few pages of the book. Many of the deed indexes have been compiled and typed in modern times. While this is a convenience, the accuracy and completeness of these indexes is not always perfect. It is always a good idea to consult the original deed book indexes during the research.

TAX RECORDS

HISTORICAL BACKGROUND

Tax lists for early Kentucky are a valuable supplement to the years between the census and deed records. Even if an early Kentucky settler did not bother to record his deed, neglected to make an entry or claim, or failed to record inheritance of land, property ownership may still be documented using appropriate tax records (Sutherland 1986, v). During the 200 years of compiling tax records and collecting taxes, the system has changed little.

In 1781, Virginia tax laws stipulated that every county be divided into precincts, and annually appoint one of the justices for each precinct to take a list of all free males above the age of twenty-one who were subject to a poll tax. Similarly, Kentucky counties were organized into tax districts, and a tax commissioner appointed for each district. The tax commissioners were responsible for calling on each person subject to taxation in his district and for obtaining a written list of taxables.

Until 1828, tax reports, also called tithables lists, were completed during required military musters. Under this system of taxation, a commissioner functioned within the confines of his military company. After giving ten days' notice, each commissioner attended the muster of his company in April and June to receive lists of taxable persons. Included within this category were white men over twenty-one and slaves over sixteen years of age, who were both subject to a poll tax not exceeding $1.50 per person per year, and those owning property within the bounds of his militia company.

Assessments were made as of 10 March. Because widows and infirm persons were not required to attend the muster, it became the duty of the commissioner to make personal application to them at their homes. Single men and women not attending the muster were allowed until 1 August to submit their tax lists. All taxpayers took an oath and swore to the correctness of their lists and were required to describe their property so that the commissioner would be able to estimate its value.

After 1828, the district tax commissioner was required to visit the residence of each citizen to obtain the list of tithables. The citizen incurred no penalty for failure to turn in a tax list unless called upon for it at his home.

In 1837, the requirements of the assessment procedure were that each taxpayer had to fix a sum, under oath, of total worth. This sum was not to include the exemption of $300, lands outside the state, the growing crop, one year's crop then on hand, and articles made at home for domestic use.

Before the abolition of slavery, the tax commissioner was required to list the number of free blacks in the county in a separate column. After abolition, all men over twenty-one years old were tithable, and slaves were eliminated from the lists in 1863. In the same year, the poll was raised from a maximum of $1.50 to $3 per person, per year.

Beginning in 1874, the voting precinct became the tax district. At this time, each taxpayer was furnished with a blank tax form to complete the listing of taxable estate, real, personal, and mixed. Prior to 1874, the taxable property of blacks, mulattoes, and Indians were listed in a separate book. By 1892, the commissioners were required to make separate books for each district as well as each city and town.

In 1892, the commissioner had new tax schedules prepared by the state auditor of public accounts. These schedules were completed by the taxpayer who assigned value to each item. The commissioner fixed his judgment of the proper valuation. Notice had to be given to the taxpayer if this value was higher.

TAX EXEMPTIONS

Exemptions from taxes were granted for a number of reasons. Women and free blacks only appeared on the tax lists if they owned land. White females were exempt, but were named when responsible for the tax of free white males over twenty-one or slaves in their household. When a man died, his widow usually appeared until the estate was settled or until she remarried (Thompson 1985, 96). Tax exemptions were granted for a variety of reasons and are shown in table 5.5.

TABLE 5.5 Tax Exemptions Granted

Ministers

Revolutionary or French and Indian War Veterans

Deceased Persons (if a man was deceased, his tax was paid by his estate). If the list indicated a "white male tithable over sixteen," then the deceased may have left a son who was being taxed.

Widows. If a widow was taxed, then she must have had a male over sixteen living in the household, perhaps a son

Poor and Disabled

White females

Source: Thompson 1985, 96.

TAX RECORDS MAINTAINED

The commissioner was required to make four general lists, arranged alphabetically, showing by columns the date of receipt of each list, each person chargeable with the tax, the number and quantity of each kind of property, and the number of free males over the age of twenty-one years. These four copies were distributed as follows: the tax commissioner, the sheriff to guide tax collection, the county clerk who certified the list, and the state auditor of public accounts.

The tax commissioner received a list of solvents from the sheriff who recorded this list in his tax books. He was required to transmit to the Kentucky State Auditor a list of all fines, additional taxes, and all taxpayers who had moved to outside the county.

The tax commissioner also kept records of delinquent taxpayers, those who failed to make a return, refused to give a list on oath, or who made a fraudulent return. These tax evaders were subject to a triple tax. Delinquent tax lists survive for some counties and can be valuable because they establish residence of mobile ancestors, and because of the information they contain. Most delinquent lists will show the reason for the delinquency including death, insolvency, exemptions of various types, and migrations of the family. Some assessors listed the state or county where the family "removed to" as well.

CONTENT OF TAX RECORDS

The information contained on tax lists varies from year to year, but the basic information has included the following at various times:
- name of person chargeable with the tax
- names or number of other taxable males
- names or number of slaves in the household
- number of acres of land and value per acre
- name of the nearest watercourse
- name of person who entered the land and in whose name patented
- name of the person for whom it was surveyed
- blacks over sixteen and total blacks
- horses and mares, cattle
- number of four-wheeled riding carriages, billiard tables, and ordinary licenses

Some indexes for tax lists exist by county. However, the usual arrangement of the lists within the county is by district and then usually in a rough alphabetical order. Some commissioners have devised unique methods of arranging the lists such as by the person's first name.

AVAILABILITY OF TAX RECORDS

Specific information regarding the availability of tax records for each county can be found in chapter 8. However, as a general rule, tax lists are available in Kentucky from 1792 to 1866 in the Kentucky archives research room. There are also Internal Revenue Assessment Lists for Kentucky from 1862 to 1866 available in the archives.

FEDERAL CENSUS RECORDS

Kentucky has federal censuses or census substitutes for the years 1790 to 1920 currently available. Statewide indexes are available from 1790 to 1870. Soundex or miracode indexes are available for 1880, and 1900 to 1920; thus, all Kentucky censuses now have at least partial statewide indexes. In addition, there are many county indexes that have been compiled by local researchers. These county indexes are available at the historical society and the local county libraries.

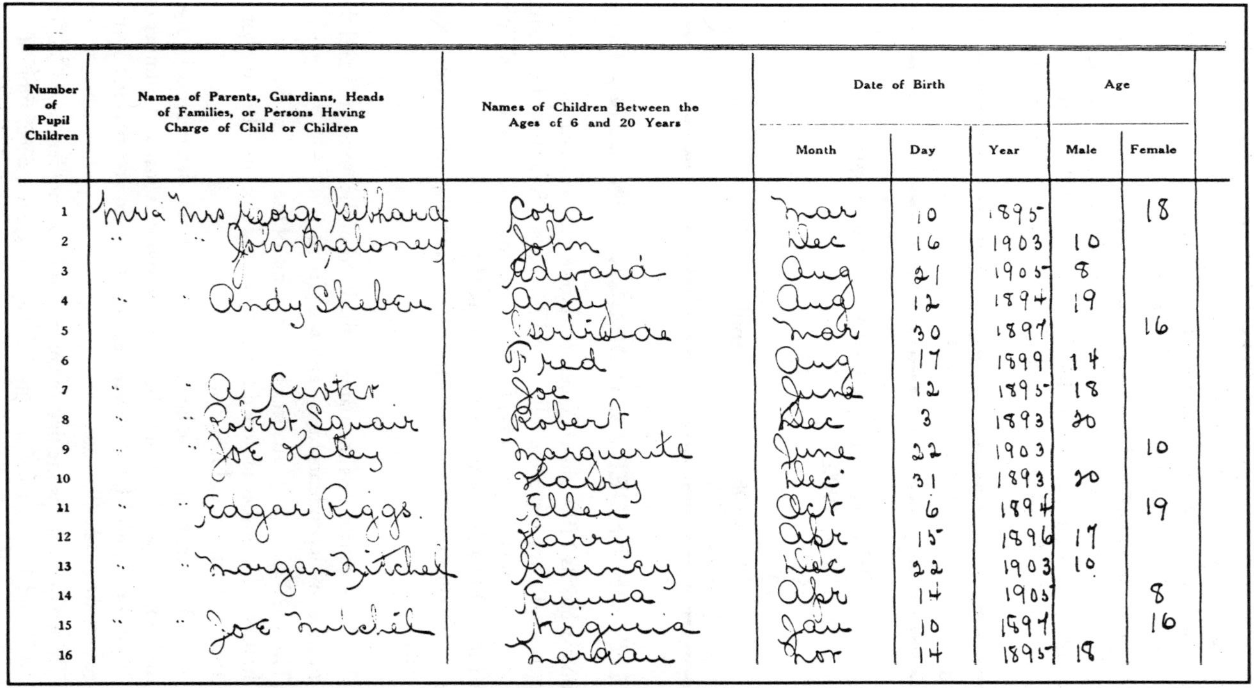

Number of Pupil Children	Names of Parents, Guardians, Heads of Families, or Persons Having Charge of Child or Children	Names of Children Between the Ages of 6 and 20 Years	Date of Birth: Month	Day	Year	Age: Male	Female
1	Mrs" Mrs George Kebhara	Cora	Mar	10	1895		18
2	" " John Maloney	John	Dec	16	1903	10	
3		Edward	Aug	21	1905	8	
4	" " Andy Sheben	Andy	Aug	12	1894	19	
5		Gertrude	Mar	30	1897		16
6		Fred	Aug	17	1899	14	
7	" " A Carter	Joe	June	12	1895	18	
8	" " Robert Squair	Robert	Dec	3	1893	20	
9	" " Joe Haley	Marguerite	June	22	1903		10
10		Harry	Dec	31	1893	20	
11	" " Edgar Riggs.	Ellen	Oct	6	1894		19
12		Harry	Apr	15	1896	17	
13	" " Morgan Mitchel	Gurney	Dec	22	1903	10	
14		Emma	Apr	14	1905		8
15	" " Joe Mitchel	Virginia	Jan	10	1897		16
16		Morgan	Nov	14	1895	18	

FIG. 5.4 Kenton County School Census for 1913-4. (Kentucky State Archives)

No known state-conducted census exists for Kentucky, only the federal census. The listing of Kentucky "census" records recently published are partial tax lists for some counties, not actual census records (Eakle and Cerny 1984, 115).

The census day is that day set aside for the official count to begin. All people who were alive on the census day were to be counted. The census taker was to show all persons in the family as of 1 June. This means that children born between 1 June and the enumerator's visit were excluded. Family members who had died, but were living 1 June, were listed. A family who was living on 1 June with another family was supposed to be listed with that family (*Bluegrass Roots* 1982, 39).

TABLE 5.6   Official Census Dates

1790 to 1820	First Monday in August
1830 to 1900	1 June
1910	15 April
1920	20 January
1930 to 1980	1 April

CONTENT OF FEDERAL POPULATION CENSUS

Kentucky lost its 1790 and 1800 census. However, these two censuses have been reconstructed using taxpayers rolls. The 1790 census is estimated to include approximately seventy-five percent of the 8,352 total households originally enumerated in 1790 by the census bureau (Purvis 1982, 258).

The information available in each of the Kentucky federal censuses is described below.

- The 1810 census lists the name of the head of the household and the number of dependents in age and sex groups.
- The 1820 and 1830 censuses list the name of the head of the household, number of dependents by age and sex, and the number and age of slaves and free blacks.
- The 1840 census lists the head of the household, dependents by age and sex groups, slaves, number of employed persons, and number of "deaf and dumb," blind, insane, idiots, students, and persons over twenty who were illiterate.
- The 1850 census is the first census to list householders by name. The 1850 and 1860 census also gives the age, sex, race, occupation of males over fifteen, value of real property, place of birth, whether mar-

ried within the year, whether in school, persons over twenty who could not read or write, and whether deaf, "dumb," blind, insane, idiot, pauper, or convict. Some of the Kentucky census takers noted in the occupation column that a person was a Revolutionary War soldier. Others recorded not only the state of birth, but also the county in Kentucky where the person was born. There is a published statewide index for the 1850 to 1870 Kentucky censuses that is available at the archives and the historical society. The 1850 and 1860 slave censuses list the name of the slave owner, the number of slaves in age and sex groups, number manumitted, deaf, "dumb," blind, insane, or idiot. There are a few scattered lists that include the name of the slave as well.

· The 1870 census lists the same information as the 1850 census plus personal property, father and mother of foreign birth, month of birthday (if born during the census year), and if the right to vote is denied. A statewide index for the 1870 Kentucky census is now available.

· The 1880 census lists the same information as the 1870 plus the place of birth of the mother and father. There is a soundex for 1880 of families who had living with them children under the age of ten.

· The 1890 census lists were also destroyed. The Union Veterans and the widows of Union Veterans of the Civil War still exists, however. There is also an 1890 tax list available for Kentucky, but it is unindexed.

· The 1900 census lists the same information as the 1880 census plus the month and day of birth, marital status, years married, number of children, number of children living, education, and whether one can read, write, and speak English. The miracode is available for the 1900 census for Kentucky at the archives and the historical society.

· The 1910 census includes the following information: name; relationship to head of household; sex; race; age at last birthday; marital status; length of present marriage; number of children; number of living children; place of birth; place of birth of parents; if foreign born, year of immigration and citizenship status; language spoken; occupation; type of industry employed in; if employer, employee, or self-employed; if unemployed, number of weeks unemployed in 1909; ability to read and write; if attended daytime school since 1 September 1909; if home is rented or owned; if home is owned free or mortgaged; if home is a house or a farm; if a survivor of the Union or Confederate army or navy; if blind in both eyes; and if "deaf and dumb." The archives in Frankfort, the historical society, and the

Public Library of Cincinnati and Hamilton County have the 1910 census soundex.

A PICTURE OF KENTUCKY IN 1880

An analysis by Ford (1981) of the early Kentucky population census reveals a great deal about Kentucky life. For example, Kentucky's population in the 1880 federal census was typical of an agrarian population with very high birth and death rates. The median age was only eighteen years, compared to thirty in 1980. Only ten percent of Kentucky's population was over fifty years old in 1880. By the time the 1880 census was taken, the average family size in Kentucky stood at 5.5. This represented a slight decline from the average family size in the 1850 census at 5.8 (Ford 1982, 10).

BIRTH RATES

The Kentucky birth rate calculated from the 1880 census was 34.9 births per thousand, about eleven percent higher than the national rate at that same time. Estimates adjusted to reflect the age distribution of Kentucky would suggest that the rate was actually somewhat higher, at around forty to forty-two births per thousand. That rate is about 2.5 times higher than the 1980 birth rate in Kentucky (Ford 1981, 10).

DEATH RATES

The annual death rate in Kentucky was fourteen deaths per thousand population in 1880. The true rate, adjusted for the age structure, was probably closer to twenty per thousand. The crude death rate in developing countries today is generally in the range of eleven to thirteen per thousand (Ford 1981, 10).

The 1880 census indicated a high infant mortality rate in Kentucky. One out of every six Kentucky babies died before it was a year old, compared with only one of eighty today. This rate was almost certainly higher in the cities and among Kentucky African-Americans. The city of Louisville, which may have had better reporting but higher death rates, registered a rate of 222 per thousand recorded births indicating that nearly one in five babies died before its first birthday (Ford 1981, 10-19).

Because families were large, most families would have experienced the loss of a young child or infant. Diphtheria, whooping cough, scarlet fever, enteritis, cholera, and fevers of various kinds claimed hundreds of young lives.

MIGRATION RATES

Kentucky has been a state that families migrated through. Analysis of the population figures shows that the state has probably lost more people to migration than it attracted every decade since 1820, with the exception of the 1840s. This trend of population loss continued until the 1970-80 decade when Kentucky recorded its first net migration gain in 130 years (Ford 1981, 7-12).

For example, an analysis of interstate migration, by counting the state of birth, of Kentucky residents in 1880 shows that there were about 454,000 native Kentuckians living in other states—about 51,000 more than had been counted in 1870. Of these 454,000 who had moved to other states, nearly seventy-five percent were located in these states: Missouri, Indiana, Illinois, Texas, Kansas, and Ohio.

At the same time, the number of Kentucky residents born in other states had only grown from 176,000 to about 187,000 in 1880. In summary, Kentucky was losing its natives to the western movement. Most of the immigrants to Kentucky, about eighty percent of the nonnative residents, excluding foreign immigrants, came from these five states listed in order of size of contribution: Tennessee, Virginia, Ohio, Indiana, and North Carolina (Ford 1981, 7-12).

RELIABILITY OF THE KENTUCKY CENSUS

An analysis of the 1870 and 1880 Kentucky censuses (Ford 1982) shows that the Kentucky censuses have a number of problems. Ford found that Kentucky's white population was probably under-reported in the 1870 census by about 6.5 percent. This means that about seven out of 100 people are not listed in the 1870 census. Indexing errors could add to this number. In 1880 census, the rate of omission appears to be about twelve percent or twelve in 100. While the precise rate is unknown, the rate of under-reporting was probably greater for black Kentuckians (Ford 1982; *Bluegrass Roots* 1983, 64).

AVAILABILITY OF KENTUCKY CENSUS

There are at least four complete sets of Kentucky federal censuses covering the years 1810 to 1920 in the state. The archives, Filson Club, the historical society, and the Kenton County Library have all available censuses for Kentucky including the indexes and the soundex/miracode. The University of Kentucky has all Kentucky county censuses for 1810 to 1900; however, they do not have the soundex/miracode. The Cincinnati Public Library also has a complete set of the Kentucky censuses and soundex/miracodes to 1920.

SPECIAL CENSUSES

In addition to the population schedules, federal censuses for mortality, manufacturing, and agriculture are available for the years 1850 to 1880. In this section, the federal agricultural census along with the military and school census are discussed.

AGRICULTURAL CENSUS

The federal agriculture census from 1850 to 1880 lists each Kentucky farm along with information about its size, products, livestock, and value. These censuses can provide wonderful insights into the farming activities and products of Kentucky ancestors.

TABLE 5.7	Agricultural Census Information Collected 1850 to 1880

1850 TO 1870 CENSUSES

Name of the owner, agent, or manager of the farm
Improved and unimproved acres (and woodland acres in 1870)
Cash value of farm
Value of farming implements and machinery
Number of livestock: horses, asses and mules, milch cows, working oxen, other cattle, sheep, swine
Value of livestock
Bushels of wheat, rye, Indian corn, oats, peas and beans, sweet potatoes, barley, buckwheat, clover seed, grass seeds, maple sugar, cane sugar
Pounds of rice, tobacco, wool, butter, cheese, hops, flax, silk cocoons, beeswax and honey
Value of orchard products, market produce, homemade manufacturers, animals slaughtered
Gallons of wines, molasses
Tons of hemp

1880 CENSUS

Name of person who conducts the farm and tenure status (owns, rents, or share crops)
Acres of land tilled, pasture, woodland, unimproved
Value of farm, implements and machinery, livestock, total farm productions
Labor costs
Grasslands acreage and products
Number and loss of livestock: working oxen, milch cows, calves and cattle, sheep, swine, poultry

Acres and bushels of cereals (barley, buckwheat, Indian corn, oats, rye, wheat); fibers (cotton, flax, seed, straw, fiber, hemp); sugars (cane and molasses); Irish and sweet potatoes; tobacco

Acres and amount of products from orchards (peach and apple), vineyards (grapes and wine), nurseries, and market produce

Amount of dairy products produced: milk, butter, cheese

Source: U.S. federal census 1850-80.

While the agricultural census is not indexed, it is arranged by neighborhood. Locate the ancestor first in the population census, then search that precinct in the agriculture lists. Another way of locating these farms is through notations made in some population censuses referring to the farm number in the agricultural census. These numbers may or may not refer to some meaningful system the census taker used to record farms. The archives, historical society, and university special collections library have these censuses.

MILITARY CENSUS

The second page of the 1840 census lists Revolutionary War soldiers. These are available at the Kentucky archives, university special collections library, and the Kentucky Historical Society.

SCHOOL CENSUS

The General Assembly of Kentucky required a school census be kept beginning in 1888. Census reports of children between the ages of six and eighteen were prepared annually. As a result, this census is a valuable source of birth dates of individuals who attended public schools in Kentucky and its timing makes it especially valuable as a supplement to the missing 1890 federal census.

Information contained in the census includes name and address of the child, race, date of birth, age, sex, school grade, and names and addresses of parents or guardian. In some cases, census cards for each child of school age have been kept. The data on these may include the school district, name of the child, race, sex, date and place of birth, address, school and grade, date entered, name of person the child lives with, and cause for withdrawal from school. Parental information includes names, occupation, and whether living or dead.

Records on black schools are also available in some cases. These records may include the name of children between six and eighteen, their parents' names, date of birth, age, sex, and address of child.

The Kentucky school censuses are kept at the local boards of education or the county clerks' offices. Scattered censuses are also available at the Kentucky archives and the Kentucky Historical Society. The state archives has school censuses dated 1901 to 1942, which are included in the Department of Education, Superintendent of Public Instruction Record Group 09001.

In addition, the Kentucky Department of Education Library in Frankfort is currently being organized. It may be possible that some additional old census records will be uncovered as the project is completed. Microfilmed school census records are listed in chapter 8 under the appropriate county.

MILITARY RECORDS

Revolutionary soldiers made up a significant proportion of early Kentucky settlers; thousands of pensions attest to the fact that many Virginian soldiers settled in Kentucky after the Revolution. And Kentuckians continued to fight in large numbers in all American wars. The service and pension records generated as a result of military service for Kentuckians are generally identical to records maintained for other states. Therefore, the focus will be on the location and special problems of Kentucky military records.

INDIAN WAR RECORDS 1783–1811

The state archives recently acquired the compiled service records of Kentuckians who served in the Indian Wars between 1783 and 1811. These men served in the Indian War of 1790-95 and the Tippecanoe Campaign of 1811. The collection includes the members of various units, as well as scouts, spies, and staff officers.

REVOLUTIONARY WAR RECORDS

The Kentucky State Archives has the *General Index to Compiled Military Service Records of Revolutionary War Soldiers*, index to pension applications, and census of Revolutionary War pensioners for all states. Other sources in the archives include the Order Books of General James Wilkinson, commanding general of the United States Army from 1796 to 1808.

The Kentucky Historical Society has a list of Revolutionary soldiers buried in Kentucky as well as the Kentucky DAR *Year Book*. The society also has lists of veterans who filed pensions by county. The 1835 *Pension Roll of the Secretary of War* should also be consulted for Revolutionary War soldiers and is available at most Kentucky libraries (Secretary of War Report 1959).

TABLE 5.8	Revolutionary War Records Dates
26 August 1776	Invalid pensions for officers and soldiers, half pay during disability, continental line.
24 May 1780	Widows and orphans of Continental officers, half pay for seven years, rescinded 29 July 1789.
21 October 1780	Service pension for life of officers of Continental Army only, rescinded 4 August 1790.
28 July 1789	Federal government assumes state invalid pensions, continental line.
3 March 1804	Federal government assumes all of South Carolina invalid pensions, continental line.
3 March 1805	Invalid pensions extended to those disabled since the war by war wounds, continental line.
10 April 1806	Invalid pensions extended to volunteers, militia, and state troops.
1813	Military records burned in War of 1812, including pension applications prior to 1813.
18 March 1818	Service pension act authorized. Act of 1820 removed many.
15 May 1828	Service pension for officers and soldiers eligible for pension under resolution of 21 October 1780, full pay for life.
7 July 1832	First service pension for all Revolutionary soldiers and sailors, continental and state. Widows and orphans entitled to balance due.
4 July 1836	Widows allowed pension of 1828, married during last term of service or before 3 November 1783.
7 July 1836	Widow pension if married before 1 January 1794.
3 March 1837	Widow entitled to pension even if remarried.
3 February 1853	All widows entitled to pension.
1869 and 1906	Last Revolutionary pensioner and widow dies.

Source: *Bluegrass Roots* 1987, 88.

WAR OF 1812 RECORDS

Pension abstracts and an index to the pensions are available for the War of 1812. A roster of militia officers as well as muster rolls of soldiers from Kentucky and Virginia is available for use in research.

CIVIL WAR RECORDS

Kentuckians fought on both sides of the Civil War, despite the fact that it was officially neutral and a border state. However, Kentucky clearly sided with the Union. Three times as many soldiers served in the Union Army as with the Confederates (Ford 1981, 3). Nevertheless, it is wise to check both Confederate and Union records if a soldier cannot be found.

The archives, the university special collections library, and the historical society have the index to the Adjutant General's Reports for the Union and Confederate armies. The Military Records and Research Library has Union and Confederate Civil War muster rolls including unit histories, casualty lists, and other documentation. The Military Library also has Civil War discharges not reflected in the Adjutant General's Report dated 1861 to 1865.

UNION RECORDS

The archives has 515 rolls of microfilm containing the compiled service records of volunteer Union soldiers belonging to units from Kentucky. These compiled records are arranged by the organization unit, the most specific of which is the regiment or independent battalion or company. At the front of most of the unit records is a "record of events" card giving its stations, movements, or activities.

Within each unit's records, the individual soldiers' service records are arranged alphabetically by surname. In order to use these records, first locate the name in the index to determine the unit he served with, then consult the unit's records for his personal records.

A soldier who served in the war may not be found in this collection for a number of reasons. In some cases, a soldier may have served in a home guard unit or other state unit and may not have been called into the federal service. He may have served in a unit other than Kentucky or in the regular army. His records could have been lost or destroyed. He could have served under a different name, or his name could be misspelled.

CONFEDERATE RECORDS

Volunteer Confederate soldiers' records include 136 rolls of microfilm of compiled service records for Kentucky units and are organized in the same manner as the Union records. Additional sources for Confederates within this record group include card abstracts and a citizens' file.

Card abstracts include vague entries in the original records for those soldiers whose place of service is difficult to determine. Other references in this series are for civilian service. The National Archives has a Provost Marshall File and the Citizens' File that lists these civilians.

Confederate Pension Applications. The General Assembly passed the Confederate Pension Act on 4 March 1912 for the compensation of Kentucky Confederate veterans who were ineligible for federal pensions. The Department of Confederate Pensions maintained these records dating from 1912 to 1946.

There are fifty rolls of film that give the following information for each Confederate applicant: name, address, age at time of application, military service history, superior officer's name, statements of witnesses, and a verification by the county judge. Applications from widows of veterans are intermingled and are identical in content and format. Supporting documents may include affidavits, letters, and memoranda.

The applications and the printed index to these records have been microfilmed and are available for research use in the archives. A good finding aid is Alicia Simpson's *Inventory of Confederate Pension Applications* (1978).

Kentucky Confederate Home Records. The Confederate Veterans' Home was established by an act of the General Assembly in 1902. The facility, which was at Pee Wee Valley in Oldham County, was closed in 1934. The Military Library in Frankfort has these records and its staff will search them if sufficient information is provided. A 1912 list of inmates is available; records dating from 1902 to 1917 are in the inventory. The archives also has microfilms of these records.

Other Confederate Records. The Louisville Military Prison registers from 1862 to 1864 lists prisoners-of-war bound for prison camps in Ohio, Indiana, and Illinois. The archives recently completed its set of these records along with records of McLean's Barracks (another Civil War prison in Cincinnati that held Kentucky confederates). A register compiled in 1912 of Confederate prisoners who died in federal prisons and hospitals is also available at the archives. The historical society has applications for membership to the Frankfort chapter of the Daughters of the Confederacy.

Kentucky soldiers and civilians who supported the South during the war could request a pardon from President Andrew Johnson. These amnesty applications for Kentucky date from 1865 to 1867. These records are available for research at the Kentucky archives.

TABLE 5.9 Military Interest Groups In Kentucky

Kentucky Civil War Roundtable 814 Sherwood Drive Lexington 40502	Revolutionary War Roundtable 23 Public Square Elizabethtown 42701

Civil War Roundtable
University Archives
Eastern Kentucky University
Cammack 26
Richmond 40475

Society of War of 1812
5608 Apache Road
Louisville 40207

Louisville Civil War Roundtable
Box 1861
Louisville 40201

Source: Fugate, Betty K. 1989–90. *The 1989–90 Directory of Kentucky Historical Organizations.*
Frankfort: Kentucky Historical Society and the Historical Confederation of Kentucky.

LATER WARS AND MILITARY RECORDS

Rosters, muster rolls, and casualty and wounded lists exist for the Mexican and Spanish War, World War I, World War II, Korea, and Vietnam. Lists of the Kentucky National Guard dating as far back as 1865 have been preserved in the Kentucky Military Library.

Selective Service records for World War I are available and can be used for genealogical information. Almost every male resident of the United States born between the years of 1873 and 1900 was required to register for the draft, even though he might not have served. There are approximately twenty-four million registration cards nationwide that contain the following pieces of information: birth date, race, citizenship, occupation, employer, nearest relative, and marital status.

Write to Archives Branch, Federal Records Center, 1557 St. Joseph Avenue, East Point, Georgia 30044. A street address is necessary if the man lived in a city.

AVAILABILITY OF MILITARY RECORDS IN KENTUCKY

Kentucky has rich sources for military research. The National Society of the Sons of the American Revolution has its national headquarters in Louisville. The Military Records and Research Library can also provide help in locating military records of a Kentucky ancestor. Chapter 2 outlines the holdings of these libraries. Chapter 8 inventories military records and pension records available on microfilm at the archives, historical society, and University of Kentucky special collections library.

KENTUCKY NATURALIZATION RECORDS

HISTORICAL OVERVIEW

Prior to 1792 and statehood, the naturalization laws of Virginia applied to Kentucky. In May of 1779, the Virginia Assembly declared that, all "white persons born within the territory of this commonwealth, and all who have resided therein two years" and all who later migrate into the state, shall become citizens. In October 1783, the Virginia Assembly replaced the 1779 law with an act requiring that aliens appear before "some court of record" and declare their intention to remain in the state and to swear their loyalty to the commonwealth of Virginia.

In March 1790, the United States Congress passed the first naturalization act. From that date until 1906, when the Bureau of Immigration and Naturalization was created, more than twenty successive federal naturalization laws were enacted. A comprehensive act passed in 1802 remained in effect, with modifications, for 104 years. This law enabled aliens to become citizens after a residence of five years by swearing an oath before a circuit or district court of the United States, a district or supreme court of the territories, or a court of record, in any state, with common law jurisdiction, a seal, and a clerk.

The Federal Naturalization Act of 1802 and its later amendments were repealed in June 1906. At this time, the Bureau of Immigration and Naturalization was created, which provided uniform rules for naturalization proceedings. As in the 1802 act, authority to naturalize aliens was conferred on federal district and circuit courts and on state courts having common law jurisdiction, a seal, and a clerk.

As of 1 January 1912 the United States Circuit Courts were abolished and in March of 1940, the Kentucky General Assembly repealed the 1892 constitutional provision permitting naturalization in state courts. Since 1940, only federal district courts have granted citizenship to aliens in Kentucky (*Bluegrass Roots* 1984, 63).

CONTENT OF NATURALIZATION RECORDS

Declarations of intention, also known as first papers, are typically made by completing a simple form giving the person's name, age, place of birth, date of departure from the home country, date of arrival, and port of entry in the United States.

The naturalization record, or second papers, may contain more information. These records may include the country and sometimes town where the person was born, his date of immigration to the United States, and perhaps his length of

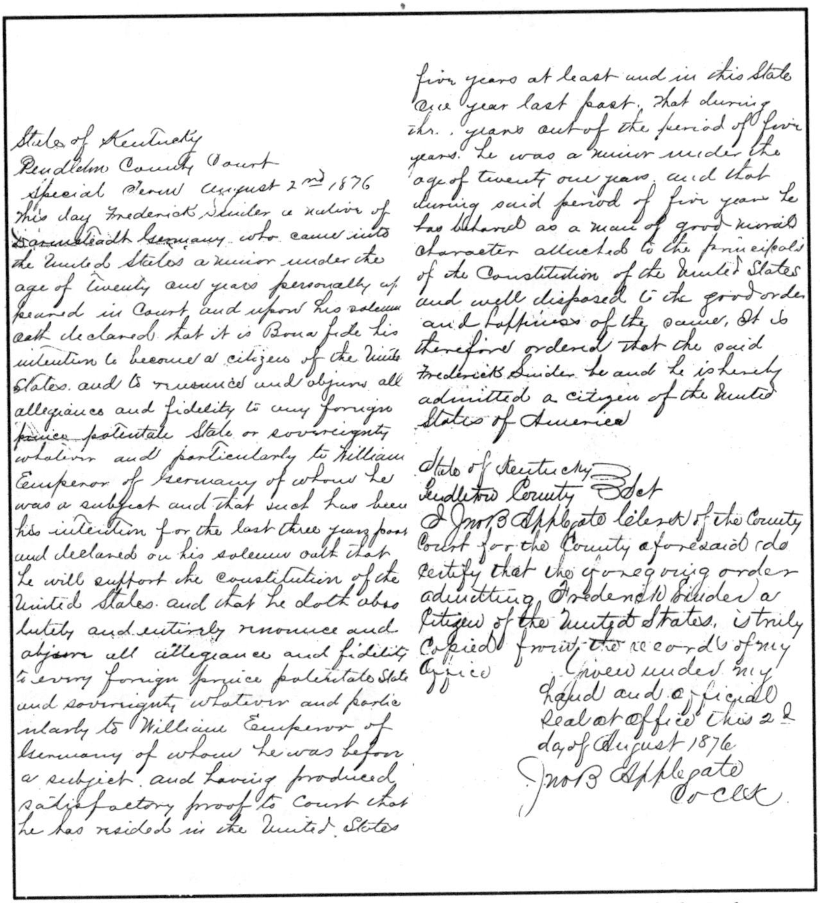

State of Kentucky
Pendleton County Court
Special Term August 2nd 1876
This day Frederick Snider a native of Darmstadt Germany who came into the United States a minor under the age of twenty one years personally appeared in Court and upon his solemn oath declared that it is Bona fide his intention to become a citizen of the United States and to renounce and abjure all allegiance and fidelity to any foreign prince potentate State or sovereignty whatever and particularly to William Emperor of Germany of whom he was a subject and that such has been his intention for the last three years past and declared on his solemn oath that he will support the constitution of the United States and that he doth absolutely and entirely renounce and abjure all allegiance and fidelity to every foreign prince potentate State and sovereignty whatever and particularly to William Emperor of Germany of whom he was before a subject and having produced satisfactory proof to Court that he has resided in the United States five years at least and in this State one year last past, that during thr.. years out of the period of five years he was a minor under the age of twenty one years and that during said period of five years he has behaved as a man of good moral character attached to the principals of the Constitution of the United States and well disposed to the good order and happiness of the same, It is therefore ordered that the said Frederick Snider be and he is hereby admitted a citizen of the United States of America

State of Kentucky
Pendleton County Sct
I Jno B Applegate Clerk of the County Court for the County aforesaid do certify that the foregoing order admitting Frederick Snider a citizen of the United States, is truly copied from the records of my office
Given under my hand and official seal at office this 2d day of August 1876
Jno B Applegate
Co Clk

FIG. 5.5 Naturalization order, 1872. (Pendleton County Clerk Order Book)

residence in the county of record. Women were not required to file naturalization certificates; naturalization of their husbands or fathers was sufficient.

In Kentucky, the naturalization is typically recorded in the county clerk's order book. There is no strict format to these naturalizations. However, the text usually describes the petitioner's nativity, perhaps date when he arrived in the county, and other personal or occupational information.

AVAILABILITY OF NATURALIZATION RECORDS

Naturalizations that occurred between 1802 and 1906 could be filed in United States, state, or local courts.

The most common place to find such records in Kentucky is the county's circuit or county court. However, any court of record could file a naturalization; therefore, all courts should be checked. For example, the police court in Jefferson County recorded many naturalizations because it was open in the evenings when it was more convenient for workers to stop by after work. A few Kentucky counties, Jefferson County is one example, maintained special Declaration of Intentions and Naturalization Certificate books.

If the naturalization was filed with the federal courts, the courts most likely to have the records for later naturalizations are the federal district courts in the eastern and western districts of Kentucky. Chapter 3 gives specific information and address data for these courts. The original records are held by the National Archives in Atlanta; however, the order books are still maintained by the court clerk.

Since June of 1906, the Bureau of Immigration and Naturalization has maintained the records on all immigrants naturalized. If the alien was granted citizenship in a federal district or circuit court, the documents will be in that federal court. For naturalizations after 1906, write to the Federal Bureau of Immigration and Naturalization. Ask for Form G-641, which is used to request the records. The address is 425 I Street, Washington, D. C. 20536.

BANKS OF THE COMMONWEALTH OF KENTUCKY

Throughout Kentucky's history, banks have been chartered to offset financial instability or establish commerce in the new frontier. The Old Bank of Kentucky was chartered in 1806 to facilitate commerce and settlement of the frontier. Its principal location was Frankfort, but by 1817, thirteen other branches were opened in these cities: Lexington, Russellville, Louisville, Washington, Bardstown, Paris, Danville, Hopkinsville, Shelbyville, Winchester, Richmond, Springfield, and Glasgow.

However, the bank also suffered from financial instability; it suffered losses during the 1819 Panic and, as a result, its operations were restricted in 1822. The branches of the bank ceased operation on 1 May 1824. Its main office in Frankfort closed in 1835. The bank's affairs were finally settled in 1870.

The Old Bank of Kentucky records in the Kentucky archives date from its charter in 1807 to 1871. Its records include 491 volumes and four rolls of microfilm. Consult the finding aid by Jeffrey M. Duff, *Inventory of the Records of the Bank of Kentucky, 1806–1835* (Duff 1976) for a complete and detailed listing of these records.

Books of the Principal Bank in Frankfort include *Bill Books* and *Bills for Collection* dating from 1807 to 1834. These records include the date a note was discounted, the name of the person, time of the note, and financial data. Arrangement of the books is chronological.

The Bank of the Commonwealth of Kentucky was chartered by the general assembly in 1820 to offset the financial instability that followed the War of 1812 characterized by massive land speculation, unsecured borrowing, and the creation of more than a hundred different currencies. The speculative bubble burst in 1819. At that time, many Kentuckians faced bankruptcy and demanded help from the state. The legislature chartered the bank to lend money to Kentucky citizens to pay debts and purchase goods.

The principal bank was in Frankfort. Branches were located in these judicial districts: Flemingsburg, Falmouth, Lexington, Louisville, Hartford, Princeton, Greensburg, Mount Sterling, Somerset, Winchester, and Bowling Green.

Loans were made from 1820 to 1830. The remaining money and records were sent to Frankfort. This bank's records date from 1820 to 1850 and consist of 303 volumes. Records include minute books, resolutions, letter books, ticklers, and account ledgers.

CHAPTER 6

SPECIAL PEOPLE: KENTUCKY WOMEN AND AFRICAN-AMERICAN FAMILIES

Searching for women and African-Americans in Kentucky can prove difficult because of their unique and changing legal status. African-Americans and women in Kentucky are not as visible in Kentucky history or records. They often changed surnames and were sometimes legally prohibited from acting in their own behalf, marrying, buying property, or making other contracts. Nevertheless, legal sources promise to tell us a great deal about the status and role of these early Kentuckians, perhaps more than many other currently available historical sources.

Because of these factors, researching Kentucky women and African-American Kentucky families requires special efforts if the details of their lives are to be discovered and appreciated. In this chapter, the legal status and historical events that influenced the lives and livelihood of Kentucky women and African-Americans are outlined. Special sources and techniques will also be discussed that will help to find the trail of these special Kentuckians.

KENTUCKY WOMEN

HISTORICAL REVIEW: WOMEN'S STATUS IN VIRGINIA

The study of legal history in colonial American life indicates that women were denied full legal status. In early Virginia, a woman could neither execute a will nor enter into a legal contract without the permission of her husband. Upon marriage, she relinquished control of all property to her husband. Voting privileges were, of course, denied to women in colonial Virginia whether single or married (Speth and Hirsch 1983, 12).

Women's status within the family was influenced by the officially established Anglican Church, and their status in the larger society was determined by the legal institutions of colonial Virginia. Colonial Virginia statutes, in turn, followed the basic tenets of the English common law tradition as it affected women. The common law is not written but is based on tradition and judicial precedent.

WOMEN, THE LAW, AND MARRIAGE

In both England and Virginia, a woman's legal status, civil obligations, and privileges were to a large extent determined by her marital status (Speth and Hirsch 1983, 7–8). A single woman, or *feme sole*, had the same legal rights as a man. A single adult woman could enter into contracts, sue her debtors, and dispose of her personal and real property by either will or deed. Once a woman married, however, she became a *feme covert*, and this legal autonomy ended.

Upon marriage, a woman's husband assumed her legal duties and certain rights to her property. For example, she lost complete control over her personal property. Her husband could dispose of her personal property as he wished. Her livestock, jewels, furniture, even her clothes belonged to her husband. Any wages she earned or property she inherited *during the course of the marriage* belonged to her husband.

Beginning with a 1748 statute, however, the House of Burgesses began to protect the interests of women's property rights. This act ordered that a man must obtain his wife's written permission to convey or sell any of his wife's land. The lawmakers provided that the woman had to be examined privately, apart from her husband, by the justices of the local court to determine if she was agreeable to the sale of the land. The Burgesses ordered further that if she was too ill to travel to court, the justices would go to her and conduct a private examination (Speth and Hirsch 1983, 9).

This 1748 law also changed inheritance to wives. In 1662, the Virginia House of Burgesses had ordered that when a man died intestate, his widow received a third of his estate. The 1748 law specified the wife's dower interest in different types of property. She was now guaranteed a life interest of one-third of her husband's land, slaves, and his personal property (Speth and Hirsch 1983, 10). Allowance was also made for a widow to contest the will if she so chose. If she contested the will, the justices of the court would appoint a commission to divide the testator's estate and ensure that the wife received her one-third (Speth and Hirsch 1983, 10).

Although a man could not sell property without his wife's consent, he could use it as he wished. All rents or profits accruing from use of the property belonged to the husband. At her death, the husband controlled her land, if they had children.

He became a tenant for life; and at his death, the land reverted to the couple's children (Speth and Hirsch 1983, 7–8).

Husbands also retained power, based on the 1748 law, to appoint guardians for his children and to apprentice them out to learn a trade while their mother was still alive (Speth and Hirsch 1983, 11).

WOMEN, THE LAW, AND DIVORCE

In colonial Virginia, divorce or separation was often neither economically feasible nor legally easy to arrange. In England, it was possible to break the spiritual contract of marriage in an ecclesiastical court. This religious institution could grant divorces. However, Virginia had no such courts, and so there was no colonial agent that could grant a total divorce. Occasionally, a local county court could grant a legal separation. Because marriage was a religious matter, however, the courts were hesitant to act in these cases and granted separations only in extreme and unusual circumstances (Speth and Hirsch 1983, 12).

In 1827, the Virginia General Assembly authorized superior courts to grant divorces from "bed and board" on the grounds of cruelty, adultery, and fear of bodily harm. These decrees were basically separation agreements where marital obligations were suspended. The wife surrendered claims on her husband, and he renounced rights to her property. By these measures, the woman had established a separate estate. The bed and board decrees did not allow the parties to remarry. Complete divorces were only allowed in cases of impotence at the time of marriage, bigamy, and idiocy. Statutes in 1848 and 1853 allowed complete divorce for adultery, desertion, and a number of other cases (Lebsock 1984, 68–70).

WOMEN AND THEIR ROLES

While the early colonial laws were certainly repressive, recent studies by legal historians have documented a disparity between the actual role versus the legal status of women during the colonial period. These studies have found that laws regarding women were not always followed among families that drew up and filed wills. Among the population of early Virginians who had property to bequeath, it appears that the laws were proscriptive rather than descriptive of reality. The conclusion seems to be that traditional historians have sometimes confused the legal paradigms of colonial times with the true role of women (Speth and Hirsch 1983, 1–6, 13).

For example, Virginia statutory law dictated that when a man died intestate, the eldest son was to receive the bulk of his father's real estate. An equal share of the father's property was divided equally among all children, both male and female. The widow was to receive one-third of the intestate's land, slaves, and personal property. At the widow's death, the real estate reverted to the couple's eldest son (Speth and Hirsch 1983, 15).

However, an analysis of 394 wills probated between 1735 and 1755 conducted on records of Amelia, Prince Edward, and Mecklenburg counties in

Virginia showed substantially different behaviors. This analysis shows that male testators diverged significantly from the inheritance patterns proscribed by the laws regulating property distribution of intestates. Approximately twenty percent of the testators bequeathed land to their daughters. About three-quarters of the testators bequeathed more than one-third of their estate to their wives.

This pattern of inheritance varied by the age of the testator at the time of the death. Elderly men tended to give all property to adult children and grandchildren and charged the eldest son with seeing that his mother was supported. Younger men with minor children tended to give their wives far more than their dower, possibly with the expectation that this would enable her to support the family after his death (Speth and Hirsch 1983, 14-18). Sixty-five percent of the widows received control over real estate that they used to maintain themselves and their children during their widowhood (Speth and Hirsch 1983, 28).

Testators in this analysis generally left custody of their children to their wives. Less than three percent of the fathers appointed a guardian other than their wives. In these cases, the testators were quite wealthy and tended to rely on business acquaintances to oversee the substantial commercial legacies they had left their children.

Testators also relied on their spouses to serve as executors of their estates. Again, this practice varied with the age of the testator. The spouse was favored if there were minor children, and the eldest son was favored if he was old enough to take on the responsibility (Speth and Hirsch 1983, 21-23).

It was assumed that in early colonial Virginia widows could easily remarry and did so quickly after the death of her husband. An analysis of recorded marriages in the counties of Amelia, Prince Edward, and Mecklenburg shows that only nine percent of the widows did, in fact, remarry. The age of the widow, of course, is the best predictor of remarriage. Widows with adult-aged children tended not to remarry (Speth and Hirsch 1983, 28-29).

PRIMOGENITURE LAWS

The ability of daughters to inherit from their fathers also changed dramatically during this period. Primogeniture laws were generally revoked by all states soon after the Revolution (Shammas 1987b, 64-66). By 1790, Virginia's inheritance laws were reflective of those in the other states: intestate settlement dictated equal division of real and personal property among the children and a one-third life estate to the widow. The widow inherited the entire estate if there were no other kin alive at the time of the death (Shammas et al. 1987b, 63-64). Thus, by 1800 in Virginia, as in most states, sons and daughters received equal shares, both real and personal, of their father's estate.

If the most significant event for women and inheritance in the eighteenth century was the abolition of primogeniture, then the most significant event in the nineteenth century was the change in a married woman's position as heir and testator. From about 1850 on, Virginia, as most states, allowed married women, rather than their husbands, the ownership and control over all personal and real property they had inherited or had been given. This meant that women could will their property (Shammas et al. 1987, 103).

An analysis of early testators in Pennsylvania found that in the 1790s, only seventeen percent of the testators were women. By the 1890s, 38.5 percent of the testators were women. These female testators exhibited substantially different behaviors than did their male counterparts. For example, three-quarters willed their husbands less than intestacy would have awarded him. Women were much more likely to name their daughters as executrix of the estate. Only about eight percent of widowers named daughters compared to fifteen percent of widows. Widows were also more likely to favor their daughters with a greater inheritance if one child received a greater share than another. (Shammas et al. 1987, 118–20).

WOMEN'S STATUS IN KENTUCKY

As in Virginia, Kentucky statute granted significantly different rights to the *feme sole*, as a single, widowed, or divorced woman, than to the *feme covert*, a married woman. For the early Kentucky woman then, marriage marked a turning point in her potential legal autonomy. There were, nevertheless, areas in which she could, and did, make decisions about her life, including dissolution of the marriage, disposition of property, and her children.

WOMEN'S PROPERTY RIGHTS

Kentucky property laws regarding women were especially repressive, even for the South. A compiler of Kentucky statutes noted that marriage operated as an absolute gift to the husband; that all personal property, along with rents and profits from the property, that the wife had at the time of her marriage went to her new husband (Stanton 1867, 2:8–9).

For women, control over her property came piecemeal. An act of the Kentucky General Assembly in 1838 allowed establishment of a separate estate for women, including married women. Under this law, it was legal for bank and other stock to be transferred to a woman for her exclusive use. This property could not be transferred, be liable to vest in the husband, nor be subject to his debts. The woman could dispose of the property by will, if unmarried, or with the consent of her husband, if married (Loughborough 1842, 251–53).

An act passed in 1846 was aimed at protecting the property rights of married women. Before this act, the husband upon marriage became entitled absolutely to all the personal estate and slaves belonging to his wife, and this right continued after her death (Stanton 1867, 2:9). In 1846, however, the husband did not acquire an interest in his wife's real estate, chattels real, or slaves owned at the time of her marriage or acquired by her after marriage. He was, however, allowed the right to rent his wife's property for not more than three years and to hire out her slaves for not more than one year (Stanton 1867, 2:8).

168   LIN   COVINGTON DIRECTORY.   LLO

Telephone
South 557.

Henry Linnemann.   Henry Moore

Linnemann & Moore,

UNDERTAKERS.

31-33 East Eleventh St.,

COVINGTON, KY.

Lindsly Mary L saleslady h 635 Philadelphia
Linehan Daniel C painter h 61 E 20th
—Margaret wid Jas J h 123 E 11th
Lipfoot Chas A clk h 316 Madison Av
—Chas T coal 225 Scott h 15 Byrd
Link Gustav tailor h 1520 Nancy
—Henry vet surg 923 Glenn Av Latonia
Linn Catherine wid Jacob h 1557 Holman Av
—Cecil tobaccowkr h 17 Neave
—Culver carp h 17 Neave
—Harriet wid Edward h 17 Neave
—Homer lab h 17 Neave
—John h 17 Neave
—Pearl h 17 Neave
Linneman Edward B secy and treas West-
ern German Savings Bank junc 9th and
Pike h 819 Greer Av
—Gus bds 58 E 5th
LINNEMANN A. C. & E. J. MOORE,
(Augustus C. L. & E. J. Moore Estate)
Undertakers and Embalmers, 717 and
719 Madison Av.; Telephone South 125
—Augustus C (A C L & E J Moore) h 1181
Bank Lick
LINNEMANN BERNARD J.,
Cashier Citizens National Bank, s.e.c.
Madison Av. and Pike; Residence, 33 E.
11th
—Dora M cashr 28 Pike h 103 W 8th
—Frank saloon 164 Pike h 809 Greer Av
—Geo, U S storekpr U S Int Rev Office h 33
E 11th
—Harry clk h 809 Greer Av
—Harry F safemkr h 1131 Bank Lick
—Henry (L & Moore) h 35 E 11th
—J B queensware 148 Pike h 103 W 8th
—Jos W salesman h 1416 Garrard
—Julia dressmkr h 103 W 8th
—Mrs Mary shoes 73 E 11th h 35 E 11th
LINNEMANN & MOORE,
(Henry L. & Henry M.) Undertakers
and Embalmers, 31 and 33 E. 11th; Tel-
ephone South 557
Linskey Julia M h 132 W 5th
—Martin carp h 182 W 5th
—Norine V clk h 132 W 5th

Linsky Bridget A bkpr 532 Madison Av h
1824 Holman Av
—John J gateman h 1824 Holman Av
—Mary h 1824 Holman Av
Linstead Catherine M milliner h 315 Warren
—Frances R steno h 315 Warren
—Geo W h 315 Warren
—John A condr h 317 Warren
Linville Lee painter h 2005 Mackoy Av
—Mary talloress bds 17 W 4th
—Wm L watchman bds 15 W 4th
Linz Barbara h 137 Center Latonia
—Barbara domestic 519 Greenup
—Lizzle h 137 Center Latonia
—Pius h 137 Center Latonia
Liphart John lab bds 519 Crawford Av
Lipp Mrs Iola nurse h 2018 Madison Av
—Mrs Virinda I h 43 Sterrett Av
Lippincott Anna wid Woodrow h 50 Livings-
ton W Covington
—J Chester elect'n h 50 Livingston W Cov-
ington
Lipscomb Mrs Alma h 1314 Scott
—Amanda wid J A h 159 Center Latonia
—Chattie tchr h 159 Center Latonia
—Davis cementwkr bds 49 E Saratoga
—Eli res Kenton County Infirmary Latonia
—John M porter h 106 Saratoga
—Joshua res Kenton County Infirmary La-
tonia
List Elmer uphol wks 157 Pike
—Geo H mill hand h 316 E 16th
Listerman C Wm tinner h 8 w s Nancy nr
Patton
Litfin Harry plstr h 107 Lewis
—Jos shoes 809 Scott
Litkenhaus Leah nurse Kenton County In-
firmary Latonia
Litmer Harry ironwkr bds 164 W 5th
Littell Chas E secy h flat L The Woodford
Littleford Betty short' hand school h flat 12
n w c 6th and Greenup
—Geo wh lumber h flat 12 n w c 6th and
Greenup
Litton Belle steno h 259 W 4th
—Mrs Belle B h 259 W 4th
—Mark steno h 259 W 4th
Litzler Agnes talloress h 706 Crescent Av
—Barbara wid John B h 706 Crescent Av
—John R pipeftr h 706 Crescent Av
—Oscar tinner h 706 Crescent Av
Lively Augustus ins solicitor 11 E 5th h 832
Scott
—Benj P fireman h 1509 Madison Av
—C M chairman Y M C A R R Dept 17th
and Madison Av also engr h 102 E 19th
—Edwin M engr h 1509 Madison Av
—Florence E h 1509 Madison Av
—Robt A engr h 1509 Madison Av
Liverpool & London & Globe Ins Co of Eng-
land n w c 5th and Madison Av
Livezey T Elwood, U S storekpr-gauger, U S
Int Rev Office h n w c 8th and Scott
Livingston Ann wid Nicholas h 1036 Lee
—Isaac Newton tobaccowkr h 1036 Lee
Livsey Jas L mgr branch The Common-
wealth Coal & Coke Co e s Russell Av h
15th and 16th rms 812 Madison Av
Llewellyn Wm T carp 106 W 7th
Lloyd Dudley C car inspector h 1730 Greenup
—Ella wid Thomas h 414 Philadelphia
—Geo W engr h n w c 17th and Garrard
—Harvey R switchman h 1902 Scott
—Jos lab h rear 4 s s Short Bremen

FIG. 6.1 Women workers and heads of households can be found in city
directories. (Covington City Directory, 1910-1911)

Twenty years later, another act was passed to improve the status of women. The act of 14 February 1866 allowed a married woman to act as a feme sole under certain conditions. For example, if her husband abandoned her, lived separately and apart from her, was not a resident of the state, or was confined to a prison for more than a year, she could be empowered to act as a feme sole (Stanton 1867, 2:10-11; Bullock and Johnson 1873, 2:522).

In 1894, in a reiteration of the 1846 statute, it was confirmed that, "marriage shall give to the husband . . . no estate or interest in the wife's property real or personal owned at the time or acquired after the marriage." It allowed women to hold a separate estate for her exclusive use and free from the debts, liabilities, or control of her husband (Barbour and Carroll 1894, 773-74). Women were now allowed to acquire and dispose of property, make contracts, bring suits, and be sued (Barbour and Carroll 1894, 774-76).

DISSOLUTION OF MARRIAGE

Divorce in the Early South. In the South, a divorce could be granted for mental cruelty (then called "personal indignities"), physical violence, and infidelity. The definition of indignity was sometimes liberally interpreted to include any kind of inappropriate behavior such as thievery, verbal abuse, cursing, ridicule, mistreating children, lack of industriousness or good management, and wastefulness.

Custody of children was typically given to the father since, according to English common law, a father had first rights to his children (Censer 1981, 43). In cases when children were awarded to the mother, the fitness of the mother and the incapacity of the husband usually had to be established (Censer 1981, 43).

There is evidence that formal divorces were more frequently granted to middle and upper class women. For example, one Southern court argued that lower class women might expect rough physical treatment and not be offended by it. However, the argument continued, this behavior would be unacceptable by women of education and refinement and, thus, be a legitimate reason for divorce (Censer 1981, 27-39).

Divorce in Kentucky. Kentucky's divorce laws reflected the general attitude toward divorce that existed in the larger society. By a statute passed in 1809 by the Kentucky General Assembly, a man could obtain a divorce if the wife voluntarily left his "bed and board" for three years, if she lived with another man, or committed a felony.

A woman, on the other hand, could be granted a divorce if abandoned by her husband for two years, if he lived in adultery, was convicted of a felony, or where his treatment of her was "so cruel, barbarous, and inhuman as actually to endanger her life" (Littell 1822, 442). The spouse at fault for the divorce was evidently important, since this had implications for remarriage and for division of any property the couple owned jointly or that was brought to the marriage.

An 1820 statute reiterated that the circuit courts were empowered to grant divorces on the same grounds as the 1809 law. Kentucky divorce statute later defined grounds for divorce as cruel and inhuman treatment "as to indicate a settled aversion to the spouse which would destroy permanently one's peace and happiness" (Sears 1989, 3-4). According to an 1829 precedent, cruelty in Kentucky divorce statutes meant an actual personal violence or the reasonable apprehension of it, or such a course of treatment as endangers life or health and renders cohabitation unsafe (Sears 1989, 11). An 1847 divorce case established that if a woman continued to live with her husband after acts of violence, this was proof that she did not consider herself in danger and so was not grounds for divorce (Sears 1989, 12).

By 1894, Kentucky statute provided for divorce to the wife in cases of (1) abandonment for one year; (2) habitual drunkenness for not less than one year; or (3) cruel beating or injury, attempt at injury or probable danger to her life. Husbands were granted divorces in cases of (1) abandonment for one year, (2) habitual drunkenness for not less than one year; or (3) adultery by the wife or such lewd, lascivious behavior on her part as proves her to be unchaste without actual proof of an act of adultery (Barbour and Carroll 1894, 768-70).

Under the early statutes, the offending party could not remarry as long as the former spouse lived. The earliest law stated that the offending party could not be released from "the pains and penalties which the law prescribes against a marriage whilst a former husband or wife is living" (Littell and Swigert 1822, 443). By 1873, divorced parties could remarry, but only one divorce was permitted to any person, except in those cases when the person was found not at fault for the divorce (Bullock and Johnson 1873, 524).

The husband's title to the wife's land resulting from the marriage ceased with the legal dissolution of that union. A divorce restored the wife's right to the immediate possession of her land (Barbour and Carroll 1894, 771). Provision was made for alimony for the support of the wife and division of property by the courts with "due regard to each party and the children" (Littell and Swigert 1822, 443).

Divorce records may be found in the circuit court records in the county of residence that will show a divorce as a chancery or equity case. Early divorces were also recorded in the Acts of Kentucky as late as 1850. See chapter 4 for other details of Kentucky divorce records.

KENTUCKY'S OLD INHERITANCE LAWS AND WOMEN

Kentucky inheritance laws were generally consistent with the rest of the country. A woman inherited one-third of her husband's real and personal property for life if there was no will (Littell and Swigert 1822, 444). If there was no living kin, then the wife inherited the estate. A woman could make a will if she had a separate estate by deed or devise. A husband, on the other hand, inherited his wife's entire estate upon her death for life if there were children of their marriage. If there were no children of the marriage, the husband inherited no real property, but all his wife's personal property (Shammas 1987b, 232-33).

Wills and Probate. Although a woman could dispose of her separate estate via will by 1867, as late as 1888 when the Equal Rights Association was formed, Kentucky was the only state that did not permit a married woman to will property that would otherwise descend to her husband's heirs (Stanton 1867, 457; Sears 1989, 3). She could only make a will to devise separate estate property. Property given or devised to her with the express intention of it being under her control and not for the use of her husband was a separate estate.

By 1894, however, there was a statute that allowed a married woman of sound mind and over the age of twenty-one to dispose of her estate by last will and testament, subject to certain other provisions of the act (Barbour and Carroll 1894, 784).

Widows could and did make wills nevertheless. Widows could, according to an 1705 statute, bequeath the crop from their land and tenements (Littell and Swigert 1822, 445). Some widows did not make wills but relinquished the dower after the death of their spouses and subsequently lived in the household of a child, usually a daughter or eldest son. These dower relinquishments are recorded in the deed books. Because widows often settled their estates in this manner, or because they had no property to relinquish other than their dower, it is often difficult to establish with certainty the death dates of early Kentucky women.

KENTUCKY WOMEN IN THE RECORDS

DEEDS AND DOWER

Kentucky women could, and did, transfer property. A man was not required to have his wife's signature when he bought property, but her consent was required for the sale of any property they held since she held a dower interest in his estate. However, in the early Virginia deeds where a husband's property was entailed, land could descend to the eldest son without the wife's signature or consent. Nevertheless, most deeds will include the wife's name and a statement that documents she was interviewed separate and apart from her husband and freely consented to the sale. Relinquishments of dower are typically recorded in the deed books in Kentucky. These transactions indicate that the women are consenting to sale of the property in which she has an interest.

MARRIAGE RECORDS

In early Virginia and Kentucky law, the marriage bond could not be arranged by the bride or her mother (Conrad 1988, 104). As a result, a male relative of the bride and the groom would obtain the marriage license from the county clerk based on the bond executed. The bond was usually posted by the groom and a male kinsman of the bride-to-be, often a brother.

MARRIAGE CONTRACTS

Pre-nuptial agreements, while not commonplace, did exist particularly for widows who wanted to protect the property of their children. As a feme sole, a widow could enter into a contract with a prospective spouse to protect her property. These agreements are filed in the deed books and in county order books. Kentucky law allowed for ante-nuptial contracts, by which each party renounced all right to the property of the other that the marriage would otherwise give. As early as 1842, it was ruled that these agreements did not necessarily bar a decree for alimony in the case of a divorce (Loughborough 1842, 33).

URBAN AND IMMIGRANT WOMEN

Tracking women, and especially immigrant women who lived apart from their families, is often difficult. Immigrant women were not required to file for naturalization although some did. A woman's citizenship status depended upon the status of her husband or father. However, Kentucky's city directories can be helpful in locating these women. City directories commonly list single and married women. Their occupation or place of employment may also be given. By noting the address of the household, one can consult the directory further to establish the family with whom these independent women were living.

AFRICAN-AMERICAN GENEALOGY AND RECORDS IN KENTUCKY

Slavery came to Kentucky from Virginia as settlers brought their chattels with them over the mountains and through the Cumberland Gap. In 1790, there were almost 12,000 slaves in Kentucky out of a total population of about 75,000 (McDougle 1918:8). By 1860, the last census prior to the Civil War, a quarter of a million, or eighteen percent of the Kentucky population, was enslaved. There were also 10,684 free blacks living in Kentucky in 1860 (Collins 1976, 2:257–61).

As a border state with ambivalent attitudes toward slavery, Kentucky served both as a slave market for the South, as well as a strategic key in the underground railroad. Due to its location, Kentucky was in favorable geographic position to supply slaves to the South. It is estimated that 1,000 to 1,500 slaves annually were transported to southern markets from Kentucky; others estimate as high as 5,000 (McDougle 1918:23). Harriett Beecher Stowe is said to have gathered material for *Uncle Tom's Cabin* while visiting Kentucky. It was in Washington near Maysville that she witnessed a slave sale that inspired the account in her book.

On the other hand, Kentucky's location as a border state meant it played a strategic role in the underground railroad. Covington is supposed to have been an

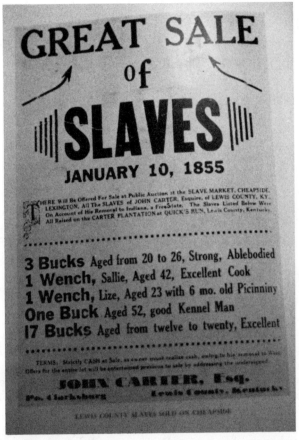

FIG. 6.2 Advertisement for Lewis County slave sale, 1855. (*Slavery Times in Kentucky*, J.W. Coleman)

important last stop in the railroad before slaves crossed safely over the Ohio River to the Union North (Coleman 1971).

AFRICAN-AMERICAN POPULATION AND MIGRATION IN KENTUCKY

African-Americans in Kentucky have been more mobile than other Kentuckians. In 1850, African-Americans made up at least 21 percent of the Kentucky population; by 1880 the numbers had declined to 16.5 percent. The trend has continued through recent times as the latest census figures show that the proportion of African-Americans in Kentucky hovers at about seven percent (Ford 1982, 15).

As a result, an understanding of the migrations within the state and outside of it will be helpful in tracking down these families constantly on the move. The first such mass migration was the Back-to-Africa Movement in the 1830s and 1840s.

THE BACK-TO-AFRICA MOVEMENT IN KENTUCKY

Free blacks and former slaves began settling the territories that would become Liberia in 1822. The American Colonization Society, which helped sponsor the migration, was founded by abolitionists who felt that shipping blacks to Africa would lead to the abolition of slavery and simultaneously avoid the potential social problems posed by numerous former slaves joining American society.

The number of blacks who returned to Africa from Kentucky is uncertain. According to Coleman, the Kentucky Colonization Society transported only about 297 blacks to Africa (Coleman 1940, 287). It is known that the Kentucky Colonization Society raised over a thousand dollars to pay for sending blacks to Liberia and that periodic exodus of slaves and freedmen from Kentucky to Liberia continued until 1856 (Clark 1960, 204-07). The Kentucky Heritage Society also notes that the Liberian theme is an important one in Kentucky since "many" blacks left Kentucky for Liberia in the 1830s and 1840s.

There were also a few private efforts to aid African-Americans wishing to return to Africa. For example, in 1833, Reverend Bibb liberated thirty-two of his slaves and provided them with money for their trip to Liberia. In the same year, 106 blacks gathered at Louisville where they were sent to Liberia through New Orleans. An outbreak of Asiatic cholera in 1833 resulted in many deaths of these refugees to Africa.

A group of former Kentuckians settled in a Liberian community that they named Clay Ashland in honor of Henry Clay, one of the state's prominent supporters of the American Colonization Society.

Some records of the Colonization Society are in the Chicago Historical Society, Archives and Manuscripts Department, Clark Street at North Avenue, Chicago, Illinois 60614. These records consist of about 100 items. There are no lists of people who were sent to Africa. The collection consists of correspondence and agents names. They do have, however, lists of captured Africans recommended to the society and other letters.

URBANIZATION OF KENTUCKY AFRICAN-AMERICANS

African-Americans have not only migrated out of the state, but since 1880, have also tended to migrate within the state from the rural areas to the cities. By 1880, there were 20,000 blacks in Louisville, 7,600 in Lexington, and 3,200 in Frankfort. Despite this movement, eighty-two percent of Kentucky blacks continued to live in rural Kentucky in 1880 (Ford 1982, 15-16).

Even before the Civil War, in the larger Kentucky towns, a small black middle class emerged consisting of free blacks and slaves who were allowed to work for their own wages. Many of these free blacks lived in their own households and were engaged in nonfarming occupations such as stone masons, wagon makers, carpenters, and barbers (Peters 1987, 178). Some free blacks married slaves and, when they did, they would often buy their spouse's freedom.

OUT MIGRATION OF BLACKS FROM KENTUCKY

Kentucky's third constitution in 1850 had a significant impact on the migration of free blacks out of the state. The 1850 legislation required that any slave freed after the constitution's adoption had to leave the state within thirty days. In addition, any free black entering or returning to Kentucky for over thirty days could be imprisoned for up to one year (Brown 1989, 428–29).

After the Civil War, great numbers of Kentucky blacks moved to the cities and outside the state to search for jobs or to escape harassment by whites in the rural areas. Between 1860 and 1870, there was a decline of nearly 14,000 Kentucky blacks at a time when the white population grew by nineteen percent. Part of the decline was because post-Civil War Kentucky was industrializing; and, as a result, jobs were not as plentiful in agriculture as they once had been. In addition, many blacks fled the state upon the withdrawal in 1869 of the Freedmen's Bureau to larger northern cities. As a result of frequent movements, these families are difficult to trace.

AFRICAN-AMERICAN RECORDS IN KENTUCKY

Genealogy for African-Americans is divided into two periods: before and after the Civil War. Before the war, genealogical techniques used to track black families is necessarily quite different than those used for white families. Research conducted on African-Americans after the war, for the most part, consists of consulting the same types of records as research for whites. There are still special sources and factors to consider, however.

The intention of this summary is to identify some of those special sources and historical events that influence research on African-American families in Kentucky. Numerous books and articles have been published on black genealogy. A special bibliography of resources for Kentucky's black families can be found in appendix 4 of this book.

PRE-CIVIL WAR RECORDS

Slave Importation Declarations. Affidavits were required of new residents to Kentucky if they transported slaves into the state with them. The owners of slaves were required to declare that the slaves were for their own use and not for sale. The records will often list not only the number, but the name, gender, and age of the slaves, and sometimes the last residence of the owner. Some of these certificate books dating from as early as 1808 and to as late as 1853 are in the archives.

Plantation Records. Many plantations maintained records on virtually every aspect of their operations. While many of these were destroyed during and after the Civil War, some have survived. The Library of Congress has a number of plantation records, family accounts, and diaries of the Old South (Blockson 1977, 70–71). However, the most numerous and richest sources are at the local level.

In Kentucky, one of the best sources for plantation records is the University of Kentucky special collections library. The library has records of several plantations located in the Fayette County area. For example, the archives has the papers of the Wickliffe Preston family, one of the largest slave owners in the area. The Piedmont Plantation papers from 1852 to 1858 and farm account papers including the overseer papers dating from 1844 to 1857 are also available. Other plantation records are in the process of being inventoried and will soon be available. These records can be located by checking the special manuscript card index in the special collections library.

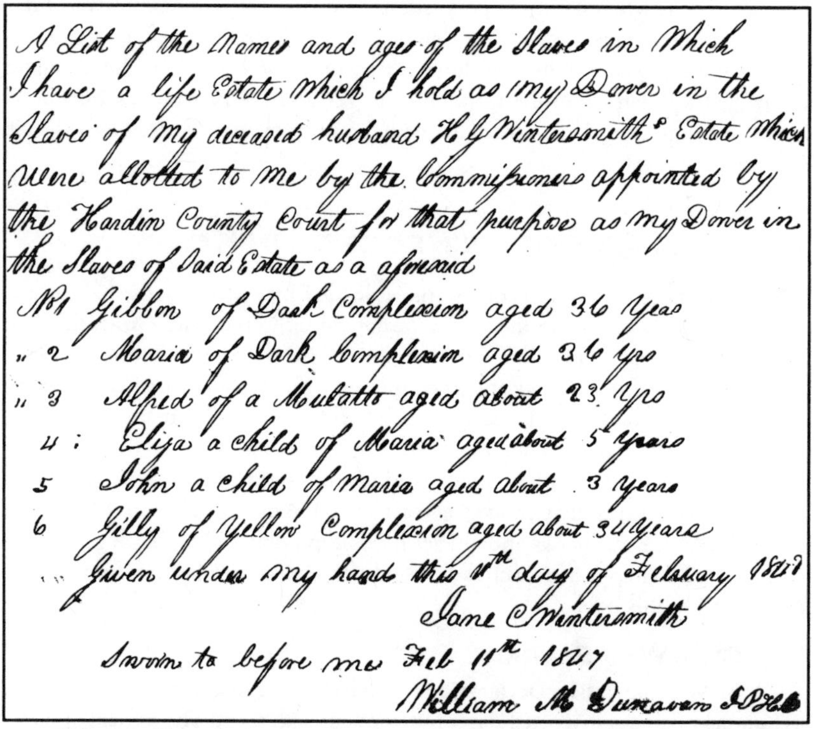

A List of the Names and ages of the Slaves in Which I have a life Estate Which I hold as my Dower in the Slaves of my deceased husband H G Wintersmith's Estate which were allotted to me by the Commissioners appointed by the Hardin County Court for that purpose as my Dower in the Slaves of said Estate as aforesaid

No 1 Gibbon of Dark Complexion aged 36 Years
" 2 Maria of Dark Complexion aged 36 yrs
" 3 Alfred of a Moulatto aged about 23 yrs
4 : Eliza a child of Maria aged about 5 years
5 John a child of Maria aged about 3 years
6 Gilly of Yellow Complexion aged about 34 years
Given under my hand this 11th day of February 1847
Jane C Wintersmith

Sworn to before me Feb 11th 1847
William M Dunavan JPHC

FIG. 6.3 Slave dower of widow Jane C. Wintersmith, 1847. (Hardin County Dower and Chattels Book)

Emancipation Records. Prior to the Civil War, Kentucky county courts presided over the emancipation of slaves. Slave holders could free slaves by two means: through a document entered into the court record, or through a will. An

1800 act of the Kentucky General Assembly permitted slaves to be emancipated by will. Courts then recorded the emancipation and issued a decree of freedom to the former slave. The former owner or his executor sometimes had to post bond to insure that the former slave did not become a public charge (Ireland 1972, 30).

If a deed of emancipation is found, a marriage may follow soon afterwards; this is particularly likely if a black man "buys" a woman. Free blacks often married slaves but, in order to do so, had to obtain their freedom first. Mothers would buy their offspring and then set them free. Below is an example of an emancipation document:

> "I do hereby emancipate and set free from further servitude my daughter, Delphia, whom I purchased from Judge James Simpson. Given under my hand this 26th day of October 1850." Jemina (Her Mark) Clark. (Clark County Order Books appearing in *Bluegrass Roots* 1986, 141).

Emancipation records in Kentucky can be found in various records including deed books, special manumission record books, wills, and county order books.

The trick in finding these records in Kentucky is to discover the county clerk's filing method. Slave emancipations, as well as other transactions for blacks, may be filed under the *first* name of the former slave, the surname of the owner, or the first name of the person who may have purchased the slave such as a mother or spouse. Slaves sometimes changed their names when they changed owners.

Emancipations are sometimes grouped on a single page of the deed index. They may be at the end of the deed book index on a separate page. There are documented examples of emancipations being listed under "S" for slave , "C" for colored, and "E" for emancipations. A good imagination is needed to find these records. If no sales or emancipations are found in a particular county, it will be necessary to scan the entire index to discover the method employed by the clerk.

Apprenticeship Bonds for Freedmen. These records were indentures of apprenticeship by which African-American children were bound to masters until a specified age was reached. The child and master, date, trade to which apprenticed, terms of indenture, and signatures of parties are shown on the bond (Kentucky Public Works Administration 1937, 212).

Kentucky Hiring Practices. Large slave owners commonly hired out their slaves. The traditional day for hiring slaves was 1 January. Large crowds of slave holders, prospective employers, and bystanders congregated at the county seat to make such arrangements. The slave could sometimes veto the deal, but this was usually not part of the agreement (Sears 1989, 5).

These contracts were usually for a year at a time, although some contracts were for a specific task. This practice seems to have been particularly common when the original owner died and was an especially attractive option for large rural slave owners. Slaves were then sent to town to work in the ropewalks, mills, and factories. These blacks worked and lived on their own. For example, until Kentucky law prohibited it, blacks could and did negotiate their own contracts and paid their master on a monthly basis (Wade 1967, 126–27).

These employment agreements can be found in the county order books under the name of the slave owner. The orders usually give the name, age, amount of wages, type of work, and the length of service.

Census Records. Beginning in 1790, free black household heads were listed in the federal census. Slaves who were hired out would be enumerated in the census with their owners prior to 1850, even though they may have worked and lived elsewhere. The first enumeration of all Kentucky blacks by individual family members' names began with the 1870 census. Although census takers attempted to enumerate individual black family members, the 1880 census was more complete than the 1870 enumeration.

One note of caution, however, while black families are included in the census, companies that have produced commercial indexes of the census did not always include black families (Eakle and Cerny 1984, 580).

Slave schedules collected by the Census Bureau are available for Kentucky for 1840 to 1860. In 1840, slaves are listed along with the Revolutionary veterans on page two of the schedule. In 1850 and 1860, slaves were enumerated separately by the name of the owner. While the census only enumerates slaves by age and gender, there are a few 1850 Kentucky census enumerations that list not only the numbers in each category as required but also the names of the slaves.

Mortality schedules list deaths for the twelve months prior to the census, and thus provide a death register for the state for that year. These registers typically under-report deaths by about thirteen percent, and slave deaths were probably more under-reported than white deaths. However, these records are still an important source for blacks since deaths are recorded by name along with whether the person was a slave or free (Eakle and Cerny 1984, 103). These are available for the 1850 to 1880 census years.

White Family Records. Pre-Civil War research for Kentucky blacks will necessarily rely heavily on records of associated white families. Analysis of the records, diaries, wills, bibles, and cemeteries of white families will often yield information on the blacks living and working with them. Some family cemeteries have a black section; many of which are noted as black. Kentucky Bible records will sometimes include a notation about blacks associated with the family.

Church and Cemetery Records. In Kentucky, the black church has served as a focal point of black family life as it has elsewhere. Where their records survive, they can provide valuable information about black ancestors. Many of the larger cities such as Lexington have exclusively black churches and cemeteries. In addition, some pioneer church records include their black members in their minutes and lists of members. Among those in the central Kentucky region who mention black members are the Providence Church in Clark County, Bryan's Station Baptist Church in Lexington, and the Stamping Ground Baptist Church.

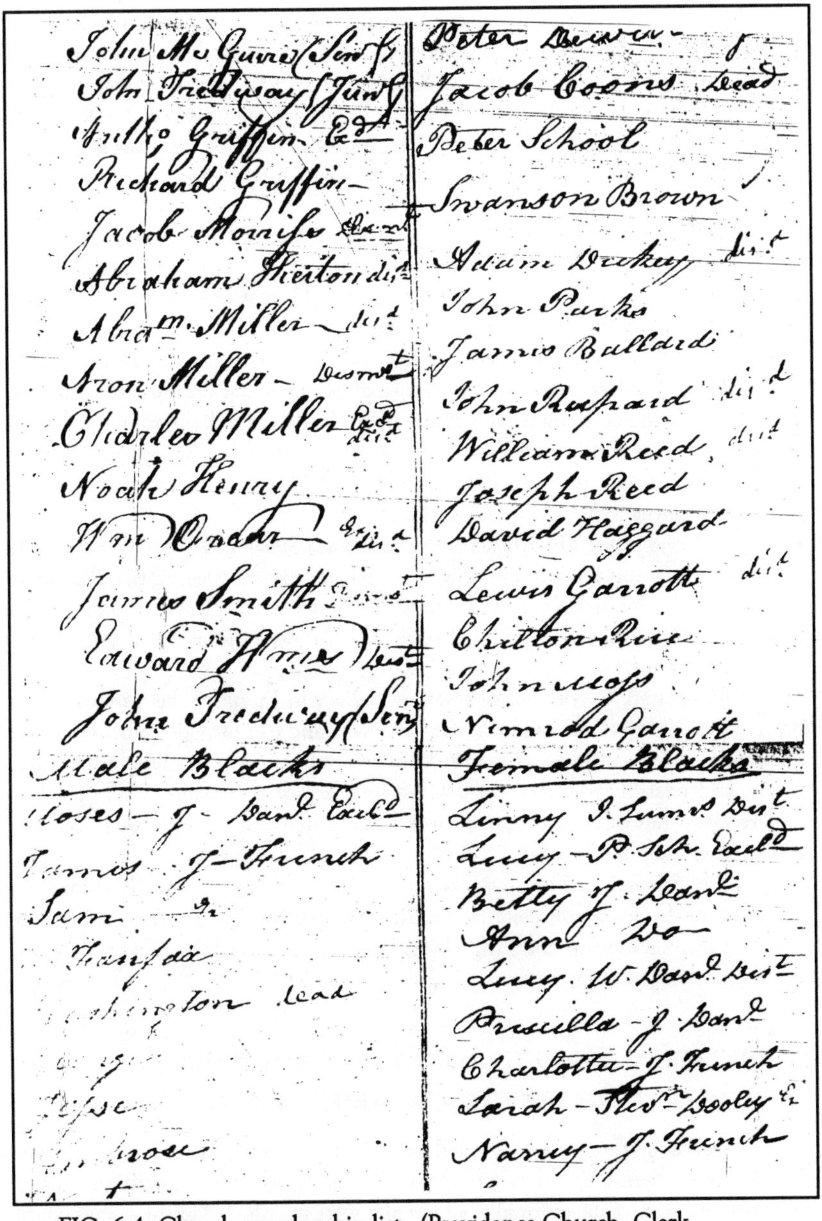
John McGuire (Senr)
John Tredway (Junr)
Anthony Griffin Exd
Richard Griffin
Jacob Morris Dismt
Abraham Shelton dist
Abram Miller dist
Aron Miller Dismt
Charles Miller Exd dist
Noah Henry
Wm Ondar Ex dist
James Smith Dismt
Edward Wms dist
John Tredway Senr
Male Blacks
Moses – J. Dand. Excld
James J. French
Sam Do
Fanfax
...hington dead

Peter Dewar J
Jacob Coons Dead
Peter School
Swanson Brown
Adam Dickey dist
John Parks
James Ballard
John Ruspard dist
William Reed, dist
Joseph Reed
David Haggard
Lewis Garrott dist
Chilton Rice
John Moss
Nimrod Garrott
Female Blacks
Linny J. Lums Dist
Lucy – P. Sch. Excld
Betty J. Dand.
Ann Do
Lucy W. Dand. Dist
Priscilla – J. Dand.
Charlotte – J. French
Sarah – Revd Dooley Ex
Nancy – J. French

FIG. 6.4 Church membership list. (Providence Church, Clerk County)

Military Records. Blacks have served in all U.S. wars. Over 5,000 blacks fought in the Continental army in the Revolutionary War; another thousand fought for the British and were known as King of England soldiers. Many of these eventually escaped to Nova Scotia. When the British left after the war, 1,400 former slaves went to London, Halifax, or the West Indies with them. *The Book of Negroes,* available in the National Archives, includes the names of these British sympathizers (Blockson 1977, 50-51).

Blacks were also active in the War of 1812, but by 1842, army regulations excluded blacks. During the Spanish-American War, blacks served in the Ninth and Tenth U.S. Cavalry. Over 350,000 blacks fought in World War I; and almost a million fought in World War II (Blockson 1977, 52-54).

The archives has produced a special publication, *List of Black Servicemen Compiled from the War Department Collection of Revolutionary War Records.* This list includes all soldiers known or presumed to be black. The names are listed alphabetically and include a reference to the complete source where more information can be found. It is available free from the Publications Sales Branch of the National Archives in Washington, D. C. 20408.

The Negro in the Military Service of the United States 1639-1886 is available on microfilm in the National Archives. The *Index to Compiled Service Records of Volunteer Union Soldiers who Served with United States Colored Troops* is a microfilm publication available at the National Archives that gives the name of the soldier, his rank, and unit.

The Military Records and Research Library in Frankfort keeps records on the "colored" troops that fought in the Civil War and can provide information on these men. Information recorded on U.S. colored troops may include their age, owner, and possibly the name of a wife who filed for a pension. There are also scattered histories of black troops from Kentucky that can be very valuable; some of these include photographs.

Vital Statistics. The first attempts at maintaining early birth records in Kentucky are far from complete as discussed earlier; however, they may be more complete for black births than for whites because the records were seen as a way to register their property interests.

KENTUCKY COURT JURISDICTION AND RECORDS FOR AFRICAN-AMERICANS

Local courts were empowered to try cases that involved free African-Americans in Kentucky. They also heard prosecutions against felonious slaves. Prosecutions against slaves for alleged felonies were transferred to the circuit courts in 1819 (Ireland 1972, 30). Justice of the Peace courts maintained special jurisdiction over criminal and freed blacks as well. Consult chapter 3 for details of court jurisdiction for African-Americans in Kentucky.

Civil War Migrations and Aftermath

While the Emancipation Proclamation was effective 1 January 1863, it was not until 18 December 1865 that the Thirteenth Amendment officially ended slavery in the United States. Kentucky refused to ratify the Thirteenth Amendment, to nullify the slave code, to provide for destitute freedmen, or to protect African-Americans in Kentucky against the white supremacists such as the Regulators after the Civil War.

As a result, Kentucky blacks faced formidable challenges: the challenge to find work when education had been denied in an economy that was industrializing; and the challenge to live peaceably when vigilantes were terrorizing blacks. Many Kentucky blacks were unable to withstand the harsh persecution in the rural areas; and thousands of blacks took to the road and established shanty towns on the outskirts of Kentucky's towns and cities.

As a result, the Freedmen's Bureau decided in January of 1866 to extend its work to Kentucky. The Kentucky area was originally part of Tennessee's jurisdiction; therefore, some of its records are filed in that record group. When the Freedmen's Bureau phased out its operation in Kentucky in 1868, many blacks began to leave the state in anticipation of an end to protection (Webb 1986, 346–49).

Post-Civil War Records

A number of post-Civil War court records were maintained separately for blacks and whites. The practice persisted only briefly in some counties. In other cases, records, particularly marriage records, were maintained separately for blacks until as late as the 1960s.

On the other hand, in deeds, cemeteries, and biographies, there is typically no notation of race. Nevertheless, some Kentucky clerks were thoughtful enough to have indicated a person's race on the deed index or in the document itself. County biographies, popular in Kentucky in the late 1800s, contain a number of black biographies, although they may not mention that the person was African-American.

Records that have been maintained separately in Kentucky are discussed below.

Marriage Indexes and Records. Beginning in 1866, blacks in Kentucky could register existing marriages by paying $2. These records are called Declarations of Freedmen or Declarations of Marriage. Many existing marriages may not have been recorded because of the fee involved. Some counties kept marriage records for blacks and whites in separate volumes beginning after the Civil War and continuing until as late as the 1960s.

Vital Statistics. Separate lists sometimes exist for black births beginning with the early 1852 series as well as those in the years following 1874. Compliance with registration laws may have been superior for black births than for whites. This is particularly probable for the Lexington area records. The records will often list the owners name and the mother's name if a slave. Records of free blacks may include the names of both parents. Black marriages were often maintained separately in the 1874 vital records series.

School Records. Kentucky maintained a high school for blacks that drew students from across the state. The Lincoln Institute was a residential school, and so its records should be investigated even though the school is outside the family's normal place of residence. There was also a black Kentucky School for Deaf and Blind children. These reports contain lists and photographs of some of the students. Records of both these institutions are in the Kentucky archives. In addition, the Kentucky Normal School, which eventually became Kentucky State University, has a growing archives of information on black families and black leaders in Kentucky.

FREEDMEN'S BUREAU RECORDS

The Freedmen's Bureau was established just before the end of the Civil War to assist newly emancipated slaves to adjust to their freedom. The bureau was the government's first attempt at a large scale welfare program (Webb 1986, 345–46).

The bureau aided in certifying slave marriages, assisted with labor contracts, issued rations and clothing to new freedmen, leased land, operated hospitals and freedmen's camps, and provided transportation to refugees and freedmen returning to their homes or relocating to another part of the country. It also helped black soldiers and sailors file and collect claims for bounties and paid pensions (Linder 1981). Unfortunately, the bureau only operated for a short time. By 1869, it had nearly stopped functioning and was totally discontinued by 1872.

REFUGEE CAMPS

In Kentucky, the bureau established refugee camps at Camp Nelson, Camp Dick Robinson, and in major towns and cities of the state (Webb 1986, 346–47).

FREEDMEN'S BUREAU SCHOOLS

African-American schools after the Civil War were coordinated by the Freedmen's Bureau. These schools for black children were separately financed by taxes on property owned by blacks. School attendance was compulsory but the average daily attendance was still only about fifty-five percent for white students and about thirty-one percent for black students. In 1880, twenty-two percent of Kentucky whites were illiterate while seventy percent of the blacks were reported as illiterate (Ford 1982, 17–18).

At the end of the war, a total of fifty-four schools for freedmen were established in Kentucky with sixty-seven teachers and 3,259 students. By 1867, the number of schools had increased to ninety-six and served 5,000 of a potential 37,000 blacks between the ages of sixteen and eighteen (Webb 1986, 349). By

1868, there were 135 day schools and one night school in operation with twenty-one white and 144 black teachers serving 6,023 students. By the end of the year, there were 249 freedmen schools with an enrollment of 10,300 students (Webb 1986, 354).

By the time the schools ceased operation under the bureau's supervision, over 20,000 students had received basic education (Webb 1986, 350). The bureau paid the rent for the school houses; subscriptions from parents and religious denominations paid the rest. The per pupil expenditure was only fifty cents per year in the 1880s for black pupils, while the white per pupil expenditure was $1.50. The average salary for a white teacher was $133 annually, while black teachers earned only $50. (Webb 1986, 347-49.)

BUREAU HOSPITALS AND VETERAN AID

Hospitals were set up in Kentucky by the bureau in Louisville, Covington, Lexington, Mt. Sterling, Paducah, and Owensboro. The bureau helped more than 1,100 black Kentucky soldiers to receive bounties through the bureau during 1868. Many more were eligible, but it was difficult to locate claimants since a large number of freedmen were constantly on the move. There were also sharp lawyers and bounty brokers who swindled the freedmen out of their claims in Kentucky (Webb 1986, 350-53).

IMPACT OF THE FREEDMEN'S BUREAU

Reports from evaluators of the Freedmen's Bureau indicated that the status of Kentucky blacks was slowly improving in some areas. The conditions in northern Kentucky were improving because of the need for labor. Conditions in central Kentucky were reported as satisfactory. Violence was continuing in eastern Kentucky, however. A report from the bureau indicated that a majority of the freedmen were being employed at fair wages and enjoyed better health. Many were using their bounties to buy land and houses, and were taking advantage of the educational opportunities of the bureau (Webb 1986, 349).

CONTENT OF BUREAU RECORDS

Records in the Freedmen's Bureau can be categorized into two major groups: the Washington office and the state offices. Records in both groups consist of letters, school reports, administrative reports, and a variety of orders. Individual level information is available, but difficult to locate (Blockson 1977, 100).

Linder (1981) reports that records of the Bureau of Refugees, Freedmen, and Abandoned Lands include some valuable items for black genealogy: marriage certificates of freed slaves, registers, and other records containing information about slave families.

Records for Kentucky Freedmen's Bureau consist almost entirely of statistical school reports. Individual names of pupils are not listed. The names of the schools and the numbers of pupils studying various courses by school neighborhood is, however, given.

AVAILABILITY OF BUREAU RECORDS

Records of the Freedmen's Bureau for Kentucky's records have been microfilmed. Records for the Freedmen's Savings and Trust Company in Louisville for the years 1865 to 1874 have been microfilmed; similar Lexington records exist for 1870 to 1874 (Eakle and Cerny 1984, 582).

The manuscript records of the Bureau of Refugees, Freedmen, and Abandoned Lands are in the custody of the National Archives in Washington, D. C. Many of them have been microfilmed and are available at each of the eleven regional federal archives. These core holdings are listed in table 6.1.

TABLE 6.1	Freedmen's Bureau Records in the Federal Archives
M752	Registers and Letters Received by the Commissioner of the Bureau of Freedmen, 1865–1872. 74 rolls.
M742	Selected Series of Records Issued by the Commissioner of the Bureau of Freedmen, 1865–1872. 7 rolls.
M798	Records of the Assistant Commissioner for the State of Georgia, Bureau of Freedmen, 1865–1869. 36 rolls.
M799	Records of the Superintendent of Education for the State of Georgia, Bureau of Freedmen, 1865–1870. 28 rolls.

Source: Amico and Burton 1989, 8–10.

ORAL HISTORY PROJECT AND OTHER ARCHIVES

The University of Kentucky special collections staff has maintained a fairly active oral history project of black Kentuckians for the past twenty years. There are approximately 250 to 300 interviews of blacks dealing with a variety of topics. The structure of the interview depends upon the interest of the researcher but generally follows a chronological recounting of the person's life. Contact the special collections library for specific information about these interviews, their subjects, and the topics covered.

Kentucky State University in Frankfort is in the process of upgrading its archives of black Kentucky family information. At the present time, their holdings are limited mainly to black literature and the black leadership in Kentucky.

LOCATING AFRICAN-AMERICAN RECORDS

Kentucky's marriage, vital statistics, and tax records are often maintained separately by race. Separate school census lists were also kept for blacks and whites during the late 1880s.

Some clerks unfailingly indicated the race of a person in each transaction, whether it involved the sale of a piece of property or a marriage. Other clerks did not. Some clerks maintained black records in separate volumes for a time and then changed their practices. Some counties placed black transactions at the end of the book or in a separate section of the book. Therefore, if a record cannot be found, scan the entire document to ensure that black records are not tucked away in a separate section.

In chapter 8 of this reference, when it was possible to distinguish between black and white tax and marriage lists, a notation was made in the county microfilm inventories. These entries were noted and listed separately for ease of identification. However, simply because no notation is made about black records, does not indicate that none exist, only that they were not labeled or that there were no identifiable separate lists.

CHAPTER 7

FLESHING OUT THE GHOSTS: USING SECONDARY RESOURCES IN KENTUCKY

Family history would be an empty study of names and dates if it were not possible to flesh out these ghosts of our pasts. One of the greatest pleasures in genealogy is to learn how families lived, to understand their experiences including their ideology, the social milieu, and their physical environment. In fact, stories of the personal lives and times of our ancestors, handed down from generation to generation, seem to be the motivation and inspiration that initially interests many family historians to pursue the quest to know more about these distant figures.

In a sense, this is what genealogy is about. We often settle for simply completing the skeletal remains of a person's life: dates of birth, marriage, and death. Fortunately, that is not necessary in Kentucky, where there are rich resources to help flesh out the everyday lives and history of its people.

Secondary resources generated outside the court's legal system provide insights into the world our ancestors inhabited as well as personal information not available through any other means. In building a Kentucky family history, secondary sources such as newspapers, church records, and other original manuscript sources should not be overlooked as sources of valuable information and clues. The most important and accessible of these sources for Kentucky are discussed in this chapter. These resources can also be important sources of data to study Kentucky's social history.

FIG. 7.1 Office of the *Kentucky Gazette*, 1787. (*The Story of Kentucky*, Connelly 1890)

NEWSPAPERS

Kentucky is fortunate to have an exceptional collection of old newspapers. In the nineteenth century, most small- to medium-size Kentucky towns had one, and often two, newspapers (Sprague 1984b, 5–8). Personal biographical information as well as important events were reported in these local papers. For example, births and deaths that occurred prior to uniform reporting in 1911 can sometimes be established via announcements in local papers. News articles of county weeklies give glimpses into the everyday life of Kentucky ancestors not available through any other means. As a result, Kentucky newspapers are a valuable source of information for the social and family historian. Below are a few tips to help evaluate and locate information from Kentucky's newspapers.

EVALUATING NEWSPAPER INFORMATION

While newspapers are a rich source of information, there are also pitfalls in researching newspapers. There are biases, problems with the timing of reporting, and inaccurate data. Information found in newspapers should be evaluated and verified by primary documents whenever possible.

BIASES

The early Kentucky newspapers were often political organs of the booster press genre. The significance of this observation for researchers is that incidents perceived to be negative may not appear in the local newspaper (Sprague 1984b, 5-8). In order to find an account, it may be necessary to consult newspapers in surrounding areas. The Lexington and Louisville papers often carried abbreviated accounts of stories from throughout the state.

TIMING OF EVENTS

Since many of the local papers were weeklies, stories were not necessarily published immediately. Some significant news stories may not be carried in the local paper because it was old news by the time the paper was printed. Everyone already knew the story (Sprague 1984b, 7).

As a result of delays in reporting, it is wise to search for obituaries or announcements at least several weeks after the death date. Searches in the few weeks preceding the death may yield stories that hint at an impending event. For example, reports of grave illnesses, visits by relatives, particularly those living at a distance, may mean that the last visits prior to an anticipated death had begun.

INACCURACIES

Events hastily reported may be in error. Newspaper stories then and now contain inaccurate statements. For example, obituaries may not report all survivors or may incorrectly report their names and relationships. Dates may be wrong.

REGIONAL SEARCHES

Kentucky newspapers commonly shared news stories with surrounding area newspapers. Therefore, if an article can not be located, or if there are no newspapers for the dates of interest, consult papers in nearby cities or counties. If the town is located close to the state border, or even if it has ties to other areas or towns, those papers should also be examined. For example, a Grant County newspaper, which shares no border with Indiana, briefly carried a weekly neighborhood column describing events in a small town in Indiana.

Regional searches are also necessary to locate elderly or widowed parents who left home in their declining years to live with a son or daughter. The hometown papers in Kentucky often carried announcements of the deaths of their long-time residents who had moved away prior to their deaths.

CONTENT OF NEWSPAPER ARTICLES

Local Kentucky newspapers contain a vast amount of information of importance to the genealogist. Of course, newspapers will report vital events such as births, marriages, and deaths. But in addition to these personal items, feature

B. M. G. Heath.

B. M. G. Heath, one of the oldest and most substantial citizens of the county, who passed into the Great Beyond several weeks ago, was born in Georgia Dec. 9, 1812. When he was one year of age his parents moved to Livingston county, Ky., and purchased a farm in that portion of Livingston county which afterwards formed Crittenden. From that early date until his death, February 5th, 1902, eighty-eight years afterward, Mr. Heath was a resident of this county. He was a son of Riland and Annie Heath, who raised a family of nine children. Five are still living. They are Robert, John and Nannie of this county, Harrison of Glasgow, Tenn., and Enoch of Martin, Tenn. The latter is the youngest child, aged 60 years.

Mr. Heath was united in marriage with Miss Narcissa Williams of this county in 1840. They lived happily until her death forty-five years later. Seven children blessed this union, of which three are living, viz: John S. of Weston, Leroy of Corbin, and Callie of St. Louis, Mo. Amanda died in Missouri several years ago. Three died while young. In 1853 Mr. Heath joined the Masonic order at Marion. He was a charter member of Zion Hill Lodge and lived a true and faithful Mason. Forty years ago he joined the Methodist church at old Mt. Zion. He was a devoted christian. After a long life of eighty-nine years he passed peacefully away at his home near Weston.

FIG. 7.2 Obituary of B.M.G. Heath. (*Crittenden Press* 27 February 1902, p. 4)

stories, editorials, political events, notices of sales, advertisements, and want ads provide insights into the lives and times of early Kentuckians.

DEATH RECORDS

Many early Kentucky obituaries are quite detailed. Some give the names of parents and siblings, dates of migration to Kentucky, and major events in the person's life. For example, a death announcement in the *Winchester Sun* in the 1890s gave the maiden name, parents' names, and the siblings of a ninety-year-old widow. Since the marriage certificate could never be found, it was the only way her father's name could have been discovered. A will subsequently found in an adjoining county confirmed the parentage.

All information in a death announcement should be carefully evaluated for genealogical information. Pallbearers listed are often sons, brothers, or sons-in-law. The funeral home and burial place will also be noted. Armed with this information, additional information can be obtained from the historical society and the genealogical society to obtain a complete list of the cemetery's burials and perhaps even funeral home records.

Announcements regarding settlements of estates or notices to make claims on estates prior to settlement can also appear in the newspapers. If the family farm had to be sold, it might have been advertised in the real estate section of the paper.

NEIGHBORHOOD COLUMNS

Newsy neighborhood columns were fairly common in most Kentucky papers. Some continue to publish these wonderful glimpses into Americana today. These local columns provide intriguing and invaluable insight into the everyday lives of Kentuckians that is simply not available from any other source. While the style of these accounts of Kentuckians at leisure and at work may seem amusing today, the events are the same: family visits, bad weather, trips to market, farms for sale, stock trading, illnesses, marriages, births, and deaths. Accounts of who visited whom and who bought and exchanged goods with whom are reported and should be studied for clues regarding family relationships.

IMAGES

The image and photographic record of Kentucky history that newspapers have preserved is another motivation for searching this source. Some Kentucky newspapers are beginning to archive their photographic collections at local libraries to the benefit of both. Even before photographs, however, images have been preserved by newspapers. For example, an obituary appearing in a western Kentucky paper showed not only the usual information on the gentleman's life, when he came to Kentucky from Virginia, his parents' and siblings' names, but also a quarter-page ink sketch (see figure 7.2).

AVAILABILITY OF KENTUCKY NEWSPAPERS

Kentucky is fortunate to have many old newspapers still in existence today and readily accessible to researchers. For example, the Filson Club in Louisville has very strong holdings of old Kentucky newspapers. The largest collection of Kentucky newspapers is housed at the University of Kentucky.

The university library began microfilming papers in 1954 and, as a result, now has over 8,000 reels of Kentucky newspapers dating from 1788 to the present. The university currently continues to subscribe to newspapers in all counties of the state.

In addition to its own holdings, the university is expanding its scope by involvement in the Kentucky Newspaper Project funded by a grant from the National Endowment for the Humanities. The goal of this exciting project is to locate, inventory, catalog, and preserve all Kentucky and out-of-state newspapers held in the state. This project is part of a similar project being conducted nationwide.

The first phase of the project is now complete after visits to over 160 Kentucky newspaper repositories. A *Kentucky Union List of Newspapers*, on microfiche, is available to all institutions or individuals who wish to purchase a copy. Approximately 14,000 newspaper titles have been identified. Information in the union list includes the dates and locations of the newspapers.

The second phase of the project will entail microfilming the papers and will be continued with the support of the National Endowment for the Humanities. At this time, over 675,000 newspaper pages have been preserved. The new grant will increase that number to nearly 946,000 pages.

The information from this project will also be available to libraries throughout the country via a computer library network and database known as OCLC. In addition, the University of Kentucky makes its microfilm newspaper holdings available for out-of-state interlibrary loan. Loan requests must include specific dates and titles or geographical locations of materials requested. For further information on interlibrary loans and restrictions on use of original papers, contact your local library who will be responsible for the loan transaction. To purchase a copy of the Union List microfiche, send $10 to Kentucky Newspaper Project, M. I. King Library, University of Kentucky, Lexington, Kentucky 40506-0391.

Newspapers available on microfilm in the archives and Kentucky Historical Society are inventoried in chapter 8 under the county of publication. Statewide newspapers are listed in the last section on Kentucky. The university's newspaper collection is not indexed in this volume.

KENTUCKY NEWSPAPER INDEXES

An important source for early Kentucky ancestors is Karen Green's index to the *Kentucky Gazette* (Green 1983; 1985). The gazette was the first newspaper published in Kentucky. Green's indexes include references to all Kentuckians appearing in the paper along with a summary of the article. There is a place name, subject, and every-name index. While pioneers from all of Kentucky may be included, entries from the central Kentucky counties are most frequent. Stories include coverage of elections, land disputes, lists of stray animals, dead letter lists, military lists, obituaries, and other events of early Kentucky life.

The University of Kentucky has, in addition to an alphabetic card catalog of its newspaper holdings, a chronological listing of its holdings that date from 1672 to 1909. This drawer is located behind the reference desk in the newspaper and microfilm room.

The Kenton County Library in Covington is an outstanding example of what can be accomplished with newspapers as a genealogical tool. The library has a card index of early Kentucky newspapers that includes a few statewide newspapers such as the *Kentucky State Journal* and the *Daily Commonwealth*, as well as local northern Kentucky papers such as the *Covington Journal*, *The Ticket*, *Kentucky Post*, and *The Times Star*. The years covered by this index are 1835 to 1925 and 1984 to 1990. There are currently over 340,000 citations. The *Kentucky Post* indexing begins with 1892. Events indexed are births, deaths, marriages, as well as local and national events. This project represents the most extensive local newspaper index in Kentucky.

The Cincinnati library, just across the river from the Kenton County Library, has a good collection of German language newspapers dating from as early as 1828. Due to the proximity, there are many references to Kentuckians. There is also a newspaper index to vital events, which includes events on a systematic basis since 1940. An index of obituaries, not death notices, was begun in the nineteenth century. Since August 1988, death notices have been indexed systematically.

The *Louisville Courier Journal* has an index of subjects from 1917 to 1977. This index is available in the Louisville Library, the University of Kentucky, the Lexington Public Library, and the Kentucky archives library (not the microfilm research room) in Frankfort.

A newspaper of particular interest to Irish-Catholic families is the *Kentucky Irish American* which ran from 1898 to 1968. Obituaries and personal columns are common in this paper.

The Lexington Public Library newspaper sources include a listing of funeral notices dating from 1806 to 1887, and a local history index that was gleaned from newspapers. The *Lexington Herald* and *Lexington Leader* index to their photographic archives from 1944 to 1974 is also available. Early newspapers available at the Lexington library are shown in table 7.1.

TABLE 7.1	Early Kentucky Newspapers Available in the Lexington Public Library

Kentucky Gazette	(1787–1910)
Kentucky Statesman	(1849–73)
Kentucky Reporter and Observer	(1808–72)
Lexington Daily Press	(1870–94)
Lexington Herald	(1888–1982)
Lexington Leader	(1888–1982)
Lexington Herald and Leader	(1983–)
Lexington Transcript	(1879–94)

While searching newspapers can be slow and tedious work, the rewards can be exciting. Access to Kentucky newspapers is improving and indexes are slowly becoming available.

KENTUCKY CHURCH RECORDS

EARLY FRONTIER RELIGION

Religion was an important part of early Kentucky frontier life. Apart from the spiritual impact, it was important not only for the ready social organization it provided, but also for the social opportunities it offered to an isolated people. Many early settlers traveled to Kentucky in voluntary bands formed for mutual assistance and defense. These groups often consisted of family, neighbors, or fellow church members (Finger 1984, 82:39). Examples include the famous "Traveling Church" of Captain Billy Bush and Rev. James Quissenberry who settled Boonesboro in Madison County in 1785; and the Lutherans of Madison County, Virginia who settled in Louisville, and central and northern Kentucky in the early 1800s.

The impact of religion on Kentucky frontier life was accentuated by numerous religious colonies and missionary efforts. A number of religious groups felt Kentucky needed more religion. Bishop Asbury observed that in Kentucky, "good religion and good land are not so easily matched together" (Finger 1984, 84:341).

While the Baptists were the first organized religion in Kentucky, they were soon joined by the Presbyterians. In 1784 the Presbyterian Rev. David Rice came to central Kentucky to organize three meeting places: Salt River (now extinct), Concord (now Danville), and Cane Run (now Harrodsburg) (Dietz 1973, 38). The Shakers sent missionaries to Kentucky from New York in 1805 (Ardery 1987, 85:316). Two Shaker colonies were established in early Kentucky at Pleasant Hill near Harrodsburg in 1805 and at South Union in Logan County in 1807. Several waves of German Lutherans came from the Virginia counties of Madison, Culpepper, and Orange to Kentucky beginning in 1806 and settled in central and northern Kentucky as well as Louisville.

In 1808, Bardstown became a Catholic see since Kentucky was the site of early Catholic settlement. Prior to 1808, the entire Catholic population in the United States was under one bishop. In 1808, Pope Pius VII approved the creation of four American sees: Boston, New York, Philadelphia, and Bardstown. The Bardstown Diocese included Kentucky, Tennessee, and the Northwest Territory. St. Joseph's Cathedral thus became the first Catholic cathedral west of the Alleghenies. In 1841, the see was moved to Louisville (Coleman 1971, 63).

THE GREAT REVIVAL

Revivalist frontier religion peaked in Kentucky in 1801 with Rev. Barton Stone's great revival at Cane Ridge in present-day Bourbon County. Rev. McGready and his followers, arriving in Kentucky in 1796, are credited with sparking a series of evangelistic meetings at his Red River Church (Ardery 1987, 85:316). During the period 1787 until 1805, McGready's powerful preaching attracted many Kentuckians to his revivals. Since people came from long distances to attend the meetings, they camped overnight. These camp meetings facilitated development of an extraordinary religious fervor in Kentucky known as the Great Revival (Coleman 1971, 52–54).

At its peak, it was estimated that twenty to thirty thousand people gathered at Cane Ridge in 1801. Witnesses told of roads jammed with wagons, carriages, horsemen, and persons on foot moving to the camp. Eighteen Presbyterian ministers along with many Baptist and Methodist preachers were present, sometimes addressing the crowd simultaneously. The revival lasted until the food gave out—nearly a week (Ardery 1987, 85:312–14). From these meetings, a coalition eventually emerged between Rev. Stone's and Rev. Alexander Campbell's groups. In 1832, followers of Stone and Alexander united to form the Christian Church, or as they called themselves, the Disciples of Christ. By 1860, nearly a quarter of the 192,000 Disciples of Christ were Kentuckians (Ardery 1987, 85:318).

The revival in some ways heralded the end of a dangerous frontier in which settlers had neither the time, resources, nor sense of security that would permit them to venture from their homes for any length of time. The revivals also served important social functions in providing opportunities to meet with and visit neighbors, a fact attested to by the presence of liquor peddlers at the camp meetings (Finger 1984, 82:350).

The "profound awakening" faded as congregations grew, formal worship solidified, and a better educated ministry became commonplace. However, it was against this backdrop of religious fervor and revivalism that Kentucky frontier religion developed and grew.

SCOPE OF KENTUCKY CHURCH RECORDS BY DENOMINATION

In Kentucky, the scope, quality, availability, and time periods covered by church records vary considerably by denomination. The scope often depends upon practices and educational levels of individual ministers as well as the church's religious beliefs. The first major religious representations in Kentucky were the Baptists, Episcopalians, Presbyterians, Methodists, and Catholics. Each of these groups had different methods and philosophies of record keeping. Therefore, a brief overview of Kentucky church history will facilitate use of the records and interpretation of information found.

BAPTIST CHURCH RECORDS

The value and consistency of record keeping by the Kentucky Baptists is variable. This can be attributed to a couple of factors. First, Baptists were among the first pioneers on the Kentucky frontier. In addition, the early pioneers had less opportunity and time to keep records, and literacy levels were generally lower in the population at that time. Another factor influencing the value of such records is that Baptists believe in adult or believer baptism rather than baptism at infancy. This means that their baptismal records are not always helpful in establishing birth dates or parentage.

While this practice renders baptismal records of limited use in establishing birth dates, their records can still include valuable information. Clerks, in culling membership rolls, sometimes added death dates or the date a person transferred membership. Funeral and marriage information can sometimes be found in the minister's private papers. The best source of information about Kentucky Baptist Churches is the Southern Baptist Seminary in Louisville. However, this archive does not have records that would be of general genealogical use, but does have historical records of the church and its ministers.

OTHER PROTESTANT CHURCH RECORDS

The Presbyterians and Episcopalians practiced infant baptism and kept excellent records. While the Methodists doctrinally practiced infant baptism, they have been strongly influenced by the Kentucky Baptist presence. As a result, the Methodists baptized few infants during parts of the nineteenth century. This was true in the eastern part of the state even until recent times.

The Christian Churches, Disciples of Christ, and Churches of Christ in Kentucky also practiced adult baptism. Since 1832, the Churches of Christ have practiced adult baptism.

The Evangelical and Reformed Historical Society in Lancaster, Pennsylvania is associated with the Lancaster Theological Seminary of the United Church of Christ. If your ancestor belonged to the German immigrant church, which was called the German Reformed Church of the Evangelical Church, consult this source. There are many churches of this background in Kentucky, particularly in the Louisville, Cincinnati, and Covington areas.

CATHOLIC CHURCH RECORDS

Prior to 1811, when the first bishop arrived in Bardstown, Kentucky was under the jurisdiction of the bishop and the archbishop of Baltimore; thus, the diocesan archives were in Maryland. The first Catholic diocese formed in the United States dates only to 1790. Therefore, for Catholic records of Kentuckians prior to 1790, it is necessary to consult English and continental sources including London and especially Rome. These records would be in addition to what would be found in local parish church records.

Pre-Revolutionary War Catholic records are almost nonexistent. Records that do exist are in the custody of local parish priests, although some Catholic records are reported to be preserved in the Provincial House, Society of Jesus, 5704 Roland Avenue, Baltimore, Maryland 21210.

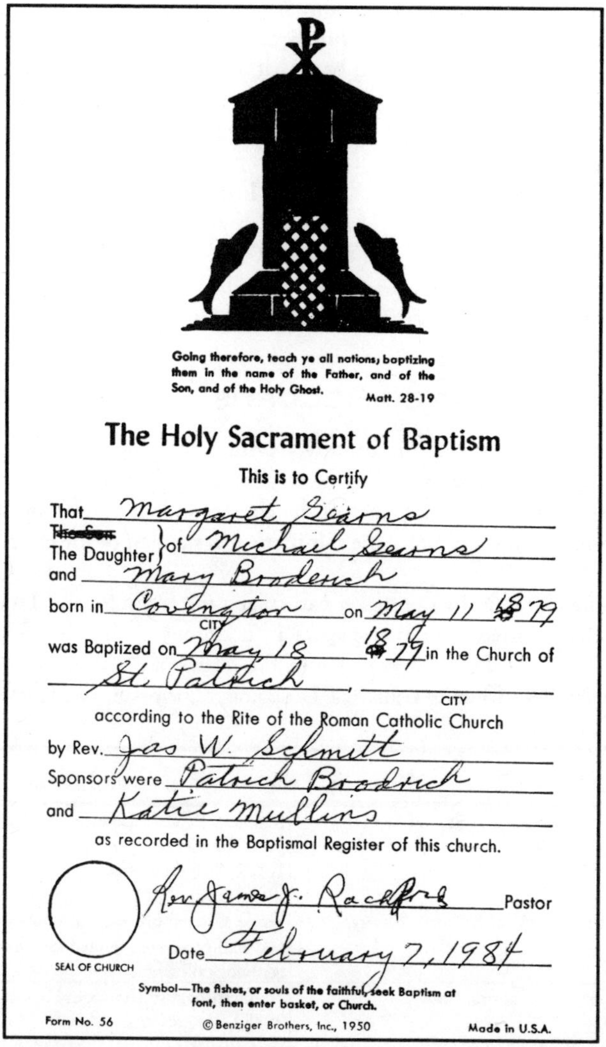

Going therefore, teach ye all nations; baptizing them in the name of the Father, and of the Son, and of the Holy Ghost. Matt. 28-19

The Holy Sacrament of Baptism

This is to Certify

That Margaret Gearns

~~The Son~~ / The Daughter of Michael Gearns

and Mary Broderick

born in Covington (CITY) on May 11 1879

was Baptized on May 18 1879 in the Church of

St. Patrick, ______ (CITY)

according to the Rite of the Roman Catholic Church

by Rev. Jas W. Schmitt

Sponsors were Patrick Broderick

and Katie Mullins

as recorded in the Baptismal Register of this church.

SEAL OF CHURCH

Rev James J. Rackford Pastor

Date February 7, 1984

Symbol—The fishes, or souls of the faithful, seek Baptism at font, then enter basket, or Church.

Form No. 56 © Benziger Brothers, Inc., 1950 Made in U.S.A.

FIG. 7.3 Baptism record of Margaret Gearns, 1879. (St. Patrick's Church, Covington)

On the whole, Catholic churches have kept excellent records of all vital events. Catholic records will include records of births, baptisms, marriages, deaths, and communions along with burial registers. Confirmation records are kept at the diocesan level. The problem, however, is that access to these records is extremely limited. Access to these records is difficult due to lack of facilities, space for storage, confidentiality of the records, and the fragile nature of the records.

In Kentucky, most old Catholic records have been transferred to diocesan archives. In Kentucky, after 1841, this means Louisville and Covington. Some records may still be available at the church. Some records for the northern Kentucky Catholic churches are reported to be in Mt. Sterling. However, the Mt. Sterling office is not able to confirm this. In Louisville, the parish records are still held by the church; the chancery keeps records of closed churches only.

A genealogical group has organized to promote a family reunion of descendants of Maryland Catholics to Kentucky. Information about the group can be obtained from Descendants of Maryland Catholics to Kentucky, c/o M. Moore, 380 Summers Lane, Bardstown, Kentucky 40004. Research information including publications, etc., that cover the Catholic families of this region is available from the Nelson County Genealogy Roundtable and Historical Society.

CHURCH RELATED RECORDS

Beginning early in this century, printed worship bulletins and church newsletters have become sources of information about births, baptisms, marriages, and deaths as well as the activities of the church and its parishioners. These are usually available in the church, the minister's private files, or the church historical society.

Some churches in Kentucky, particularly the Catholic and Lutheran churches, published their own newspapers in addition to church newsletters and bulletins. Some of these are available in the University of Kentucky library and other city libraries including Louisville, Lexington, Cincinnati, and Kenton County.

TABLE 7.2   Kentucky Religious Archives and Resources*

Louisville Presbyterian Theological Seminary 1044 Alta Vista Road Louisville 40205 502-895-3411 Scope: local and general Kentucky history.	Kentucky Baptist Convention Archives P.O. Box 43433 10702 Shelbyville Road Middletown 40243 Scope: Church histories, directories of pastors and staff personnel; limited information of a genealogical nature.
Kentucky Baptist Historical Society Box 43433 Middletown 40243-0433 502-245-4101 Scope: Church history only; very limited information on Kentucky ministers; no resources available to do genealogical research.	Southern Baptist Theological Seminary 2825 Lexington Road Louisville 40280 502-897-4807 Scope: Kentucky Baptists and affiliated churches.
Jewish Genealogical Society of Louisville 3600 Dutchmans Lane Louisville 40205	American Jewish Archives 3101 Clifton Avenue Cincinnati, Ohio 45220

*   These libraries are *not* genealogical libraries and do not have the resources to conduct research. When addressing these societies, include a stamped, self-addressed envelope.

INTERPRETATION AND CONTENT OF CHURCH RECORDS

Records kept by Kentucky churches that are most useful to the genealogist are membership lists and records of vital events and burials. Many churches kept records of current members in good standing and some wrote comments on their lists. Death notations will sometimes have the date and place the person died and even the cause of death, thus providing a valuable alternative for information about deaths prior to 1911.

Minute books maintained by some churches can be valuable for genealogy. These minute books can contain notes regarding family members moving to another area or being admitted to the church upon arrival to Kentucky or dismissed from the church. The term "dismissal" in Baptist circles means that a member left to join another church. A person who was dismissed was often given a letter of reference to present to their next church as a recommendation for admission.

There were times, however, when churches did ask its members to worship elsewhere. Accounts of members being admonished or censured for various acts can be found in the church records. The language in these cases might be "excluded" or "disfellowshipped." In the case of minor offenses, the member was asked, or ordered, to repent or publicly apologize. Some acts were so serious a violation that repentance was not acceptable, or the member may have refused to repent or admit the error of his ways. In these cases, the member may have been excluded from the church and detailed accounts of the act, votes of other members, and discussions on the transgressions may be found.

The early Clark County Providence Church records, established by relatives of Daniel Boone and Captain Billy Bush, contain such accounts of its members' indiscretions. These records, available at the University of Kentucky special collections library and the Kentucky Historical Society, contain lists of members of the church, as well as information about attendance, transgressions, and sins of its early pioneer members. Accounts of unacceptable behaviors of church members were debated in the church with the member given the opportunity of self-defense. Public apologies or other outcomes of these discussions are also recorded in the minutes of the church. The Providence Church records are simply one example of the church records that exist in Kentucky archives and libraries.

AVAILABILITY OF KENTUCKY CHURCH RECORDS

The Kentucky Historical Society maintains a good collection of church histories and records. The society maintains a file drawer, organized by county, of unpublished church histories from churches throughout the state. In addition, the society has a strong collection of church histories. These histories include lists of members, communion lists, details of the church business dealings, family group lists, and lists of its ministers. Some histories, such as the Baptist histories, contain biographies of ministers serving its churches.

The Filson Club as well as the University of Kentucky special collections library have significant holdings of church histories and church related documents among their manuscripts. Local libraries in Kentucky are sometimes the beneficiaries of defunct churches' records, so these should be consulted as well. In addition, the microfilmed records of churches are listed in chapter 8.

It should be noted that, with the exception of the Jewish group, none of the groups listed in table 7.2 have a genealogical mission. They have neither the resources nor the records to do genealogical research. Their records generally consist of information on ministers and church histories. Most of the church member lists are maintained by the churches. Many Kentucky church records are maintained out of the state; consult the address list compiled by Harrison in his excellent article on Kentucky church records for these national archives and repositories (Harrison 1984, 42–55).

CEMETERIES

Both state and local groups are active in recording information from and preserving the family cemeteries that are so important to Kentucky genealogy. As a result, these sources are constantly growing.

The Kentucky Historical Society has been working on a statewide Cemetery Records Project since 1976. By 1987, over one million grave sites had been recorded. These will be entered into a computerized data base (Harney 1987, 5). At this time, not all are indexed. These counties are considered complete and have resulted in books: Ballard, Boyd, Carroll, Clinton, Garrard, Greenup, Hart, Henry, Lee, Magoffin, Owen, Taylor, and Whitley. In addition, the best collection of private family cemetery lists can be found at the historical society in their county files. The historical society does not search these files; interested individuals are requested to visit the society or to hire a researcher to do so.

Bluegrass Roots and *Kentucky Ancestors* regularly publish small family cemetery tombstone inscriptions. Gravestones that have appeared in *Bluegrass Roots* have been indexed to 1984 (Harney 1985).

The Kentucky DAR chapters have also been active in preserving family cemeteries. They have published a multivolume set of Kentucky cemeteries that is well indexed. The collection of this data began as early as World War II, and as a result, some stones that are no longer legible and accessible are included in these records.

Some early Lexington cemetery records can be found in the Margaret I. King Library. There are approximately fourteen cubic feet of records dating back to the founding of the Lexington Cemetery in 1849. The Lexington Cemetery is in the process of computerizing its records. They will then permit the University of Kentucky library to transfer this same information to microfilm for genealogists and other scholars (*Bluegrass Roots* 1985, 57).

Kentucky has six national cemeteries. The national cemetery had its beginnings in the Civil War. There were forty national cemeteries established in 1866 by the United States legislature. A huge reburial program was undertaken at the end of the war. By 1870, some 300,000 Civil War dead in seventy-three national cemeteries were reinterred. In Kentucky, the interrments included 2,203 dead, from five areas of Kentucky, being moved to Camp Nelson. Frankfort sent 104 dead; Richmond, 241; London, 266; Covington, 437; and from the Perryville Battle of 1862, 975 bodies were removed to be buried at Camp Nelson. One hundred and forty-three additional men were disinterred from towns surrounding the camp and family plots.

The Camp Nelson cemetery contains a total of 5,374 burials as of the end of 1975. Of these, 1,245 are unknown soldiers from the Civil War (*Bluegrass Roots* 1981, 97-99).

TABLE 7.3	Kentucky's National Cemeteries
Camp Nelson National Cemetery 6980 Danville Road Nicholasville 40356 606-885-5727	Lexington National Cemetery 833 West Main Street Lexington 40507 Phone Camp Nelson for information
Cave Hill National Cemetery 701 Baxter Avenue Louisville 40204 502-893-3852	Mill Springs National Cemetery RD No. 1 Box 172 Nancy 42544 606-636-6470
Danville National Cemetery 377 North First Street Danville 40422 Phone Camp Nelson for information	Zachary Taylor National Cemetery 4701 Brownsboro Road Louisville 40207 502-893-3852
Lebanon National Cemetery Lebanon 40033 502-692-3390	

Source: *Bluegrass Roots* 1981, 97-99.

CITY DIRECTORIES
AND URBAN SOURCES

Directories for Kentucky's largest cities are available and provide a valuable resource for tracking the more mobile urban Kentuckians. By examining these directories for related family names, as well as the surname of interest for persons listed at the same address, a fairly complete picture of the household composition may be obtained.

Inaccuracies in these directories are possible. Neighbors were sometimes the informants for the information just as they are today. It appears that in some Kentucky directories as much as a year passed between the time information was collected and the publication of the directory. As a result, data may be outdated, and some people listed in the directory may have died in the previous year.

Lexington and Louisville directories are available in those city libraries. Lexington directories began in 1806 and have continued uninterrupted to the present day; Louisville directories are available from 1832 to the present. The northern Kentucky cities also have a strong collection of city directories. For example, the Kenton County Library has a set of directories for various Cincinnati metropolitan cities dating from 1834 to the present. Some of these directories have been microfilmed and are also available in the archives. The Covington and Newport directories dating from 1834 to 1903 are available there. Smaller surrounding cities are also available for scattered years. See chapter 8 for the details of the microfilm holdings at the archives.

Many municipal and city records have been microfilmed and are available at the Kentucky State Archives. These microfilm holdings are listed in chapter 8 under the county where the city is located. These records generally deal with the operations of the city but often include materials that may be helpful to the researcher.

KENTUCKY MANUSCRIPTS, SPECIAL
COLLECTIONS AND PRINTED SOURCES

DRAPER MANUSCRIPTS

An extremely rich source of information on early Kentucky and its pioneers can be found in the Draper manuscripts. Lyman Copeland Draper made it his life's work to rescue the history of the Revolutionary heroes. With the support of family, Draper gathered reminiscences, documents, and information that was intended to be a series of volumes on the settlement and history of the West. Draper gathered much of the work himself. He took several research trips in the 1840s gathering materials for his work. His work continued through correspondence until his death in 1891.

Rev. Shane was a major informant and co-worker of Draper in the central Kentucky area. His work focused on collecting interviews of aging Kentucky pioneers regarding their travels to Kentucky, battles with Indians, and other aspects of frontier life.

The Draper manuscripts include nearly 500 volumes of records generally covering the period 1740 through the War of 1812. The majority of the information collected by Mr. Draper was generated between the years 1840 and 1891. There are journals, diaries, interviews, military records, muster rolls, business records, maps, and papers of other historians. Draper was interested in history and life-styles, not genealogy. However, there is a great deal of genealogical material in the personal interviews of the aging Kentucky pioneers.

The Kentucky Papers consist of thirty-seven volumes. An index to interviews as well as a subject index has been published by the Wisconsin Historical Society (Weaks 1979). In addition to the Kentucky papers, the following series in the Draper manuscripts should also be consulted for Kentucky material: Simon Kenton Papers, Daniel Boone Papers, Draper's Chronicles of Border Warfare, and the King's Mountain Papers. Some of these interviews have been transcribed and are published in the *Kentucky Historical Society Register*.

The original Draper manuscripts are in the Historical Society of Wisconsin where Draper became the corresponding secretary. However, microfilm copies are available in many major genealogy libraries and other larger libraries. (*Bluegrass Roots* 1987, 1). In Kentucky, the following libraries have complete copies of the Draper manuscripts: Filson Club, Kentucky Historical Society, Murray State University, Kentucky archives, University of Kentucky, and Western Kentucky University. The Louisville Library reports that it has "about half" of the Draper manuscripts. Copies of the Draper manuscripts may be purchased from Chadwyck-Healey, Inc., 1101 King Street, Alexandria, Virginia 22314; 703-683-4890.

GOVERNORS' PAPERS

An overlooked source of genealogical and historical information in Kentucky is a collection of materials known as the Governors' Papers. Papers of the governors from Isaac Shelby through William Fields, covering the years 1792 to 1927, have been appraised and microfilmed. The most important series for the genealogist is the Executive Journal, which is a record of the official actions of the governor. Information about an individual can be found if he/she was a local or state official, a military officer, or a criminal who appealed for clemency. Pardons, respites, and fines remitted are given. Nominees for a government post may have submitted a good deal of biographical data.

Militia returns are available, particularly for the years 1812 to 1820, in these records. Officers' ranks and dates of commissions are shown. Filed with the returns are muster rolls of the officers and enlisted men along with the numbers of horses, saddles, and rifles issued to each person. For example, there is an 1844-48 militia muster roll in the papers of William Owsley. The Preston Leslie papers covering the years 1871 to 1875 also contain a roster for militia for the city of Louisville.

Criminals are indexed in the Executive Journal under the heading, "Pardons, Remissions, Respites, and Rejected Petitions." The journal entry will give the action taken and the date of any action. Various supporting documents such as the trial transcripts, letters, and arrest warrants may also be filed with the petition (Place 1983, 52-54).

SPECIAL GENEALOGY COLLECTIONS

The Kentucky Historical Society has a guide to their manuscripts. These manuscripts include family collections, correspondence, diaries, scrapbooks, and other papers.

The genealogical research and family collections of several prolific genealogists have been microfilmed and preserved at libraries in the state. Two of the larger collections are the Ardery Collection for Bourbon and surrounding counties and the Barton Collection for Pendleton and northern Kentucky counties.

The historical society and University of Kentucky special collections library have both the Barton and Ardery collections. The archives has the Barton collection. The University of Kentucky special collections library also has a card index of family names as well as many individuals included in the Barton Collection. In chapter 8, these special family collections are listed under the heading of genealogy or family histories.

KENTUCKY ORAL HISTORY PROJECT

The Kentucky Oral History Project collects interviews of elderly and prominent Kentuckians and makes them available at the state archives. The archives has tape recorders to enable patrons to listen to the tapes.

The University of Kentucky also has a nationally recognized oral history interview program that emphasizes prominent Kentuckians and university officials. While the focus of the oral history interview is not on Kentucky family history per se, some information about early times in Kentucky can be found in this interesting and valuable source. The program began in the early 1970s to document the history and culture of the commonwealth more thoroughly. The project now contains over 2,600 interviews on a wide range of topics and subjects.

PRINTED SOURCES

Kentucky is fortunate to have many active historians and genealogists interested in publishing their works. The most comprehensive collection of print materials, including county and church histories, family histories, compilations and indexes of local records, historical and genealogical journals, and general Kentucky history books, is held by the Kentucky Historical Society. The University of Kentucky special collections library is strong in its general Kentucky history collection and its appalachian histories and materials.

Two sources can be used to keep up-to-date with the ever growing numbers of privately printed Kentucky material. First, recently published manuscripts and references pertaining to Kentucky are reviewed quarterly in *Kentucky Ancestors* and in *The Register*. Second, the Historical Confederation has instituted a Kentucky Publications Survey that includes privately printed materials and works published for and about Kentucky history and genealogy. An updated list of these publications may be obtained from the Confederation if provided with a long, self-addressed stamped envelope.

KENTUCKY BIOGRAPHIES AND INDEXES

In Kentucky, county biographical books were popular from the late 1870s through the 1910s. These biographies consisted of county or regional collections of personal portraits that were included in the volumes for a fee. These biographical sketches contain a great deal of genealogical and personal information about their subjects. The articles may be quite long and may include information on three or four generations of families, their migrations, occupations, and accomplishments.

The information contained in these biographies was typically provided by the subject of the article, but that does not necessarily mean the information is completely accurate. Mistakes were made and events put in a favorable light. The books were supported by preselling copies of the book to those who appeared in them. Nevertheless, these biographies can be insightful and informative.

A number of indexes make these biographies easily accessible. Some volumes have separately printed indexes; others have indexes as part of the original works. The best collection of these indexes is available at the historical society. The University of Kentucky special collections library has most of the biographies plus a comprehensive card index of twenty of Kentucky's standard biographies including the works by Perrin and Kerr's History of Kentucky. Another good index of these biographies is Cook's compilation (Cook 1986). His work is not an every-name index, but an index to the subject of the biography.

Indexing Projects, Computer Databases, and Other Special Aids

Indexing Aids

The accessibility of information in journal articles and other publications depends upon good indexes. Kentucky has a number of important indexing projects and compilations that aid use of the vast amount of information in its many journals. Over forty Kentucky genealogical and historical journals are indexed in *PERSI*, the Ft. Wayne Library index publication. Another important work is Harney's every-name index to the *Bluegrass Roots*, which covers the period from 1973 to 1984 (Harney 1985). A number of Kentucky and Virginia historical journals have already been indexed in the scholarly historical journals index. These historical abstracts are usually available at college and university libraries.

One particularly valuable index is Cook and Trapp's *Kentucky Genealogical Index* (Cook and Trapp 1985). This index contains an every-name index to the following genealogical publications: *Kentucky Ancestors* (1965–80), *Eastern Kentuckian* (1965–80), *Kentucky Genealogist* (1950–80), and *Bluegrass Roots* (1974–80).

Both of these works are available at the Kentucky Historical Society library as well as most Kentucky public libraries.

Computer Database Searching

The use of national databases, now available through computer networks such as GENIE, plus various commercial databases that include historical journals, will become increasingly more accessible and fruitful in searching for Kentucky ancestors. In addition, there is a statewide movement to begin indexing and computerizing projects under the leadership of Mr. Brian Harney of the Kentucky Genealogical Society. In the future, this project will become an invaluable research tool.

Kentucky Family Files and Group Sheet Project

Family files can be a treasure chest of undocumented clues on Kentucky ancestors. Many public libraries maintain family files. The Kentucky Historical Society Library has the largest collection of family files statewide. They also maintain a card index of researchers for specific family lines.

The Kentucky Genealogy Society also maintains family files and has encouraged its members to submit family group sheets. These group sheets are maintained in the society's research room at the Kentucky archives. The University of Kentucky special collections library also maintains family files; a listing of their files was given in *Bluegrass Roots* (1984, 149–52).

KENTUCKY BIBLE RECORDS

A number of projects have been aimed at collecting and publishing Kentucky family Bible records. The most important of these statewide is the DAR project. Most Kentucky libraries have copies of the DAR volumes of Kentucky family Bibles. The scope of the project is statewide and its volumes are well indexed. In addition, *Kentucky Ancestors* recently published a matriarch/patriarch index of family Bible records, which appeared in the *Kentucky Ancestors* and *The Register* (*Kentucky Ancestors* 1989, 14–22).

KENTUCKY MAPS AND PLACE LOCATORS

GENERAL REFERENCES

Kentucky has excellent maps and two excellent finding guides. A *Guide to Kentucky Place Names*, by Thomas P. Field (1961), is invaluable for locating small villages, creeks, neighborhoods, and even family cemeteries. Another excellent source for locating historical places is *Kentucky Place Names*, by Rennick (1984). Jillson's *Pioneer Kentucky* (1934) has a good list of early stations and settlements. Obscure towns can be located by writing to U.S. Board of Geographic Names, 523 National Center, Reston, Virginia 22092. They maintain records of town name changes in the United States.

Kentucky County Maps (available from C. J. Puetz, 601 West Seymour, Appleton, Wisconsin 54911) contains detailed highway maps of all 120 Kentucky counties including state and county roads, family cemeteries, churches, creeks and other landmarks. These maps are invaluable for finding Kentucky backroads. This reference is also available at the Kentucky Historical Society bookshop.

The best maps for ancestor and cemetery hunting, however, are those published by the University of Kentucky Geological Survey. These maps are available from the Survey by writing Room 106, Mining and Mineral Resource Building, University of Kentucky, Lexington, Kentucky 40506-0056; 606-257-3896. These maps also show family cemeteries, church sites, and all roads, including unpaved dirt roads, for the dedicated cemetery and creek hunter. The archives and the University of Kentucky map room have complete sets of these maps.

FIG. 7.4 Gazetteer of Boone County, 1883. (D.J. Lake & Company, Philadelphia)

HISTORICAL MAPS AND GAZETTEERS

In the late 1880s, a company by the name of Lake and Company published a series of gazetteers for some Kentucky counties. These are available mostly for northern and central Kentucky counties. The best collections of these maps are at the Kentucky Historical Society and the University of Kentucky special collections library.

The Kentucky archives has a map collection dating from the 1700s as well as some of the county atlases published in the 1880s. The Kentucky Historical Society also has a good collection of Kentucky county gazetteers. These are listed in table 7.4.

TABLE 7.4	Historical Maps and Gazetteers Held by the Kentucky Historical Society and University of Kentucky
1884*	Bath and Fleming counties
1883*	Boone, Kenton and Campbell counties
1861	Bourbon, Clark, Fayette, Jessamine, and Woodford counties topographical map
1877*	Bourbon, Clark, Fayette, Jessamine, and Woodford counties
1876	Boyle and Mercer counties
1884*	Bracken and Pendleton counties
1883*	Carroll and Gallatin counties
1878	Christian County precinct map
1876	Daviess County
1882	Franklin County
1914	Fulton County plat map
1879	Garrard and Lincoln counties
1880	Graves County
1880*	Henderson and Union counties
1882*	Henry and Shelby counties
1885	Hickman County plat map
1858	Jefferson County property holders map
1876	Jefferson County—City of Louisville

1879*	Jefferson and Oldham counties
1899	Larue County farmhouse map
1876*	Madison County
1877*	Marion and Washington counties
1876*	Mason County
1879	Montgomery County (reprint of 1870 edition)
1882	Nelson and Spencer counties
1880	Owen County
1879	Scott County precinct map

---

*   Indicates the map is available both at the society and at the University of Kentucky special
collections library.

Source for society holdings: Ms. Linda Anderson, Kentucky Historical Society Staff, 10 October
1990, personal correspondence.

A special resource for urban areas are the Sanborn insurance maps of
Kentucky cities and towns. These detailed maps depict the structure and size of
each building. For most cities in this collection, there are maps covering a period
of time from the mid-1880s to the 1920s to 1940s. The University of Kentucky
map department as well as the Kentucky archives have copies of these maps.

UNIVERSITY OF KENTUCKY MAP DEPARTMENT

The University of Kentucky's map department maintains a collection of
maps, atlases, gazetteers, guidebooks, and cartobibliographies. It is well organized
and extensive. Microfilmed historical maps are also available in the newspaper
room in the main library. In the special collections library, the university also
houses approximately 550 original and facsimile rare Kentucky maps.

Kentucky maps held by the university include maps of most incorporated
towns and cities, county and district highway maps, road and railroad maps, and
other thematic maps, all covering different periods in Kentucky history. The
Kentucky geological topographic sheets at the scale of 1:24,000 and the United
States 1:250,000 maps are housed in this collection.

The university's collection also includes city maps for all major United States
and world cities as well as a number of historic city maps. The library has highway
maps for all the states, and county highway maps for Kentucky and bordering
states.

The university's map department also has a detailed series of maps of many
areas of the world along with finding aids to locate even small villages in Europe,

England, and Ireland. The map department is a depository for the Army's Defense Mapping Agency and, as a result, has many detailed maps of the world. Finally, gazetteers for many states of the United States are available in addition to the United States Board on Geographic Names gazetteers for many countries of the world.

CHAPTER 8

INVENTORY OF COUNTY MICROFILMED HISTORICAL RECORDS

Kentucky courthouses were burned, flooded, struck by lightning, hit by tornadoes, neglected, and even deliberately set on fire during the Civil War. Man-made as well as natural disasters have taken their toll to the point that the loss for some counties is nearly total. However, because of the existence of state, federal, church, cemetery, other private records, and rerecordings of destroyed records, some early records are available for nearly all counties.

In this chapter, an inventory of all microfilmed court records and other primary genealogical resources available at the three largest archival libraries is provided for each of Kentucky's 120 counties.

Other important county information is provided in addition to the inventory of primary court records including addresses of the county clerk's office, libraries, and genealogical and historical societies. Dates of the county's formation, parent counties, and other relevant courthouse information have also been included for each county.

Each week, additional materials are added to the holdings of the Kentucky archives and the Kentucky Historical Society. While the majority of these new acquisitions represent modern records rather than early Kentucky records of interest to the historian and genealogist, corrections or updates to any of the information provided in this inventory are invited and welcomed.

County Data and Resources

County Clerk's Office

Below each county's name, the county clerk's telephone number, city, and zip code are provided.

Local Libraries

Many, though not all, local libraries maintain local history and genealogical collections. Therefore, the county's main library is indicated with its address and telephone number. This data was obtained from the *Directory of Kentucky's Libraries and Archives* (Kentucky Department for Libraries 1988). It is always wise to contact the library or archives prior to a visit for the most current information on hours.

Historical and Genealogical Groups

Addresses of local county genealogical and historical societies were obtained from the most recent version of *The Directory of Kentucky Historical Organizations* (Fugate 1989). Only countywide societies are listed. Consult *The Directory* for additional, specialized organizations.

The organizations and groups listed in this reference often depend heavily on volunteers, and none undertake genealogical or historical research. When corresponding for information, please send a stamped, self-addressed envelope for a reply. Limit questions to one or two brief queries and enclose a small fee to cover the work or copies you are requesting.

County and Other Courthouse Data

Courthouse construction and disaster dates have been compiled and reported in this chapter where applicable. Chapter 7 has complete details on these construction and disaster dates.

When corresponding with courts, it is important to remember that most do not have the staff to do in-depth research. It is wise to limit your requests for documents to only one or two and to be as specific as possible in the request. Enclose a stamped, self-addressed envelope for a reply and a small fee to cover the work or copies you request. Since the Kentucky archives typically has early court records, it is usually more fruitful to contact them or the historical society first with your brief query. They also maintain lists of professionals who perform research for others.

MICROFILMED RECORDS

Following the general county information, is an inventory of each of Kentucky's 120 counties' *microfilmed* records and their location at the Kentucky State Archives (abbreviated "A"), Kentucky Historical Society (abbreviated "H"), and University of Kentucky special collections library (abbreviated "U"). Records that have not been microfilmed are NOT included in this inventory. In some counties, these nonmicrofilmed materials can be quite substantial; in other counties, inconsequential.

METHODOLOGY OF THE INVENTORY

Information on microfilmed records at the historical society, the archives, and the University of Kentucky special collections library was taken from inventory books available at each site. The information was entered directly into a laptop computer and later electronically uploaded to an MS-DOS personal computer. All data was verified and proofread twice against the original inventory. Records from each site were then merged and sorted using utility and database software.

While every effort was taken to ensure the accuracy of the information, there were problems with the accuracy of the inventories at each of the libraries. The archives, whose records are in the best condition, is currently editing these guide books and, as a result, new information may come to light during this process. The historical society's microfilm drawers should be consulted when trying to locate records listed in this inventory, since not all records are consistently included in its various inventory books. The records at the University of Kentucky special collections library are indexed in a number of places, and the librarian should be consulted if a record shown here is not found in the main inventory books.

EXPLANATION OF CODES AND INVENTORY ABBREVIATIONS

In order to conserve space, a few simple conventions and abbreviations have been used.

GENERAL COUNTY INFORMATION

The address shown beneath the county name is the address of the county clerk's office and its phone number. The public library, historical and genealogical societies, if any, are listed without the county name. For example, "Genealogical Society" and "Public Library" in the Boone County section should be understood to mean "Boone County Genealogical Society" and "Boone County Public Library."

INVENTORY ABBREVIATIONS

Additional abbreviations and codes used to conserve space are shown in tables 8.1 and 8.2.

TABLE 8.1	Microfilm Inventory Left-hand Column Codes
H	Kentucky Historical Society
U	University of Kentucky Special Collections Library
A	Kentucky Department of Libraries and Archives

TABLE 8.2	Microfilm Inventory Text Abbreviations
IN*	Indexed (indicates original records and index exists for these records)
PIN	Partially Indexed
UNIN	Unindexed
EX	Except
SY	Scattered Years
SA	Scattered Articles
SI	Scattered Issues
Misc.	Miscellaneous
Vol.	Volume
?	Dates are uncertain or unknown
(number)	Number shown after the Revolutionary War pensions represents number of pensioners
Order Books	County Clerk Order, unless otherwise stated

*   If an index is known to exist or if records are known to be unindexed, this is indicated. However, if there is no notation, there was no indication as to whether the record is indexed or not.

References to "Military Records—Veterans Graves" data at the Kentucky Historical Society indicates that the Society has information on graves of veterans buried in the county, indexed by the Public Works Project in 1939. There are five volumes of these lists. There is a similar reference to "Military Records—Revolutionary and 1812 Pensions," often with a number in parentheses beside it. This indicates there are abstracts of veterans filing pensions from that county. The number in parenthesis indicates the number of abstracts that exist for that county. These abstracts were done by Annie Walker Burns.

DATES

The dates of the records are inclusive and continuous unless otherwise indicated. For example, if the years are shown as 1792-1800, this indicates records are available for the entire period, unless there is an exception list following the entry.

Slight variations in the dates, usually by one year, of seemingly similar or identical films exist in some counties. These errors or variations were recorded as they appear in each site's inventory.

KENTUCKY MICROFILM INVENTORY

ADAIR COUNTY

Columbia 42728
502-384-2801

Public Library	Genealogical Society	Historical Society of Adair
307 Greensburg Street	P.O. Box 613	County
Columbia 42728	Columbia 42728	809 Greensburg Street
502-384-2472		Columbia 42728

Adair County was formed in 1802 from Green County. The present courthouse on the public square was constructed by 1884. It replaced the courthouse built in 1806 after the county was formed.

H	?-?	Bible Records
H	1921	Church Records—Presbyterian, Christian, Baptist
A	?-?	Church Records—Various Churches
A	1810-1904	Civil Order Books—Circuit Court (IN)
U	1876-1902	Commonwealth Court Orders
A	1876-1902	Criminal Order Books—Commonwealth Order Books
U	1801-1904	Deed Books

A	1802–1905	Deed Books
H	1802–1960	Deed Books (IN)
A	1802–1941	Deed Index
U	1801–1941	Deed Index—Grantors and Grantees
U	1866–1909	Deeds—Commissioners
A	1873–1909	Deeds—Commissioners
U	1877–1941	Deeds—Commissioners—Index
A	1802–1806	Marriage Bonds
H	1802–1926	Marriage Bonds
U	1853–1872	Marriage Bonds
A	1853–1914	Marriage Bonds
A	1802–1912	Marriage Bonds and Certificates
U	1872–1916	Marriage Bonds and Certificates
H	1802–1954	Marriage Bonds and Consents
U	1802–1872	Marriage Certificates
A	1839–1865	Marriage Certificates
H	1802–1916	Marriage Index
A	1802–1916	Marriage Records (IN)
U	1802–1970	Marriage Records—General Index
U	1802–1840	Marriage Register
A	1802–1872	Marriage Register
A	1815–1862	Marriages
A	?–?	Military Records—Civil War Records and Letters
A	1912–1912	Military Records—Confederate Home Inmates
H	?–?	Military Records—Revolutionary and 1812 War Pensions (62)
H	?–?	Military Records—Veterans Graves
U	1827–1829	Misc. Records—Depositions, Deeds, Wills, etc.
A	1897–1900	Newspapers—*Adair County News*
H	1868–1921	Newspapers (SA)
A	1802–1903	Order Books
H	1950–1956	Order Books
H	1817–1907	Order Books (PIN)
A	1802–1940	Order Books Index
U	1802–1903	Orders (EX 1816)
U	1802–1941	Orders General Index
U	1810–1904	Orders—Circuit Court
A	1802–1892	Tax Book (EX 1832, 1834, 1839)
H	1802–1878	Tax Book (EX 1832, 1834, 1839)
H	1852–1907	Vital Statistics (SY)
U	1791–1930	Will Books
A	1804–1960	Will Books
H	1804–1960	Will Books
A	1804–1970	Will Index
U	1791–1970	Will Index

ALLEN COUNTY

Scottsville 42164
502-237-3706

Public Library	Historical Society
Public Square	P.O. Box 393
Scottsville 42164	Scottsville 42164
502-237-3861	

Allen County was formed in 1815 from parts of Barren and Warren counties. The courthouse burned on 2 October 1902 destroying some of its records.

A	1865–1911	Apprenticeship Book (IN)
A	1816–1864	Deed Books (IN)
A	1877–1885	Deed Books—Commissioners
A	1864–1885	Deeds (Burned Records)
A	1902–1916	Marriage Bonds (IN)
A	1815–1865	Marriage Records—DAR (IN)
H	?–?	Military Records—Revolutionary and 1812 War Pensions (27)
A	1880–1885	Minute Book—Financial Board
A	1826–1837	Minute/Order Books (IN)
H	1839–1941	Newspapers (SA)
A	1815–1923	Surveyors Record Book
H	1815–1878	Tax Book (EX 1818, 1830, 1832, 1834, 1839–40, 1864)
A	1815–1892	Tax Book (EX 1830, 1832, 1834, 1839, 1891)
H	1852–1904	Vital Statistics (SY)

ANDERSON COUNTY

Lawrenceburg 40342
502-839-3041

Public Library	Historical Society
114 N. Main Street	114 N. Main Street
Lawrenceburg 40342	Lawrenceburg 40342
502-839-6420	

Anderson County was formed in 1827 from parts of Franklin, Mercer, and Washington counties. There were two courthouse disasters: on 26 October 1859 and another on 13 January 1915 in which only a very few records were destroyed—Order Book D and Mortgage Book B.

U	1837–1871	Administrator and Guardian Bonds
A	1837–1869	Administrator Bonds (IN from 1852)
H	1852–1915	Administrator and Executor Bonds
H	1837–1871	Administrator and Guardian Bonds
U	1852–1915	Administrators and Executors Bonds

H	1829–1973	Church Records—Baptist, Christian
A	1798–1906	Church Records—Salt River Baptist
U	1886–1915	Death Records—Funerals by Rev. Moore
U	1827–1866	Deed Books
A	1827–1986	Deed Books
H	1827–1866	Deed Books (IN)
A	1827–1966	Deed Books Cross Index
H	1827–1897	Deed Index
U	1827–1897	Deed Index
A	1852–1915	Executors Bonds (IN)
U	?–?	Family Bible and Cemetery Records
A	1886–1935	Funeral Records of Rev. Moore
U	?–?	Genealogy—Diary of Henry Terrell—Civil War
U	?–?	Genealogy—Family Records
A	1852–1871	Guardian Bonds (IN)
A	1831–1984	Marriage Bonds (IN)
U	1831–1866	Marriage Bonds
H	1831–1866	Marriage Bonds
A	1837–1865	Marriage Bonds (arranged by year)
A	1831–1987	Marriage Index
A	1866–1909	Marriage License and Bonds—Black (IN)
A	1842–1865	Marriage Records—Grooms List
A	1886–1935	Marriage Records of Rev. Moore
U	1842–1865	Marriages
H	?–?	Military Records—Veterans Graves
A	1944–1974	Minute Books—Lawrenceburg
A	1820	Misc. Records—DAR—Cemetery, Church, Marriage
A	1906	Newspapers—*Anderson News*—Souvenir Supplement
H	1862–1938	Newspapers (SA)
H	1827–1848	Order Books
U	1827–1848	Order Books
A	1827–1873	Order Books
U	1853–1872	Order Books
H	1831–1868	Processioners Book A
A	1830–1948	Processioners Record Book (IN)
U	1831–1868	Processioners Records
A	1827–1892	Tax Book (EX 1831-32, 1834, 1836, 1838–80)
H	1827–1837	Tax Book (EX 1831-32, 1834, 1836)
H	?–?	Tax Records—Taxpayers papers—date unknown
H	1852–1878	Vital Statistics (SY)
H	1827–1930	Will Books
U	1827–1930	Will Books
A	1827–1985	Will Books (IN)

BALLARD COUNTY

Wickliffe 42087
502-355-5168

Ballard/Carlisle/Livingston Library System
Mailing Address:
P.O. Box 428
Bardwell 42023
Physical Location:
Wickliffe
502-335-3460

Ballard-Carlisle Co. Historical
   and Genealogical Society
Box 212
Wickliffe 42087

Ballard County was not formed until 1842 from parts of McCracken and Hickman counties. The first county seat was Blandville. The county seat was moved to Wickliffe in 1882 after the first courthouse was burned on 17 February 1880. It is reported that all records were destroyed by this fire, except one book that happened to be in the circuit clerk's home the night of the fire. However, some re-recordings do exist.

A	1880–1901	Administrator and Executor Register
A	1878–1920	Administrator and Executor Settlements—Index
A	1880–1887	Administrator Bonds (IN)
A	1882–1912	Appraisements, Inventories, and Sales Books—Index
A	1864–1897	Case Files Index—Circuit Court
A	1867–1897	Case Files Index—Court of Common Pleas
A	1842–1895	Case Files—Circuit Court Plaintiff Index
A	1880–1927	Claims Allowed—List
A	1880–1884	Coffee House Bonds (IN)
A	1880–1897	Constable Bonds (IN)
A	1896–1900	Criminal Order Books
A	1880–1922	Deed Index (re-recordings of burned records)
A	1873–1967	Deed Books
A	1880–1887	Deed Books—Commissioners
A	1842–1963	Execution Book (IN from 1856)
A	1868–1892	Execution Book—Court of Common Pleas
A	1880–1909	Executors and Administrators Settlements (IN)
A	1880–1921	Executors Bonds (IN)
A	1880–1890	Guardian Bonds (IN)
A	1880–1901	Guardian List
A	1880–1904	Guardian Settlement Books (IN)
A	1883–1920	Guardian Settlements Index
A	1875–1877	Judgment Book—Common Pleas
A	1863–1867	Judgment by Default Book
A	1880–1914	Marriage Bonds—Black (IN)
A	1880–1912	Marriage Bonds (IN)
A	1879–1884	Marriage Register
H	1879–1914	Marriage Register and Bonds
A	1880–1943	Mechanic Liens (IN)

H	?-?	Military Records—Veterans Graves
A	1880-1923	Minister Bonds (IN, pages missing)
A	1880-1890	Mortgage Book (PIN)
A	1880-1900	Mortgage Books Index
H	1868-1882	Newspapers (SA)
A	1880-1892	Order Books
A	1880-1968	Order Books—General Index
A	1842-1902	Order Books (IN)
A	1867-1892	Order Books (IN from 1870)
A	1881-1964	Plat Book
A	1879-1891	Register of Sales, Replevin, and Other Bonds
A	1880-1917	Road Order Books and Register (PIN)
A	1880-1888	Sheriffs Settlement Book
A	1880-1923	Surveyor Bonds
H	1843-1884	Tax Book (EX 1879-83)
A	1843-1892	Tax Book (all years)
H	1852-1894	Vital Statistics (SY)
A	1879-1924	Will Books
H	1879-1924	Will Books

BARREN COUNTY

Glasgow 42141
502-651-3783

Mary W. Weldon Public Library 107 West College Glasgow 42141 502-651-2824	South Central Kentucky Historical and Genealogical Society P.O. Box 80 Glasgow 42141	Historical Society Rt. 7 Glasgow 42141

Barren County was formed in 1799 from parts of Green and Warren counties. The first courthouse was a log building and was succeeded by five other buildings over the years.

U	1848-1881	Administrator Bonds
A	1848-1869	Administrator Bonds (IN)
H	1804-1942	Church Records—Baptist Association Minutes
A	1800-1807	Deed Book—Quarter Sessions Court
U	1798-1866	Deed Books
A	1801-1866	Deed Books
H	1866-1902	Deed Books
A	1798-1935	Deed Index
U	1798-1935	Deed Index Grantors and Grantees
A	1813-1930	Equity Case Files—Plaintiff Index
A	1813-1865	Equity Case Files—Circuit Court
U	1813-1931	Equity Case Index
U	1813-1931	Equity Judgments and Index

U	1799–1813	Execution Book
A	1799–1813	Execution Book—Circuit Court (IN)
A	1848–1882	Executor Bonds (IN)
H	?–?	Genealogy—Gorin
A	1852–1867	Guardian Bonds (IN)
U	1852–1867	Guardian Bonds
A	1835–1865	Inventory Books (IN)
U	1835–1865	Inventory Books
H	1865–1909	Inventory Books
A	1848–1872	Marriage Bonds (IN 1849-55)
U	1848–1872	Marriage Bonds
H	1799–1913	Marriage Bonds (IN)
H	1799–1811	Marriage Bonds Index
H	1798–1851	Marriage Index—Brides and Grooms
U	1798–1933	Marriage Index—Brides and Grooms
H	1868–1870	Marriage Licenses and Certificates
A	1799–1870	Marriage Records Files
U	1799–1834	Marriage Records Index and Marriages
A	1799–1933	Marriage Records—General Index to Bonds
U	1799–1883	Marriage Register
A	1799–1900	Marriage Register
U	1829–1870	Marriages
H	?–?	Military Records—Revolutionary and 1812 Pensions (69)
U	1799–1802	Minute Book
A	1878–1983	Minute Books (Glasgow)
A	1799–1802	Minute/Order Book—Quarter Sessions (IN)
H	1930–1959	Misc. Records—POA, Release Deeds, etc.
A	1852–1866	Mortgage Book
U	1852–1866	Mortgage Book
A	1861–1949	Newspapers—*Free Press* and *Evening Journal*
H	1873–1948	Newspapers (SA)
U	1798–1870	Order Books
U	1813–1866	Order Books
H	1870–1903	Order Books
A	1799–1903	Order Books (PIN)
A	1813–1866	Order Books—Circuit Court (1835-37, IN only)
U	1799–1883	Surveyor's Books
A	1799–1908	Surveyor's Books
A	1799–1892	Tax Book (EX 1818, 1830-32, 1837-39, 1867, 1873-84)
H	1799–1872	Tax Book (EX 1818, 1830-32, 1837-39, 1867-69 White)
H	1798–1827	Tax Receipts
H	1852–1878	Vital Statistics (Scattered, EX 1858-76)
U	1798–1834	Will Books
H	1798–1943	Will Books
A	1799–1884	Will Books
U	1798–1959	Will Books Index
A	1798–1960	Will—Inventory and Settlement Books Index

BATH COUNTY

Owingsville 40360
606-674-2613

Bath Memorial Library
P.O. Box 136
Main Street
Owingsville 40360
606-674-2531

Bath County was formed in 1811 from part of Montgomery County. It was named for the medicinal springs in the area. The Owingsville courthouse burned on 21 May 1864. No records appear to be lost. The 1864 fire was accidentally set when federal soldiers overturned a stove while trying to leave upon learning that Confederate troops would soon arrive.

A	1866	Business Records—Day Book—Dr. Willis Connors
A	1879–1977	Case Files Off Docket Index
H	?–?	Church Records
H	1901–1932	Church Records—Baptist Association Sessions
A	1887–1977	Civil Order Books—Circuit Court (IN)
A	1886–1977	Criminal Order Books (IN)
U	1811–1866	Deed Books
A	1811–1986	Deed Books—Index
H	1829–1880	Idiot Returns
A	1860–1865	Judgments by Default Book—Circuit Court (IN)
H	1812–1855	Marriage Bonds
U	1853–1855	Marriage Bonds
H	1932–1933	Marriage Bonds
A	1812–1855	Marriage Bonds (EX 1840–41, 1843–44, 1852)
U	1812–1865	Marriage Bonds—Loose
A	1867–1917	Marriage Books
H	1851–1860	Marriage Licenses
U	1851–1860	Marriage Licenses
H	1811–1865	Marriage Records
A	1857–1865	Marriage Records
U	1811–1865	Marriage Records—Misc.
H	1817–1851	Marriage Records of Rev. "Racoon" John Smith
H	1799–1900	Marriage Register
U	1811–1917	Marriage Returns
H	1867–1917	Marriage Returns
A	1811–1856	Marriage Returns (PIN)
H	1792–1794	Military Records—Muster Rolls
H	?–?	Military Records—Veterans Graves
A	1819–1825	Minute Book
U	1819–1825	Minute Book
A	1834–1845	Minute Book—Circuit Court

A	1913–1922	Minute Book—Circuit Court
A	1912–1971	Minute Book—City Council of Owingsville
U	1848–	Misc. Records—Depositions, Deeds, Wills, etc.
H	1872–1881	Newspapers (SA)
A	1811–1882	Order Book—Circuit Court (IN)
U	1830–1867	Order Books
A	1874–1892	Order Books (IN)
A	1874–1892	Order Books (IN)
A	1811–1867	Order Books (IN from 1830)
A	1908–1985	Ordinance Book—Owingsville
A	1813–1823	Record Book—Circuit Court
A	1811–1892	Tax Book (EX 1832, 1836, 1848–69, 1871–78, 1880–85)
H	1811–1870	Tax Book (EX 1832, 1836, 1848–69)
H	1852–1901	Vital Statistics (SY)
H	1811–1896	Will Books
U	1811–1896	Will Books
A	1811–1984	Will Books
H	1811–1959	Will Books Index
A	1811–1897	Will Settlement Book—General Cross Index

BELL COUNTY

Pineville 40977
606-337-6143

Pineville Public Library	Middlesboro-Bell County	Historical Society
Tennessee Avenue	Library	P.O. Box 1344
and Walnut Street	Box 1677	Middlesboro 40965
Pineville 40977	126 S. 20th Street	
606-337-3422	Middlesboro 40965	
	606-248-4812	

Bell County was formed in 1867 from parts of Knox and Harlan counties. It also appears from census maps that a small tract of land went from Whitley County to Bell between the 1870 and 1880 census. The Wilderness Road, one of the first Kentucky wagon roads, was built in 1796 and runs through the county. County offices in Pineville were damaged in a 1976 flood. While most of the flood-damaged records of permanent value were salvaged, there was a loss of records in the earlier fire in 1914 and perhaps in a 1918 fire.

A	1888–1897	Case Files Off Docket Index
A	1888–1897	Case Files Off Docket Index—Common Pleas
A	1893–1939	Civil Case Files Index—Defendant and Plaintiffs
A	1953–1977	Civil Case Files Index—Circuit Court
A	1888–1892	Civil Order Books—Common Pleas Court
A	1888–1962	Civil Order Books (IN)
A	1893–1961	Criminal Order Books (IN)
A	1867–1940	Deed Book Index

U	1867–1901	Deed Books
A	1867–1962	Deed Books
A	1877–1901	Deed Books—Commissioners
U	1867–1935	Deed Index Grantees
U	1867–1941	Deed Index Grantors
U	1877–1907	Deeds—Commissioners
A	1930–1953	Equity Case Files—Plaintiff Index
H	1829–1880	Idiot Returns
U	1875–1921	Inventory and Appraisements
A	1875–1921	Inventory and Appraisements
A	1877–1902	Land Sold for Taxes Book
A	1869–1911	Marriage Bonds
U	1869–1897	Marriage Bonds
H	1890–1911	Marriage Bonds
U	1893–1911	Marriage Bonds and Certificates
A	1867–1937	Marriage Books—Bride and Groom Index
A	1938–1966	Marriage Books—Groom Index
H	1867–1937	Marriage Index—Brides and Grooms
U	1867–1937	Marriage Index—Brides and Grooms
H	1867–1892	Marriage Register
U	1869–1892	Marriage Register
A	1870–1892	Marriage Register
H	1867–1937	Marriages
U	1938–1966	Marriages Index—Grooms
H	?–?	Military Records—Veterans Graves
H	1875–1965	Newspapers (SA)
A	1867–1903	Order Books
U	1867–1903	Order Books (EX 1876–81)
A	1875–1893	Order Books (IN)
A	1936–1938	Order Books—Circuit Court (IN)
U	1875–1901	Orders—Circuit Court
A	1930–1953	Ordinary Case Files—Plaintiff Index
A	1888–1920	Real Estate Register—Middlesborough Company
A	1874–1919	Settlement Book
U	1874–1919	Settlement Book
A	1896–1928	Sheriffs Land Sold for Taxes (EX 1904–19) (PIN)
A	1870–1913	Survey Book—General Index
A	1869–1885	Survey Book (IN)
A	1867–1887	Survey Order Books
U	1870–1913	Surveyor's Book
A	1870–1913	Surveyor's Book
A	1880–1892	Tax Book
H	1874–1878	Vital Statistics (EX 1877, births; 1874, marriages)
U	1869–1920	Will Books
A	1869–1920	Will Books (IN)
H	1869–1920	Will Books (IN)

BOONE COUNTY

Burlington 41005
606-334-2112

Public Library
7425 U.S. Highway 42
Florence 41042
606-371-6222

Historical Society
259 Main Street
Florence 41042

Boone County was formed in 1799 from Campbell County. The first court met at the home of James Marshall. The second courthouse was built in 1817 replacing an early log structure of 1801. There was a courthouse fire in the late 1880s, but records were stored in another building.

A	1866-1884	Administrator and Executor List
H	1862-1884	Administrator Bonds
U	1867-1935	Administrator Bonds
H	1902-1935	Administrator Bonds
A	1902-1935	Administrator Bonds (IN)
A	1820-1860	Administrator—Executor and Guardian Bonds (IN)
U	1876-1932	Administrator—Executor and Guardian Settlements
U	1874-1901	Births and Deaths
H	1804-1851	Business Records—Account Books
H	?-?	Cemetery Records—Belleview Plots (IN)
H	1824-1965	Church Records—Baptist and Lutheran
A	1874-1977	Civil Case Files—Circuit Court
U	1799-1912	Deed Books (IN)
A	1799-1914	Deed Books (IN)
H	1799-1878	Deed Books (IN)
U	1799-1914	Deed Index
A	1799-1914	Deed Index
H	1822-1893	Estray Book
U	?-?	Family Histories, Cemetery Records, etc.
H	1666-1879	Genealogy—Randall Family
H	1789-1800	Genealogy—Tanner's Captivity
A	1860-1938	Guardian Bonds (IN)
U	1854-1920	Guardian Bonds
H	1820-1938	Guardian Bonds and Reports
A	1866-1884	Guardian List
A	1854-1882	Guardian Report Book (IN)
H	1829-1880	Idiot Returns
H	1876-1923	Inventory Books
U	1876-1923	Inventory Books
A	1876-1923	Inventory Books (IN)
H	1798-1865	Marriage Bond Originals
U	1798-1913	Marriage Bonds
A	1798-1913	Marriage Bonds (some unarranged)

H	1817–1903	Marriage Bonds—Mixed
U	1849–1914	Marriage Books
U	1884	Marriage Books
H	1799–1914	Marriage Books (1847, 1848, 1851 part missing)
A	1871–1914	Marriage Books (IN)
H	1817–1901	Marriage Licenses, Certificates, and Bonds (SY)
H	1861–1865	Military Records—Civil War—Adjutant General Abstracts
H	1875	Military Records—Civil War—Enrolled Militia
H	1863	Military Records—Civil War—Exemptions
H	1864	Military Records—Civil War Draft to Union Army
H	?–?	Military Records—Revolutionary War Pensions(41)
H	?–?	Military Records—Veterans Graves
U	1875–1922	Minute Books
A	1890–1914	Minute Books (some missing years)
H	1875–1922	Minute Books
H	1916–1921	Minute Books
H	1830–1858	Municipal Government in Florence, Kentucky
H	1834–1956	Newspapers (SA)
H	1799–1914	Order Books
U	1799–1914	Order Books
A	1799–1914	Order Books (PIN)
H	1896–1904	School Census
H	1914–1915	School Census
H	1932–1934	School Census (EX 1933)
H	1897–1934	School Census—Black (SY)
A	1896–1897	School Census Districts 1–55
A	1876–1932	Settlement Books (IN)
H	1876–1932	Settlement Books
A	1821–1893	Stray Book
U	1821–1893	Stray Book
A	1869–1913	Tavern Keeper Bonds (IN to 1900)
H	1869–1913	Tavern Keepers Bonds
U	1869–1913	Tavern Keepers Bonds
A	1799–1894	Tax Book (EX 1817–18, 1830, 1832, 1838)
H	1799–1878	Tax Book (EX 1818, 1830, 1832, 1838)
A	1933–1967	Tax Book (most years, EX 1934–38)
H	1852–1878	Vital Statistics (EX 1860, 1862–74)
H	1852–1879	Vital Statistics—Births (EX 1860, 1863–73)
A	1849–1850	Vital Statistics—Deaths
A	1874–1899	Vital Statistics (SY)
A	1880–1881	Vital Statistics (scattered and some blacks)
H	1800–1915	Will Books
U	1800–1915	Will Books
A	1800–1918	Will Books
A	1800–1856	Will Books—General Index
H	1800–1866	Will Index
U	1800–1855	Will Index

BOURBON COUNTY

Paris 40361
606-987-2430

Paris-Bourbon County Public Library	Duncan Tavern Historic Center
701 High Street	(D.A.R. John Fox Library)
Paris 40361	323 High Street
606-987-4419	Paris 40361
	606-987-1788

Bourbon County was formed in 1786 from Fayette. The first court was held at Mt. Lebanon in the home of James Garrard on 16 May 1786. Paris, originally known as Hopewell, changed its name to Paris in 1790. A courthouse fire on 8 May 1872 burned the second courthouse built by the Metcalfe brothers. Some records were destroyed in this fire; however, in a second fire in 1901, no records were lost.

A	1810–1841	Deed Book—Circuit Court
U	1786–1865	Deed Books (IN)
A	1786–1874	Deed Books—General Cross Index
H	1786–1794	Marriage Bonds
U	1786–1862	Marriage Bonds
A	1794–1845	Marriage Bonds
A	1786–1794	Marriage Bonds—Misc.
A	1785–1851	Marriage Records—Grooms List—DAR
A	1799–1930	Marriage Records Index
H	1817–1851	Marriage Records of Rev. Racoon Smith
A	1789–1930	Marriage Register and Few Deeds at End of 1930
U	1790–1930	Marriage Register Index
A	1788–1793	Marriage Returns
A	1861–1862	Marriage Returns
A	1808–1865	Marriages and Deaths—Kentucky Straight Bourbon List
A	1808–1865	Marriages and Deaths—Private Compilations
H	?–?	Military Records—Revolutionary and 1812 Pensions (69)
H	?–?	Military Records—Veterans Graves
A	1894–1986	Minute Books (SY)
A	1862–1982	Minute Books—Common Council of Paris
U	1780–1812	Misc. Records—Depositions, Deeds, Wills, etc.
U	1700	Misc. Old Documents
A	1786–1790	Misc. Old Documents
H	1808–1946	Newspapers (SA)
A	1882–1899	Newspapers—*Semi-Weekly Bourbon News*
A	1786–1866	Order Books
U	1786–1866	Order Books
A	1875	Poll Books
U	1875	Poll Books
A	1885	Poll Books

A	1787–1892	Tax Book (EX 1794, 1832, 1834)
A	1786–1871	Will Books
U	1786–1871	Will Books (IN)
H	1786–1871	Will Books (IN)
A	1780–1890	Will Index (nos. 1–10,149)
H	1786–1890	Will and Estate Proceedings Index

BOYD COUNTY

Catlettsburg 41129
606-739-5116

Public Library	Eastern Kentucky	Historical Society	Catlettsburg
1740 Central Ave.	Genealogical Society	2734 Jackson Avenue	Historical Society
Ashland 41101	P.O. Box 1544	Ashland 41101	3420 Spring Street
606-329-0090	Ashland 41101		Catlettsburg 41129

Boyd County was formed in 1860 from parts of Carter, Greenup, and Lawrence counties. The county has had two courthouses—built in 1861 and in 1912.

A	1948–1986	Audit Reports—Water Works and City—Ashland
A	1960–1985	Budget of City—Ashland
A	1860–1953	Civil Case Files Index—Equity
A	1860–1953	Civil Case Files Index—Ordinary
A	1924–1940	Civil Case Files Index—Ordinary
A	1860–1953	Civil Case Files—Circuit Court Index
A	1939	Code of Ordinances and Resolutions—Ashland
A	1911–1940	Criminal Case Files—Defendant Index
A	1876–1973	Criminal Order Books (IN)
A	1860–1866	Deed Books
U	1860–1866	Deed Books
A	1860–1929	Deed Books—Grantor Index
U	1860–1929	Deed Index
A	1860–1865	Marriage Bonds (PIN)
A	1861–1939	Marriage Bonds and License Books—Grooms and Brides
U	1860–1939	Marriage Index—Grooms and Brides
U	1860–1867	Marriages
H	?–?	Military Records—Veterans Graves
A	1858–1985	Minute Books—Ashland
A	1860–1979	Minute Books—Catlettsburg
A	1860–1869	Minute/Order Books (IN)
A	1868–1876	Newspapers—*Catlettsburg Sentinel* and *Big Sandy Herald*
H	1869–1882	Newspapers (SA)
A	1860–1949	Order Books—Circuit Court (IN)
U	1860–1869	Order Books
A	1939–1977	Ordinance Book—Ashland
A	1978–1985	Ordinance Book—Ashland (IN)

A	1895-1986	Ordinance Books—Catlettsburg
A	1939-1985	Resolution Book—Ashland (PIN)
H	1860-1878	Tax Book
A	1860-1892	Tax Book (EX 1885)
H	1859-1907	Vital Statistics—Births (SY)
H	1875-1878	Vital Statistics—Deaths
H	1875-1907	Vital Statistics—Marriages (EX 1876, 1879-1905)
A	1860-1899	Will Books
U	1860-1899	Will Books
A	1874-1962	Will Books—General Index
U	1860-1961	Will Index

BOYLE COUNTY

Danville 40422
606-238-1110

Danville-Boyle County Public Library Third Street at Broadway Danville 40422 606-236-8466	Genealogical Association P.O. Box 273 Rt. 1 Gravel Switch 40328	Danville-Boyle County Historical Society P.O. Box 1122 Danville 40422

This county was formed in 1842 from parts of Lincoln and Mercer counties. The courthouse burned in 1860 with some loss of records.

A	1895-1977	Civil Case Files Index
A	1898-1977	Criminal Order Books (IN)
U	1842-1865	Deed Books
A	1842-1986	Deed Books
A	1842-1882	Deed Index
U	1842-1882	Deed Index
H	1829-1880	Idiot Returns
A	1842-1984	Marriage Bonds and Consents (IN)
U	1842-1866	Marriage Bonds
A	1866-1943	Marriage Books—Black (IN)
A	1842-1985	Marriage Books—Groom and Bride Index
A	1867-1908	Marriage Declaration—Freedmen (IN)
A	1836-1988	Minute Books—Danville
A	1936-1985	Minute Books—Junction City
A	1941-1958	Mortgage Books
H	1843-1950	Newspapers (SA)
A	1842-1977	Order Books—Circuit Court (IN)
U	1842-1868	Order Books
A	1842-1868	Order Books (IN)
A	1928-1932	Tax Book
A	1849-1892	Tax Book (EX 1851-54, 1865-67, 1874, 1877-79)
H	1849-1892	Tax Book (EX 1851-55, 1865-67, 1874, 1877-79)

H	1852–1907	Vital Statistics (SY)
U	1842–1897	Will Books
A	1847–1986	Will Books
A	1842–1921	Will Index
U	1842–1921	Will Index

BRACKEN COUNTY

Brooksville 41104
606-735-2952

Knoedler Memorial Library
Main Street
Augusta 41022
606-756-3911

Bracken was formed in 1797 from parts of Campbell and Mason counties. The first county seat was Augusta. There was a courthouse fire on 20 April 1848 that resulted in some record loss.

U	1797–1866	Deed Books
A	1797–1897	Deed Books—General Cross Index
A	1797–1866	Deed Books—Index
U	1797–1866	Deed Index
H	1829–1880	Idiot Returns
A	1856–1875	Marriage Bonds (IN)
A	1797–1870	Marriage Bonds (unarranged)
U	1798–1864	Marriage Bonds—Loose
A	1851–1876	Marriage List—DAR
A	1851–1876	Marriage List—DAR
U	1856–1875	Marriage Records and Bonds
U	1797–1890	Marriage Register and Index
A	1797–1890	Marriage Registers
A	1797–1890	Marriage Registers—Cross Indexes
H	?–?	Military Records—Revolutionary and 1812 Pensions (111)
H	?–?	Military Records—Veterans Graves
A	1880–1884	Newspapers—*Bracken Bulletin* and *Chronicle*
H	1868–1902	Newspapers (SA)
A	1797–1866	Order Books (A–G)
A	1797–1866	Order Books General Index (Books A–H)
U	1797–1866	Order Books with Index Book
A	1797–1831	Tax Book (EX 1798, 1800, 1814, 1818, 1830)
H	1797–1817	Tax Book (EX 1798, 1800–01, 1803, 1814)
H	1819–1835	Tax Book (EX 1830, 1832)
H	1837–1878	Tax Book (EX 1859–62, 1869–75)
A	1837–1892	Tax Book (EX 1859–62, 1869–75)
H	1852–1905	Vital Statistics (SY)
U	1798–1866	Will Books (IN)

A   1798–1866   Will Books (IN)

BREATHITT COUNTY

Jackson 41339
606-666-4035

Public Library	Genealogical Society	Historical Society
1024 College Avenue	c/o Public Library	Quicksand 41363
Jackson 41339	Jackson 41339	
606-666-5541	606-666-5541	

Breathitt was formed in 1839 from parts of Clay, Estill, and Perry counties, with the county seat originally named Breathitt. The name was changed in 1845 to Jackson. Offspring counties include Owsley, Wolfe, Lee, and Knott. According to some sources, Confederate troops burned the courthouse, at least partially, in July of 1866. However, this fire may actually have been set at the jail. A second fire in 1873 destroyed most of the county's records except for a circuit court order book dated 1839–49 and a few criminal and civil order books.

A	1870–1977	Case Files Off Docket Index
A	1960–1968	Civil Case File Plaintiff Index
A	1977	Civil Case File Plaintiff Index
U	1890–1901	Civil Cases–Circuit Court Common Pleas
A	1890–1892	Civil Order Books–Common Pleas (IN)
A	1865–1979	Civil Order Books–Circuit Court (IN)
U	1890–1900	Commonwealth Cases–Circuit Court
A	1917–1963	Criminal Case Files Off Docket General Index
A	1893–1954	Criminal Order Books (IN)
A	1870–1961	Deed Book Index
U	1873–1901	Deed Books
A	1873–1984	Deed Books
A	1878–1917	Deed Books–Commissioners
U	1870–1961	Deed Index–Grantors and Grantees
U	1878–1917	Deeds–Commissioners
H	1878–1925	Deeds–Commissioners
A	1873–1912	Guardian Bonds (IN)
U	1873–1912	Guardian Bonds
H	1829–1880	Idiot Returns
A	1970–1984	Lease Books
A	1873–1939	Marriage Bonds–General Cross Index
A	1873–1983	Marriage Bonds (IN)
H	1873–1939	Marriage Bond Index
H	1873–1916	Marriage Bonds
U	1872–1916	Marriage Bonds and Certificates
U	1873–1939	Marriage Index–Brides and Grooms
H	?–?	Military Records–Veterans Graves

A	1911–1984	Misc. Contract Books (PIN)
A	1915–1983	Mortgage Books
H	1873–1882	Newspapers (SA)
A	1899–1984	Order Book–Fiscal (IN from 1909, EX 1945–58)
U	1879–1903	Order Books
U	1873–1888	Order Books (EX 1880–82)
A	1873–1977	Order Books (IN)
U	1839–1893	Orders–Circuit Court
A	1885	Poll Books
U	1885	Poll Books
A	1875	Poll Books
H	1887	Tax Book
A	1840–1892	Tax Book (EX 1863–64, 1868–86)
H	1840–1867	Tax Book (EX 1863–64)
H	1852–1878	Vital Statistics (SY)
U	1884–1925	Will Books
H	1884–1973	Will Books (IN)
A	1884–1984	Will Books (IN)

BRECKINRIDGE COUNTY

Hardinsburg 40143
502-756-2246

Public Library	Historical Society	Breckinridge County Archives
248 Main Street	P.O. Box 498	County Courthouse
Hardinsburg 40143	Hardinsburg 40143	P.O. Box 538
502-756-2323		Hardinsburg 40143
		502-756-2246

This county was formed in 1800 from Hardin County. On 28 December 1864, guerrillas set fire to the courthouse, but citizens saved both the building and its records. It burned again in February of 1958 with some loss of records.

A	1894–1983	Church Records–Baptist
A	1894–1983	Church Records–Corinth Baptist
A	1881–1985	Criminal Order Books (IN from 1886)
A	1799–1987	Deed Books
U	1800–1880	Deed Books
A	1800–1987	Deed Books–General Cross Index
A	1800–1816	Deed Books (IN)
U	1800–1911	Deed Index
U	1800–1861	Deeds–Commissioners
A	1852–1875	Guardian Bonds (IN from 1856)
U	1852–1875	Guardian Bonds
A	1852–1914	Marriage Bonds (IN)
U	1852–1914	Marriage Bonds
A	1858–1879	Marriage Register

U	1858-1879	Marriage Register
H	?-?	Military Records—Revolutionary and 1812 Pensions (147)
H	?-?	Military Records—Veterans Graves
A	1892-1985	Minute Books (Cloverport)
A	1969-1983	Minute Books (Irvington)
A	1964-1973	Minute Books—Water and Sewer Commission (Cloverport)
A	1878-1903	Newspapers—*Breckinridge News*
H	1885-1949	Newspapers (SA)
A	1803-1941	Order Books (IN from 1809)
A	1800-1803	Order Books—Quarter Sessions (IN)
A	1926-1954	Order Books—Cloverport
H	1800-1835	Tax Book (EX 1810, 1818, 1830, 1832, 1836)
A	1800-1839	Tax Book (EX 1810, 1818, 1832, 1836)
H	1837-1875	Tax Book (EX 1840-48, 1874)
A	1849-1892	Tax Book (EX 1876-78, 1880-81)
A	1935-1971	Tax Book—Cloverport
H	1852-1904	Vital Statistics (SY)
U	1800-1965	Will Books
A	1800-1965	Will Books (IN)

BULLITT COUNTY

Shepherdsville 40165
502-543-2513

Ridgway Memorial Library	Genealogical Society	Historical Society
Second and Walnut Streets	Box 960	P.O. Box 317
Shepherdsville 40165	Shepherdsville 40165	Brooks 40109
502-543-7675		

This county was formed in 1797 from Jefferson and Nelson counties. Shepherdsville, one of the oldest towns in Kentucky, was settled ca. 1781 and formerly known as Mud Garrison. It was located on the Wilderness Road from Fort Harrod to Louisville and the Falls of the Ohio.

U	1854-1856	Birth and Death Certificates
A	1865-1894	Civil Case Files Index—Circuit Court
A	1853-1980	Civil Case Files Off Docket Index
A	1797-1864	Civil Case Files—Common Law and Chancery Index
A	1803-1957	Civil Case Files—Equity Index
A	1874-1957	Civil Case Files—Ordinary Index
A	1797-1864	Civil Case Files—Ordinary Index
A	1969-1977	Civil Order Books Circuit Court (IN)
A	1867-1977	Criminal Case Files General Index
A	1969-1977	Criminal Order Books—Circuit Court (IN)
A	1820-1842	Deed Books—Circuit Court
A	1797-1803	Deed Books—Quarter Sessions (IN)

U	1797–1901	Deed Books
A	1797–1902	Deed Books
A	1966–1983	Deed Books
A	1797–1910	Deed Books General Cross Index
U	1820–1842	Deed Books—Circuit Court
U	1797–1909	Deed Index
H	1774–1934	Genealogy—Hogland Oakes Family
A	1872–1881	Marriage Bonds (IN)
A	1907–1911	Marriage Bonds (IN)
U	1872–1911	Marriage Bonds
H	1797–1823	Marriage Licenses
A	1824–1911	Marriage Licenses and Certificates
U	1797–1911	Marriage Licenses and Certificates
H	1824–1897	Marriage Licenses and Certificates
H	1797–1911	Marriage Records
A	1797–1830	Marriage Register
U	1797–1872	Marriage Register
A	1797–1872	Marriage Register (IN)
A	1882–1907	Marriage Register (IN)
H	1787–1861	Military Muster Rolls by Cpl. Reuben Field
H	?–?	Military Records—Revolutionary and 1812 Pensions (34)
H	1876	Newspapers—Articles
U	1797–1900	Order Books
A	1797–1900	Order Books (PIN)
H	1797–1847	Tax Book (EX 1828–29, 1832, 1836, 1843)
A	1797–1892	Tax Book (EX 1828–29, 1836, 1843, 1848–49, 1852–58)
H	1850–1875	Tax Book (EX 1852–58)
H	1852–1907	Vital Statistics (SY)
U	1796–1935	Will Books
H	1796–1935	Will Books (IN)
A	1796–1935	Will Books (IN)

BUTLER COUNTY

Morgantown 42261
502-526-5676

Public Library	Historical and Genealogical Society
P.O. Box 247	P.O. Box 435
125 Ohio Street	Morgantown 42261
Morgantown 42261	
502-526-4722	

Butler County was formed in 1810 from parts of Logan and Ohio counties. In 1873, a new courthouse was built to replace the county's first courthouse, which burned in 1872.

A	1840–1908	Case Files Index—Circuit Court
A	1810–1897	Civil Case Files—Circuit Court Index
A	1810–1858	Civil Case Files—Equity
A	1810–1890	Civil Order Book—Circuit Court (IN)
A	1882–1885	Commissioners Report of Sales Books
A	1811–1948	Criminal Case Files—Circuit Court—Index
U	1810–1876	Deed Books
A	1809–1876	Deed Books—Index
A	1839–1841	Deed Books—Commissioners
U	1795–1883	Deed Index
A	1811–1847	Docket Book—Circuit Court
A	1821–1841	Execution Book—Circuit Court
A	1856–1882	Guardian Bonds (IN)
U	1856–1882	Guardian Bonds
A	1851–1905	Judgment Book—Circuit Court (IN)
A	1855–1905	Judgments from Inferior Courts (IN)
U	1856–1878	Marriage Bonds
A	1894–1897	Marriage Certificate Book (IN)
A	1856–1983	Marriage License and Bonds (IN)
A	1814–1984	Marriage Record Book—General Index
A	1814–1903	Marriage Register
U	1823–1893	Marriage Register
A	1814–1865	Marriage Register (IN)
U	1814–1929	Marriage Index
H	?–?	Military Records—Revolutionary and 1812 Pensions (98)
H	?–?	Military Records—Veterans Graves
A	1860–1875	Militia Book (1860, 1863, and 1875)
A	1848–1898	Minute Book—Circuit Court
A	1880–1940	Newspapers—*Green River Republican* (SI)
H	1873–1908	Newspapers (SA)
A	1874–1880	Order Book—Common Pleas (IN)
A	1881–1893	Order Book—Criminal (IN)
A	1859–1864	Order Book—Equity and Criminal (IN)
U	1810–1880	Order Books
A	1810–1880	Order Books (IN)
A	1843–1884	Processioners Book
A	1812–1843	Record Books—Circuit Court
A	1851	Record of Justices' Districts
A	1892–1905	Roster—Attorneys—Circuit Court
A	1811–1892	Tax Book (EX 1817, 1824, 1832, 1836)
H	1811–1875	Tax Book (EX 1817, 1824, 1832, 1836)
H	1853–1907	Vital Statistics (SY)
H	1812–1912	Will Books
U	1812–1912	Will Books
A	1813–1912	Will Books (IN)

CALDWELL COUNTY

Princeton 42445
502-365-6754

Public Library
114 S. Harrison Street
Princeton 42445
502-365-2884

This county was formed in 1809 from Livingston County. The first courthouse was built in 1820 from crude logs. The second courthouse, built in 1840, burned on 15 December 1864 with some loss of records.

A	1877–1914	Administrator and Guardian Settlements (IN)
A	1852–1920	Administrator Bonds
U	1852–1920	Administrator Bonds
A	1916–1984	Deed Books—General Cross Index
A	1809–1973	Deed Books—Index
A	1809–1942	Deed Index
U	1811–1913	Deed Books and Index
A	1852–1919	Guardian Bonds (IN)
U	1852–1919	Guardian Bonds
U	1822–1849	Inventory Books (EX 1832–36)
U	1850–1915	Inventory Books
A	1820–1915	Inventory Books (IN)
A	1852–1912	Marriage Bonds
U	1809–1912	Marriage Bonds
U	1808–1911	Marriage Licenses
A	1809–1850	Marriage List from Private Materials
A	1808–1911	Marriage Records
A	1809–1872	Marriage Register
H	?–?	Military Records—Revolutionary and 1812 Pensions (38)
H	?–?	Military Records—Veterans Graves
A	1865–1873	Minute Book
H	1834–1882	Newspapers (SA)
U	1801–1915	Order Books
A	1818–1915	Order Books (PIN)
A	1857–1861	Order Books—Quarterly Court
A	1829–1837	Probate Record Book
U	1877–1914	Settlements
A	1809–1892	Tax Book (EX 1831–32, 1834, 1836, 1849–80)
H	1809–1848	Tax Book (EX 1831, 1832, 1834, 1836)
H	1852–1878	Vital Statistics (SY)
U	1809–1968	Will Books
A	1809–1968	Will Books and General Index
U	1809–1962	Will Index

CALLOWAY COUNTY

Murray 42071
502-753-3923

Public Library	Pogue Library	Genealogical Society	Jackson Purchase
710 Main Street	Murray State University	1405 Main Street	Historical Society
Murray 42071	Murray 42071	Murray 42071	Rt. 2; P.O. Box 10
502-753-2288			Murray 42071

This county was formed in 1821 from Hickman County. In 1823, the first public building erected in the Jackson Purchase area was the courthouse in Wadesboro, the county seat from 1822 to 1842. In 1843, Murray became the county seat, and the original log building was moved to Murray State University where it is used as a private residence. There was a courthouse fire in 1906 that destroyed some records, according to some sources.

H	1854–?	Church Records—Disciples of Christ Church
A	1953–1977	Civil Case Files—Circuit Court Index
A	1934–1984	Deed Book—Cemeteries of Murray
U	1823–1875	Deed Books
A	1823–1956	Deed Books
U	1822–1885	Deed Index
A	1822–1956	Deed Index
H	1823–1846	Marriage Register
U	1823–1846	Marriage Register
A	1823–1846	Marriage Register and Ministers' Returns
H	?–?	Military Records—Veterans Graves
A	1914–1984	Minute Books—Murray
A	1958–1984	Minute Books—Planning Commission of Murray
H	1873–1938	Newspapers (SA)
A	1967–1984	Pension Fund of Police and Firemen of Murray
A	1823–1863	Tax Book (EX 1830, 1832, 1839, 1853–58)
A	1865–1892	Tax Book (EX 1876–78, 1881)
H	1823–1875	Tax Book (EX 1830, 1832, 1839, 1853–58, 1864)
H	1852–1907	Vital Statistics (SY)
U	1836–1885	Will Books
A	1836–1885	Will Books
A	1836–1885	Will Index

CAMPBELL COUNTY

Newport 41072   Alexandria 41001
606-292-3845   606-635-2151

Public Library	Campbell/Pendleton	Northern Kentucky	Heritage League and
Fourth and Monmouth	Historical Group	University	Historical Society
Newport 41071	37 Homestead Place	Highland Heights	212 Linden Avenue
606-291-4770	Ft. Thomas 41075	41076	Southgate 41071
		606-572-5456	
		606-572-6312	
		(Reference)	

This county was formed in 1795 from parts of Harrison, Mason, and Scott counties. The first court was held in Wilmington (now Burlington, in Boone County) in 1794 and later relocated to Newport. Both Newport and Alexandria serve as county seats, and there are records at both locations. Check both series of records when researching this county. Because of overlap in the courthouse records, some duplicate listings of records may appear in the list below.

A	1863–1920	Administrator and Executor Bonds (vols. 3–4)
A	1795–1897	Administrator and Executor Bonds Index (vols. 1–3)
U	1795–1897	Administrator and Executor Bonds
U	1863–1920	Administrator and Executor Bonds
A	1874–1913	Administrator Bonds
U	1874–1913	Administrator Bonds—Second Series
A	1974–1977	Affidavit of Descent—Alexandria
A	1974–1976	Articles of Incorporation
H	1906	Birth Records—Newport
A	1950–1973	Building Inspectors Reports—Cold Springs
A	1974–1986	Building Permits—Cold Springs
A	1795–1934	Case Files—Index
A	1795–1802	Case Files—Quarterly Court
H	?–?	Cemetery Records—Evergreen, St. Stephens, etc.
A	1834–1903	City Directories—Various Cities
H	1884–1905	Deaths—Newport
H	1916–1928	Deaths—Newport
A	1795–1856	Deed Books
U	1795–1911	Deed Books
A	1858–1909	Deed Books
A	1858–1911	Deed Books
A	1863–1885	Deed Books
A	1885–1912	Deed Books
A	1795–1856	Deed Books and Index—Alexandria
A	1863–1912	Deed Books (IN)
A	1854–1911	Deed Books—Second Series—Alexandria
U	1863–1912	Deed Books—Second Series
A	1974–1977	Deed Books—Alexandria
A	1886–1905	Deed Books—Newport

A	1974-1977	Deed Books—Newport
U	1795-1896	Deed Index
U	1865-1873	Deed Index—Second Series
A	1974-1977	Encumbrances
U	1870-1928	Executors and Administrators List
A	1863-1918	Executors Bonds
U	1863-1918	Executors Bonds
H	?-?	Genealogy—Taylor, Marshall, etc.
A	1863-1912	Guardian Bonds
U	1863-1912	Guardian Bonds
U	1869-1947	Guardian Bonds
A	1863-1912	Guardian Bonds (vols. 1-8)
A	1863-1945	Guardian Bonds Index
A	1878-1916	Guardian Bonds and Settlements
U	1869-1929	Guardian—Administrator and Executor Bonds Index
H	1829-1880	Idiot Returns
A	1941-1965	Incorporation of City—Cold Springs
A	1814-1963	Inventories and Sales—Index
U	1814-1967	Inventories and Sales—Index
A	1876-1912	Inventories and Settlements
U	1876-1912	Inventories and Settlements
A	1974-1976	Inventories and Settlements
H	1780-1835	Land Records—Forfeited Lands, Transfers, etc.
A	1795-1800	Marriage Bonds
U	1795-1913	Marriage Bonds
A	1800-1911	Marriage Bonds
A	1876-1901	Marriage Bonds
A	1907-1911	Marriage Bonds
U	1854-1911	Marriage Bonds—Second Series
A	1855-1912	Marriage Bonds, Consents, and Registers
A	1879	Marriage Bonds—County
U	1900-1914	Marriage Certificates
A	1854-1911	Marriage Index
U	1830-1900	Marriage Records
U	1855-1912	Marriage Records—Second Series
U	1795-1840	Marriage Records by Myrtice Kraft
A	1830-1851	Marriages
A	1836-1914	Marriages
A	1795-1914	Marriages and Index
U	1795-1914	Marriages Index
U	1855-1912	Marriages Index—Second Series
H	?-?	Military Records—Revolutionary and 1812 Pensions (428)
H	?-?	Military Records—Revolutionary and 1812 Pensions
H	?-?	Military Records—Veterans Graves
A	1870-1984	Minute Book (Bellevue)
A	1870-1896	Minute Book Circuit Court—Alexandria
A	1974-1976	Minute Book—Public Parks—Newport

U	1870-1896	Minute Books
A	1870-1984	Minute Books—Bellevue
A	1941-1986	Minute Books—Cold Springs
A	1951-1986	Minute Books—Crestview Hills
A	1962-1985	Minute Books—City of Villa Hills
A	1973-1976	Minutes—Public Properties Corporation—Alexandria
A	1975-1986	Minutes—Supplemental Boards—Cold Springs
U	1802-1831	Misc. Records—Depositions, Deeds, Wills, etc.
A	1974-1977	Misc. Book—Newport
A	1974-1977	Mortgage Book
H	1859-1900	Newspapers (SA)
A	1960-1985	Oaths of Office—Cold Springs
A	1951	Order Book—Alexandria
A	1974-1977	Order Book—Newport
U	1815-1914	Order Books
A	1863-1915	Order Books (vols. 1-9)
A	1795-1914	Order Books (vols. A-14)
A	1895-1915	Order Books (vols. 10-16)
U	1863-1915	Order Books—Second Series
A	1888-1968	Ordinance Books—Bellevue
A	1888-1968	Ordinance Books—Bellevue
A	1941-1985	Ordinances (IN, Cold Springs)
A	1950-1986	Resolutions—Cold Springs
A	1962-1985	Resolutions Index—Cold Springs
U	1879-1918	Settlements
A	1879-1892	Tax Book
A	1795-1879	Tax Book (EX 1810 1831-32)
H	1795-1837	Tax Book (EX 1810, 1831-32)
H	1839-1875	Tax Book (EX part of 1840, 1847, 1872)
A	1799-1984	Tax Book (Villa Hills)
H	1852-1907	Vital Statistics (SY)
U	1794-1926	Will Books
A	1976	Will Books—Alexandria
A	1887-1895	Will Books (IN)
U	1863-1913	Will Books—Second Series (vols. 1-8)
A	1794-1926	Will Books—Index
U	1863-1913	Wills Index—Second Series (vols. 1-37)

CARLISLE COUNTY

Bardwell 42023
502-628-3233

Ballard/Carlisle/Livingston County Library
Mailing Address:
P.O. Box 428
Bardwell 42023
Physical Location:
Wickliffe,
502-335-3460

Historical and Genealogical Society
P.O. Box 212
Wickliffe 42087

This county was formed in May of 1886 from part of Ballard County. The county's first courthouse was completed in 1887 and only replaced after a courthouse fire on 22 October 1980 that destroyed some of the county tax books.

A	1885–1976	Case Files Index—Circuit Court
A	1953–1977	Complaint—Order and Judgment—Circuit Court (IN)
A	1886–1977	Criminal Order Books (IN)
A	1886–1969	Deed Books—General Cross Index
A	1886–1984	Marriage Record Book (IN)
A	1886–1907	Marriage Record Book—Blacks (IN)
A	1886–1915	Marriage Records
H	1886–1937	Marriage Register
U	1886–1937	Marriage Register
A	1886–1976	Marriage Register (IN)
H	?–?	Military Records—Veterans Graves
H	1879–1882	Newspapers (SA)
A	1893–1962	Order Books—Circuit Court (IN)
A	1886–1892	Order Books—Common Pleas (IN)
A	1886–1892	Tax Book
H	1901–1907	Vital Statistics—1901, 1904, and 1907 (No Births)
A	1886–1927	Will Books (IN)

CARROLL COUNTY

Carrollton 41008
502-732-4487

Public Library
136 Court Street
Carrollton 41008
502-732-6352

Port William Historical Society
311 Park Avenue
Carrollton 41008

When the county was formed in 1838 from parts of Gallatin, Henry, and Trimble counties, Port William was renamed Carrollton. The present courthouse was built in 1884.

H	1910–1916	Business Records—Burley Tobacco Company
H	1830–1902	Business Records—Smith, Tailor, Parker
H	1859–1985	Cemetery Books—Oddfellows Lodge
H	1850–1929	Church Records—Ghent Baptist Church
H	1795–1836	Deed Books
A	1795–1885	Deed Books
U	1795–1885	Deed Books
A	1795–1965	Deed Index
U	1838–1965	Deed Index—Grantors and Grantees
A	1931–1933	Lease Book
A	1837–1912	Marriage Bonds
A	1837–1938	Marriage Bonds (IN)
U	1837–1912	Marriage Bonds
H	1837–1912	Marriage Bonds Books
H	1837–1938	Marriage Index—Brides and Grooms
U	1837–1938	Marriage Index—Brides and Grooms
H	1836–1911	Marriage Licenses, Certificates, and Returns
U	1840–1911	Marriage Licenses, Certificates, and Returns
A	1836–1911	Marriage Records (in alphabetized order)
H	?–?	Military Records—Revolutionary and 1812 Pensions (61)
H	?–?	Military Records—Veterans Graves
A	1967	Newspapers—*Carroll News Democrat*—Special Edition
A	1852–1855	Newspapers—*Carroll Times and Courier*
H	1843–1937	Newspapers (SA)
U	1838–1881	Order Books
A	1838–1881	Order Books (IN)
H	1857–1874	Private Records—Treasurer's Book of Masons
H	1840–1875	Tax Book
A	1840–1892	Tax Book (EX 1876–78)
H	1852–1878	Vital Statistics (SY)
H	1838–1920	Will Books
U	1838–1920	Will Books
A	1838–1921	Will Books (IN)

CARTER COUNTY

Grayson 41143
606-474-5188

Carter was formed in 1838 from parts of Greenup and Lawrence counties. The present courthouse is the county's second and was finished in 1907.

A	1914–1940	Civil Case Files—General Cross Index
A	1838–1977	Civil Case Files—Circuit Court (IN)
A	1876–1977	Criminal Order Books (IN)
U	1838–1867	Deed Books
A	1838–1958	Deed Books—General Cross Index
A	1879–1929	Deed Books—Commissioners (IN)

U	1838–1919	Deed Index
H	1829–1880	Idiot Returns
H	1838–1866	Marriage Bonds
A	1838–1866	Marriage Bonds
U	1838–1866	Marriage Bonds
H	1838–1875	Marriage Books
A	1882–1957	Marriage Books—General Cross Index
H	1822–1857	Marriage Index
U	1883–1920	Marriage Index
A	1838–1875	Marriage Register and Ministers Returns (IN)
U	1838–1875	Marriages
A	1863–1864	Military Discharges (at end of Deed Book 7)
A	1922–1986	Minute Books—Grayson (IN from 1931)
A	1956–1978	Minute Books—Utility Commissions—Grayson
H	1873–1946	Newspapers (SA)
A	1893–1910	Newspapers—Various Papers (SI)
A	1838–1977	Order Book—Circuit Court (IN)
A	1852–1869	Order Books
U	1854–1864	Orders
A	1976–1985	School Census (Books 20–31)
A	1896–1916	School Census (EX 1901–05 1907 1912) (PIN)
A	1918–1934	School Census (EX 1919 1921 1931) (Books 1–19)
A	1897–1901	School Superintendent Record Book
A	1839–1892	Tax Book (EX 1840, 1847–51, 1876–78)
H	1839–1875	Tax Book (EX 1840, 1847–51)
H	1852–1907	Vital Statistics (SY)
U	1835–1886	Will Books
A	1840–1886	Will Books—Includes Inventories and Bills
H	1835–1886	Will Books (IN)

CASEY COUNTY

Liberty 42539
606-787-6471

Public Library	Bicentennial Heritage Corp.
P.O. Box A	Box 574
Rt. 1	Liberty 42539
Liberty 42539	
606-787-9381	

Casey County was formed in 1807 from Lincoln County. There have been three courthouses; the third and current courthouse was designed in 1887 and completed in 1889.

U	1852–1900	Administrator Bonds
A	1852–1900	Administrator Bonds (PIN)
A	1870–1890	Appraisements—Inventory and Settlement Books

H	1820	Church Records–Association of Baptists Minutes
A	1851–1986	Civil Case Files–Plaintiff Index
A	1851–1984	Civil Case Files Index–Defendants
A	1894–1939	Criminal Case Files–Defendant Index
A	1889–1977	Criminal Order Books (IN)
A	1877–1905	Deed Book–Commissioners (IN)
U	1807–1902	Deed Books
A	1807–1986	Deed Books
U	1807–1962	Deed Index–Grantors and Grantees
A	1807–1962	Deed Index
U	1892–1941	Deeds of Partition
A	1892–1946	Deeds of Partition (IN)
U	1871–1905	Deeds–Commissioners
A	1865–1896	Guardian Bonds (PIN)
U	1865–1892	Guardian Bonds
U	1878–1890	Inventory Books
A	1872–1899	Marriage Bonds
U	1872–1905	Marriage Bonds
U	1807–1935	Marriage Index for Register
U	1807–1911	Marriage Register
U	1807–1911	Marriage Register
A	1807–1911	Marriage Register (PIN)
A	1807–1935	Marriage Registers–Cross Index
H	?–?	Military Records–Revolutionary and 1812 Pensions (102)
H	?–?	Military Records–Veterans Graves
H	1834–1879	Newspapers (SA)
A	1807–1977	Order Book–Circuit Court (IN)
U	1807–1840	Order Books
U	1817–1901	Order Books
A	1817–1901	Order Books (PIN)
U	1825–1902	Order Books–Circuit Court
A	1893–1905	Settlements
U	1893–1904	Settlements
A	1931–1939	Tax Book
A	1967–1977	Tax Book
H	1807–1875	Tax Book (EX 1818, 1832, 1834, 1836, 1839, 1863)
A	1807–1862	Tax Book (EX 1818, 1832, 1836, 1839)
A	1864–1899	Tax Book (EX 1867–78, 1893–97)
H	1852–1907	Vital Statistics (SY)
H	1809–1936	Will Books
U	1809–1936	Will Books
A	1809–1936	Will Books (IN)

CHRISTIAN COUNTY

Hopkinsville 42240
502-887-4105

Hoptown-Christian County Library 1101 Bethel Street Hopkinsville 42240 502-887-4263	Genealogical Society 6445 Pine Lane Hopkinsville 42240	Historical Society 3700 Bradshaw Pike Hopkinsville 42240

This county was formed in 1797 from part of Logan County. The courthouse burned in mid-December of 1864, and some records may have been destroyed. The current courthouse was built in 1869.

U	1875–1917	Administrator and Executor Settlements
A	1922–1956	Case Files—Criminal (IN)
A	1874–1887	Civil Case Files (IN)
A	1888–1977	Civil Case Files (IN)
A	1929–1953	Civil Order Books—Equity (IN)
A	1880–1977	Civil Order Books (IN)
A	1876–1977	Criminal Order Books (IN)
A	1797–1841	Deed Books
A	1797–1912	Deed Books
U	1797–1912	Deed Books
A	1797–1915	Deed Index
U	1797–1915	Deed Index
U	1827–1912	Guardian Bonds
A	1824–1912	Guardian Bonds and Settlements
A	1797–1914	Marriage Bonds
U	1797–1914	Marriage Bonds
U	1818–1944	Marriage Index—Grooms
A	1818–1841	Marriage Index
A	1797–1911	Marriage Licenses
U	1797–1911	Marriage Licenses
H	?–?	Military Records—Revolutionary and 1812 Pensions (594)
H	?–?	Military Records—Veterans Graves
A	1894–1981	Minute Books—Russellville City Clerk (IN)
H	1835–1944	Newspapers (SA)
A	1807–1886	Order Book—Circuit Court (IN)
A	1876–1885	Order Book—Commonwealth Causes (IN)
U	1797–1915	Order Books
A	1835–1915	Order Books
A	1875–1917	Settlements
A	1797–1848	Tax Book (EX 1818, 1832, 1834, 1840–47)
H	1797–1848	Tax Book (EX 1818, 1832, 1834, 1840–47)
H	1855–1875	Tax Book (EX 1858–67, 1869–74)
A	1855–1892	Tax Book (EX 1869–74, 1876–78)
H	1852–1907	Vital Statistics (SY)

A	1797–1921	Will Books
U	1797–1921	Will Books
A	1797–1910	Will Books (IN)
U	1797–1910	Will Index
A	1797–1910	Will Index

CLARK COUNTY

Winchester 40391
606-745-0280

Public Library
109-111 S. Main Street
Winchester 40391
606-744-5661

Historical Society
122 Belmont Avenue
Winchester 40391

This county was formed in 1793 from Fayette and Bourbon counties. At that time, Clark County included all the present counties of Montgomery, Bath, Menifee, Powell, Wolfe, Harlan, and Letcher; as well as the greater portion of what is now Breathitt, Perry, and Knot; large portions of Estill, Lee, Leslie, Morgan, and Magoffin; and small portions of Pike, Floyd, Knox, and Nicholas. The current Winchester courthouse was built from 1853 to 1855. Henry Clay made his first and last speech there. Clark County was closely associated with the establishment of Boonesboro; therefore, also check Madison County records.

U	1822–1863	Church Records—Friendship Records—Minutes
U	1793–1903	Church Records—Lublegrud Records—Minutes
A	1793–1903	Church Records—Lublegrud Baptist Church
A	1802–1805	Church Records—North District—Baptist
A	1780–1833	Church Records—Providence Church
U	1780–1833	Church Records—Providence Church Proceedings
A	1793–1903	Church Records
A	1797–1801	Deed Books—Quarter Court Sessions (IN)
A	1793–1865	Deed Books
U	1793–1865	Deed Books
A	1803–1807	Deed Books—Circuit Court
U	1793–1959	Deed Index
A	1793–1959	Deed Index
U	1795–1814	Depositions
U	?–?	Family Records—William Haggard Diary
H	1829–1880	Idiot Returns
A	1956–1982	Licensing Board—Winchester Clerk
H	1784–1862	Maps—Early Settlements—Bush, etc. (four maps)
A	1793–1850	Marriage Bonds
A	1793–1850	Marriage List
A	1793–1850	Marriage List
U	1793–1800	Marriage Records

A	1829–1853	Marriage Returns (IN)
U	1793–1850	Marriages
H	?–?	Military Records—Confederates from Winchester
H	1787–1861	Military Records—Muster Rolls of Various Units
H	?–?	Military Records—Revolutionary and 1812 Pensions (652)
H	?–?	Military Records—Veterans Graves
A	1794–1983	Minute Books—Clerk of Winchester (IN)
A	1863–1874	Minute/Order Books
H	1822–1920	Newspapers (SA)
H	1878–1929	Newspapers—*Winchester Democrat* (SA)
A	1793–1798	Order Books—Quarter Court Sessions
A	1793–1853	Order Books
U	1801–1874	Order Books
U	1830–1852	Order Books
A	1981–1983	Order Books—City Clerk of Winchester
A	1895–1983	Ordinance Book—City Clerk of Winchester
U	1875	Poll Books
A	1875	Poll Books
H	1794–1842	Processioners Record Book—Depositions (IN)
A	1795–1842	Processioners Record Book (IN)
U	1805–1857	Processioners Record Book
A	1954–1974	Public Officials Bonds—Winchester
H	1793–1798	Quarter Session Clerk Record Book (IN)
A	1950–1985	Resolution Book—Clerk of Winchester (IN)
H	1793–1839	Tax Book (EX 1798, 1808, 1832)
A	1792–1892	Tax Book (EX 1798, 1832, 1840–50, 1855, 1875–80)
H	1850–1874	Tax Book (EX 1855–56, 1874)
A	1862–1892	Tax Book—Blacks (EX 1875–80)
H	1852–1904	Vital Statistics (SY)
A	1793–1850	Will Abstracts—Historical Society
H	1793–1865	Will Books
U	1793–1868	Will Books (IN)
A	1793–1868	Will Books (IN)
A	1793–1854	Will Index
U	1793–1854	Will Index and Settlements
H	1793–1854	Will Index and Settlements

CLAY COUNTY

Manchester 40962
606-598-2544

Public Library
211 Bridge Street
Manchester 40962
606-598-2617

Genealogical and Historical Society
P.O. Box 394
Manchester 40962

This county was formed in 1807 from parts of Floyd, Knox, and Madison counties. Areas in Clay have been used to form parts of Perry, Laurel, Leslie, Breathitt, Owsley, and Jackson. On 20 January 1936 there was a courthouse fire.

A	1808-1906	Administrator and Executor List
A	1852-1887	Administrator Bonds (IN)
A	?-?	Civil Case Files Off Docket Index
A	1810-1812	Commissioners Tax Book
A	1823	Commissioners Tax Book
A	1934-1956	Criminal Case Files Index
A	?-?	Criminal Case Files Off Docket General Index
A	1807-1986	Deed Books (IN)
A	1852-1916	Guardian Bonds (IN)
A	1879-1909	Guardian List Book
H	1829-1880	Idiot Returns
A	1878-1933	Inventory and Appraisements Books
A	1855-1953	Inventory, Appraisement, Sale, and Settlement Books
A	1875-1921	Marriage Bonds (PIN)
H	1875-1921	Marriage Bonds
A	1806-1923	Marriage Records—Groom Index (SY)
A	1807-1922	Marriage Records (SY)
A	1807-1851	Marriage Register
A	1874-1903	Marriage Register and Returns
A	1851-1881	Marriage Register (IN)
H	1807-1851	Marriage Register—Certificates and Licenses
H	1867-1872	Marriages
H	?-?	Military Records—Revolutionary and 1812 Pensions(130)
H	?-?	Military Records—Veterans Graves
A	1853	Militia Roll—Upper Horse Creek
H	1876-1954	Newspapers (SA)
A	1809-1886	Order Books (PIN)
A	1855-1886	Order Books (PIN)
A	1875-1931	Settlements
A	1836-1838	Surveys Recorded—County Clerk
A	1807-1879	Tax Book (EX 1810, 1812-25, 1827, 1832, 1839, 1876-78)
A	1883-1892	Tax Book (EX 1891)
H	1807-1875	Tax Book (EX 1810, 1827, 1832, 1839)
A	1814	Tax Book—Delinquent and Solvent

A	1880	Vital Statistics
H	1852–1907	Vital Statistics (SY)
H	1830–1965	Will Books
A	1826–1965	Will Books (IN)

CLINTON COUNTY

Albany 42602
606-387-5943

Public Library
Burkesville Road
Albany 42602
606-387-5989

Historical Society
104 Cumberland
Albany 42602

This county was formed in 1836 from Cumberland and Wayne counties. The courthouse was burned once during the Civil War by guerillas in 1864, and most of the old county records were lost. It burned in 1980 and again lost some records.

A	1864–1910	Administrator Bonds
U	1864–1910	Administrator Bonds
U	1872–1907	Administrator Settlements (IN)
A	1872–1907	Administrator Settlements (IN)
H	1804–1942	Church Records—Baptist
A	1864–1969	Civil Order Books—Circuit Court (PIN)
A	1865–1977	Civil Orders (IN)
A	1976–1977	Civil Orders (IN)
U	1864–1907	Deed Books
A	1853–1986	Deed Books (IN)
U	1864–1931	Deed Index—Grantors and Grantees
U	1878–1915	Deeds—Commissioners
A	1878–1915	Deeds—Commissioners
A	1974–1980	Financial Statements Book—County Court
A	1864–1915	Guardian Bonds
U	1864–1915	Guardian Bonds
A	1871–1913	Guardian Settlements
A	1932–1960	Guardian Settlements
U	1871–1913	Guardian Settlements
A	1865–1977	Indictments Index
A	1871–1913	Inventories and Sales
U	1871–1913	Inventories and Sales
A	1874–1896	Land Book
U	1874–1896	Land Book
A	1877–1980	Lease Book (IN from 1917)
A	1978–1980	Leases General Index
A	1878–1980	Leases Index
A	1972–1980	Marriage Bonds

U	1859-1902	Marriage Bonds (Black 1860-80 bonds not filmed)
A	1866-1869	Marriage Bonds—Blacks and Mulattoes
A	1918-1972	Marriage Bonds (IN)
A	1859-1934	Marriage Bonds (PIN)
H	1864-1958	Marriage Index and Register
A	1864-1958	Marriage Index and Register
U	1864-1958	Marriage Index to Bonds
A	1859-1902	Marriage Register
H	1865-1885	Marriage Register
U	1865-1885	Marriage Register
H	1859-1902	Marriages
H	?-?	Military Records—Revolutionary and 1812 Pensions (174)
A	1919-1979	Military Records—Veterans Discharge Book
H	?-?	Military Records—Veterans Graves
A	1872-1931	Mortgage Books—Real Estate (PIN)
A	1900-1974	Mortgage Books (UNIN)
A	1974-1980	Mortgage Books—Real Estate
A	1978-1980	Mortgages—General Index
H	1868-1880	Newspapers (SA)
U	1864-1902	Order Books
A	1864-1980	Order Books (IN)
A	1889-1974	Order Books—Fiscal Court
U	1864-1908	Order Books—Circuit Court
A	1864-1908	Order Books—Circuit Court (IN)
A	1902-1966	Order Books—Circuit Court Commonwealth (PIN)
A	1975-1980	Order Books—Fiscal Court
A	1872-1980	Probate Records—Settlements (UNIN)
A	1948-1980	Sheriffs Settlements Book
A	1874-1945	Suits Off Docket Cross Index
A	1837-1862	Tax Book
A	1864-1875	Tax Book
A	1879-1892	Tax Book
H	1837-1875	Tax Book (EX 1863)
H	1852-1904	Vital Statistics (SY)
H	1863-1943	Will Books
U	1863-1943	Will Books
A	1863-1980	Will Books

CRITTENDEN COUNTY

Marion 42064
502-965-3403

Public Library	Historical Society
204 West Carlisle Street	P.O. Box 25
Marion 42064	Marion 42064
502-965-3354	

Marion was called Oxford when Crittenden was formed in 1842 from part of Livingston County. Marion became the county seat in 1844. Civil War guerrillas, on 25 January 1865, burned the courthouse. Some of the county records have been reported lost in this fire. A second fire in May of 1870 also destroyed some records.

U	1842–1878	Administrator and Executor Bonds
A	1843–1876	Administrator and Executor Bonds
A	1843–1984	Deed Books (IN to 1913)
U	1842–1913	Deed Books
A	1842–1987	Deed Books (IN)
A	1877–1962	Deed Books—Commissioners (UNIN)
U	1842–1968	Deed Index—Grantors and Grantees
A	1842–1928	Guardian Bonds
U	1878–1928	Guardian Bonds
U	1853–1871	Guardian Bonds
U	1842–1878	Guardian Lists
A	1842–1913	Inventory Books
U	1852–1924	Inventory Books
U	1842–1913	Inventory Books
A	1842–1914	Marriage Bonds
H	1853–1914	Marriage Bonds
U	1853–1914	Marriage Bonds
A	1948–1958	Marriage Bonds
U	1842–1911	Marriage Licenses
A	1858–1911	Marriage Licenses
H	1842–1911	Marriage Licenses and Bonds
A	1842–1910	Marriage Register
H	1842–1910	Marriage Register
U	1842–1910	Marriage Register
H	?–?	Military Records—Veterans Graves
A	1879–1900	Newspapers—*Crittenden Press* (SI)
H	1868–1882	Newspapers (SA)
H	1852–1857	Newspapers—*Marion Post*
A	1921–1973	Oil and Gas Leases (UNIN)
A	1843–1915	Order Books
U	1843–1968	Order Books
A	1913–1980	Plats Recorded in Deed Book
U	1843–1919	Settlement Books

A	1843–1919	Settlement Books
H	1842–1875	Tax Book
A	1843–1875	Tax Book
A	1879–1892	Tax Book
H	1852–1907	Vital Statistics (SY)
A	1843–1968	Will Books
H	1843–1968	Will Books
A	1962–1980	Will Books (UNIN)

CUMBERLAND COUNTY

Burkesville 42717
502-864-3726

Public Library
P.O. Box 440
114 W. Hill Street
Burkesville 42717
502-864-2207

This county was formed in 1799 from Green County. Burkesville was laid out in 1798 and originally given the name Cumberland Crossing. Its name was changed about twenty years later to Burkesville. The courthouse burned on 3 January 1865 and again on 3 December 1933, with loss of records.

A	1875–1931	Administrator Settlements
U	1875–1931	Administrator Settlements
H	?–?	Bible Records
H	1882–1901	Business Records—Dr. Hutchins' Accounts
H	?–?	Cemetery Records—Family Cemeteries
H	?–?	Cemetery Records Index
H	1800–1850	Census Index
H	1860–1880	Census Abstract
H	1820–1823	Circuit Court Records Index
A	1874–1955	Civil Case File—Defendant Index Circuit Court
A	1874–1934	Civil Case File—Plaintiff Index Circuit Court
H	1820–1889	Court Records (scattered)
U	1799–1901	Deed Books
A	1799–1986	Deed Books (IN)
H	1799–1867	Deed Books (IN)
U	1799–1934	Deed Index—Grantors and Grantees
A	1815–1912	Genealogical Records—Misc.
A	1815–1912	Genealogy—Bibles, Cemeteries, Wills, etc.
H	?–?	Genealogy—Families South of Cumberland River
A	1875–1910	Guardian Settlements
U	1875–1910	Guardian Settlements
A	1882–1888	Marriage Bonds (IN)
A	1893–1899	Marriage Bonds (IN)

U	1882–1899	Marriage Bonds and Certificates
H	1799–1817	Marriages
H	?–?	Military Records—Revolutionary and 1812 Pensions (243)
H	?–?	Military Records—Veterans Graves
A	1962–1985	Minute Books—City Clerk—Burkesville
H	1900–1910	Newspapers—Obituaries, etc.
H	1873–1930	Newspapers (SA)
A	1934–1978	Order Book—Circuit Court (IN)
A	1982–1985	Ordinance Book—Burkesville
A	1982–1985	Resolution Book—Burkesville
A	1799–1945	Survey Records (IN)
H	1799–1945	Survey Records (IN)
U	1799–1964	Surveyor Books
A	1799–1964	Surveyor Books (IN)
A	1879–1892	Tax Book
A	1799–1857	Tax Book (1799, 1805, 1833, 1837, 1840–57 only)
H	1799–1875	Tax Book (SY)
H	1852–1907	Vital Statistics (SY)
H	1852–1862	Vital Statistics Index
U	1815–1912	Will Books
A	1815–1912	Will Books (IN)
H	1815–1912	Will Books (IN)

DAVIESS COUNTY
Owensboro 42301
502-685-8434

Public Library 450 Griffith Avenue Owensboro 42301 502-684-0211	Historical Society 450 Griffith Avenue Owensboro 42301	Society of Kentucky Pioneers 11129 Pleasant Ridge Rd. Utica 42376	West Central Kentucky Family Research Association P.O. Box 1932 Owensboro 42302

This county was formed in June of 1815 from part of Ohio County. The county seat was originally called Yellow Banks, but the name was later changed to Owensborough in 1817 and then Owensboro. There was a courthouse fire on 4 January 1865, but records had been moved to a Methodist church nearby before the fire was set.

A	1834–1852	Administrator and Guardian Bonds
U	1834–1902	Administrator Bonds
A	1834–1904	Administrator Bonds (IN from 1852)
A	1852–1853	Birth Records
A	1860	Birth Records
A	1875–1876	Birth Records
U	1852–1876	Births and Deaths
H	1810–1969	Church Records—Methodist, Baptist, Christian, etc.

A	1824–1841	Church Records—St. Lawrence Church
A	1937–1954	Civil Case Files—On Docket General Index
A	1816–1984	Civil Case Files Index
A	1875–1981	Criminal Case Files Defendant Index
A	1852–1860	Death Records
A	1875–1876	Death Records
A	1815–1901	Deed Books
U	1815–1901	Deed Books
A	1983–1985	Deed Books
A	1815–1964	Deed Books (IN)
U	1815–1964	Deed Index—Grantors and Grantees
A	1871–1902	Deeds—Commissioners
U	1871–1902	Deeds—Commissioners
A	1817–1841	Deeds—Commissioners—Circuit Court (IN)
A	1878–1904	Executor Bonds (IN)
U	1878–1904	Executor Bonds
A	1846–1901	Guardian Bonds
U	1846–1901	Guardian Bonds (EX 1868–70)
A	1815–1967	Marriage Bonds (IN)
A	1852–1909	Marriage Bonds (IN)
U	1815–1909	Marriage Bonds
U	1815–1967	Marriage Index—Grooms and Brides
H	1815–1967	Marriage Index—Grooms and Brides
H	1818–1909	Marriage Licenses and Bonds
A	1815–1853	Marriage Returns
H	?–?	Military Records—Revolutionary and 1812 Pensions (148)
H	?–?	Military Records—Veterans Graves
A	1983–1984	Misc. Book—County Court
A	1968–1969	Newspapers—*Owensboro Star*
H	1868–1882	Newspapers (SA)
U	1837–1901	Order Books
A	1837–1903	Order Books (IN from 1847)
A	1815–1901	Order Books—Circuit Court (IN)
A	1979–1983	Order Books—County Judge
A	1848–1902	Settlement Books (IN from 1861)
U	1848–1902	Settlement Books
A	1815–1892	Tax Book (EX 1832, 1838, 1873–78, 1884)
H	1815–1875	Tax Book (EX 1832, 1838, 1849)
H	1853–1874	Vital Statistics (SY)
A	1812–1909	Will Books
H	1812–1909	Will Books
U	1812–1909	Will Books
H	1815–1969	Will Index
A	1815–1969	Will Index
U	1815–1969	Will Index

EDMONSON COUNTY

Brownsville 42210
502-597-2624

Public Library
P.O. Box 219
Brownsville 42210
502-597-2146

Historical Society
Allen Hurst Farm
13790 Louisville Road
Smith Grove 42171

This county was formed in 1825 from parts of Grayson, Hart, and Warren counties. The only Edmonson courthouse built for the purpose was completed in 1873. An earlier building had been converted from an "old dwelling" and was used until 1872 when the first floor collapsed.

U	1825–1878	Deed Books
A	1825–1878	Deed Books (PIN)
U	1825–1916	Deed Index—Grantors and Grantees
A	1825–1916	Deed Index
A	1843–1876	Guardian Bonds (IN from 1853)
U	1843–1875	Guardian Bonds
A	1843–1954	Marriage Bonds (IN)
U	1843–1877	Marriage Bonds
A	1843–1877	Marriage Bonds (IN from 1865)
U	1843–1954	Marriage Index
U	1825–1907	Marriage Records
A	1825–1907	Marriage Register—Whites only (IN)
A	1825–1870	Marriage Returns
H	?–?	Military Records—Veterans Graves
H	1876–1880	Newspapers (SA)
U	1831–1876	Order Books
A	1831–1876	Order Books (IN from 1865)
A	1825–1892	Tax Book (EX 1832, 1839, 1876–78)
A	1825–1892	Tax Book—Blacks (EX 1832, 1839, 1876–78)
H	1825–1875	Tax Book (EX 1832 and 1839)
H	1852–1893	Vital Statistics (SY)
U	1826–1948	Will Books
H	1826–1948	Will Books
A	1826–1948	Will Books (IN)

ELLIOTT COUNTY

Sandy Hook 41171
606-738-5421

This county was formed in 1869 from parts of Carter, Lawrence, and Morgan counties. There was a fire in the courthouse on 19 December 1957 that destroyed some records.

U	1869–1941	Deed Books
A	1869–1978	Deed Books (IN)
U	1869–1970	Deed Index—Grantors and Grantees
H	1829–1880	Idiot Returns
A	1956–1978	Lease Book (IN)
U	1934–1963	Marriage Licenses and Certificates
A	1934–1963	Marriage Record Book (IN)
H	?–?	Military Records—Veterans Graves
A	1957–1979	Misc. Book—County Court (IN)
A	1961–1972	Mortgage Book (IN)
H	1876–1881	Newspapers (SA)
U	1902–1932	School Census
A	1902–1932	School Census Report Books (EX 1913-17, 1921-31)
H	1869–1875	Tax Book
A	1869–1892	Tax Book (EX 1876-78)
H	1874–1878	Vital Statistics
A	1958–1984	Wills

ESTILL COUNTY

Irvine 40336
606-723-5156

Public Library
246 Main Street
Irvine 40336
502-723-3030

Historical and Genealogical Society
P.O. Box 221
Ravenna 40472

Estill was formed in 1808 from parts of Clark and Madison counties. In October 1864, soldiers burned the court house, according to some sources, or burned the jail, according to others. In 1865 the courthouse collapsed and was replaced by another in 1867. The current courthouse was built in 1941.

U	1808–1870	Deed Books
A	1808–1984	Deed Books
A	1808–1885	Deed Books (IN)
U	1808–1885	Deed Index—Grantors and Grantees
A	1879–1925	Deeds—Commissioners (IN from 1906)
H	1829–1880	Idiot Returns
U	1820–1866	License Certificates
H	1808–1868	Marriage Bonds
U	1809–1817	Marriage Bonds
A	1809–1868	Marriage Bonds
U	1819–1851	Marriage Bonds
U	1840–1843	Marriage Bonds
U	1852–1869	Marriage Bonds
U	1808–1839	Marriage Bonds—Loose
A	1915–1920	Marriage Books—Blacks (IN)

A	1808–1817	Marriage Books (IN)
A	1851–1985	Marriage Books (IN)
A	1808–1857	Marriage Certificates
H	1808–1857	Marriage Certificates
U	1808–1857	Marriage Certificates
U	1852–1869	Marriage Records
A	1809–1869	Marriage Register
H	1852–1867	Marriage Register
A	1852–1962	Marriage Register (IN)
H	?–?	Military Records–Revolutionary and 1812 Pensions (29)
U	1853–1869	Minute Books–Executor Bond
A	1921–1985	Minute Books–Ravenna
A	1918–1985	Minute Books–Irvine (PIN)
A	1808–1860	Minute/Order Books
A	1927–1967	Newspapers–*Estill Herald*
H	1868–1938	Newspapers (SA)
A	1854–1908	Order Books (IN from 1884)
A	1893–1985	Order Books–Fiscal court (IN)
U	1808–1869	Order–Minutes and Records
U	1811–1867	Surveyors Land Book
A	1811–1867	Surveyors Land Book
H	1808–1875	Tax Book (EX 1810, 1828, 1832, 1838–39)
A	1808–1892	Tax Book (EX 1810, 1828, 1832, 1838–39, 1876–78)
H	1852–1878	Vital Statistics (SY)
A	1936–1972	Voter Registration Forms–Cancelled (IN)
A	1936–1972	Voter Registration Forms (in alphabetical order)
H	1808–1928	Will Books
A	1808–1982	Will Books (IN)
U	1808–1928	Will Books

FAYETTE COUNTY
Lexington 40507
606-253-3344

Public Library	Genealogical Society	University of Kentucky	Lexington Stake Family
140 E. Main Street	P.O. Box 8113	Special Collections	History Center
Lexington 40507	Lexington 40533	Margaret I. King	1789 Tates Creek Road
606-231-5500		Library North	Lexington 40502
		Lexington 40506	606-269-2722
		606-257-8611	

Fayette was formed in 1780 as one of the original Kentucky counties of Virginia. Therefore, early tax records for Fayette show up as Virginia records. Forty counties and parts of eighty others were formed from Fayette. In the early days of the county, records were kept in the homes of officials. A large portion of records was in the home of Levi Todd, the county clerk, when his home burned on 31 January 1803. Most records were destroyed. The legible records remaining were copied by a special committee. A second fire on 14 May 1897 also destroyed some early records including quarter session records and deeds. Some of these were rerecorded, and there is an existing index.

H	1906–1910	Birth Records—Lexington
H	1888–1926	Birth Records—Lexington (IN)
A	1794–1796	Burned Records (IN)
H	?–?	Burned Records (IN)
U	?–?	Burned Records—Reconstructions
A	1867–1941	Causes—Index to Commonwealth Causes
U	1852–1903	Commissioner's Book
A	1886–1902	Death Records
H	1894–1910	Death Records—Burial Permits—Lexington
H	1898–1907	Death Records—Burial Transits—Lexington
U	1803–1819	Deed Book—Circuit Court
U	1794–1802	Deed Book—District Court (SY)
U	1794–1954	Deed Books
A	1970–1984	Deed Books (vols. 1000–1342)
A	1782–1959	Deed Books (vols. A–V 666)
A	1794–1807	Deed Books—Circuit Court
A	1803–1819	Deed Books—Circuit Court
A	1794–1802	Deed Books—District Court
A	1782–1806	Deed Books—Trustees (incomplete)
A	1970–1985	Deed of Release Books
A	1793–1800	Deeds and Other Burned Records (IN)
A	1852–1903	Division of Lands Estates
A	1976–1985	Encumbrance Book (IN)
H	1782–1817	Entry Books (IN)
H	1793–1930	Genealogy—Misc. Manuscripts
A	1803–1817	Guardian Bonds
U	1803–1870	Guardian Bonds
A	1823–1870	Guardian Bonds
A	1803–1815	Guardian Settlements
U	1803–1815	Guardian Settlements
H	1829–1880	Idiot Returns
A	1883–1977	Inventories and Appraisements (IN)
A	1791–1825	Land Trial Records
A	1973–1979	Ledgers—General for Lexington Urban Co. Govt.
A	1983–1984	Ledgers—General for Lexington Urban Co. Govt.
A	1803–1898	Marriage Bonds
H	1803–1898	Marriage Bonds
U	1803–1898	Marriage Bonds
A	?–?	Marriage Bonds
U	1785–1852	Ministers Bonds and Returns
A	1782–1830	Minute Book—Trustees
A	1830–1854	Minute Book—Trustees
A	1781–1986	Minute Books—Lexington

U	1785-1849	Misc. Records—Depositions, Deeds, Wills
A	1970-1985	Misc. Books—County (IN)
A	1973-1985	Mortgage Books (IN)
A	1974-1985	Mortgage Books—Condominium (IN)
A	1869-1874	Newspapers—*Apostolic Times*
A	1886-1899	Newspapers—*Bluegrass Blade*
A	1787-1910	Newspapers—*Kentucky Gazette*
A	1820	Newspapers—*Lexington Advertiser*
A	1834-1836	Newspapers—*Lexington Intelligencer*
A	1864-1865	Newspapers—*National Unionist*
H	1795-1949	Newspapers (SA)
H	1787-1910	Newspapers—*Kentucky Gazette* (SA)
H	1808-1830	Newspapers—*Kentucky Reporter* (SA)
H	1799-1822	Newspapers—*Western Spy* (SA)
A	1845-1846	Newspapers—*The True American* (SA)
A	1819	Newspapers—*The Western Monitor*
A	1803-1985	Order Books
U	1803-1856	Order Books
H	1803-1856	Order Books (IN)
A	1974-1985	Order Books (IN)
A	1790-1936	Order Books General Index
A	1790-1930	Order Books Index—Police Court
A	1837-1891	Order Books—Police Court—Lexington (EX 1881-83) (UNIN)
A	1837-1891	Order Books—Police Court—Lexington (UNIN)
A	1852-1968	Partitions and Division of Land
A	1974-1978	Payroll Register—Lexington Urban Co. Govt.
A	1875	Poll Books
U	1875	Poll Books
A	1898-1910	School Census
U	1898-1910	School Census
A	1869-1889	School Records—University of Kentucky Matriculate Register
A	1876-1977	Settlement Books (IN)
A	1796-1973	Suits Index—Circuit Court
A	1783-1820	Surveys
A	1817-1876	Surveys—Old
A	1787-1875	Tax Book (EX 1798, 1832)
H	1787-1875	Tax Book (EX 1798, 1832)
A	1880-1892	Tax Book (EX 1881-82)
A	1815-1859	Tax Book—Lexington
H	1798	Taxable Property List
A	1911-1985	Veterans Discharge Book (IN)
H	1852-1905	Vital Statistics (SY)
U	1793-1955	Will Books

H	1793-1967	Will Books (IN)
A	1793-1984	Will Books (IN)
U	1793-1900	Will Index

FLEMING COUNTY

Flemingsburg 41041
606-845-8461

Public Library
303 South Main Cross
Flemingsburg 41041
606-845-7851

Historical Society
207 E. Main Street
Flemingsburg 41041

This county was formed in 1798 from Mason County. Fleming's first courthouse was built by 1799 and was believed to be of log. The second was completed in 1830 and the third in 1952.

H	1901-1932	Church Records—Baptist Association
U	1797-1866	Deed Books
A	1984-1986	Deed Books
A	1798-1870	Deed Books (PIN)
A	1798-1962	Deed Index
U	1797-1845	Deed Index—Grantors and Grantees
H	1829-1880	Idiot Returns
H	1780-1835	Lands Forfeited, transfers, etc.
A	1866-1965	Marriage Bonds—Black (IN)
A	1798-1986	Marriage Bonds (IN)
A	1837-1984	Marriage Bonds (PIN)
H	1798-1891	Marriage Book
H	1798-1962	Marriage Index
U	1799-1961	Marriage Index
H	1798-1894	Marriage Records
A	1798-1962	Marriage Records Index
H	1817-1851	Marriage Records of Rev. Racoon Smith
A	1867-1870	Marriage Register (Black)
A	1798-1914	Marriage Register (IN from 1873)
U	1798-1888	Marriages
A	1867-1871	Marriages—Declarations—Black (IN)
H	?-?	Military Records—Veterans Graves
A	1897-1912	Newspapers—*Ewing Enquirer* (SI)
H	1846-1903	Newspapers (SA)
A	1798-1803	Order Book—Circuit Court
A	1798-1802	Order Book—Quarter Sessions
A	1851-1855	Order Book—Quarterly Court
A	1859-1869	Order Book—Quarterly Court
U	1798-1863	Order Books
A	1802-1866	Order Books

A	1798–1863	Order Books (PIN)
A	1798–1892	Tax Book (EX 1816–18, 1823, 1830, 1835–36, 1876–78)
H	1798–1875	Tax Book (EX 1816, 1818, 1823, 1830, 1832, 1835–36)
H	1852–1907	Vital Statistics (SY)
H	1798–1871	Will Books
U	1798–1871	Will Books
A	1798–1986	Will Books (PIN)
A	1798–1962	Will Index
H	1798–1962	Will Index
U	1789–1962	Will Index

FLOYD COUNTY

Prestonsburg 41653
606-886-3816

Public Library
North Arnold Avenue
Prestonburg 41653
606-886-2981

Auxier Historical Society
Luck Coal Co., Store Building
P.O. Box 409
126 Railroad Street
Auxier 41602

This county was formed in 1800 from Fleming, Mason, and Montgomery counties. A few records were destroyed in a courthouse fire in April of 1808. A large number of eastern Kentucky counties were taken from Floyd County; as a result, these records should be consulted when doing early eastern Kentucky genealogy.

A	1808–1940	Civil Cases—Circuit Court Index
A	1960–1978	Criminal Order Books (UNIN)
A	1915–1934	Deed Books—Includes Commissioners Deeds
A	1808–1986	Deed Books
U	1810–1901	Deed Books
A	1810–1969	Deed Index
U	1810–1969	Deed Index—Grantors and Grantees
A	1934–1952	Defendants Index to Circuit Court Civil Cases
U	1803–1860	Early Marriage Records by Jillson
U	1856–1865	Execution Book
A	1852–1888	Guardian Bonds
U	1852–1888	Guardian Bonds
U	1868	Inventory Books, Appraisements, Sales
H	1829–1880	Idiot Returns
A	1808–1851	Marriage Bonds
U	1808–1916	Marriage Bonds
A	1866–1916	Marriage Bonds
A	1803–1914	Marriage Certificates
A	1810–1965	Marriage Index
U	1810–1965	Marriage Index

A	1808–1918	Marriage Records
H	?–?	Military Records—Revolutionary and 1812 Pensions (817)
H	?–?	Military Records—Veterans Graves
A	1913–1973	Misc. Book (IN)
H	1846–1882	Newspapers (SA)
U	1808–1901	Order Books
A	1810–1937	Order Books (IN)
U	1893–1903	Order Books—Commonwealth Court
A	1893–1903	Order Books—Commonwealth
A	1811–1901	Order Books—Circuit Court
A	1951–1978	Order Books—Circuit Court (IN)
U	1810–1937	Order Books Index
A	1806–1928	Survey Book (IN from 1865)
A	1793–1793	Tax Book
A	1837	Tax Book
A	1840	Tax Book (EX 1876–78)
H	1793–1875	Tax Book (EX 1794–1836, 1838–39, 1862–64)
U	1840–1875	Tax Book (also includes 1793, 1837)
H	1852–1904	Vital Statistics (SY)
H	1860–1924	Will Books
U	1860–1924	Will Books
A	1860–1924	Will Books

FRANKLIN COUNTY

Frankfort 40601
502-875-8702

Paul Sawyier Public Library	Kentucky Genealogical Society	Historical Society
305 Wapping Street	Box 153	104 Dakota Road
Frankfort 40601	Frankfort 40602	Frankfort 40601
502-223-1658		

Franklin County was formed shortly after statehood in 1795 from parts of Mercer, Shelby, and Woodford counties. Frankfort is the spot where Kentucky's original three counties, Jefferson, Fayette and Lincoln, came together. Many state records are in the Franklin County records because of its role as site of the state capitol.

H	1860–1890	Cemetery Account Book of Frankfort and Owners
H	1877–1913	Cemetery Records and Lot Owners
H	1891–1979	Cemetery Records—Frankfort Cemetery
A	1966–1977	Civil Case Files (IN)
U	1803–1821	Court Records—General
U	1795–1866	Deed Books
A	1803–1847	Deed Books
H	1795–1804	Deed Books—Includes Lands Now in Carroll
A	1795–1866	Deed Index

U	1795–1866	Deed Index
A	1794–1802	Deeds—District Court
U	1794–1802	Deeds—District Court
A	1795–1807	Deeds—Quarter Session Court
A	1786–1802	District Court Chancery
A	1828–1851	Estate Settlements
U	1824–1877	Executor and Administrator Bonds
A	1832–1864	Executor Bonds
A	1974–1977	Fiscal Case Files—Defendant Index
H	?–?	Genealogy—Manuscripts and Family Papers
A	1832–1864	Guardian Bonds
U	1832–1864	Guardian Bonds
A	1795–1865	Marriage Bonds
U	1795–1865	Marriage Bonds
A	1810–1879	Marriage Records
U	1810–1879	Marriage Records
A	1795–1830	Marriage Records—Brides Index
U	1795–1830	Marriage Records—Brides Index
U	1795–1865	Marriages and County History
H	?–?	Military Records—Revolutionary and 1812 Pensions (588)
H	?–?	Military Records—Veterans Graves
A	1861–1867	Militia—Lists of Enrolled Militia
A	1869	Militia—Lists of Enrolled Militia
U	1809–1820	Misc. Records—Depositions, Deeds, Wills
A	1810–1956	Newspapers—*Argus of Western America*
A	1833	Newspapers—*Argus of Western America*
A	1825–1830	Newspapers—*Argus of Western America*
A	1810–1821	Newspapers—*Argus of Western America*
A	1837–1838	Newspapers—*Commonwealth*
A	1844–1851	Newspapers—*Daily Commonwealth*
A	1854–1861	Newspapers—*Daily Commonwealth*
A	1872–1873	Newspapers—*Daily Kentucky Yeoman*
A	1833–1872	Newspapers—*Frankfort Commonwealth*
A	1844–1849	Newspapers—*Frankfort Commonwealth*
A	1859–1862	Newspapers—*Frankfort Commonwealth*
A	1870–1878	Newspapers—*Frankfort Commonwealth*
A	1890–1916	Newspapers—*Frankfort Courier* (SI)
A	1909–1911	Newspapers—*Frankfort News*
A	1911–1912	Newspapers—*Frankfort News Journal*
A	1884–1908	Newspapers—*Frankfort Roundabout*
A	1908–1909	Newspapers—*Frankfort Weekly News*
A	1957	Newspapers—*Franklin County News*
A	1869–1876	Newspapers—*Kentucky Free Mason*
A	1795–1905	Newspapers—*Kentucky Journal*
A	1906–1910	Newspapers—*Kentucky State Journal*
A	1843–1844	Newspapers—*Kentucky Yeoman* (IN)
A	1800–1814	Newspapers—*Palladium*

H	1798–1956	Newspapers (SA)
A	1804–1940	Newspapers (SI)
A	1912–1961	Newspapers—*State Journal* (SI)
A	1895–1891	Newspapers—*The Capital/Daily Capital*
A	1819–1828	Newspapers—*The Commentator*
A	1885–1891	Newspapers—*The Daily Capital*
A	1898	Newspapers—*The Headlight*
A	1851–1865	Newspapers—*Tri-Weekly Commonwealth*
A	1877–1884	Newspapers—*Tri-Weekly Kentucky Yeoman* (IN)
A	1860–1861	Newspapers—*Tri-Weekly Commonwealth*
A	1885	Newspapers—*Truthful Witness*
A	1864–1882	Newspapers—*Weekly Kentucky Yeoman* (IN)
A	1877–1880	Newspapers—*Weekly Roundabout*
A	1879–1884	Newspapers—*Weekly Roundabout* (SI)
A	1806–1808	Newspapers—*Western World*
U	1795–1867	Order Books
U	1795–1834	Order Books Index
A	1795–1867	Order Books Index
U	1875	Poll Books
A	1875	Poll Books—Convention (with Garrard County Book)
A	1875	Poll Books Franklin
U	1795–1807	Quarter Sessions Court Records
H	1786–1802	Records—Chancery Court
A	1896	School Census
A	1915–1917	School Census
A	1921	School Census
A	1932	School Census
A	1934	School Census
H	1896–1934	School Census
U	1828–1851	Settlements of Estates
A	1795–1855	Suits Index—Circuit Court
H	1795–1875	Tax Book (EX 1798–1800, 1832, part of 1862)
A	1795–1892	Tax Book (EX 1800, 1832, 1876–78)
H	1797–1818	Tax Book (SY)
H	1852–1909	Vital Statistics (SY)
A	1795–1880	Will Books
U	1795–1880	Will Books

FULTON COUNTY

Hickman 42050
502-236-2727

Public Library	Genealogical Society	Hickman Branch Library
312 Main Street	P.O. Box 31	902 Moscow Avenue
Fulton 42041	Fulton 42041	Hickman 42050
502-472-3439		502-236-2464

This county was formed in 1845 from part of Hickman County. The county seat of Hickman was originally known as Mills' Point in honor of an early settler, James Mills. The name was changed in 1837 to Hickman.

A	1840–1880	Case Files—Circuit Court
U	1853–1882	Cases—Equity
U	1846–1872	Cases—Ordinary
U	1878	Death List of Yellow Fever Epidemic Dead
A	1845–1876	Deed Books
U	1845–1876	Deed Books
A	1925–1985	Deed Books
A	1919–1984	Deed Index
A	1845–1887	Deed Index
U	1845–1887	Deed Index
U	?–?	Family Cemetery Records
A	1845–1878	Marriage Bonds (IN)
U	1845–1878	Marriage Bonds
U	1845–1875	Marriage Docket Book
A	1845–1875	Marriage Register
H	?–?	Military Records—Veterans Graves
A	1845–1876	Minute/Order Books (IN from 1856)
A	1841–1843	Newspapers—*Commercial Appeal Herald*
A	1879–1899	Newspapers—*Hickman Courier* (SI)
A	1856–1857	Newspapers—*Hickman Times*
H	1847–1894	Newspapers (SA)
A	1845–1848	Newspapers—*Weekly Commercial Standard*
U	1845–1876	Order Books
H	1846–1875	Tax Book (EX 1862)
A	1846–1892	Tax Book (EX 1876–78)
H	1852–1904	Vital Statistics (SY)
H	1845–1923	Will Books
U	1845–1923	Will Books
A	1845–1923	Will Books (IN)

GALLATIN COUNTY

Warsaw 41095
606-567-5411

Public Library
P.O. Box 258
209 Market Street
Warsaw 41095
606-567-2786

Historical Society
P.O. Box 405
Warsaw 41095

Gallatin was formed in 1799 from portions of Franklin and Shelby counties. From 1804 to 1831, Warsaw was known as Fredericksburg. Gallatin's original county seat was in Port William (now Carrollton) until 1838 when it was moved to Warsaw. All records of the original Gallatin County, including northern Owen, eastern Trimble, and all of present-day Gallatin and Carroll counties, are intact.

U	1826–1852	Administrator Bonds
A	1826–1852	Administrator Bonds
H	1826–1852	Administrator Bonds
H	?–?	Cemetery Records
A	1801–1807	Deed Books—Circuit Court (IN)
U	1799–1901	Deed Books
A	1799–1985	Deed Books (IN)
A	1798–1957	Deed Index
U	1798–1942	Deed Index—Grantors and Grantees
H	1805–1810	Docket Books
H	1799–1879	Estray Book
H	1798–1948	Genealogy—History of Gallatin County
A	1826–1855	Guardian Bonds (IN from 1852)
H	1829–1873	Guardian Bonds (EX 1849–51)
U	1829–1854	Guardian Inventory
U	1829–1873	Guardians Bonds
H	1829–1852	Inventory Report to Court
U	1799–1907	Marriage Bonds
H	1799–1911	Marriage Bonds
U	1852–1898	Marriage Bonds—Original
A	1852–1898	Marriage Bonds (PIN)
U	1799–1941	Marriage Index
A	1799–1818	Marriage Records
A	1819–1911	Marriage Records
A	1799–1941	Marriage Records General Index
U	1799–1914	Marriage Register
H	1799–1911	Marriage Register and Index
A	1799–1914	Marriage Register and Returns Books
H	?–?	Military Records—Revolutionary and 1812 Pensions (564)
H	?–?	Military Records—Veterans Graves
A	1869–1897	Minute Books

U	1869–1897	Minute Books
U	1868–1873	Minute Books—Circuit Court
H	1869–1897	Minute Books
H	1843–1882	Newspapers (SA)
U	1799–1916	Order Books
A	1799–1916	Order Books (majority IN)
U	1805–1810	Rule Docket
A	1799–1810	Rule Docket Book—Quarter Sessions Court
A	1799–1879	Stray Book
U	1799–1879	Stray Book—Lost Property
A	1799–1892	Tax Book (EX 1832, 1834, 1876–78)
H	1799–1875	Tax Book (EX 1832, 1834, 1837–39)
H	1852–1878	Vital Statistics (SY)
U	1800–1964	Will Books
H	1917–1964	Will Books
A	1800–1964	Will Books (IN from 1817)

GARRARD COUNTY

Lancaster 40444
606-792-3071

Public Library	Historical Society
101 Lexington Street	101 Lexington Street
Lancaster 40444	Lancaster 40444
606-792-3424	606-792-3424

Garrard was formed in 1797 from parts of Lincoln, Madison, and Mercer counties. Lancaster was named in 1798 for Lancaster, Pennsylvania, from which many early setters orginated.

H	?–?	Cemetery Records
H	1824–1924	Church Records and Histories—Baptist
A	1868–1941	Civil Suits Index Circuit Court
A	1797–1964	Deed Books
U	1797–1866	Deed Books
A	1797–1984	Deed Index
H	1797–1935	Deed Index—Grantees
U	1797–1935	Deed Index—Grantors and Grantees
U	1807–1846	Depositions—Circuit Court
A	1813–1827	Depositions—Circuit Court
A	?–?	Genealogical and Church Records of Forrest Calico
H	?–?	Genealogy
H	1797–1869	Marriage Bonds
U	1853–1869	Marriage Bonds
A	1797–1958	Marriage Index
U	1797–1958	Marriage Index
H	1797–1958	Marriage Index

U	1797–1853	Marriage Records
A	1797–1869	Marriage Records
H	?–?	Military Records—Revolutionary and 1812 Pensions (793)
A	1895–1900	Newspapers—*The Central Record*
H	1848–1924	Newspapers (SA)
A	1895–1900	Newspapers—*The Central Record*
A	1908–1914	Newspapers—*The Central Record*
H	1797–1825	Order Books
A	1797–1855	Order Books
U	1797–1869	Order Books
A	1797–1912	Order Books—Circuit Court (IN from 1804)
A	1820–1890	Poll Books (for 1820, 1840, 1870, and 1890 only)
U	1854–1892	Poll Books (SY)
U	1879	Poll Books
A	1879	Poll Books—Convention
A	1797–1892	Tax Book (EX 1798, 1831–32, 1834, 1876–78)
H	1797–1875	Tax Book (EX 1798, 1831–33, 1834)
H	1852–1878	Vital Statistics
H	1797–1866	Will Books
U	1797–1866	Will Books
A	1797–1866	Will Books (IN)
U	1797–1957	Will Index
A	1797–1957	Will Index

GRANT COUNTY

Williamstown 41097
606-824-3321

Public Library	Historical Society
107 N. Main Street	15 Cherry Grove Road
Williamstown 41097	Williamstown 41097
606-824-4723	

Grant County was formed in 1820 from Pendleton County. At that time, it contained all current territory except areas subsequently added from Campbell, Harrison, Boone, and Owen. The courthouse, the third on the site, was completed in 1939 replacing an earlier brick building that dated back to 1856.

H	1910–1916	Business Records—Burley Tobacco Company
A	1820–1978	Case Files Index—Circuit Court
H	?–?	Cemetery Records—Williamstown
A	1874–1880	Criminal Order Books (IN)
A	1953–1977	Criminal Order Books (IN)
U	1820–1866	Deed Books
A	1820–1927	Deed Books (IN)
A	1820–1872	Deed Index
U	1820–1872	Deed Index

A	1821–1898	Family Genealogy—Clark Family
H	?–?	Genealogy—Barton Collection
A	1838–1871	Guardian Settlement Books (PIN)
U	1838–1871	Guardian Settlement Books
H	1832–1865	Marriage Bonds
U	1832–1867	Marriage Bonds
A	1875–1919	Marriage Books (IN)
H	1820–1857	Marriage Certificates
A	1866–1878	Marriage Record Book (IN)
A	1820–1890	Marriage Register
H	1820–1890	Marriage Register
U	1820–1890	Marriage Register
A	1882–1908	Marriage Register—Black
A	1857–1858	Marriage Returns Book
H	?–?	Military Records—Revolutionary and 1812 Pensions (309)
H	?–?	Military Records—Veterans' Graves
H	1868–1970	Newspapers (SA)
U	1820–1869	Order Books
A	1820–1869	Order Books (IN EX 1834–45)
A	1820–1977	Order Books—Circuit Court (IN)
A	1820–1891	Tax Book (EX 1832, 1834, 1839, 1853, 1863, 1876–78)
H	1820–1875	Tax Book (EX 1832, 1834, 1839, 1853, 1863)
H	1852–1907	Vital Statistics
H	1820–1866	Will Books
U	1820–1866	Will Books
A	1820–1866	Will Books (IN)

GRAVES COUNTY

Mayfield 42066
502-247-1676

Public Library
Sixth and College
Mayfield 42066
502-247-2911

Genealogical Society
P.O. Box 245
Mayfield 42066

This county was formed in 1824 from Hickman County. There was a courthouse fire in 1864 and again on 18 December 1887 in which early records were destroyed.

A	1953–1977	Case Files Index—Civil Circuit Court
A	1883–1953	Case Files Index—Common Law Cross
A	1936–1977	Case Files—Criminal Index
A	1866–1953	Case Files—Equity Cross Index
A	1883–1963	Church Records
U	1948–1963	Church Records—Christian, Methodist
A	1883–1962	Church Records—Register, Minute Books, etc.

U	1825–1963	Church Records—Rolls, Records and Histories
U	1849–1963	Church Records—Sedalia Methodist
A	1887–1951	Deed Books
A	1916–1974	Deed Index
U	?–?	Family Bible Records and Histories
A	1837–1963	Family Bible Records and Misc. Records
A	?–?	Genealogy—Family Bibles and Other Records
U	1887–1915	Marriage Register
A	1887–1915	Marriage Register (PIN)
H	?–?	Military Records—Revolutionary and 1812 Pensions (116)
H	?–?	Military Records—Veterans' Graves
H	1863–1879	Newspapers (SA)
A	1946–1977	Order Books—Civil (IN)
A	1953–1977	Order Books—Civil Circuit Court (IN)
A	1964–1978	Order Books—Criminal (IN)
A	1824–1891	Tax Book (EX 1832, 1836, 1838, 1876–79, 1888–90)
H	1824–1875	Tax Book (EX 1832, 1836, 1838)
H	1852–1907	Vital Statistics

GRAYSON COUNTY

Leitchfield 42754
502-259-3201

Public Library
P.O. Box 512
130 E. Market Street
Leitchfield 42754
502-259-5455

Historical Society
Box 64
Leitchfield 42754

This county was formed in 1810 from Hardin and Ohio counties. One Grayson County courthouse was burned by the Confederates on 24 December 1864. The second courthouse burned on 16 June 1896, and only three record books were saved. The third courthouse, built ca. 1898, was also burned on 3 April 1936, but in that fire all records were saved.

A	1896–1912	Deed Books
U	1896–1912	Deed Books
A	1896–1964	Deed Index
U	1896–1964	Deed Index
A	1896–1918	Deeds—Commissioners
U	1896–1918	Deeds—Commissioners
A	1896–1913	Marriage Bonds—Black (IN)
A	1896–1968	Marriage Bonds—Grooms Index
A	1896–1912	Marriage Bonds (IN EX 1898–99)
U	1896–1912	Marriage Bonds and Certificates
U	1896–1968	Marriage Index—Bonds and Certificates (Grooms)
H	?–?	Military Records—Revolutionary and 1812 Pensions (207)

H	?-?	Military Records—Veterans' Graves
A	1903–1985	Minute Books (Leitchfield)
A	1942–1943	Newspapers—*Grayson County News*
A	1890–1890	Newspapers—*Grayson Gazette* (26 October only)
H	1876–1880	Newspapers (SA)
A	1906–1916	Order Books
U	1906–1916	Order Books
A	1901–1911	Settlement Books (IN)
U	1901–1911	Settlement Books
A	1810–1891	Tax Book (EX 1832, 1835, 1876-78, 1887-90)
H	1810–1875	Tax Book (EX 1832, 1835)
H	1852–1907	Vital Statistics
H	1896–1925	Will Books
U	1896–1925	Will Books
A	1896–1925	Will Books (IN)

GREEN COUNTY

Greensburg 42743
502-932-5386

Public Library
116 South Main Street
Greensburg 42743
502-932-7081

Historical Society
P.O. Box 276
Greensburg 42743

This county was formed in 1793 from Lincoln and Nelson counties. The second Green County courthouse was built in 1804 by Stone Hammer Metcalfe who later became the tenth governor of Kentucky. It is the oldest courthouse still standing in Kentucky. The current courhouse was completed in 1931.

A	1852–1892	Administrator Bonds
U	1852–1892	Administrator Bonds
H	1812–1956	Church Records (Church of Christ, Baptist)
U	1793–1904	Deed Books
A	1793–1972	Deed Books
H	1793–1904	Deed Books
A	1793–1902	Deed Index
U	1793–1952	Deed Index—Grantors and Grantees
U	1837–1841	Deeds—Commissioners
A	1837–1911	Deeds—Commissioners
U	1887–1911	Deeds—Commissioners
U	1848–1922	Guardian Bonds
A	1848–1915	Guardian Bonds
U	1852–1874	Guardian List
A	1812–1839	Inventory Books
U	1812–1885	Inventory Books—Includes Settlement Books and Sales
A	1839–1885	Inventory Books, Settlements, and Sales

H	1854–1913	Marriage Bonds
A	1854–1914	Marriage Bonds
A	1842–1902	Marriage Bonds (vols. D–S)
A	1873–1897	Marriage Bonds (vols. K–Q)
A	1842–1863	Marriage Bonds (IN)
U	1793–1900	Marriage Licenses and Certificates
A	1793–1900	Marriage Licenses and Certificates
U	1793–1902	Marriage Records (Certificates and Bonds)
A	1793–1860	Marriage Records—Ministers Returns
U	1793–1860	Marriage Records—Ministers Returns
A	1793–1861	Marriage Register (IN)
H	?–?	Military Records—Revolutionary and 1812 Pensions (979)
H	?–?	Military Records—Veterans' Graves
A	1962–1985	Minute Books—Greensburg and Index
A	1795–1819	Minute Books—Greensburg
A	1907–1985	Minute Books—Greensburg
A	1795–1819	Minute Books—Greensburg Board of Trustees
A	1907–1961	Minute Books—Greensburg Board of Trustees
U	1800–1806	Misc. Records—Depositions, Deeds, Wills
H	1787–1861	Muster Rolls
H	1876–1880	Newspapers (SA)
A	1794–1852	Order Books
A	1794–1901	Order Books
U	1794–1901	Order Books
A	1794–1906	Order Books
H	1794–1906	Order Books
A	1794–1899	Order Books—Circuit Court
U	1801–1901	Order Books—Circuit Court
U	1803–1822	Order Books—Circuit Court
A	1803–1822	Record Books—Circuit Court
U	1895–1902	School Census
A	1895–1906	School Census
A	1855–1901	Settlement Books
U	1855–1901	Settlement Books
H	1795–1875	Tax Book (EX 1798, 1824–26, 1833, 1838–39)
A	1795–1892	Tax Book (EX 1798, 1824–26, 1831–33, 1838–39, 1876–79)
H	1852–1904	Vital Statistics
A	1793–1913	Will Books
H	1793–1959	Will Books
U	1793–1913	Will Books

GREENUP COUNTY

Greenup 41144
606-473-3151

Public Library	Historical Society
203 Harrison Street	607 Riverside Dr.
Greenup 41144	Wurtland 41144
606-473-6514	

This county was formed in 1804 from part of Mason County. Greenup was incorporated in 1818 as Greenupsburg, but the name changed to Greenup in 1872. There have been three Greenup courthouses and no fires.

A	1811–1869	Deed Books
H	1811–1869	Deed Books
U	1811–1869	Deed Books
A	1940–1955	Deed Books
A	1815–1868	Deed Index
H	1815–1868	Deed Index
U	1815–1868	Deed Index
A	?–?	Genealogy—Family Histories
U	1803–1866	Marriage Bonds
H	1803–1865	Marriage Bonds
A	1803–1866	Marriage Bonds
H	?–?	Military Records—Revolutionary and 1812 Pensions (350)
H	?–?	Military Records—Veterans' Graves
A	1966–1986	Minute Books—Board of Council of Russell
A	1943–1984	Minute Books—Chinnville
A	1926–1930	Minute Books—Chinnville (Raceland)
A	1904–1966	Minute Books—City Council of Russell
H	1843–1954	Newspapers (SA)
A	1845–1977	Newspapers (SY, SA)
U	1838–1846	Order Books
A	1838–1863	Order Books
H	1838–1863	Order Books
A	1809–1965	Order Books—Civil and Criminal (IN)
A	1807–1816	Order Books—Circuit Court (IN)
A	1920–1980	Suits Off Docket—Circuit Court Index
A	1839–1892	Tax Book (EX 1840, 1853, 1857, 1876–78)
H	1839–1875	Tax Book (EX 1840, 1853)
H	1852–1904	Vital Statistics
H	1822–1870	Will Books
A	1822–1870	Will Books
U	1822–1870	Will Books

HANCOCK COUNTY

Hawesville 42348
502-927-6117

Public Library	Genealogical Society	Historical Society
P.O. Box 249	Old Courthouse	Box 605
Court Street	Hawesville 42348	Hawesville 42348
Hawesville 42348		
502-927-6760		

This county was formed in 1829 from parts of Breckinridge, Daviess, and Ohio counties. The second courthouse, completed in 1868, was restored in 1978.

A	1863–1912	Administrator Bonds
U	1863–1912	Administrator Bonds
A	1897–1959	Administrator Bonds
A	1879–1926	Criminal Order Books (IN)
U	1829–1901	Deed Books
A	1829–1974	Deed Books
A	1914–1935	Deed Books—Master Commissioners
A	1829–1952	Deed Index
U	1829–1959	Deed Index
U	1863–1918	Executor Bonds
A	1863–1934	Executor Bonds
A	1863–1914	Guardian and Executor Bonds
U	1863–1893	Guardian Bonds
A	1913–1940	Guardian Bonds
A	1853–1932	Land Records—Division of Lands
A	1862–1904	Marriage Bonds
U	1862–1904	Marriage Bonds
A	1914–1974	Marriage Bonds
A	1829–1861	Marriage Licenses
U	1829–1861	Marriage Licenses
A	1829–1900	Marriage Records
U	1829–1900	Marriage Records
A	1900–1914	Marriage Register
A	1902–1966	Marriage Register (IN from 1925)
A	1866–1914	Marriage Returns (IN)
H	?–?	Military Records—Veterans' Graves
H	1875–1879	Newspapers (SA)
U	1834–1901	Order Books
A	1834–1901	Order Books
A	1906–1965	Order Books
A	1839–1971	Order Books—Circuit Court
U	1839–1902	Order Books—Circuit Court
A	1893–1972	Order Books—Fiscal Court
A	1866–1920	Order Books—Quarterly Court (IN from 1871)
A	1894–1906	School Census

U	1894-1902	School Census (EX 1898)
A	1857-1864	Settlement Books
U	1857-1864	Settlement Books
A	1874-1965	Settlement Books
A	1829-1892	Tax Book (EX 1832, 1834, 1876-78)
H	1829-1875	Tax Book (EX 1832, 1834)
H	1852-1907	Vital Statistics
H	1830-1928	Will Books
A	1830-1973	Will Books
U	1830-1928	Will Books

HARDIN COUNTY

Elizabethtown 42701
502-765-2171

Public Library	Historical Society	Ancestral Trails	Revolutionary War
201 West Dixie Street	128 N. Main	Historical Society	Roundtable
Elizabethtown 42701	Elizabethtown 42701	P.O. Box 573	23 Public Square
502-769-6337		Vine Grove 40175	Elizabethtown 42701

This county was formed in 1793 from Nelson County. The present courthouse was completed in 1934 in the middle of the town square. There was a loss of records on 23 December 1864 due to a courthouse fire. The third courthouse also burned on 6 December 1932 and was replaced in 1934.

A	?-?	Cemetery Records and Lots Register—Elizabethtown
A	1852-1980	Church Records—New Salem Baptist Church
A	1795-1904	Civil Suits General Cross Index
A	1909-1982	Civil Suits Index
A	1867-1867	Common Pleas Case Files and Index
A	1881-1951	Criminal Order Books (IN)
U	1793-1876	Deed Books
A	1793-1947	Deed Books (IN)
U	1795-1904	Deed Index
A	1892-1911	Ledger Books—Elizabethtown
A	1793-1911	Marriage Bonds and Consents
U	1793-1861	Marriage Bonds, Consents, and Licenses
U	1793-1896	Marriage Index
U	1862-1911	Marriage Licenses and Certificates
U	1793-1914	Marriage Register
A	1793-1914	Marriage Register (IN)
H	?-?	Military Records—Revolutionary and 1812 Pensions (512)
A	1893-1979	Minute Books—Elizabethtown (PIN)
A	1931-1986	Minute Books—Trustees of West Point
A	1793-1799	Minute/Order Index—Quarter Sessions Court
U	1795-1795	Misc. Records—Depositions, Deeds, Wills, etc.
A	1869-1934	Newspapers—*Elizabethtown News* (SI)

A	1830-1909	Newspapers—Elizabethtown (SI)
H	1868-1941	Newspapers (SA)
U	1793-1875	Order Books
A	1798-1875	Order Books
A	1799-1896	Order Books (IN From 1804)
A	1853-1977	Order Books—Circuit Court (IN)
A	1933-1946	Order Books—Circuit Court (IN)
A	1799-1825	Order Books—Quarter Sessions (IN)
A	1794-1925	Suits—Quarter Sessions Index
A	1920-1962	Tax Book
H	1793-1834	Tax Book (EX 1793, 1798, 1818, 1831-32)
A	1793-1846	Tax Book (EX 1798, 1818, 1831-32, 1835, 1838)
H	1836-1875	Tax Book (EX 1838, 1847)
A	1848-1892	Tax Book (EX 1876-78)
H	1852-1874	Vital Statistics
A	1793-1915	Will Books
U	1793-1915	Will Books
A	1793-1838	Will Books Abstracts

HARLAN COUNTY

Harlan 40831
606-573-3636

Public Library	Harlan Heritage Seekers	Harlan Genealogical Society
Central Street at Third	P.O. Box 853	P.O. Box 1498
Harlan 40831	Harlan 40831	Harlan 40831
606-573-5220		

This county was formed in 1819 from Knox County. The county seat of Harlan was known as Mount Pleasant until 1912. The courthouse was burned in October of 1863 in reprisal for the burning of the courthouse of Lee County, Virginia. However, the county records in the nearby clerk's office were saved.

A	1888-1903	Administrator Bonds
U	1888-1903	Administrator Bonds
H	1879-1891	Birth and School Records
A	1820-1960	Deed Books
U	1820-1901	Deed Books
A	1820-1961	Deed Index
U	1820-1961	Deed Index—Grantors and Grantees
A	1871-1901	Deeds—Commissioners
U	1871-1901	Deeds—Commissioners
H	1829-1880	Idiot Returns
A	1917-1918	Lease Book
A	?-?	Maps—Right of Way
A	1830-1956	Marriage Bonds Index
H	1830-1956	Marriage Bonds Index

A	1820-1946	Marriage Books—General Index
A	1947-1979	Marriage Books Cross Index
U	1820-1956	Marriage Index—Brides and Grooms
U	1870-1916	Marriage Licenses and Bonds
U	1818-1905	Marriage Register
A	1820-1916	Marriage Register
U	1914-1914	Marriage Register
H	1820-1916	Marriage Register and Returns
A	1958-1960	Military Records—Veterans' Discharges
H	?-?	Military Records—Veterans' Graves
H	1868-1881	Newspapers (SA)
U	1820-1904	Order Books
A	1820-1904	Order Books (EX 1861-83)
A	1897-1897	School Census
U	1897-1897	School Census (in Marriage Register pp. 6-53)
A	1943-1980	Suits Off Docket Index—Circuit Court
A	1910-1977	Tax Book
A	1820-1892	Tax Book (EX 1830, 1832, 1839, 1876-78)
H	1820-1875	Tax Book (EX 1830, 1832, 1839)
H	1852-1904	Vital Statistics
A	1936-1972	Voter Registration Record Forms
A	1850-1920	Will Books
H	1850-1920	Will Books
U	1850-1920	Will Books

HARRISON COUNTY

Cynthiana 41031
606-234-2232

Public Library
P.O. Box 217
103 S. Church
Cynthiana 41031
606-234-4881

Historical Society
P.O. Box 411
Cynthiana 41031

Harrison was formed in 1794 from parts of Bourbon and Scott counties. The present courthouse in Cynthiana was completed in 1853 after a courthouse fire on 24 January 1851 in which some records were destroyed.

A	1863-1869	Administrator Bonds
U	1863-1869	Administrator Bonds
H	1863-1869	Administrator Bonds
H	1801-1960	Church Records (Baptist, Christian)
H	1794-1905	Death Records—Deceased Estate Index
H	1914-1981	Death Records—Funeral Home—Rees, Whaley (PIN)
A	1794-1866	Deed Books
H	1794-1866	Deed Books

U	1794–1866	Deed Books
A	1794–1894	Deed Index
H	1794–1894	Deed Index
U	1794–1894	Deed Index
A	1794–1905	Estates Index
U	1794–1905	Estates Index
H	1780–1835	Forfeited Lands, Transfers, etc.
H	?–?	Genealogy–Family Records and Manuscripts
A	1854–1869	Guardian Bonds
H	1854–1869	Guardian Bonds
U	1854–1869	Guardian Bonds
H	1829–1880	Idiot Returns
U	1794–1923	Judgments Index–Circuit Court
A	1794–1921	Judgments and Suits–Circuit Court
H	1794–1921	Judgments and Suits–Circuit Court (IN)
A	1794–1836	Judgment Bundles–Circuit Court–Suits
H	?–?	Judgment Case Files–Circuit Court (IN)
U	1796–1863	Marriage Bonds
H	1796–?	Marriage Bonds
A	1854–1869	Marriage Bonds
U	1854–1869	Marriage Bonds
U	1794–1867	Marriage Bonds and Licenses
A	1794–1893	Marriage Bonds Index and Files
H	1794–1893	Marriage Index
U	1794–1893	Marriage Index
A	1794–1828	Marriage Register
A	1832–1867	Marriage Register
U	1832–1867	Marriage Register
U	1794–1852	Marriage Returns
H	1814–1832	Marriage Returns
H	?–?	Military Records–Revolutionary and 1812 Pensions (323)
H	?–?	Military Records–Veterans' Graves
H	1796–1863	Minute Books
H	?–?	Minute Books (A–C and G–N)
U	1776–1801	Misc. Records–Depositions, Deeds, Wills, etc.
A	1896–1909	Newspapers–*Cynthiana Democrat*
A	1850–1902	Newspapers–*Cynthiana News* (SI)
H	1837–1882	Newspapers (SA)
A	1896–1937	Newspapers–*The Log Cabin*
H	?–?	Order Books (vols. A–Z, 26–29, 30–32)
A	1794–1865	Order Books–Circuit Court
H	1794–1865	Order Books–Circuit Court
U	1794–1865	Order Books–Circuit Court
U	1794–1867	Record Books
H	1794–1867	Record Books
U	1794–1921	Suit Bundles–Circuit Court
H	1794–1875	Tax Book (EX 1798, 1820, 1831–32, 1836)

A	1794–1891	Tax Book (EX 1798, 1820, 1831–32, 1836, 1876–78)
H	1852–1878	Vital Statistics
A	1795–1870	Will Books
H	1795–1870	Will Books
U	1795–1870	Will Books
H	1794–1905	Will Index

HART COUNTY

Munfordville 42765
502-524-2751

Public Library
P.O. Box 337
East Third Street
Munfordville 42765
502-524-1953

Historical Society
P.O. Box 606
Munfordville 42765

This county was formed in 1819 from parts of Hardin and Barren counties. There was a courthouse fire on 3 January 1928 that resulted in some loss of records.

A	1928–1953	Case Files Index—Circuit Court
H	?–1960	Cemetery Records (PIN)
A	?–?	Church Records
H	1803–1898	Church Records—Baptist and Presbyterian
A	1928–1985	Deed Books
A	1939–1949	Easements—Right of Way
H	?–?	Genealogy
A	?–?	Genealogy—Collections, History, Cemeteries
A	1930–1937	Mineral Leases
H	?–?	Military Records—Revolutionary and 1812 Pensions (169)
H	?–?	Military Records—Veterans' Graves
A	1903–1984	Minute Books—Munfordville (PIN)
A	1886–1887	Newspapers—*Hart County News*
H	1834–1882	Newspapers (SA)
A	1819–1823	Order Books
H	1819–1823	Order Books
U	1819–1823	Order Books
A	1928–1977	Order Books—Circuit Court (IN)
A	1931–1977	Order Books—Criminal (IN)
A	1819–1892	Tax Book (EX 1830, 1834, 1836–39, 1876–78)
H	1819–1875	Tax Book (EX 1832–34, 1836, 1838–39)
H	1852–1907	Vital Statistics (SY)

HENDERSON COUNTY

Henderson 42420
502-826-3906

Public Library
101 S. Main Street
Henderson 42420
502-826-3712

Genealogical and Historical Society
P.O. Box 715
Henderson 42420

Henderson was formed in 1799 from Christian County. The 1843 courthouse was razed in 1964, and a new courthouse was begun on the same site.

A	1853–1903	Administrator Bonds
U	1853–1903	Administrator Bonds
A	1797–1901	Deed Books
U	1797–1901	Deed Books
A	1798–1984	Deed Index
U	1798–1968	Deed Index—Grantors and Grantees
A	1877–1903	Deeds—Commissioners
U	1877–1903	Deeds—Commissioners
A	1871–1909	Executor and Administrator Bonds
U	1871–1909	Executor and Administrator Bonds
U	1875–1905	Executor and Administrator Settlement Books
U	1853–1902	Executor, Administrator, and Guardian Bonds
U	1868–1910	Guardian List
A	1868–1910	Guardian List
A	1853–1901	Guardian Bonds
A	1875–1901	Guardian Settlement Books
U	1882–1901	Guardian Settlement Books
U	1840–1906	Inventory and Appraisement Books
A	1840–1893	Inventory and Appraisement Books
A	1810–1900	Marriage Bonds
U	1810–1900	Marriage Bonds
A	1808–1968	Marriage Index—Brides and Grooms
U	1808–1968	Marriage Index—Brides and Grooms
U	1864–1900	Marriage Licenses and Certificates
A	1864–1900	Marriage Licenses and Returns
A	1977–1985	Minute Books—City of Henderson (IN)
U	1827–1827	Misc. Records—Depositions, Deeds, Wills
U	1802–1802	Misc. Records—Depositions, Deeds, Wills, etc.
A	1891–1895	Newspapers—*Daily Journal*
A	1898–1899	Newspapers—*Henderson Daily Journal* (SI)
A	1880–1884	Newspapers—*Henderson Weekly Reporter*
H	1821–1882	Newspapers (SA)
A	1829–1829	Newspapers—*The Columbian*
A	1816–1902	Order Books
U	1816–1902	Order Books
A	1875–1905	Settlement Books

A	1880-1884	Tax Book
H	1799-1875	Tax Book (EX 1805-07, 1832, 1838)
A	1799-1892	Tax Book (EX 1805-07, 1832, 1838, 1876-78, 1880-84)
A	1923-1958	Tax Book—(White and Black)
H	1852-1907	Vital Statistics (SY)
A	1799-1915	Will Books
U	1799-1915	Will Books
A	1800-1966	Will Index
U	1800-1966	Will Index

HENRY COUNTY

New Castle 40050
502-845-2934

Public Library	Historical Society
P.O. Box 147	P.O. Box 570
Eminence Terrace	New Castle 40050
Eminence 40019	
502-845-5682	

Henry County was formed in 1799 from Shelby County. The county's second courthouse burned in 1804 with some loss of records. Its third courthouse was built in 1875 and is still standing.

H	1800-1900	Cemetery Records
H	1912-1962	Death Records—Funeral Home
A	1799-1901	Deed Books
U	1799-1901	Deed Books
A	1799-1888	Deed Index
U	1799-1888	Deed Index
A	1880-1970	Deed Index
U	1877-1970	Deed Index—Grantors and Grantees
U	1800-1875	Marriage Licenses and Bonds
A	1800-1911	Marriage Licenses and Bonds
U	1875-1911	Marriage Licenses, Bonds, and Certificates
H	?-?	Military Records—Revolutionary and 1812 Pensions (1,464)
H	1853-1885	Newspapers (SA)
A	1803-1901	Order Books
U	1803-1901	Order Books
H	1799-1875	Tax Book (EX 1810, 1831-32, 1836, part of 1873)
A	1800-1901	Tax Book (EX 1810, 1828, 1831-32, 1876-78)
A	1902-1973	Tax Book (EX 1893-1900, 1903, 1924-25, 1950)
H	1852-1877	Vital Statistics (SY)
A	1800-1910	Will Books
H	1800-1910	Will Books
U	1800-1910	Will Books

H	1800–1970	Will Index
A	1800–1970	Will Index
U	1800–1970	Will Index

HICKMAN COUNTY

Clinton 42031
502-653-2131

Public Library
209 Mayfield Road
Clinton 42031
502-653-4684

Historical Society
333 W. Clay Street
Clinton 42301

This county was formed in 1821 from parts of Caldwell and Livingston counties in the original Jackson Purchase. The county seat at the time of formation was Columbus. Court business was transacted in the home of William Tipton near the Columbus Ferry landing for the years 1821 to 1823. In 1829 the county seat was moved to Clinton.

A	1822–1905	Case Files—Circuit Court
A	1839–1923	Civil Case Files Index
A	1922–1978	Civil Case Files Index
A	1822–1857	Civil Case Files Index—Common Law
A	1822–1954	Civil Case Files Index—Equity (few after 1954)
A	1855–1923	Civil Case Files Index—Ordinary
U	1832–1937	Court Cases (SY)
A	1885–1977	Criminal Case Files—Indictments Index
A	1885–1978	Criminal Order Books (IN)
U	1822–1877	Deed Books
A	1822–1888	Deed Books
A	1822–1887	Deed Index
U	1822–1887	Deed Index
A	1846–1886	Marriage Bonds
U	1846–1886	Marriage Bonds
A	1931–1984	Marriage License and Bonds (IN)
A	1822–1918	Marriage Register
U	1822–1918	Marriage Register
A	1868–1875	Military Lists
H	?–?	Military Records—Revolutionary and 1812 Pensions (124)
A	1867–1875	Newspapers—*Columbus Dispatch*
A	1867–1875	Newspapers—*Columbus Dispatch* (SI)
H	1853–1882	Newspapers (SA)
U	1822–1881	Order Books
A	1822–1918	Order Books (IN)
A	1835–1977	Order Books—Civil (IN)
A	1867–1892	Order Books—Common Pleas Court (IN EX 1882–87)
A	1856–1861	Order Books—Equity and Criminal Court

A	1822–1892	Tax Book (EX 1830–33, 1876–78)
H	1822–1875	Tax Book (EX 1830–33)
H	1804–1827	Taxes on Land
H	1852–1904	Vital Statistics (SY)
A	1822–1906	Will Books
H	1822–1906	Will Books
U	1822–1906	Will Books
A	1941–1986	Will Books (IN)

Hopkins County

Madisonville 42431
502-821-7361

Public Library	Genealogical Society	Historical Society
31 S. Main Street	P.O. Box 51	107 Union Street
Madisonville 42431	Madisonville 42431	Madisonville 42431
502-825-2680		

Hopkins was formed in 1807 from Henderson County. There was a courthouse fire in 1829 that destroyed records. The county's third or fourth courthouse was burned in December of 1864.

U	1870–1919	Administration Settlement Books
A	1910–1919	Administration Settlement Books
A	1846–1910	Administrator Bonds
U	1846–1913	Administrator Bonds
A	1861–1961	Business Records—Bank and Trust Companies
H	1812–1849	Church Records—Baptist
U	1807–1912	Deed Books
A	1807–1939	Deed Books (IN)
U	1807–1939	Deed Index—Grantors and Grantees
U	1852–1932	Executor Bonds
A	1852–1932	Executor Bonds
A	1846–1913	Guardian Bonds
U	1846–1913	Guardian Bonds
A	1860–1913	Inventory Books and Appraisements
U	1888–1913	Inventory Books and Appraisements
A	1880–1898	Inventory Books of Estates
U	1807–1912	Marriage Bonds
A	1858–1912	Marriage Bonds
A	1810–1911	Marriage Index
U	1892–1912	Marriage Index
U	1807–1892	Marriage Index and Register
A	1806–1911	Marriage Licenses
U	1806–1911	Marriage Licenses
A	1807–1864	Marriage Register
H	?–?	Military Records—Revolutionary and 1812 Pensions (384)

A	1892–1912	Newspapers—*Earlington Bee*
H	1868–1903	Newspapers (SA)
A	1807–1904	Order Books
U	1807–1904	Order Books
H	1807–1830	Tax Book (EX 1809–10, 1818)
A	1807–1862	Tax Book (EX 1809–10, 1818, 1831–32, 1834, 1836)
H	1833–1875	Tax Book (EX 1834, 1836, 1863)
A	1864–1889	Tax Book (EX 1876–78)
H	1852–1907	Vital Statistics (SY)
A	1806–1930	Will Books
U	1806–1930	Will Books Index

JACKSON COUNTY

McKee 40447
606-287-7800

Public Library
P.O. Box 160
D Street
McKee 40447
606-287-8113

Jackson was formed in 1858 from parts of Clay, Estill, Laurel, Owsley, Madison, and Rockcastle counties. The Old Warrior's Trail (or Old Boone Trail) passes through the edge of Jackson County. The path was followed by explorers as early as 1674. The county's third courthouse was destroyed by fire in 1949.

U	1858–1902	Deed Books
A	1858–1975	Deed Books
A	1858–1903	Deed Index
U	1858–1903	Deed Index
A	1878–1907	Deeds—Commissioners
U	1878–1910	Deeds—Commissioners
U	1859–1873	Executor Bonds
A	1859–1873	Executor Bonds (PIN)
A	1882–1913	Executor Bonds (SY)
A	1872–1920	Guardian Settlement Books
U	1872–1920	Guardian Settlement Books
H	1829–1880	Idiot Returns
A	1858–1897	Marriage Bonds
U	1858–1903	Marriage Bonds
A	1898–1901	Marriage Records
A	1858–1906	Marriage Register
H	1858–1906	Marriage Register
U	1858–1906	Marriage Register
A	1938–1986	Minute Books—City Council of McKee
A	1858–1909	Order Books (IN)

U	1858–1909	Order Books
U	1858–1901	Order Books—Circuit Court
A	1858–1901	Order Books—Circuit Court (IN)
A	1968–1986	Ordinances and Resolutions of McKee
H	1858–1875	Tax Book
A	1858–1892	Tax Book (EX 1876–78)
H	1858–1904	Vital Statistics (SY)
H	1860–1969	Will Books
U	1860–1969	Will Books
A	1860–1969	Will Books (IN)

JEFFERSON COUNTY

Louisville 40202
502-625-6374

Louisville Free Public Library	Louisville Genealogical Society	Jeffersontown and Southeast
Fourth and York Streets	P.O. Box 5164	Jefferson County Historical
Louisville 40203	Louisville 40205	Society
502-561-8600, ext. 616		2432 Merriwood Drive
		Jeffersontown 40299
Filson Club	National Society–Sons of	Louisville Civil War Roundtable
1310 South Third Street	American Revolution	P.O. Box 1861
Louisville 40208	1000 S. 4th Street	Louisville 40201
502-635-5083	Louisville 40203	
	502-589-1776	

Jefferson was one of the original Kentucky counties of Virginia and was formed in 1780. Louisville was originally known as Fort Nelson. The current courthouse was built during the years 1835-42 by Gideon Shryock and completed by 1860. It was designed to be used as a state house should the state capitol ever be moved to Louisville.

A	?–?	Baptismal and Marriage Records
A	1898–1910	Birth Records—Index and Records for Louisville
A	1887–1892	Chancery (Vice) Law and Equity Court Cross Index
A	1782–1842	Chancery Court (Old) Defendants—Circuit Court
A	1835–1890	Chancery Court Defendants Index
A	1872–1890	Chancery Court Index (Plaintiffs and Cross Index)
H	1781–1892	Chancery Court Records Index
A	1829–1941	Church Records—Christ Church Registers (IN)
A	1842–1950	Church Records—Fifth Street Baptist
A	1844–1964	Church Records—Green Street Baptist Church
A	1894–1981	Church Records—Hill Street Baptist Church
A	1865–1949	Church Records—St. John's Evangelical
A	1834–1978	Church Records—St. Paul's Episcopal

A	1930–1982	Civil Service Minutes and Appeals—Louisville
A	1781–1865	Common Law Defendants—Circuit Court
A	1781–1865	Common Law Plaintiffs—Circuit Court
A	1865–1882	Common Pleas Court—Defendants
A	1865–1875	Common Pleas Index to Suits
A	1865–1892	Common Pleas—Plaintiffs
A	1866–1910	Death Records—Index and Records for Louisville
H	1783–1794	Deed Books
A	1783–1911	Deed Books
U	1783–1911	Deed Books (UN)
A	1783–1892	Deed Index—Grantees
A	1783–1869	Deed Index—Grantors
H	1796–1870	Deeds—Division Books
U	1797–1870	Division Books 1 and 2
H	1775–1881	Entry Books (index from Jillson's entries)
H	?–?	Genealogy
A	1962–1979	General Ledger—City Clerk of St. Matthews
A	1886–1938	Index Book—Fiscal Court
A	1800–1910	Inventory Books and Settlements Index
A	1938–1976	Journal Book—Trustees of Shively
A	1846–1846	Land Records—Resident Lands Sold for Taxes
A	1846–1846	Land Sold for Taxes—Jefferson Co.
A	1913–1913	Map Index—Louisville and Jefferson Co.
U	1866–1866	Marriage Bonds
U	1781–1856	Marriage Bonds and Licenses
U	1852–1914	Marriage Bonds and Licenses
U	1784–1826	Marriage Bonds and Register
A	1853–1915	Marriage Licenses and Certificates
U	1853–1915	Marriage Licenses and Certificates
U	1908–1916	Marriage Licenses—Black
A	1780–1916	Marriage Licenses and Bonds
A	1852–1915	Marriage Licenses and Bonds—Black
A	1784–1911	Marriage Register
H	1784–1911	Marriage Register
U	1784–1911	Marriage Register
H	?–?	Military Records—Revolutionary and 1812 Pensions (940)
A	1784–1829	Minute Book (most years)
A	1971–1987	Minute Index—Louisville
A	1975–1987	Minute Book—Louisville
A	1894–1986	Minute Book—Trustees of North Middletown
H	1780–1817	Minute Books
U	1784–1829	Minute Books
A	1950–1985	Minute Books—City Council of St. Matthews
A	1983–1985	Minute Books—City Council—City of Plantation
A	1897–1918	Minute Books—Louisville (PIN to 1822, IN from 1946)
A	1951–1966	Minute Books—Planning Commission—St. Matthews
A	1960–1985	Minute Books—Trustees City of Plantation

A	1886–1978	Minute/Order Books—Fiscal Court
A	1911–1977	Minutes—Board of Education—Anchorage
A	1951–1986	Minutes—City Council of West Buechel City Clerk
A	1828–1851	Minutes—Common Council of Louisville and Index
A	1780–1901	Minutes—Court
A	1911–1917	Minutes—Fire Department—Anchorage
A	1886–1982	Minutes—Legislative Body—Anchorage
A	1779–1779	Minutes—Louisville
A	1781–1828	Minutes—Trustees and Commissioners of Louisville
U	1793–1888	Misc. Records—Depositions, Deeds, Wills
A	1981–1987	Municipal Orders of West Buechel
A	1903–1913	Naturalization—Declarations of Intention
A	1893–1912	Naturalization Books—Circuit Court
A	1910–1913	Naturalization Certificates—Circuit Court
A	1851–1906	Naturalization Index
A	1896–1900	Naturalization Letters
A	1893–1905	Naturalization Records—Petitions
A	1910–1912	Naturalization and Petition Records—Circuit Court
A	1896–1906	Naturalizations—County Court (PIN)
A	1851–1868	Newspapers—*Daily Louisville Democrat*
H	1849–1936	Newspapers—*Louisville Anzieger*
A	1851–1868	Newspapers—*Louisville Daily Courier*
A	1830–1868	Newspapers—*Louisville Daily Journal*
A	1917–1950	Newspapers—*Louisville Leader*
A	1844–1850	Newspapers—*Louisville Morning Courier*
H	1838–1945	Newspapers (SA)
A	1858–1860	Newspapers—*The Guardian* (Catholic weekly)
A	1907–1912	Newspapers—*The Jeffersonian*
A	?–?	Occupational License Registers of St. Matthews
H	1780–1900	Order Books
A	1784–1785	Order Books
H	1784–1785	Order Books
A	1836–1897	Order Books—Louisville Police Court (PIN)
U	1781–1901	Order Minutes
A	1890–1898	Ordinance and Resolution Book—South Louisville
A	1950–1987	Ordinance Book—City of St. Matthews (IN)
A	1971–1985	Ordinance Book—Louisville (IN from 1974)
A	1954–1986	Ordinances of West Buechel (IN)
U	1875–1875	Poll Books
A	1875–1875	Poll Books—Constitution
A	1976–1986	Resolutions of West Buechel (IN)
A	1871–1901	School of Pharmacy—University of Louisville
A	1872–1977	Suits Cross Index—Chancery and Equity Courts
A	1872–1890	Suits Index—Chancery Court
A	1805–1860	Suits Index—Chancery Court Cross Index
A	1893–1977	Suits Index—Circuit Court
A	1969–1974	Tax Assessments and Collection Rolls

A	1966–1979	Tax Bills—Anchorage
A	1883–1883	Tax Book
A	1789–1875	Tax Book (EX 1798, 1815–16, 1832)
H	1789–1875	Tax Book (EX 1798, 1815–16, 1832)
H	1870–1875	Tax Book—Blacks
A	1834–1885	Tax Book—Louisville (UN)
A	1937–1979	Tax Book—Shively
A	1967–1986	Tax List—City of St. Matthews
A	1951–1986	Tax Registers—City of St. Matthews
H	1852–1910	Vital Statistics—Birth, Death, and Marriage
U	1866–1910	Vital Statistics—Louisville
H	1852–1859	Vital Statistics (SY)
H	1783–1901	Will Books
A	1784–1901	Will Books
U	1784–1901	Will Books
H	1784–1919	Will Index
A	1784–1919	Will Index
U	1784–1919	Will Index
A	1833–1872	Will Index and Abstracts—DAR

JESSAMINE COUNTY

Nicholasville 40356
606-885-4161

Public Library
101 South Second Street
Nicholasville 40356
606-885-3523

Historical Society
139 Lowry Lane
Wilmore 40390

Jessamine County was formed in 1799 from the southern part of Fayette County. Court sessions were first held at the tavern of Fisher Rice when the county was first formed. The present building was completed in 1878.

H	1840–1974	Church Records—Baptist
A	1883–1892	Civil Suits Index—Common Pleas
A	1954–1981	Civil Suits Index—Quarter Sessions
A	1799–1848	Civil Suits—Quarter Sessions Index
A	1849–1967	Common Law Index to Suits—Quarter Sessions
A	1953–1966	Criminal Order Book—Police Court—Nicholasville
A	1876–1977	Criminal Order Books (IN)
A	1850–1977	Criminal Suits Index—Quarter Sessions
H	1799–1865	Deed Books
A	1799–1974	Deed Books
A	1799–1947	Deed Index
H	1799–1947	Deed Index
U	1799–1865	Deed Index—Grantors and Grantees
A	1850–1967	Equity Suits Index—Quarter Sessions Court

H	1829–1880	Idiot Returns
A	1799–1867	Marriage Bonds
A	1799–1867	Marriage Licenses and Bonds (IN)
U	1799–1867	Marriage Licenses and Bonds (IN)
H	1799–1867	Marriage Licenses and Bonds (IN)
H	?–?	Military Records—Revolutionary and 1812 Pensions (285)
A	1887–1985	Minute Book—Board of Council of Nicholasville
U	1790–1864	Misc. Records—Depositions, Deeds, Wills
H	1884–1885	Newspapers (SA)
H	1799–1867	Order Books
A	1799–1867	Order Books
U	1799–1867	Order Books
A	1803–1977	Order Books—Circuit Court (IN)
H	1799–1875	Tax Book (EX 1814, 1818, 1832, 1836, 1839)
A	1799–1875	Tax Book (EX 1814, 1818, 1832, 1836, 1839)
A	1879–1911	Tax Book (EX 1906–07, 1909)
H	1852–1907	Vital Statistics (SY)
U	1799–1865	Will Books
U	1799–1865	Will Books
A	1799–1865	Will Books (IN)
H	1799–1865	Will Books (IN)

JOHNSON COUNTY

Paintsville 41240
606-789-2557

Public Library
Church and Main
Paintsville 41240
606-789-4355

Historical and Genealogical Society
P.O. Box 788
Paintsville 41240

This county was formed in 1843 from parts of Floyd, Lawrence, and Morgan counties. In 1860, part of Johnson County was used to form Magoffin, and in 1870, part of its territory was taken to help create Martin County. Paintsville was originally called Paint Station and was founded in 1790 in an area where Indian paintings were discovered on nearby cliffs.

A	1981–1983	Articles of Incorporation
A	1843–1940	Case Files Index—Circuit Court
A	1953–1977	Civil Case Files Index
U	1843–1900	Commonwealth Orders—Circuit Court
A	1876–1900	Criminal Court Order Books (IN)
A	1900–1977	Criminal Order Books (IN)
U	1843–1902	Deed Books
A	1843–1970	Deed Books
A	1975–1983	Deed Books
A	1843–1933	Deed Index

U	1843-1933	Deed Index
A	1875-1875	Deeds—Commissioners
A	1875-1935	Deeds—Commissioners
U	1877-1905	Deeds—Commissioners
H	1829-1880	Idiot Returns
A	1982-1983	Lease Books
A	1982-1983	Lis Pendens Books
A	1843-1914	Marriage Bonds
U	1843-1914	Marriage Bonds and Certificates
A	1899-1928	Military Records—Veteran Discharge Book (IN)
A	1943-1980	Military Records—Veteran Discharge Books (IN)
A	1965-1969	Mineral Lease Books
A	1908-1973	Minute Books—City Council of Paintsville
A	1967-1970	Mortgage Books
A	1983-1983	Mortgage Books
H	1862-1881	Newspapers (SA)
U	1844-1907	Order Books
A	1851-1907	Order Books
A	1983-1983	Order Books
U	1851-1904	Order Books—Circuit Court
A	1843-1977	Order Books—Circuit Court (IN)
A	1843-1938	Order Books—Circuit Court General Index
U	1843-1940	Order Index—Circuit Court Civil Cases
A	1872-1938	Ordinances and Proceedings Book—Paintsville (IN)
U	1895-1910	School Census
A	1898-1910	School Census
A	1844-1935	Survey Books (IN)
H	1844-1875	Tax Book (EX 1847)
A	1844-1892	Tax Book (EX 1847, 1876-78)
H	1852-1904	Vital Statistics (SY)
U	1854-1927	Will Books
H	1859-1927	Will Books
A	1869-1927	Will Books
A	1979-1983	Will Books

KENTON COUNTY

Covington 41011　　　　　　　　　　Independence 41051
606-491-0702　　　　　　　　　　　 606-356-9272

Public Library	Historical Society	Northern Kentucky Historical
Fifth and Scott	P.O. Box 641	Society
Covington 41011	Covington 41011	Box 151
606-491-7610		Ft. Thomas 41075

Kenton was formed in 1840 from Campbell County. Both Independence and Covington serve as county seats. The microfilm records are often mislabeled, as are the original records, at all archival locations. Therefore, it is advisable to check both series of records when researching this county. The courthouse in Independence was begun in 1840; the county's courthouse in Covington was dedicated in 1843. Covington's new courthouse was completed in 1970.

H	1867-1965	Administrator Bonds
H	1896-1910	Birth Certificates—Covington (IN)
H	1896-1910	Birth Records (IN)
A	1968-1979	Building Permits—Crescent Springs
A	1969-1970	Case Files—Circuit Court
H	?-?	Cemetery Records—Independence
A	1834-1903	City Directories—Various Cities
A	1978-1981	Civil and Criminal Case Files Index
A	1840-1977	Civil Cases Files Index
H	1848-1848	Commissioners Books
H	1852-1877	Constable Book
A	1965-1977	Criminal Order Books (IN)
H	1881-1910	Death Certificates—Covington
H	1881-1890	Death Certificates Index—Covington
H	1873-1931	Death Records—Funeral Home Account Books—Donnally
H	1881-1910	Death Records (IN)
A	1860-1901	Deed Books—Covington
H	1887-1901	Deed Books—Covington
A	1840-1904	Deed Books—Independence
H	1840-1904	Deed Books—Independence
A	1860-1900	Deed Index—Covington
H	1904-1949	Deed Index—Independence
A	?-?	Deed Index—Independence
H	1866-1954	Executions—New Series
H	1895-1902	Fiscal Court Records—Covington
H	?-?	Genealogy—Barton Collection—Other Collections
A	1841-1877	Guardian Bonds—County
A	1840-1900	Inventory and Settlement Books
A	1858-1869	Inventory and Settlement Books
H	1840-1906	Inventory and Settlement Books—Independence
A	1978-1984	Ledgers—General—Crescent Springs
A	1840-1876	Marriage Bonds
A	1907-1912	Marriage Bonds
H	1874-1910	Marriage Bonds (IN)
A	1906-1907	Marriage Certificates
H	1874-1941	Marriage Index
H	1840-1902	Marriage Licenses
A	1902-1906	Marriage Licenses
H	1840-1935	Marriage Licenses Index—Independence
H	?-?	Military Records—Veterans' Graves
H	?-?	Military Rosters
A	1826-1832	Minute Books—Covington
H	1826-1901	Minute Books—Covington

A	1963–1982	Minute Books—Crescent Springs
A	1978–1984	Minute Books—Ft. Mitchell
A	1939–1977	Minute Books—Ft. Wright
H	1868–1875	Minute Books—Independence
A	1959–1984	Minute Books—Lakeside Park
A	1864–1969	Minute Books—Ludlow (IN)
A	1910–1973	Minute and Ordinance Books—Ft. Mitchell
A	1855–1901	Mortgage Book
H	1857–1901	Mortgage Books—Independence
A	1849–1954	Naturalizations—Declarations of Intentions
H	1844–1900	Newspapers (SY)
H	1853–1908	Order Books and Index
H	1840–1848	Order Books and Index—Independence
A	1858–1901	Order Books—Covington
A	1840–1930	Order Books—Independence
A	1858–1939	Order Index
A	1871–1887	Order Books—Chancery Court
A	1848–1889	Order Books—Circuit Court—Independence (IN)
A	1962–1977	Order Books—Circuit Court—Civil Division
A	1850–1885	Order Books—Circuit Court (IN)
A	1938–1965	Order Books—Common Law—Equity and Criminal (IN)
A	1840–1977	Order Books—Criminal Cases Cross Index
A	1866–1888	Order Books—Criminal Court
A	1895–1905	Order Books—Fiscal Court
A	1840–1962	Order Books—Index to Probate
A	1949–1985	Ordinance and Resolution Books—Ft. Wright
A	1957–1976	Ordinance Books—Crescent Springs
A	1859–1927	Plat Books—Ludlow (SY)
A	?–?	Plats and Index (no dates)
A	1807–1965	Probate Bonds
A	1960–1984	Resolutions Book—Ft. Mitchell
A	1853–1878	Road Books
H	1853–1879	Road Books—Independence
A	1977–1987	School Census
A	1912–1922	School Census (EX 1915-20)
A	1915–1977	School Census Cards
H	1911–1922	School Enumeration
A	1977–1983	School Records—Attendance
H	1841–1852	Sheriffs Bonds
H	1897–1914	Tavern Keepers Bonds (with Administrator Bonds)
A	1887–1892	Tax Book—Covington
A	1840–1892	Tax Book (EX 1876-78)
H	1840–1875	Tax Book (EX 1851, 1858)
A	1975–1979	Tax Book—Ft. Mitchell
H	1852–1907	Vital Statistics (SY)
A	1936–1972	Voter Registration Records (IN)
A	1858–1915	Will Books

H	1871-1937	Will Books
H	1858-1938	Will Index
A	1858-1915	Will Index

KNOTT COUNTY
Hindman 41822
606-785-5651

Public Library
P.O. Box 667
Hindman 41822
606-785-5412

Historical Society
Hindman 41822

Knott County was formed in 1884 from parts of Breathitt, Floyd, Letcher, and Perry counties. The second Knott courthouse was built in the 1890s and burned in 1929.

A	1885-1919	Administrator Bonds
U	1885-1924	Administrator Bonds
A	1883-1906	Deed Books
U	1883-1906	Deed Books
A	1883-1968	Deed Index
U	1883-1968	Deed Index
A	1891-1924	Guardian Bonds
U	1891-1924	Guardian Bonds
A	1884-1898	Marriage Bonds
H	1884-1898	Marriage Bonds
U	1884-1898	Marriage Bonds and Certificates
A	1884-1912	Marriage Books (IN)
A	1902-1911	Marriage Licenses
H	1902-1911	Marriage Licenses
U	1902-1911	Marriage Licenses and Certificates
U	1884-1951	Marriage Records—Brides and Grooms Index
H	1884-1951	Marriage Register
A	1884-1951	Marriage Register Index
H	?-?	Military Records—Veterans' Graves
U	1888-1904	Order Books
A	1888-1904	Order Index
A	1884-1930	Surveyor Books (IN)
U	1884-1930	Surveyor Books
A	1889-1892	Tax Book
A	1889-1889	Tax Book—Blacks
A	1892-1892	Tax Book—Blacks
H	1892-1948	Will Books
U	1892-1948	Will Books
A	1892-1948	Will Books (IN)

KNOX COUNTY

Barbourville 40906
606-546-3568

Public Library	Genealogical Society	Historical Society
Daniel Boone Drive	2603 Aintree Way	P.O. Box 528
Barbourville 40906	Louisville 40220	Barbourville 40906
606-546-5339		

Knox was formed in 1800 from Lincoln County. Since its creation, parts of Knox have gone to create parts of Bell, Clay, Harlan, Laurel, Rockcastle, and Whitley. It was through the Gap in Knox that many early pioneers traveled on their way to the west. The county has had five courthouses; the present one was built in 1964.

A	1847–1850	Apprentice Bonds (in Will Book B)
H	1804–1930	Church Records—Baptist Minutes, lists, etc.
H	1800–1858	Deed Book Abstracts
U	1800–1912	Deed Books
A	1801–1956	Deed Books (IN)
U	1800–1899	Deed Index
A	1801–1936	Deed Index
H	1829–1880	Idiot Returns
H	1800–1844	Land Survey Books 1 and 2—Abstracts
H	1798–1827	Land Tax Receipts from Treasurers and Auditors
A	1800–1912	Marriage Books (IN from 1868)
U	1800–1850	Marriage Index
U	1800–1912	Marriage Licenses, Bonds, and Records
H	1800–1902	Marriage Records, Licenses, and Bonds
A	1865–1886	Marriage Register
A	1866–1869	Marriage Register—Freedmen
H	?–?	Military Records—Revolutionary and 1812 Pensions (335)
H	?–?	Military Records—Veterans' Graves
A	1921–1982	Minute Books (Corbin)
A	1904–1982	Minute/Ordinance/Resolution Books—Corbin
U	1823–1826	Misc. Records—Depositions, Deeds, Wills
A	1871–1887	Mortgage Book
H	1787–1861	Muster Rolls
H	1873–1959	Newspapers (SA)
A	1800–1816	Order Books (IN)
U	1801–1816	Order Index
A	1800–1802	Order Books—Quarter Sessions
A	1978–1985	Payroll Register—First National Bank—Corbin
A	1879–1881	Road Orders
A	1894–1905	School Census
U	1894–1905	School Census
H	1880–1905	School Census (EX 1891–97)

H	1800–1875	Tax Book (EX 1813–14, 1832)
A	1800–1892	Tax Book (EX 1813–14, 1832, 1876–78, 1890)
H	1880–1880	Tax Book Abstract
H	1852–1907	Vital Statistics (SY)
U	1862–1966	Will Books
A	1803–1966	Will Books (IN)
H	1803–1966	Will Books (IN)
U	1803–1862	Will Index
A	1803–1842	Will Index and Abstracts

LARUE COUNTY

Hodgenville 42728
502-358-3544

Public Library	Genealogical Society
201 S. Lincoln Boulevard	P.O. Box 173
Hodgenville 42748	Rt. 2
502-358-3851	Hodgenville 42748

Larue was formed in 1843 from Hardin County. Its courthouse burned on 21 February 1865 in a fire set by guerrillas. However, the records were saved.

U	1852–1858	Birth and Death Certificates
U	1896–1899	Birth and Death Certificates
H	1852–1899	Birth Certificates
H	?–?	Cemetery Records and Index
H	1852–1899	Death Certificates
H	1843–1881	Deed Books
U	1843–1881	Deed Books
A	1843–1986	Deed Books
A	1843–1935	Deed Index
H	1843–1935	Deed Index
U	1843–1935	Deed Index
A	1852–1885	Guardian Bonds
U	1852–1885	Guardian Bonds
H	1852–1885	Guardian Bonds
U	1843–1870	Inventory Books
H	1843–1870	Inventory Books
A	1843–1870	Inventory Books
A	1850–1877	Marriage Bonds (IN from 1855)
A	1847–1913	Marriage Bonds
H	1847–1913	Marriage Bonds
U	1847–1913	Marriage Bonds (PIN)
H	1843–1862	Marriage Bonds—Consents and Licenses
U	1843–1914	Marriage Bonds—Consents and Licenses
A	1843–1914	Marriage Licenses
U	1852–1861	Marriage Records—Misc.

U	1843–1914	Marriage Register
A	1843–1914	Marriage Register
H	1843–1914	Marriage Register
A	1855–1881	Marriage Register (IN)
H	?–?	Military Records—Veterans' Graves
H	1843–1920	Newspapers (SA)
A	1843–1900	Order Books
U	1859–1900	Order Books
H	1843–1900	Order Books (EX 1848–58)
A	1845–1892	Tax Book (EX 1876–78)
H	1843–1880	Tax Book (EX part of 1873, 1876–79)
A	1852–1856	Vital Statistics
A	1896–1899	Vital Statistics
H	1852–1907	Vital Statistics (SY)
A	1843–1965	Will Books
H	1843–1965	Will Books
U	1843–1965	Will Books

LAUREL COUNTY

London 40741
606-864-5158

Public Library	Historical Society
116 E. Fourth Street	P.O. Box 816
London 40741	London 40741
606-864-5759	

Laurel was formed in 1826 from parts of Clay, Knox, Rockcastle, and Whitley counties. Only one courthouse fire has been identified on 9 December 1958. A new courthouse was completed in 1961 to replace the earlier structure.

H	1853–1871	Administrator Bonds
A	1853–1871	Administrator Bonds (IN)
H	1879–1925	Administrator Settlement Books
H	1914–1916	Business Records—Grocery Register
A	1931–1985	Criminal Order Books (IN)
A	1872–1891	Deed Books
H	1843–1884	Deed Books (IN)
A	1962–1985	Deed Books (IN)
A	1826–1884	Deed Books (UNIN)
A	1826–1964	Deed Index
A	?–?	Deed Index
H	1876–1891	Deeds—Commissioners
A	1876–1891	Deeds—Commissioners (IN)
A	1898–1939	Deeds—Commissioners and Sheriffs
A	1826–1845	Executor Bonds (IN from 1826–42)
H	1826–1845	Executor Bonds

A	1853–1910	Executor Bonds (IN)
H	1853–1910	Executor Bonds
H	1875–1927	Executors Settlement Book
A	1875–1927	Executors Settlement Book (UNIN)
A	1861–1873	Fee Book (IN)
H	1861–1873	Fee Book (IN)
A	1853–1893	Guardian Bonds (IN)
H	1853–1893	Guardian Bonds
H	1829–1880	Idiot Returns
H	1826–1951	Land Survey Books
A	?–?	Maps—Geologic Atlas of Laurel County
A	1875–1904	Marriage Bonds—Blacks (IN)
A	1853–1923	Marriage Bonds (IN to 1915)
H	1826–1923	Marriage Books
A	1953–1960	Marriage Books
A	1826–1937	Marriage Index
H	1826–1937	Marriage Index
A	1826–1897	Marriage Register (IN)
H	?–?	Military Records—Veterans' Graves
U	1825–1834	Misc. Records—Depositions, Deeds, Wills
A	1959–1959	Mortgage Book
A	1956–1964	Mortgage Index
H	1787–1861	Muster Rolls
H	1891–1906	Naturalization Records—Register of Citizens
A	1891–1906	Naturalized Citizens Register (IN)
A	1895–1902	Newspapers—Corbin (SI)
H	1863–1954	Newspapers (SA)
H	1826–1889	Order Books
A	1955–1962	Order Books
A	1826–1897	Order Books (UNIN)
A	1853–1936	Order Index
H	1853–1936	Order Index
A	1955–1977	Order Books—Circuit Court (IN)
A	1879–1925	Settlement Books
A	1955–1985	Suits Off Docket—Circuit Court Index
A	1826–1951	Survey Book (IN from 1857)
A	1827–1857	Tax Book (EX 1830, 1832, 1834, 1836–39, 1856)
H	1827–1875	Tax Book (EX 1830, 1832, 1834, 1837–39, 1856)
A	1879–1892	Tax Book (EX 1891)
H	1852–1904	Vital Statistics (SY)
A	1955–1958	Will Books
A	1826–1960	Will Books (IN)
A	1826–1939	Will Books (IN)
H	1826–1939	Will Books (IN)

LAWRENCE COUNTY

Louisa 41230
606-638-4108

Public Library	Lawrence County Regional	Big Sandy Valley Historical
W. Main and Jefferson	Historical Society	Society
Louisa 41230	100 Rodburn Road, Apt. 121	Box 723
606-638-4497	Morehead 40351	Louisa 41230

Lawrence County was formed in 1822 from parts of Floyd and Greenup counties. The first courthouse was built in 1823; the third and current one was built in 1961-64.

U	1865-1907	Administrator Bonds
U	1822-1902	Deed Books
A	1822-1970	Deed Books
U	1822-1970	Deed Index
A	1886-1900	Deeds—Commissioners
U	1865-1891	Guardians Bonds
H	1829-1880	Idiot Returns
U	1871-1913	Inventory Books and Appraisements
U	1868-1916	Marriage Bonds
A	1865-1916	Marriage License and Bonds
U	1822-1859	Marriage Records
A	1822-1970	Marriage Records (IN)
H	1822-1970	Marriage Records (IN)
U	1822-1970	Marriage Records (IN)
U	1875-1893	Marriage Records—Ministers Returns
H	1858-1916	Marriage Register and Bonds
A	1858-1873	Marriage Register (IN from 1842-62)
U	1858-1876	Marriage Register, Certificates, Returns, and Bonds
A	1822-1893	Marriage Returns (PIN)
H	?-?	Military Records—Veterans' Graves
A	1897-1984	Minute Books—Louisa (IN from 1946)
A	1885-1898	Newspapers—Big Sandy News (SI)
A	1809-1810	Newspapers—Farmers Friend
H	1868-1881 ·	Newspapers (SA)
A	1822-1904	Order Books
U	1822-1904	Order Books
U	1898-1902	School Census
A	1898-1902	School Census (some lists for blacks)
H	1822-1838	Tax Book (EX 1830, 1832, 1835-36)
A	1822-1892	Tax Book (EX 1832, 1839, 1870-72, 1876-78)
H	1840-1880	Tax Book (EX 1870-72, 1876-79)
A	1891-1891	Tax Book—Blacks
H	1852-1907	Vital Statistics (SY)

H	1824-1941	Will Books
U	1824-1917	Will Books
A	1824-1917	Will Books (IN)

LEE COUNTY

Beattyville 41311
606-464-2596

Public Library
P.O. Box V
Main Street
Beattyville 41311
606-464-8014

Historical and Genealogical Society
P.O. Box 604
Beattyville 41311

Lee County was formed in 1870 from parts of Breathitt, Estill, Owsley, and Wolfe counties. The first permanent courthouse was built ca. 1873-75 and remained in use until 1976. The iron fence from the original building still remains.

A	1870-1920	Administrator Bonds
U	1870-1920	Administrator Bonds
A	1922-1967	Civil Suits—Circuit Court Index
A	1879-1977	Criminal Order Books (IN)
U	1870-1901	Deed Books
A	1870-1985	Deed Books (IN)
U	1870-1967	Deed Index
A	1870-1950	Deeds and Mortgages Index
A	1877-1907	Deeds—Commissioners
U	1879-1911	Deeds—Commissioners
A	1870-1910	Executor Bonds
U	1870-1910	Executor Bonds
U	1870-1917	Guardian Bonds
A	1870-1917	Guardian Bonds
A	1874-1916	Guardian Settlement Books
U	1874-1916	Guardian Settlement Books
U	1874-1942	Inventory Books
A	1874-1942	Inventory Books
A	1870-1913	Marriage Bonds
U	1870-1913	Marriage Bonds
A	1870-1913	Marriage Index
H	?-?	Military Records—Veterans' Graves
A	1872-1894	Mortgages
U	1872-1894	Mortgages
H	1875-1954	Newspapers (SA)
A	1870-1905	Order Books
U	1870-1905	Order Books
A	1870-1977	Order Books—Circuit Court (IN)
A	1870-1891	Tax Book (EX 1876-78)

H	1870-1884	Tax Book (EX 1876-79, 1881-83)
H	1874-1901	Vital Statistics
A	1873-1945	Will Books
U	1873-1945	Will Books

LESLIE COUNTY
Hyden 41749
606-672-2193

Public Library	Historical Society
P.O. Box 498	Leslie County Library
Main Street	P.O. Box 498
Hyden 41749	Hyden 41749
606-672-2460	606-672-2460

Leslie was formed in 1878 from parts of Clay, Harlan, and Perry counties. The first courthouse was built in 1878, and the second and present was completed in 1954.

A	1879-1988	Deed Books
A	1879-1983	Deed Index
A	1872-1916	Deeds—Commissioners
A	1893-1933	Deeds—Sheriffs
A	1877-1879	Judgments—Default (UNIN)
A	1866-1942	Judgments—Inferior Courts
A	1894-1905	Marriage Bonds (IN)
H	1884-1925	Marriage Bonds
A	1878-1987	Marriage Book and Index
A	1879-1913	Marriage Book and Index—Blacks
A	1884-1976	Marriage Bonds (IN)
H	1878-1975	Marriage Index
A	1884-1976	Marriage Index
H	1896-1911	Marriage Register
A	1883-1916	Marriage Register (PIN)
H	?-?	Military Records—Veterans' Graves
A	1881-1900	Mortgage Book (IN)
H	1878-1878	Newspapers (SA)
A	1878-1893	Order Books (UNIN)
A	1893-1906	Order Books (UNIN)
A	1888-1892	Order Books—Common Pleas
A	1873-1887	Order Books—Circuit Court
A	1878-1893	Order Books—Circuit Court
A	1881-1929	Settlement Books
A	1878-1924	Suit Index of the Circuit Court
H	1880-1884	Tax Book (EX 1881-83)
A	1879-1892	Tax Book (EX 1886)
A	1944-1982	Veteran Discharge

H	1878-1879	Vital Statistics
H	1883-1947	Will Books
A	1883-1983	Will Books

LETCHER COUNTY

Whitesburg 41858
606-633-2432

Public Library
Whitesburg 41858
606-633-7547

Historical Society
Whitesburg 41858

This county was formed in 1842 from Perry and Harlan counties. In 1751 Christopher Gist of the Ohio Land Company discovered a natural route from Kentucky to Virginia here when he came down the Ohio River and left Kentucky by way of Letcher County. Letcher has had three courthouses; the current one was built in 1965.

A	1866-1915	Administrator Bonds
U	1866-1923	Administrator Bonds
A	1875-1923	Appraisements and Inventory Books
A	1860-1923	Case Files—Plaintiff Index
A	1842-1945	Case Files—Circuit Court (IN)
A	1911-1977	Civil Case File Off Docket Index
A	1953-1977	Civil Case File On Docket Index
U	1844-1901	Deed Books
A	1848-1901	Deed Books
A	1900-1937	Deed Books
U	1844-1964	Deed Index
A	1848-1959	Deed Index
A	1881-1902	Deeds—Commissioners
U	1881-1902	Deeds—Commissioners
H	1820-1880	Idiot Returns
U	1875-1920	Inventory Books and Appraisements
A	1870-1905	Land Entry Book
A	1842-1903	Land Survey Books
U	1870-1884	Marriage Bonds
A	1871-1912	Marriage Bonds
U	1884-1912	Marriage Bonds and Certificates
A	1842-1940	Marriage Index
H	1842-1940	Marriage Index
U	1861-1884	Marriage Register
H	1875-1912	Marriage Register and Bonds
A	1941-1958	Marriage Register Index
A	1875-1884	Marriage Registers
U	1842-1958	Marriages Index—Brides and Grooms

H	?-?	Military Records—Veterans' Graves
A	1878-1893	Minute Book—Quarterly Court and Court of Claims
A	1866-1893	Minute Book—Quarterly Court (most years)
H	1921-1956	Newspapers—*Mountain Eagle*
H	1932-1949	Newspapers—*Neon*
H	1875-1882	Newspapers (SA)
A	1866-1890	Order Books
A	1890-1904	Order Books
U	1890-1904	Order Books
A	1852-1941	Order Books—Circuit Court (IN from 1867)
A	1885-1916	Processioners Report
U	1855-1947	Surveyor Books
A	1858-1927	Surveyor Books
H	1843-1880	Tax Book (EX 1853, 1862-64, 1866, 1876-79)
A	1843-1892	Tax Book (EX 1853, 1862-66, 1876-79)
H	1852-1907	Vital Statistics
A	1871-1905	Will Books
H	1871-1905	Will Books
U	1871-1905	Will Books

LEWIS COUNTY

Vanceburg 41179
606-796-3062

Public Library	Historical Society
422 Second Street	P.O. Box 212
Vanceburg 41179	Vanceburg 41179
606-796-2532	

Lewis County was formed in 1807 from Mason County. The first courthouse was at Poplar Flat in 1806. The county seat was moved to Clarksburg in 1809 and then Vanceburg where a courthouse was erected in 1865.

A	1800-1928	Church Records—Baptist
U	1800-1928	Church Records—Baptist Forks of Salt Lick
A	1807-1984	Conveyances Index
U	1807-1867	Deed Books
A	1807-1984	Deed Books
A	1807-1952	Deed Index
U	1807-1952	Deed Index
U	?-?	Family Information—Landers—Old Family Bible
U	?-?	Family Information—Wilson and Halbert
A	?-?	History of Lewis County in the World War
H	1829-1880	Idiot Returns
A	1807-1952	Ledger Book
A	1807-1867	Marriage Books
A	1852-1987	Marriage Books (IN)

U	1807-1867	Marriage Books—Brides and Grooms Index
A	1808-1962	Marriage Index—Brides and Grooms
A	1807-1852	Marriage Register
H	?-?	Military Records—Revolutionary and 1812 Pensions (177)
H	?-?	Military Records—Veterans' Graves
A	1868-1985	Minute Books—City Council of Vanceburg
H	1863-1882	Newspapers (SA)
A	1939-1969	Ordinance Book—City Council of Vanceburg (IN)
A	1982-1985	Resolution Book—City Council of Vanceburg
U	1832-1894	Surveyor Books 1-3 (PIN)
A	1831-1901	Surveys
A	1807-1833	Tax Book (EX 1813, 1818, 1822, 1832)
H	1807-1870	Tax Book (EX 1813, 1818, 1822, 1832)
A	1872-1911	Tax Book (EX 1876-78, 1907)
H	1872-1885	Tax Book (EX 1876-79, 1882, 1884)
H	1851-1878	Vital Statistics
A	1807-1867	Will Books
U	1807-1867	Will Books
A	1807-1941	Will Index
U	1807-1941	Will Index
A	1806-1877	Will Index and Abstracts—DAR

LINCOLN COUNTY

Stanford 40484
606-365-2601

Harvey Helm Memorial Library	Historical Society
301 Third Street	313 Redwood Drive
Stanford 40484	Stanford 40484
606-365-7513	

Lincoln was formed on 1 November 1780 from the original Kentucky County of Virginia. Lincoln was the largest of the counties, comprising about one third of the state. As a result of its size, fifty-eight counties have been cut from Lincoln County. From 1780 to 1786, the county seat of Lincoln was in Harrodsburg. Stanford, its current county seat, was founded in 1786 and was originally on the old buffalo path through the territory, which later became the first road in Kentucky, the old Wilderness Road. It is located near St. Asaph, or Logan's Fort, established in 1775. The first courthouse was built in 1785. Lincoln County has some of the oldest records in Kentucky, some of which are written on sheepskin.

H	1874-1926	Attachment Bonds (1874, 1878, 1891, 1922, 1926)
H	1880-1928	Bail Bonds (1880, 1908, 1924, 1928)
H	1864-1875	Bond Book—Justice of the Peace
H	?-?	Cemetery Records

H	1819-1893	Church Records—Baptist, Episcopalian, Disciples of Christ
H	1902-1913	Claims Docket
H	1877-1879	Commissioners Sales of Real Estate
H	1796-1800	Commissions and Suits
A	1781-1866	Deed Books
H	1781-1866	Deed Books
U	1781-1866	Deed Books
H	1780-1870	Deed Index
U	1780-1870	Deed Index
A	1780-1902	Deed Index
H	1854-1892	Deeds—Unrecorded Deeds List
H	1853-1888	Dockets—Claim (SY)
H	1881-1898	Dockets—Court Records
H	1863-1901	Dockets—Various Courts
H	1799-1787	Entry Records—Index to Lincoln Entries
H	1897-1912	Equity Book
H	1851-1863	Equity Docket—Index to Estate Papers
H	1808-1918	Execution Books
H	1821-1828	Execution Records
H	1930-1937	Executions for Cost—Criminal Court
H	1893-1916	Executors and Administrators List
H	1863-1901	Executors and Administrators Lists
H	1850-1852	Executor Bonds
H	1780-1835	Forfeited Lands and Sales
H	1863-1896	Guardians List
H	1899-1899	Idiot Bond Book
H	1853-1906	Journals
H	1877-1880	Judgment by Default
H	1899-1903	Judges Book
H	1883-1885	Judgment Books
H	1801-1806	Land Cases of County
H	1800-1801	Land Depositions
H	?-?	Land Office Index—Virginia (Kentucky Military District)
H	1891-1906	Land Sales—Sheriff for Taxes (dated 1891, 1897, 1906)
H	1798-1827	Land Tax Receipts—Treasurer's and Auditor's
H	1877-1880	Ledger—Common Pleas Court
H	1867-1877	Ledger—Quarterly Court
H	1857-1915	Ledgers and Indexes—Circuit Court and Dockets
H	1867-1914	Magistrates Judgments Transcript
A	1781-1865	Marriage Consents and Bonds
U	1781-1865	Marriage Consents and Bonds
H	1784-1908	Marriage Records
H	?-?	Marriage Records—DAR Report and Index
U	1781-1908	Marriage Register Index
A	1784-1908	Marriage Register Index
H	1787-1861	Military Muster Rolls

H	?-?	Military Records—Revolutionary and 1812 Pensions (565)
H	?-?	Military Records—Veterans' Graves
H	1895-1899	Minute Book—Circuit Court
H	1881-1887	Minute Books
H	1885-1939	Minute Books
U	1786-1826	Misc. Records—Depositions, Deeds, Wills
H	1868-1882	Newspapers (SA)
H	1781-1865	Order Books
U	1781-1865	Order Books
A	1781-1865	Order Books
A	1783-1786	Order Books
H	1875-1832	Order Books
H	1883-1888	Order Books
H	1796-1800	Order Books—Danville
H	1783-1802	Order Books—Supreme Court
H	1870-1926	Quarterly Court Docket
H	1870-1927	Replevin Books (dated 1870, 1921, 1926, 1927)
H	1897-1910	School Census
H	1889-1892	School Census—Blacks
H	1906-1907	School Census—Blacks
H	1895-1913	Supervisors Assessments
H	1852-1885	Tavern Keepers Bonds
H	1885-1895	Tavern Keepers Bonds—Index
A	1787-1833	Tax Book (EX 1789, 1798, 1810, 1813, 1818, 1832)
H	1787-1833	Tax Book (EX 1793, 1796, 1810, 1818, 1832)
H	1835-1911	Tax Book (EX 1836, 1871, 1882)
A	1837-1911	Tax Book (EX 1899, 1908, 1902, 1905)
H	1852-1878	Vital Statistics (SY)
A	1851-1862	Will and Administrations Abstracts—DAR
A	1781-1977	Will Books
H	1781-1865	Will Books
U	1781-1865	Will Books
H	1781-1865	Will Index
U	1781-1959	Will Index
A	1781-1984	Will Index

LIVINGSTON COUNTY

Smithland 42081
502-928-2162

Ballard/Carlisle Library System
Mailing Address:
Box 428
Bardwell 42023
Physical Location:
Wickliffe
502-335-3460

Historical and Genealogical Society
P.O. Box 163
Rt. 2
Salem 42078

This county was formed in 1798 from Christian County. The first county seat was established at Eddyville in 1799 but later moved to Centerville in 1804 and then to Salem in 1809. In 1841 the county seat was moved again to Smithland. The county records have never been destroyed by fire or other disaster; the 1845 courthouse is still in use today.

U	1853–1908	Birth Records
A	1874–1954	Civil Case Files Index–Equity and Ordinary
A	1916–1972	Criminal Case Files Index
U	1874–1881	Death Records
U	1800–1866	Deed Books
A	1800–1985	Deed Books (IN)
U	1800–1880	Deed Index
A	1800–1983	Deed Index
A	1877–1942	Deeds–Commissioners
H	1798–1827	Land Tax Receipts–Treasurer and Auditor Offices
A	1872–1984	Marriage Bonds (IN)
A	1896–1916	Marriage Bonds–Blacks (IN)
A	1866–1896	Marriage Bonds–Freedman (IN)
U	1799–1822	Marriage Bonds
A	1799–1822	Marriage Records
U	1822–1877	Marriage Register
A	1822–1894	Marriage Register (IN)
A	1866–1896	Marriage Register–Freedmen
H	?–?	Military Records–Revolutionary and 1812 Pensions (203)
H	?–?	Miitary Records–Veterans' Graves
H	1843–1882	Newspapers (SA)
U	1798–1869	Order Books
A	1799–1977	Order Books (IN from 1810)
H	1800–1861	Tax Book (EX 1832, 1834, 1839)
A	1800–1892	Tax Book (EX 1832, 1834, 1839, 1862–68, 1876–78)
H	1869–1886	Tax Book (EX 1876–80, 1882–84)
H	1852–1907	Vital Statistics
A	1886–1808	Vital Statistics–Births (EX 1882–85)
A	1853–1878	Vital Statistics–Births (SY)
A	1874–1881	Vital Statistics–Deaths
U	1799–1873	Will Books
A	1800–1985	Will Books (IN)

LOGAN COUNTY

Russellville 42276
502-726-6061

Public Library
201 W. 6th Street
Russellville 42276
502-726-6129

Genealogical Society
392 W. 7th Street
Russellville 42276

Logan was formed in 1792 from Lincoln County. The county seat was known as Logan Courthouse and Loganberry prior to being named Russellville.

A	1792–1876	Deed Books
A	1960–1964	Deed Books
U	1960–1964	Deed Books
A	1792–1936	Deed Index
A	1944–1960	Deed Index
A	1952–1960	Fiscal Court Orders
A	1831–1874	Guardian Bonds
U	1831–1874	Guardian Bonds
A	1865–1909	Guardian Lists
U	1865–1909	Guardian Lists
A	1803–?	Land Grants (Included in Order Book #3)
H	1798–1827	Land Tax Receipts
H	1780–1835	Land Forfeited, Transfers, etc.
A	1959–1964	Land—Guardian and Probate Minutes
A	1790–1950	Marriage Bonds
A	1961–1964	Marriage Bonds
U	1961–1964	Marriage Bonds
A	1935–1960	Marriage Bonds—Black
A	1818–1950	Marriage Index
A	1818–1858	Marriage Records
H	1818–1894	Marriage Records
A	1858–1885	Marriage Register
A	1871–1894	Marriage Register
H	?–?	Military Records—Revolutionary and 1812 Pensions (726)
H	?–?	Military Records—Veterans Graves
A	1959–1964	Mortgage Book
A	1960–1964	Mortgages
U	1960–1964	Mortgages
H	1873–1961	Newspapers (SA)
A	1793–1896	Order Books
U	1961–1964	Order Books
H	1796–1800	Order Books—Supreme Court (Bardstown)
A	1894–1906	School Census
A	1796–1906	Survey Index
U	1796–1906	Survey Index

H	1792–1875	Tax Book (EX 1798, 1818, 1827, 1832, 1840-68, 1870-75)
A	1792–1869	Tax Book (EX 1798, 1818, 1832, 1835, 1840-68)
A	1880–1892	Tax Book (EX 1881-82, 1888)
H	1852–1878	Vital Statistics
A	1791–1851	Will Abstracts and Index—DAR
A	1795–1903	Will Books

LYON COUNTY

Eddyville 42038
502-388-2331

Public Library	Historical Society
P.O. Box 546	P.O. Box 811
Commerce Street	Eddyville 42038
Eddyville 42038	
502-388-7720	

This county was formed in 1854 from Caldwell County. Eddyville, the current county seat of Lyon, served as the county seat of Livington County from 1799 to 1804. The county has had at least two courthouses; the current one was built in 1961.

U	1854–1869	Deed Books
A	1854–1986	Deed Books (IN)
U	1854–1898	Deed Index
A	1854–1862	Marriage Bonds
U	1854–1862	Marriage Bonds
A	1854–1878	Marriage Register
U	1854–1878	Marriage Register Book
H	?–?	Military Records—Veterans Graves
A	1894–1979	Minute Books—Eddyville
H	1876–1880	Newspapers (SA)
A	1854–1866	Order Books
U	1854–1866	Order Books
H	1863–1881	Tax Book (EX 1868-75 for Blacks, 1876-80)
A	1863–1892	Tax Book (EX 1876-78, 1883)
H	1853–1908	Vital Statistics
A	1847–1985	Will Books
U	1847–1941	Will Books

Madison County

Richmond 40475
606-623-4288

Public Library	Society of	Eastern Kentucky	Historical Society
P.O. Box 309	Boonesborough	University	201 Geri Lane
Richmond 40475	4022 Saint Ives Court	Townsend Room/	Richmond 40475
606-623-1204	Louisville 40207	Kentucky Collection	
		Crabbe Library	
		Richmond 40475	
		606-622-2820	
		(Kentucky Room)	
		606-622-1778	
		(main number)	

Madison was formed in 1786 from Lincoln County and was one of nine counties already formed when Kentucky became a state. Boonesboro was the first seat of government in what is now Kentucky. The courthouse was completed in 1850, and records there date back to 1786.

H	?-?	Cemetery Records
A	1803-1852	Circuit Court Records
A	1787-1852	Civil and Criminal Case Files Index
A	1852-1977	Civil and Criminal Circuit Court Index
A	1832-1923	Civil Suits—Common Pleas Index
A	1961-1977	Civil Suits—Circuit Court Index
A	1874-1892	Common Pleas Order Books (IN)
A	1787-1792	Court Index
A	1792-1802	Court Records—Quarter Sessions
A	1966-1981	Criminal Cases (IN)
H	1787-1864	Deed Books
U	1787-1865	Deed Books
A	1787-1956	Deed Books
A	1787-1899	Deed Index
H	1787-1899	Deed Index
U	1787-1899	Deed Index
H	1780-1835	Forfeited Lands Lists
H	1829-1880	Idiot Returns
H	1877-1892	Inventory Books
A	1780-1793	Land Entries
U	1780-1793	Land Entries
A	1780-1894	Land Entries
H	1779-1801	Land Office Index for Kentucky Military District (VA)
A	1783-1884	Land Surveys
U	1783-1884	Land Surveys
A	1804-1866	Marriage Bonds
A	1786-1866	Marriage Bonds
U	1853-1866	Marriage Bonds

H	1786–1866	Marriage Bonds (EX ca. 1859, 1831–33)
A	1869–1911	Marriage Books
U	1786–1852	Marriage Licenses Bonds Files (EX 1831–33)
U	1792–1877	Marriage Returns
A	1792–1877	Marriage Returns
H	1792–1877	Marriage Returns and Index
H	?–?	Military Records—Revolutionary and 1812 Pensions (470)
A	1896–1979	Minute Books—Richmond (PIN)
H	1787–1861	Muster Rolls
H	1813–1938	Newspapers (SA)
A	1899–1904	Newspapers—*The Citizen* (SI)
A	1887–1901	Newspapers—*The Climax*
U	1786–1864	Order Books
A	1786–1864	Order Books (some deeds included)
H	1786–1864	Order Books (PIN)
A	1805–1843	Order Books—Circuit Court Civil and Criminal (IN)
A	1843–1977	Order Books—Circuit Court Civil (IN)
A	1880–1977	Order Books—Circuit Court Criminal (IN)
A	1792–1804	Order Books—Quarter Sessions (IN)
A	1950–1962	Ordinance Book—Richmond (IN)
A	1892–1942	Plans of City Hall of Richmond
A	1950–1979	Resolution Book—Richmond (IN to 1974)
A	1787–1792	Supreme Court—Kentucky
H	1787–1847	Tax Book (EX 1798, 1810, 1832, 1838–40)
A	1787–1855	Tax Book (EX 1798, 1810, 1832, 1838–40, 1848)
H	1849–1864	Tax Book (EX 1856–60, 1862–63)
A	1861–1892	Tax Book (EX 1862–63, 1875–81, 1883, 1885)
H	1868–1874	Tax Book (EX 1869–72 black, 1873, 1874 black, 1875)
H	1852–1807	Vital Statistics
A	1787–1866	Will Books
H	1787–1866	Will Books
U	1787–1866	Will Books
H	1787–1959	Will Index
A	1787–1959	Will Index
U	1787–1959	Will Index

MAGOFFIN COUNTY

Salyersville 41465
606-349-2216

Public Library
P.O. Box 435
Main Street
Salyersville 41465
606-349-2411

Historical Society
P.O. Box 222
Salyersville 41465

The county was formed from Floyd, Johnson, and Morgan counties in 1860. In 1957, there was a courthouse disaster, but there was no loss of records because records were in fire proof vaults.

A	1895-1922	Administrator Bonds (IN)
A	1953-1977	Civil Case Files—Circuit Court on Docket Index
A	1887-1917	Commissioners Division of Land
A	1880-1910	Commissioners Sales Reports—Circuit Court
A	1889-1988	Criminal Order Books (IN)
A	1860-1891	Deed Books
H	1918-1940	Deed Books
A	1860-1891	Deed Index
A	1882-1897	Deeds of Sheriffs Land Sold for Taxes
A	1879-1900	Deeds of Sheriffs Land Sold for Taxes (IN)
A	1877-1917	Deeds—Commissioners (IN)
A	1906-1920	Guardian Bond Book (IN)
A	1873-1896	Guardian Record Book (IN)
A	1891-1913	Guardians/Trustees Covenant Book (IN)
A	1872-1941	Inventories and Appraisements (IN)
A	1867-1950	Judgments—Circuit Court from Inferior Courts
A	1873-1906	Land Records—Non-Residents Land Register
A	1870-1984	Marriage Bonds (most IN)
A	1870-1921	Marriage Bonds Book (PIN)
A	1878-1910	Marriage Certificates
A	?-?	Marriage Indexes (unidentified, no dates)
A	1860-1896	Marriage License Book (IN)
A	1860-1953	Marriage Records (arranged alphabetically)
A	1860-1949	Marriage Records Book (IN from 1906)
A	1886-1926	Marriage Register
A	1906-1925	Marriage Register (IN)
A	1893-1973	Medical Register (IN)
H	?-?	Military Records—Veterans Graves
A	1880-1905	Minute Book
A	1872-1919	Mortgage Book (IN)
H	1868-1876	Newspapers (SA)
A	1860-1901	Order Books
A	1860-1977	Order Books—Circuit Court (IN)
A	1876-1886	Order Books—Criminal Court (IN)
A	1889-1889	Poll Books
U	1889-1889	Poll Books
A	1906-1906	School Census
A	1897-1897	School Census (PIN)
A	1878-1885	School Settlements
H	1870-1870	Tax Book
A	1870-1892	Tax Book (EX 1871-79)
H	1859-1877	Vital Statistics
A	1860-1975	Will Books (IN)

MARION COUNTY

Lebanon 40033
502-692-2651

Public Library
201 East Main Street
Lebanon 40033
502-692-4698

Historical Society
Lebanon 40033

This county was formed in 1834 from Washington County. On 5 July 1863 a fire in the clerk's office was started by Morgan's Raiders reportedly to destroy treason indictments against some of his men. All records were destroyed in this 1863 fire.

A	1869–1901	Administrator Bonds
U	1869–1901	Administrator Bonds
H	1869–1901	Administrator Bonds
H	1846–1848	Business Records—Blacksmith Account Books
H	1863–1901	Deed Books
U	1863–1901	Deed Books
A	1863–1984	Deed Books
U	1863–1969	Deed Index
A	1863–1983	Deed Index
H	1861–1909	Deeds—Commissioners
A	1876–1906	Deeds—Commissioners
U	1877–1907	Deeds—Commissioners
A	1863–1906	Estate Settlements
A	1863–1885	Executor Bonds
H	1863–1885	Executor Bonds
U	1863–1885	Executor Bonds
A	1863–1902	Guardian Bonds
H	1863–1902	Guardian Bonds
U	1863–1902	Guardian Bonds
A	1861–1909	Inventory Books
H	1861–1909	Inventory Books
U	1863–1909	Inventory Books
H	1863–1901	Marriage Bonds
A	1863–1901	Marriage Bonds
U	1863–1901	Marriage Bonds
A	1863–1920	Marriage Register
H	1863–1920	Marriage Register
U	1863–1920	Marriage Register
H	?–?	Military Records—Revolutionary and 1812 Pensions (25)
H	?–?	Military Records—Veterans Graves
H	1863–1882	Newspapers (SA)
A	1863–1901	Order Books
H	1863–1901	Order Books

U	1863-1901	Order Books
A	1894-1900	School Census
H	1894-1900	School Census
U	1894-1900	School Census
H	1863-1906	Settlements
U	1863-1906	Settlements
H	1834-1875	Tax Book (EX 1838-39, 1857)
A	1834-1892	Tax Book (EX 1838-39, 1857, 1876-78)
H	1852-1904	Vital Statistics
A	1863-1912	Will Books
H	1863-1912	Will Books
U	1863-1912	Will Books

MARSHALL COUNTY

Benton 42025
502-527-3323

Public Library	Genealogical Society	Jackson Purchase Historical
1003 Poplar Street	P.O. Box 373	Society
Benton 42025	Benton 42025	Box 503; RFD 8
502-527-9969		Benton 42025

This county was formed in 1842 from Calloway County. There were two courthouse disasters in 1888 and December of 1914 that destroyed some records.

U	1848-1874	Deed Books
A	1848-1937	Deed Books
A	1944-1948	Deed Books
A	1982-1984	Deed Books
A	1848-1929	Deed Index
U	1848-1932	Deed Index
A	1848-1917	Docket Book
A	1848-1864	Marriage
U	1848-1899	Marriage Bonds
A	1848-1917	Marriage Bonds
U	1848-1917	Marriage Docket
H	?-?	Military Records—Veterans Graves
H	1868-1876	Newspapers (SA)
A	1848-1872	Order Books
U	1848-1872	Order Books
H	1843-1875	Tax Book
A	1843-1892	Tax Book (EX 1876-78, 1884)
H	1852-1907	Vital Statistics
U	1848-1933	Will Books
A	1848-1938	Will Books

MARTIN COUNTY

Inez 41224
606-298-3336

Public Library
P.O. Box 1318
Inez 41224
606-298-7766

The county was formed in 1870 from Floyd, Johnson, Lawrence, and Pike counties. Inez was originally named Eden. There was a courthouse fire in 1892 that destroyed records.

A	1925-1978	Civil Suits Index—Circuit Court
A	1878-1974	Commonwealth Order Books (IN)
A	1971-1978	Criminal Order Books (IN)
U	1870-1903	Deed Books
A	1870-1985	Deed Books
U	1870-1970	Deed Index
A	1870-1987	Deed Index
U	1873-1913	Deeds—Commissioners
A	1879-1913	Deeds—Commissioners (IN)
A	1886-1977	Leases (most IN)
A	1871-1917	Marriage Bonds
U	1871-1895	Marriage Bonds and Certificates
U	1871-1914	Marriage Register
A	1871-1914	Marriage Register
U	1902-1928	Marriages Bonds and Certificates
H	?-?	Military Records—Veterans Graves
H	1876-1882	Newspapers (SA)
A	1944-1974	Off Docket Index—Commonwealth Circuit Court
A	1870-1907	Order Books
U	1870-1907	Order Books
A	1871-1900	Order Books—Circuit Court
U	1871-1900	Order Books—Circuit Court
A	1878-1978	Order Books—Circuit Court (IN)
A	1870-1920	School Census
U	1897-1931	School Census
A	1871-1941	Suits Index
H	1870-1875	Tax Book
A	1870-1892	Tax Book (EX 1875-78, 1885)
H	1874-1878	Vital Statistics
A	1861-1941	Will Books
U	1861-1941	Will Books

MASON COUNTY

Maysville 41056
606-564-3341

Public Library	Genealogical Society	Historical Society
221 Sutton Street	P.O. Box 266	State National Bank
Maysville 41056	Maysville 41056	Maysville 41056
606-564-3286		

Mason was formed in 1789 from Bourbon County. Nineteen counties have been formed in whole or in part from Mason. Among the counties formed from the original Mason County are Pendleton, Lawrence, Pike, Morgan, Carter, Johnson, Rowan, Boyd, Magoffin, Elliott, and Martin. The original county seat for the period of 1789 to 1847 was Washington. Limestone, later renamed Maysville in 1787, was settled in 1784 and was an important port of entry for early Kentucky settlers coming down the Ohio River.

H	1819-1822	Business Records—Factory Record Book—Maysville
H	1833-1834	Business Records—Mayslick General Store
A	1876-1876	Charter of City of Maysville
A	1901-1901	Charter—Laws and Ordinances of Maysville
H	1792-1932	Church Records—Baptist, Presbyterian
A	1789-1866	Deed Books
U	1789-1866	Deed Books
A	1946-1963	Deed Books
A	1971-1981	Deed Books
A	1789-1980	Deed Index
A	1896-1981	Encumbrance Book—Real Estate (IN)
H	1829-1880	Idiot Returns
A	1942-1977	Land Sold for Taxes (IN)
A	1866-1977	Marriage Bonds
A	1926-1928	Marriage Bonds
A	1866-1976	Marriage Bonds—Blacks
U	1789-1857	Marriage Bonds
A	1789-1860	Marriage Bonds
A	1852-1866	Marriage Bonds
A	1789-1860	Marriage Bonds Index—DAR
U	1789-1860	Marriage Bonds Index—DAR
U	1852-1866	Marriage Books
A	1977-1979	Marriage Books (IN)
A	1790-1949	Marriage Index
A	1852-1979	Marriage Index
A	1866-1940	Marriage Record—Blacks
A	1874-1972	Mechanics Liens (IN)
H	?-?	Military Records—Revolutionary and 1812 Pensions (50)
A	1918-1973	Military Records—Veterans Discharges (IN)
H	?-?	Military Records—Veterans Graves

A	1968-1985	Minute Books—Board of Councilmen
A	1833-1939	Minute Books—Board of Councilmen (PIN)
A	1833-1985	Minute Books—Councilmen of Maysville (PIN)
U	1790-1806	Misc. Records (Depositions, Deeds, Wills)
A	1931-1964	Mortgage Books—Building Association (IN)
A	1925-1934	Mortgage Books—Federal Land Bank (UNIN)
A	1979-1981	Mortgage Books (IN)
A	1898-1979	Mortgage Books (IN from 1976)
A	1900-1981	Mortgage Index
A	1852-1864	Newspapers—*Dollar Weekly Bulletin* (SI)
H	1810-1936	Newspapers (SA)
A	1799-1799	Newspapers—*The Mirror* (SI)
A	1789-1980	Order Books (IN from 1870)
A	1919-1979	Order Books—Fiscal Court (IN)
A	1803-1806	Order Books—Circuit Court—Land Cases
A	1803-1977	Order Books—Circuit Court (IN)
A	1796-1802	Order Books—District Court (IN)
A	1792-1802	Order Books—Quarter Sessions (IN)
U	1789-1870	Order Books
A	1849-1977	Ordinance Book (IN)
A	1849-1977	Ordinance Book—Maysville
A	1918-1918	Ordinance—Traffic of Maysville
A	1934-1949	Right of Way Deed Books (IN)
A	1938-1940	Right of Way Easements (UNIN)
A	1876-1977	Settlements (IN)
H	1785-1789	Surveys—Fieldbook—Simon Kenton, John Marshall
A	1790-1892	Tax Book (EX 1798, 1832, 1876-78)
H	1790-1875	Tax Book—Black (EX 1798, 1832, part of 1848, 1866)
A	1969-1974	Tax Records—Estate Tax Lien Releases (IN)
H	1794-1849	Trustees Book
H	1852-1907	Vital Statistics
A	1869-1981	Will Books (PIN)
U	1791-1869	Will Books
A	1791-1869	Will Books
A	1791-1869	Will Index
A	1791-1981	Will Index

McCracken County

Paducah 42001
502-444-4700

Paducah Public Library	Genealogical and Historical Society
555 Washington Street	360 Watson Road
Paducah 42001	Paducah 42001
502-443-2664	

This county was formed in 1825 from Hickman County. Wilmington was selected as the first county seat in 1824 but moved to Paducah in 1832.

A	1957–1985	Bench Mark Book—City Commissions (IN)
A	?–?	Bible Records—Graves, McCracken, and Trigg
U	1852–1860	Birth Certificates (SY)
A	?–?	Cemetery Records
U	?–?	Cemetery Records
A	1893–1963	Church Records—Methodist and Cemetery Records
A	?–?	Church Records—Methodist and Presbyterian
U	1856–1963	Church Records—Rolls and History
A	1825–1984	Civil Case Files Index—Circuit Court
A	1830–1906	Criminal Case Files General Index
U	1852–1859	Death Certificates
U	1825–1865	Deed Books
A	1825–1913	Deed Books
A	1825–1938	Deed Index
U	1825–1938	Deed Index
A	1943–1985	Maps—Block (IN of Paducah)
A	1897–1985	Maps—Sewer Book (IN of Paducah)
A	1825–1845	Marriage Bonds
U	1825–1845	Marriage Bonds
A	1825–1866	Marriage Bonds
U	1825–1866	Marriage Bonds
H	?–?	Military Records—Veterans Graves
A	1946–1985	Monument Book—Paducah (IN)
H	1862–1882	Newspapers (SA)
A	1825–1869	Order Books
U	1825–1869	Order Books
A	1825–1836	Order Books—Circuit Court
H	1824–1837	Tax Book (EX 1830, 1832, 1834)
A	1824–1892	Tax Book (EX 1830, 1832, 1834, 1838–39, 1876–78)
H	1840–1875	Tax Book (EX 1870 blacks, 1872)
H	1852–1908	Vital Statistics
A	1852–1860	Vital Statistics—Births
A	1852–1859	Vital Statistics—Deaths
A	1857–1920	Vital Statistics—Private Birth and Death Records
A	1826–1866	Will Books
U	1826–1866	Will Books

McCREARY COUNTY

Whitley City 42653
606-376-2411

Public Library
P.O. Box 8
N. Main Street
Whitley City 42653
606-376-8738

McCreary County was not formed until 1912 from Pulaski, Wayne, and Whitley counties. When the county was first formed, Pine Knot was the temporary county seat. It was soon moved to Whitley City. There are few records for McCreary since it was formed so late, and their records were not microfilmed by the Church of Jesus Christ of Latter-day Saints in the 1960s with the other Kentucky counties. In addition, in 1927 and 1951, the first and second courthouses burned.

A	1912–1985	Deed Books
A	1912–1983	Deed Index
H	?–?	Military Records—Veterans Graves

McLEAN COUNTY

Calhoun 42327
502-273-3082

Historical Society
Box 193
Rt. 3
Calhoun 42327

This county was formed in 1854 from parts of Daviess, Muhlenberg, and Ohio counties. The county seat of Calhoun was first known as Fort Vienna and was first settled in 1788. There was a courthouse fire in 1908.

U	1867–1908	Administrator Bonds
A	1867–1908	Administrator Bonds (IN)
U	1854–1900	Deed Books
A	1854–1985	Deed Books
A	1854–1983	Deed Index
U	1854–1937	Deed Index
U	1854–1895	Inventories and Appraisements
A	1854–1895	Inventories and Appraisements (IN)
A	1854–1937	Marriage Index
U	1854–1937	Marriage Index
U	1854–1911	Marriage Register
A	1854–1911	Marriage Register (IN from 1890)
H	?–?	Military Records—Veterans Graves

A	1898-1979	Minute Books—Livermore
U	1859-1899	Order Books
A	1854-1897	Order Books (IN from 1865)
U	1854-1897	Order Books—Circuit Court
A	1854-1899	Order Books—Circuit Court (IN)
U	1847-1892	Settlements
A	1854-1892	Settlements
H	1855-1875	Tax Book
A	1855-1891	Tax Book (EX 1876-78)
H	1854-1907	Vital Statistics
U	1854-1911	Will Books
A	1854-1985	Will Books (IN)

MEADE COUNTY

Brandenburg 40108
502-422-2152

Public Library
400 Library Place
Brandenburg 40108
502-422-2094

This county was formed in 1824 from Breckinridge and Hardin counties. There was a tornado on 3 April 1974 that destroyed many historic buildings in Brandenburg, including the courthouse and some of its records.

A	1824-1977	Deed Books
U	1824-1876	Deed Books
A	1824-1904	Deed Index
U	1824-1904	Deed Index
A	?-?	Deed Index—Unrecorded Deeds
A	1877-1969	Deeds—Commissioners
H	1855-1913	Marriage Bonds
U	1855-1913	Marriage Bonds
A	1918-1922	Marriage Bonds and Affidavits by Race (UNIN)
U	1844-1855	Marriage Bonds and Consents
A	1922-1968	Marriage Bonds and Register
A	1917-1918	Marriage Bonds and Register (IN)
A	1866-1916	Marriage Bonds—Blacks or Mulattoes
A	1913-1917	Marriage Bonds—White (IN)
A	1824-1907	Marriage Bonds—Licenses and Returns
H	1824-1907	Marriage Bonds—Licenses and Returns
A	1866-1875	Marriage Declarations—Freedmen
A	1855-1913	Marriage Licenses
U	1824-1843	Marriage Licenses and Ministers Returns
U	1847-1859	Marriage Licenses and Ministers Returns
U	1859-1913	Marriage Licenses, Certificates, and Returns

A	1958–1967	Marriage List—Brides and Grooms
U	1824–1843	Marriage Records
A	1907–1912	Marriage Records
A	1824–1934	Marriage Register
H	1824–1934	Marriage Register
U	1824–1934	Marriage Register
A	1934–1976	Marriage Register (IN)
A	1866–1921	Marriage Register—Freedmen
H	?–?	Military Records—Revolutionary and 1812 Pensions (167)
A	?–?	Mortgage Index (books 1–26)
A	1824–1877	Order Books
U	1824–1877	Order Books
A	1879–1892	Tax Book
A	1824–1853	Tax Book (SY until 1837)
A	1919–1976	Veterans Discharge
H	1852–1907	Vital Statistics
A	1936–1972	Voters Registration File—Cancelled
A	1936–1972	Voters Registration Record Form
A	1824–1977	Will Books
H	1824–1932	Will Books
U	1824–1932	Will Books

MENIFEE COUNTY

Frenchburg 40322
606-768-3512

Public Library	Menifee County Roots
P.O. Box 237	P.O. Box 114
Frenchburg 40322	Frenchburg 40322
606-768-2212	

Menifee was formed in 1869 from Bath, Montgomery, Morgan, Powell, and Wolfe counties. The 1872 courthouse was replaced in 1928 with the current courthouse.

U	1869–1902	Deed Books
A	1869–1984	Deed Books
A	1869–1980	Deed Index
U	1869–1941	Deed Index
U	1871–1912	Inventories and Appraisements
A	1871–1912	Inventories and Appraisements
U	1869–1940	Marriage Bonds (IN)
A	1869–1912	Marriage Bonds
H	1869–1912	Marriage Bonds
U	1869–1912	Marriage Bonds
A	1869–1984	Marriage Books (IN)
A	1869–1940	Marriage Index

H	1869–1940	Marriage Index
U	1869–1912	Marriage Register
A	1869–1913	Marriage Register
H	?–?	Military Records—Veterans Graves
A	1869–1904	Order Books
U	1869–1904	Order Books
A	1869–1901	Order Books—Circuit Court
U	1869–1901	Order Books—Circuit Court
H	1870–1875	Tax Book
A	1870–1892	Tax Book (EX 1876–78)
H	1874–1878	Vital Statistics
A	1870–1948	Will Books
H	1870–1948	Will Books
U	1870–1948	Will Books

MERCER COUNTY

Harrodsburg 40330
606-734-5135

Public Library	Historical Society
109 West Lexington Street	P.O. Box 216
Harrodsburg 40330	220 S. Chiles Street
606-734-3680	Harrodsburg 40330

Mercer was formed in 1786 from Lincoln County. The first court for Kentucky County met at Harrodsburg and selected St. Asaph's, now Stanford, as the county seat. Harrodsburg is the oldest permanent settlment in Kentucky and the first English settlement west of the Alleghenies. There was a courthouse fire on 15 May 1928.

A	1787–1865	Case Files—Circuit Court
H	1789–1798	Court Records—District Court
H	1834–1859	Death Records
U	1786–1865	Deed Books
A	1786–1986	Deed Books
H	1786–1903	Deed Books (IN)
U	1786–1908	Deed Index
A	1786–1979	Deed Index
H	1789–1792	Execution Books—District Court
H	1780–1814	Land Records—Entry Books (IN)
A	1786–1986	Marriage Bonds (IN)
A	1786–1865	Marriage Bonds
H	1786–1865	Marriage Bonds
U	1786–1865	Marriage Bonds
A	1786–1954	Marriage Index
H	1786–1954	Marriage Index
U	1786–1954	Marriage Index

A	1786–1984	Marriage Index
A	1786–1875	Marriage Register
H	1786–1875	Marriage Register
U	1786–1875	Marriage Register
A	1786–1901	Marriage Register (PIN)
H	1789–1792	Minute Books
H	1789–1878	Minute Books
H	1796–1904	Minute Books
H	1796–1819	Minute Books (IN)
U	1780–1825	Misc. Records—Depositions, Deeds, Wills
A	1878–1879	Newspapers—*The Monthly Review*
H	1760–1819	Order Books
A	1786–1801	Order Books
U	1786–1801	Order Books
H	1786–1801	Order Books
U	1879–1879	Poll Books
A	1875–1875	Poll Books—Convention (with Garrard County book)
H	1868–1909	Reports and Records—Circuit Court
U	1786–1835	Suit Index
A	1786–1850	Suit Index
U	1786–1900	Suit Index—Circuit Court
A	1788–1865	Suit Index—Circuit Court
H	1792–1865	Suits and Judgments—Circuit Court
U	1780–1865	Suits/Judgments—Circuit Court
H	1789–1875	Tax Book
A	1789–1892	Tax Book (EX 1790–93, 1798, 1814, 1832, 1843, 1876–78)
H	1786–1892	Trustee Records of Harrodsburg
H	1852–1878	Vital Statistics
A	1848–1875	Vital Statistics—Birth, Marriage, and Death
U	1786–1865	Will Books
H	1865–1916	Will Books
A	1786–1930	Will Books (IN)
A	1784–1826	Will Books Abstracts—DAR
H	1786–1946	Will Index
U	1786–1946	Will Index
A	1786–1986	Will Index

Metcalfe County
Edmonton 42129
502-432-4821

Public Library	Historical Society
P.O. Box 626	P.O. Box 371
Main Street	Rt. 1
Edmonton 42129	Summer Shade 42166
502-432-4981	

Metcalfe was formed in 1860 from Adair, Barren, Cumberland, Green, and Monroe counties. The largest portion of the county came from Barren County. The county seat of Edmonton, originally Edmundton, was laid out in 1800. There is conflicting data regarding fires in this county. According to some sources, there were fires at the courthouse in March of 1865 and perhaps again in 1867 or 1868.

U	1898–1912	Administrator Settlements
U	1868–1902	Deed Books
A	1868–1984	Deed Books
U	1868–1963	Deed Index
A	1868–1979	Deed Index
A	1884–1902	Deeds—Commissioners
U	1884–1902	Deeds—Commissioners
U	1868–1888	Executors and Guardians Settlements
U	1867–1908	Inventory Books
A	1867–1908	Inventory Books
H	1867–1902	Marriage Bonds
A	1867–1902	Marriage Bonds
U	1867–1902	Marriage Bonds
A	1865–1895	Marriage Register
H	1865–1895	Marriage Register
U	1867–1895	Marriage Register
H	1868–1882	Mortgage Books
A	1868–1894	Order Books
U	1868–1901	Order Books
U	1893–1923	Sales Books
A	1893–1923	Sales Books
A	1868–1888	Settlements
A	1896–1912	Settlements and Administrators
H	1860–1875	Tax Book
A	1860–1892	Tax Book (EX 1883, 1876–78)
H	1851–1907	Vital Statistics (including marriage) (SY)
A	1865–1933	Will Books
H	1865–1933	Will Books
U	1865–1933	Will Books

MONROE COUNTY

Tompkinsville 42167
502-487-5471

William B. Harlan Memorial Library
500 W. Fourth Street
Tompkinsville 42167
502-487-5301

This county was formed in 1820 from Barren and Cumberland counties. The first Monroe County courthouse was burned by Confederates on 22 April 1863. Records were destroyed. The courthouse was rebuilt but burned again in 1888. This fire also resulted in record loss.

A	1881-1904	Administrator Settlements
U	1885-1901	Administrator Bonds
A	1885-1901	Administrator Bonds
H	1885-1901	Administrator Bonds
H	1799-1953	Church Records—Baptist
H	1863-1902	Deed Books
U	1863-1902	Deed Books
A	1863-1986	Deed Books (IN)
U	1863-1969	Deed Index
A	1863-1982	Deed Index
H	1938-1968	Deed Index
A	1877-1904	Deeds—Commissioners
U	1877-1904	Deeds—Commissioners
H	1885-1915	Guardian Settlements
A	1888-1915	Guardian Settlements
U	1890-1916	Guardian Settlements
H	1869-1901	Marriage Bonds
U	1869-1901	Marriage Bonds
A	1895-1901	Marriage Bonds
A	1869-1960	Marriage Index
H	1869-1960	Marriage Index
H	1863-1938	Marriage Index—Brides and Grooms
U	1869-1960	Marriage Index—Brides and Grooms
A	1863-1910	Marriage Register
H	1863-1910	Marriage Register
U	1863-1910	Marriage Register
A	1863-1904	Order Books
U	1863-1904	Order Books
H	1863-1904	Order Books—Circuit Court
A	1888-1978	Order Books—Circuit Court (IN)
A	1888-1977	Order Books—Criminal (IN)
A	1893-1903	School Census
U	1893-1903	School Census
H	1881-1904	Settlements

U	1881–1904	Settlements
H	1820–1875	Tax Book (EX 1832)
A	1820–1892	Tax Book (EX 1832, 1838, 1876–78, 1885)
A	1861–1946	Will Books
H	1861–1946	Will Books
U	1861–1946	Will Books

MONTGOMERY COUNTY

Mt. Sterling 40353
606-498-0136

Mt. Sterling-Montgomery County Library	Historical Society
241 W. Locust Street	316 N. Maysville Street
Mt. Sterling 40353	Mt. Sterling 40353
606-498-2404	

Montgomery was formed in 1797 from Clark County. Mount Sterling was originally established as Little Mountain Town in 1793. The surveyor changed the name to Sterling. There was a fire on 4 March 1851. On 2 December 1863, Confederate forces burned the courthouse, and circuit court records were destroyed. However, the county clerk records were said to be saved because they were in a different building. However, marriage records have been reconstructed to 1864 based on other records.

A	?–?	Articles of Incorporation Index of County Clerk
H	1793–1972	Church Records—Methodist
A	1849–1977	Civil Case Files—Circuit Court Index
U	1841–1866	County Court Record Book
H	1934–1976	Death Records—Funeral Home
A	1800–1919	Deed Books
U	1800–1866	Deed Books
A	1797–1961	Deed Index
U	1797–1861	Deed Index
A	1900–1986	Deeds, Mortgages, Encumbrances, Leases, and Wills
A	1929–1963	Encumbrances Book—Real Estate
H	1841–1866	Guardian Settlements
A	1864–1868	Marriage Bonds
H	1864–1868	Marriage Bonds
H	1864–1868	Marriage Bonds
A	1892–1914	Marriage Certificate Book (IN)
A	1861–1893	Marriage Certificates
H	1861–1893	Marriage Certificates
U	1861–1868	Marriage Certificates and Bonds
A	1864–1984	Marriage Record Book (IN)
A	1863–1893	Marriage Register (IN)
U	1797–1864	Marriages in Montgomery County by Hazel Boyd

A	1855–1985	Minute Books–Board of Mt. Sterling (PIN)
U	1829–1867	Misc. Records–Depositions, Deeds, Wills, etc.
A	?–?	Misc. Book–County Clerk (modern)
H	1829–1960	Newspapers (SA)
A	1853–1866	Order Books
U	1853–1866	Order Books
A	1841–1978	Order Books–Circuit Court (EX 1944–45) (IN)
A	1878–1977	Order Books–Criminal Order Books (IN)
A	1897–1900	School Census
U	1897–1900	School Census
A	1841–1866	Settlements–Fiduciary
H	1797–1875	Tax Book
A	1797–1892	Tax Book (EX 1798, 1828, 1832, 1836, 1839–64, 1876–78)
H	1852–1894	Vital Statistics (SY)
A	1797–1879	Will Books
H	1797–1879	Will Books
U	1797–1879	Will Books
A	1823–1931	Will Books (IN)
A	1834–1854	Will Index and Abstracts–DAR

MORGAN COUNTY

West Liberty 41472
606-743-3949

John F. Kennedy Memorial Library 408 Prestonsburg Street West Liberty 41472 606-743-4151	Genealogical Society P.O. Box 114 Frenchburg 40322	Historical Society P.O. Box 900 RR 1 West Liberty 41472

Morgan County was formed in 1823 from Bath and Floyd counties. There were two courthouse disasters that resulted in destroyed records: one in October of 1862 and another in 1925.

A	1823–1915	Civil Suits Plaintiff Index–Circuit Court
A	1824–1828	Common Law Cases General Index
A	1852–1906	Criminal and Civil Cross Index–Circuit Court
A	1852–1901	Criminal and Civil Order Book–Circuit Court
A	1855–1967	Criminal Case Index
A	1889–1948	Criminal Order Books
A	1895–1900	Criminal Order Books
U	1823–1901	Deed Books
A	1846–1901	Deed Books
U	1823–1970	Deed Index
A	1823–1970	Deed Index
U	1879–1907	Deeds–Commissioners

A	1879–1911	Deeds—Commissioners
H	1867–1888	Inventories and Settlements
A	1867–1888	Inventories and Settlements
U	1867–1888	Inventories and Settlements
A	1914–1916	Marriage Bonds
U	1914–1916	Marriage Bonds
A	1823–1914	Marriage Register
H	1823–1914	Marriage Register
U	1823–1914	Marriage Register
A	1889–1985	Mineral Lease Books (IN to 1978)
U	1849–1867	Misc. Records—Depositions, Deeds, Wills
A	1959–1975	Mortgage Book (IN)
U	1823–1830	Order Books
A	1823–1905	Order Books
U	1865–1905	Order Books
A	1890–1892	Order Books of Common Pleas (IN)
U	1895–1900	Order Books of the Commonwealth Court
U	1852–1901	Order Books—Circuit Court
A	1852–1954	Order Books—Circuit Court—Civil and Criminal (IN)
A	1855–1867	Probate Record Book
A	1893–1916	School Census
U	1893–1916	School Census (EX 1900, 1905–08)
A	?–?	Suits Index—Civil and Criminal (nineteenth century)
A	1916–1972	Suits Off Docket General Cross Index
U	1839–1847	Surveyor Books
A	1839–1947	Surveyor Books
H	1823–1875	Tax Book
A	1823–1862	Tax Book (EX 1832, 1834–35, 1839, 1850)
A	1865–1892	Tax Book (EX 1876–78)
H	1852–1904	Vital Statistics (SY)
A	1866–1963	Will Books (IN)
H	1866–1963	Will Books
U	1866–1963	Will Books

MUHLENBERG COUNTY

Greenville 42345
502-338-1441

Public Library
117 S. Main Street
Greenville 42345
502-338-4760

Genealogical Society
Central City Public Library
Broad Street
Central City 42330
502-754-4630

Muhlenberg County was formed in 1799 from Christian and Logan counties. Courthouses were built in 1800, 1814, 1836, and 1907.

A	1858-1913	Administrator Bonds
U	1858-1913	Administrator Bonds
U	1834-1918	Administrators and Guardian Settlements
A	1982-1984	Audit Report–Bancroft
A	1798-1913	Deed Books
A	1798-1913	Deed Books
U	1798-1913	Deed Books
A	1967-1972	Deed Books
U	1798-1896	Deed Index
A	1798-1968	Deed Index
A	1798-1968	Deed Index
A	1858-1908	Executor Bonds
U	1858-1908	Executor Bonds
A	1858-1912	Guardian Bonds
U	1858-1912	Guardian Bonds
A	1981-1986	Ledger of City Clerk–Bancroft
A	1965-1968	Maps–Sewer Line–Bancroft
A	1965-1965	Maps–Subdivision Plats–Bancroft
U	1801-1912	Marriage Bonds and Licenses
A	1801-1912	Marriage Bonds and Licenses
A	1802-1874	Marriage Books (PIN)
A	1799-1967	Marriage Index–Brides and Grooms
U	?-?	Marriage Index–Brides and Grooms
A	1970-1985	Minute Book–Bancroft
A	1836-1886	Mortgage Book (UNIN)
A	1799-1912	Order Books
U	1799-1912	Order Books
A	1970-1985	Ordinance Book–Bancroft (IN)
A	1834-1918	Settlements
A	1877-1878	Sheriffs Bonds
A	1837-1924	Stray Book
U	1837-1924	Stray Book
A	1865-1903	Tavern Keepers Bonds
U	1865-1903	Tavern Keepers Bonds
H	1799-1860	Tax Book
A	1799-1849	Tax Book (EX 1810, 1814, 1832-33, 1836-39, 1843-47)
A	1850-1891	Tax Book (EX 1851-54, 1861-65)
H	1852-1907	Vital Statistics (SY)
U	1801-1968	Will Books
A	1801-1968	Will Books (IN)
H	1801-1968	Will Books (IN)
U	?-?	Will Index

NELSON COUNTY

Bardstown 40004
502-348-5941

Public Library	Genealogical Roundtable	Historical Society
90 Court Square	P.O. Box 409	P.O. Box 311
Bardstown 40004	Bardstown 40004	Bardstown 40004
502-348-3714		

Nelson was formed in 1785 from Jefferson County. Bardstown was first named Salem and located on a Revolutionary War soldier's tract by the name of David Baird. Bardstown is the second oldest city in Kentucky, incorporating in 1788 by an act of the Virginia legislature. There have been three courthouses built: 1785, 1787, and 1892.

A	1804-1807	Account Book
U	1792-1828	Administrator–Executor and Guardian Bonds
A	1792-1828	Administrator–Executor and Guardian Bonds
A	1965-1982	Articles of Incorporation
A	1921-1977	Case Files Index–Circuit Court
A	1798-1801	Caveat Land Cases
U	1798-1801	Caveat Land Cases
U	1791-1822	Chancery Decrees (SY)
U	1878-1878	Charter and Ordinances of Bardstown
U	1785-1812	Church Records–Catholic
U	1936-1936	Church Records–Catholic–Gethsemani
U	1810-1917	Church Records–First Presbyterian of Bardstown
U	1953-1953	Church Records–First Presbyterian of Bardstown
A	1924-1924	Church Records–Gethsemane Postulates
U	1804-1807	Court Account Book
U	1795-1817	Court Issue Docket
U	1799-1801	Debtors papers
A	1784-1904	Deed Books
U	1784-1904	Deed Books
A	1908-1985	Deed Books
A	1786-1984	Deed Index
U	1786-1947	Deed Index
H	1784-1795	Deed and Record Books
U	1800-1816	Depositions to Establish Land Entries
A	1800-1816	Depositions
A	1795-1810	Depositions–Established Land Entries
A	1780-1801	Depositions–Debtor Papers
A	1975-1975	Easements–Right of Way
A	1966-1974	Encumbrance Book
A	1802-1822	Estate Papers–Sales Inventories
U	1791-1810	Execution Book–Quarter Sessions
A	1791-1810	Execution Book–Quarter Sessions (EX 1804-07)

U	1793–1815	Fee Book–Circuit Court
A	1793–1815	Fee Book–Circuit Court
U	?–?	Genealogical–Collections of Frances Farleigh
U	1794–1802	Guarantee Bonds
A	1794–1802	Guarantee Debts Bonds
U	1822–1825	Guardian Bonds
A	1832–1878	Guardian Bonds
U	1832–1878	Guardian Bonds
A	1823–1875	Guardian Settlements
U	1823–1875	Guardian Settlements
A	1865–1975	Guardian Settlements
A	?–?	History–Pictorial Supplement (clippings)
A	1966–1975	Inventory and Appraisements
A	1795–1817	Issue Docket–Quarter Sessions Court
A	1805–1807	Journal and Day Book–Bardstown
U	1805–1807	Journal and Day Book–Bardstown
U	1780–1785	Judgments
A	1905–1985	Land Ownership Books (Bardstown)
A	1972–1972	Land Sold for Taxes
A	1784–1832	Land Warrants and Misc. Records–George Mason
A	1966–1973	Lis Pendens Book
H	1785–1832	Marriage Bonds
A	1785–1913	Marriage Bonds
U	1785–1913	Marriage Bonds
A	1869–1913	Marriage Bonds–White and Black
U	1869–1913	Marriage Bonds–White and Black
H	1820–1849	Marriage Consents
A	1833–1839	Marriage Consents
U	?–?	Marriage Consents and Returns (old)
H	1831–1838	Marriage Licenses
U	1831–1853	Marriage Licenses
A	1831–1911	Marriage Licenses
A	1873–1896	Marriage Licenses
U	1854–1911	Marriage Licenses and Certificates
A	1785–1859	Marriage Register
H	1785–1859	Marriage Register
A	1785–1951	Marriage Register
U	1785–1951	Marriage Register
U	?–1881	Marriage Register
H	1785–1830	Marriage Returns
A	1836–1836	Marriage Returns
A	1803–1843	Memo Book–Circuit Court (SY)
U	1803–1843	Memorandum Books–Circuit Court
A	?–?	Military Records–Vietnam Veteran Discharges
A	1827–1980	Minute Books–Bardstown
U	1789–1827	Minute Books–Bardstown Trustees
A	1790–1849	Minute Books–Circuit Court

A	1789-1827	Minute Books—Trustees
U	1790-1849	Minute Books
H	1840-1842	Minute Books
U	1782-1833	Misc. Papers—Wills, Deeds, Bonds, etc.
A	?-?	Misc. Records—Wills, Deeds, Warrants, etc.
U	1788-1804	Misc. Records—Depositions, Deeds, Wills
A	1963-1973	Misc. Record Book
A	1875-1893	Mortgage Books
A	1965-1983	Mortgage Books
A	1825-1855	Newspapers—*Bardstown Herald* (SI)
A	1837-1866	Newspapers—Bardstown papers (SI)
U	1785-1825	Order Books
H	1790-1791	Order Books
A	1830-1902	Order Books
U	1830-1902	Order Books
A	1965-1981	Order Books
U	1796-1799	Order Books—Circuit Court
A	1796-1799	Order Books—Supreme Court
A	1785-1825	Order Books—Supreme Court (EX 1798-02, 1817-21)
A	1790-1791	Order Books—Supreme Court District of Kentucky
U	1804-1871	Order Index
A	1906-1983	Ordinance Books—Bardstown
A	1959-1974	Plat Book
A	1779-1785	Processioners Reports
A	1811-1873	Processioners Reports
U	1779-1873	Processioners Reports (EX 1786-1810)
A	1795-1802	Quarter Session
A	1785-1815	Records—Superior Court District of Kentucky
U	1795-1809	Rule Docket—Chancery References
A	1797-1809	Rule Dockets Circuit Court
A	1964-1975	Settlements
A	1964-1974	Sheriffs Settlement Book
A	1799-1807	Stray Animal Book
U	1799-1807	Stray Animal Book
H	1870-1870	Tavern Keepers Bonds
U	1870-1870	Tavern Keepers Bonds
A	1870-1870	Tavern Keepers Bonds
A	1879-1887	Tax Book
A	1888-1892	Tax Book
H	1792-1875	Tax Book (EX 1798, 1832-44, 1841-44)
A	1792-1892	Tax Book (EX 1798, 1832-34, 1841-44, 1876-87)
A	1967-1967	Tax Roll
A	1901-1919	Tax Supervisors Minute Book—Bardstown
A	1785-1791	Tithables List
U	1785-1823	Tithables List
H	?-?	Tithables List
H	1785-1788	Tithes Order Books

H	1852–1907	Vital Statistics (SY)
A	1785–1926	Will Books
U	1786–1918	Will Books
H	1790–1807	Will Books
A	1962–1983	Will Books
A	1786–1961	Will Index
U	1786–1961	Will Index
A	1784–1851	Will Index and Abstracts—DAR
U	1802–1821	Witness and Attendance Book
A	1802–1821	Witness and Attendance Book
A	1789–1847	Writs and Petitions
U	1789–1847	Writs of Ad Quoddamnum on Mill Sites

NICHOLAS COUNTY

Carlisle 40311
606-289-5591

Public Library
223 Broadway
Carlisle 40311
606-289-5595

Historical Society
Box 222
Carlisle 40311

The county was formed in 1800 from Bourbon and Mason counties. The county seat was first at Bedinger's Mill until 1804 when it was moved to Ellisville. Carlisle became the permanent seat in 1816.

U	1857–1896	Apprenticeship Indentures
H	1853–1899	Church Records—Carlisle Bible Society Minutes
A	1932–1961	Civil Case Files Index—Circuit Court
U	1800–1866	Deed Books
A	1800–1986	Deed Books (IN)
U	1800–1892	Deed Index
A	1854–1866	Guardian Bonds
U	1854–1866	Guardian Bonds
A	1857–1896	Indentures and Apprenticeships
A	1854–1870	Marriage Bonds
U	1854–1870	Marriage Bonds
A	1800–1866	Marriage Bonds and Licenses
U	1800–1866	Marriage Bonds and Licenses
A	1961–1984	Marriage Index—Grooms
A	1877–1918	Marriage Books—Black (IN)
A	1854–1934	Marriage Books (IN for most years)
A	1800–1895	Marriage Register
U	1800–1895	Marriage Register
A	1866–1960	Marriage Register—Black (IN)
A	1800–1961	Marriage Register (IN)
U	1816–1841	Minutes—Town of Carlisle

A	1867–1901	Newspapers—Carlisle Mercury (SI)
H	1886–1947	Newspapers (SA)
A	1800–1869	Order Books
U	1800–1869	Order Books
A	1895–1932	School Census
U	1895–1932	School Census
A	1800–1892	Tax Book (EX 1832, 1837, 1876–78)
U	1800–1866	Will Books
A	1800–1980	Will Books (IN)

OHIO COUNTY

Hartford 42347
502-298-3673

Public Library
413 Main Street
Hartford 42347
502-298-3790

Historical Society
P.O. Box 44
Hartford 42347

This county was formed in 1799 from Hardin County. In 1800 the first log courthouse was built over the jail. On 20 December 1864 the courthouse burned.

A	1842–1900	Administrator Bonds
U	1842–1900	Administrator Bonds
U	1799–1903	Deed Books
A	1799–1968	Deed Books (IN)
U	1799–1968	Deed Index
U	1817–1905	Deeds—Commissioners
A	1817–1912	Deeds—Commissioners
U	1817–1968	Deeds—Commissioners Index
A	1842–1885	Guardian Bonds
U	1842–1904	Guardian Bonds
A	1849–1904	Guardian Reports
U	1849–1904	Guardian Reports
A	1839–1902	Inventory Books
U	1839–1902	Inventory Books
A	1808–1901	Marriage Bonds
U	1808–1901	Marriage Bonds
U	1808–1963	Marriage Bonds Index
A	1808–1965	Marriage Index
U	1856–1871	Marriage Register
A	1856–1897	Marriage Register
A	1919–1972	Military—Veterans Discharge Book (IN)
A	1878–1981	Minute/Ordinance Books
A	1878–1981	Minute/Ordinance Books—Hartford
A	1881–1899	Newspapers—Hartford Herald (SI)
A	1891–1899	Newspapers—Hartford Republican

A	1829–1904	Order Books
U	1829–1904	Order Books
U	1851–1903	Order Books–Quarterly Court
A	1851–1902	Order Books–Quarterly Court
A	1803–1900	Order Books–Circuit Court
U	1803–1900	Order Books–Circuit Court
A	1878–1983	Ordinance Book–Board of Trustees
A	1878–1983	Ordinance Books–Hartford
A	1855–1901	Settlements
U	1855–1901	Settlements
H	1799–1875	Tax Book
A	1799–1839	Tax Book (EX 1810, 1818, 1832, 1834, 1836)
A	1841–1875	Tax Book (EX 1853-56, 1862, 1867, 1872-74)
A	1879–1891	Tax Book (EX 1881, 1883)
H	1852–1904	Vital Statistics (SY)
U	1801–1911	Will Books
A	1801–1986	Will Books (IN)
U	1801–1968	Will Index

OLDHAM COUNTY

LaGrange 40031
502-222-9311

Public Library	Historical Society
106 E. Jefferson Street	West Highway 146
LaGrange 40031	Pewee Valley 40056
502-222-1141	

This county was formed in 1824 from Henry, Jefferson, and Shelby counties. The trading center in Westport became a settlement around 1800 and served as the county seat for the years 1828 to 1838. A fire destroyed the first courthouse in 1873.

H	1840–1893	Business Records
A	1958–1977	Civil Case File Index–Circuit Court
A	1882–1977	Criminal Order Books (IN)
U	1824–1900	Deed Books
A	1824–1980	Deed Books
A	1825–1902	Deed Index
U	1825–1902	Deed Index
H	1842–1874	Docket Books
A	1891–1958	Equity Suits of Circuit Court Index
U	1824–1914	Marriage Bonds and Register
U	1824–1911	Marriage Bonds, Certificates, Consents
A	1853–1863	Marriage Bonds
U	1824–1965	Marriage Index
A	1824–1911	Marriage Records

A	1853-1965	Marriage Records Index
A	1863-1914	Marriage Register
A	1824-1853	Marriage Returns
A	1950-1985	Minute Books—City Council of LaGrange
A	1950-1985	Minute Books—LaGrange
A	1823-1901	Order Books
U	1823-1901	Order Books
A	1853-1977	Order Books—Circuit Court (IN)
H	?-?	Road Book
H	1824-1875	Tax Book
A	1824-1892	Tax Book (EX 1832, 1876-78)
H	1852-1879	Vital Statistics (SY)
H	1824-1917	Will Books
U	1824-1917	Will Books
A	1824-1917	Will Books (IN)

OWEN COUNTY

Owenton 40359
502-484-2213

Public Library	Historical Society
P.O. Box 296	c/o Owen County Library
N. Main Street	P.O. Box 296
Owenton 40359	Owenton 40359
502-484-3450	502-484-3450

Owen County was formed in 1819 from Franklin, Gallatin, Scott, and Pendleton counties. The first county seat was Heslerville until 1822. A courthouse was completed ca. 1857-58 and was occupied during the Civil War by federal groups.

A	1819-1864	Case Files Index—Circuit Court
A	1904-1971	Civil Case Files Index
A	1864-1979	Civil Case Files Index—Defendant and Plaintiffs
A	1910-1979	Criminal Case Files Index
A	1874-1880	Criminal Court Order Books (IN)
A	1913-1977	Criminal Order Books—Circuit Court (IN)
U	1819-1866	Deed Books
A	1819-1987	Deed Books
U	1819-1961	Deed Index
A	1819-1961	Deed Index
A	1838-1843	Fee Book—Circuit Court
H	1819-1849	Marriage Bonds
A	1819-1849	Marriage Bonds
U	1842-1865	Marriage Bonds
U	1850-1858	Marriage Bonds and Certificates
H	1850-1865	Marriage Bonds and Certificates

U	1819-1849	Marriage Bonds—Loose
A	1819-1863	Marriage Certificates
H	1819-1863	Marriage Certificates
U	1820-1849	Marriage Certificates
A	1850-1865	Marriage Certificates
U	1819-1940	Marriage Register
A	1819-1948	Marriage Register—Groom Index
H	1819-1948	Marriage Register—Groom Index
U	1819-1948	Marriage Register—Groom Index
U	1819-1863	Marriage Certificates
A	1820-1849	Marriages—Recorded Certificates
A	1877-1893	Minute Book—Columbus Turnpike Company
A	1819-1856	Minute Book—Circuit Court (EX 1833-52)
A	1819-1867	Order Books
U	1819-1867	Order Books
A	1819-1977	Order Books—Circuit Court (IN from 1839)
H	1819-1875	Tax Book (EX 1832-33, 1838, 1847-49, 1865)
A	1819-1892	Tax Book (EX 1832-33, 1838, 1847-49, 1865, 1876-78)
H	1852-1875	Vital Statistics (SY)
H	1820-1869	Will Books
U	1820-1869	Will Books
A	1820-1987	Will Books (IN from 1847)

OWSLEY COUNTY

Booneville 41314
606-593-5735

Public Library	Historical Society
P.O. Box 176	Rt. 2
Booneville 41314	Booneville 41314
606-593-5700	

Owsley was formed from Breathitt, Clay, and Estill counties in 1843. The county has suffered two disasters: one courthouse fire in January of 1929 and another on 5 January 1967. All county records were lost in the 1929 fire.

A	1929-1985	Deed Books
A	1929-1949	Election Commissioner's Record Book
H	?-?	Genealogy—Diary
A	1929-1951	Lease Book (IN)
A	1929-1984	Marriage Bonds (IN)
A	1929-1965	Marriage Register
A	1931-1966	Military—Veteran's Discharge Book (IN)
A	1929-1951	Mortgage Book
A	1929-1986	Mortgage Index
A	1930-1935	School Census (EX 1932-33) (IN)
H	1844-1875	Tax Book

A	1844-1892	Tax Book (EX 1876-8)
H	1852-1904	Vital Statistics (SY)
A	1930-1983	Will Books

PENDLETON COUNTY

Falmouth 41040
606-654-3380

Public Library
228 Main Street
Falmouth 41040
606-654-8535

Historical Society
200 Columbia, Apt. A1
Newport 41071

The county was formed in 1799 from Bracken and Campbell counties. Falmouth was settled in 1776 and incorporated in 1792. The county's first courthouse was completed in 1800, and its second and current one in 1848.

U	1855-1866	Administrator Bonds
A	1855-1866	Administrator Bonds (IN)
A	1798-1866	Deed Books
U	1798-1866	Deed Books
A	1798-1931	Deed Index
U	1798-1931	Deed Index
A	1780-1950	Genealogy—Barton Papers
A	1852-1858	Guardian Bonds
U	1852-1858	Guardian Bonds
A	1855-1866	Marriage Bonds (IN)
A	1799-1852	Marriage Bonds
U	1799-1866	Marriage Bonds
U	1799-1962	Marriage Licenses
U	1853-1865	Marriage Licenses
A	1805-1935	Marriage Records—Grooms List
H	1799-1843	Marriage Records
U	1799-1869	Marriage Records
A	1853-1865	Marriage Records
A	1799-1869	Marriage Records Books (IN)
A	1799-1962	Marriage Records Index
U	1827-1835	Misc. Records—Depositions, Deeds, Wills
H	1939-1946	Newspapers (SA)
U	1805-1822	Order and Minute Books
A	1799-1866	Order Books
U	1826-1866	Order Books
H	1799-1875	Tax Book
A	1799-1892	Tax Book (EX 1832, 1834, 1847-50, 1876-78)
H	1852-1879	Vital Statistics (SY)

H	1841–1871	Will Books
U	1841–1871	Will Books
A	1841–1871	Will Books (IN)

PERRY COUNTY

Hazard 41701
606-436-4614

Public Library
479 High Street
Hazard 41701
606-436-2475

Genealogical and Historical Society
Box 550
HC 32
Vicco 41773

This county was formed in 1821 from Clay and Floyd counties. There were two courthouse disasters, one in 1885 and another in 1911, that resulted in some record loss.

A	1907–1983	Contract and Chattel Mortgage Books
A	1821–1985	Deed Books
A	1821–1975	Deed Index
A	1890–1930	Deeds—Commissioners
H	?–?	Genealogy—Family Records
H	1960–1970	Lease Agreements
A	1821–1977	Marriage Books (IN from 1960)
A	1821–1963	Marriage Books Cross Index
A	1976–1984	Marriage License and Bond Book (IN)
H	1822–1897	Marriage Register and Bonds
A	1959–1977	Mineral Lease Book
U	1914–1914	Misc. Records—Depositions, Deeds, Wills
A	1895–1983	Misc. Book (IN from 1926)
A	1940–1977	Mortgage Book
A	1821–1861	Tax Book (EX 1832, 1839–41, 1846–48)
H	1821–1875	Tax Book (EX 1832, 1839–41, 1846–48, 1862–64)
A	1865–1892	Tax Book (EX 1876–78, 1890)
H	1852–1878	Vital Statistics (SY)
H	1901–1977	Will Books
A	1901–1984	Will Books

PIKE COUNTY
Pikeville 41501
606-432-6240

Pikeville Public Library	County Public Library	Historical Society
210 Pike Avenue	309 Main Street	Box 547-0547
Pikeville 41501	Elkhorn City 41522	Regina 41559
606-432-1285	606-754-5451	

This county was formed in 1822 from Floyd County. There was a courthouse disaster in 1977; however, all records were salvaged.

A	1865-1882	Case Files and Records—Circuit Court
U	1860-1867	Circuit Court Records
A	1822-1920	Civil Case Files Index
U	1820-1902	Deed Books
A	1820-1902	Deed Books
U	1820-1970	Deed Index
A	1820-1970	Deed Index
A	1867-1909	Deeds—Commissioners
U	1867-1909	Deeds—Commissioners
U	1867-1905	Marriage Bonds
A	1868-1917	Marriage Bonds
U	1868-1917	Marriage Bonds
U	1871-1883	Marriage Certificates
A	1822-1940	Marriage Index
A	1822-1871	Marriage Records
U	1822-1871	Marriage Records
U	1866-1905	Marriage Records—Ministers Returns
U	1822-1940	Marriage Records and Bonds Index
A	1822-1902	Order Books
H	1822-1902	Order Books
U	1822-1902	Order Books
U	1822-1938	Order Index
A	1822-1938	Order Index
H	1822-1938	Order Index
A	1860-1867	Record Book—Circuit Court
U	1895-1918	School Census (EX 1913)
A	1895-1917	School Census Index
H	1823-1874	Tax Book
A	1904-1914	Tax Book
A	1823-1861	Tax Book (EX 1830, 1832, 1837-53, 1856-58)
A	1865-1892	Tax Book (EX 1873, 1875-85)
H	1852-1907	Vital Statistics (SY)
A	1839-1912	Will Books
H	1839-1912	Will Books
U	1839-1912	Will Books

POWELL COUNTY

Stanton 40380
606-663-4390

Public Library
135 Breckinridge Street
Stanton 40380
606-663-4511

Red River Historical Society
Box 195
Clay City 40312

The county was formed in 1852 from Clark, Estill, and Montgomery counties. According to some sources, the courthouse and records at Stanton were burned by guerrillas in the spring of 1863. The jail and other records were burned again in 1864 destroying most records.

U	1788-1890	Chancery Decrees
U	1864-1872	Deed Books
A	1864-1970	Deed Books
A	1864-1954	Deed Index
U	1864-1954	Deed Index
H	1864-1961	Deed Index
A	1864-1871	Marriage Bonds (IN)
H	1864-1871	Marriage Bonds
U	1864-1871	Marriage Bonds
A	1863-1900	Marriage Register
U	1863-1926	Marriage Register
A	1913-1927	Marriage Register
A	1906-1977	Minute Books (Clay City)
A	1967-1971	Mortgage Book
A	1864-1875	Order Books
H	1864-1875	Order Books
U	1864-1875	Order Books
H	1852-1875	Tax Book
A	1852-1892	Tax Book (EX 1862, 1876-78, 1884-85, 1890)
H	1852-1878	Vital Statistics (SY)
U	1864-1961	Will Books
H	1864-1961	Will Books
A	1864-1961	Will Books (IN)

PULASKI COUNTY

Somerset 42501
606-679-2042

Public Library
P.O. Box 36
107 N. Main Street
Somerset 42501
606-679-8401

Historical Society
Public Library Building
North Main Street
Somerset 42501

This county was formed in 1799 from Green and Lincoln counties. There were two fires, one in 1838 and another on 7 December 1871, which destroyed the courthouse and burned some of the town. According to local sources, the clerk's office was not in this building, so most of the records were saved.

A	1864-1902	Administrator Bonds
U	1864-1902	Administrator Bonds
A	1880-1977	Civil Case File Index
A	1893-1978	Criminal Case File Index
A	1879-1887	Criminal Order Books (UNIN)
A	1879-1981	Criminal Order Books (EX 1891-93, 1907) (PIN)
U	1799-1901	Deed Books
A	1799-1919	Deed Books
U	1799-1934	Deed Index
A	1799-1934	Deed Index
U	1865-1905	Deeds—Commissioners
A	1886-1905	Deeds—Commissioners
A	1865-1901	Guardian Bonds
U	1865-1901	Guardian Bonds
A	1871-1909	Inventories and Appraisals
U	1871-1909	Inventories and Appraisals
A	1799-1901	Marriage Bonds
H	1799-1901	Marriage Bonds
U	1799-1901	Marriage Bonds (and Certificates after 1870)
H	1799-1853	Marriage Index
H	1799-1938	Marriage Index—Brides and Grooms
A	1799-1938	Marriage Index—Brides and Grooms
U	1799-1938	Marriage Index—Brides and Grooms
A	1800-1874	Marriage Records (IN)
A	1799-1853	Marriage Register
U	1799-1864	Marriage Register
A	1853-1885	Minutes—Inferior Court (Circuit Court)
A	1854-1969	Newspapers—Pulaski and Somerset Papers (SI)
A	1823-1957	Order Book—Circuit Court (EX 1830-32) (PIN)
A	1863-1885	Order Book—Circuit Court Default Judgments (UNIN)
A	1799-1902	Order Books
U	1799-1902	Order Books
U	1799-1940	Order Index
A	1799-1940	Order Index
A	1804-1901	Order Books—Circuit Court (Criminal and Civil)
U	1804-1901	Order Books—Circuit Court
A	1876-1890	Order Books—Circuit Court—Civil
A	1953-1977	Order Books—Circuit Court—Civil
A	1870-1872	Order Books—Circuit Court (UNIN)
A	1870-1884	Settlements
U	1870-1907	Settlements
A	1894-1907	Settlements

A	1893–1925	Tax Book
A	1799–1845	Tax Book (EX 1830, 1832, 1835–36, 1842)
H	1799–1845	Tax Book (EX 1830, 1832, 1835–36, 1842)
H	1847–1875	Tax Book (EX 1849–50, 1852)
A	1847–1892	Tax Book (EX 1849–50, 1876–78)
A	1801–1910	Will Books
H	1801–1910	Will Books
U	1801–1910	Will Books
A	1817–1829	Will Index—DAR

ROBERTSON COUNTY

Mt. Olivet 41064
606-724-5212

Public Library
Box 105
Court Street
Mt. Olivet 41064
606-724-5746

Historical Society
Mt. Olivet 41064

This county was formed in 1867 from Bracken, Harrison, Mason, and Nicholas counties. The current courthouse is a brick building built 1870/72.

A	1868–1983	Deed Books
H	1868–1916	Deed Books
U	1868–1916	Deed Books
A	1868–1916	Deed Index
H	1868–1916	Deed Index
U	1868–1916	Deed Index
A	1917–1954	Deeds—Commissioners
H	1867–1897	Marriage Bonds
A	1867–1911	Marriage Bonds
U	1867–1911	Marriage Bonds
U	1867–1914	Marriage Books
A	1867–1914	Marriage Books
H	1867–1914	Marriage Books
A	1867–1939	Marriage Register
H	1867–1939	Marriage Register
U	1867–1939	Marriage Register
H	1875–1971	Newspapers (SA)
A	1867–1915	Order Books
U	1867–1915	Order Books
H	1867–1915	Order Books
H	1875–1875	Settlements
A	1875–1893	Settlements
U	1875–1893	Settlements
H	1872–1892	Tax Book

A	1872–1892	Tax Book (EX 1874–78)
H	1874–1878	Vital Statistics (SY)
A	1864–1937	Will Books
H	1864–1937	Will Books
U	1864–1937	Will Books

ROCKCASTLE COUNTY

Mt. Vernon 40456
606-256-2831

Public Library	Historical Society
P.O. Box 261	Box 930
Mt. Vernon 40456	Mt. Vernon 40456
606-256-2388	

This county was formed in 1810 from Knox, Lincoln, Madison, and Pulaski counties. Mt. Vernon was originally known simply as "The Mount." The Rockcastle courthouse had a fire in 1871 that destroyed most of its early records. Local genealogists are attempting to overcome the loss of early records through establishment of other sources.

A	1872–1916	Administrator Bonds
U	1873–1917	Administrator Bonds
A	1914–1978	Criminal Suit Index
A	1865–1984	Deed Books
U	1865–1912	Deed Books (pre-1865 were destroyed by fire)
A	1865–1968	Deed Index
U	1865–1968	Deed Index
A	1877–1915	Deeds—Commissioners
U	1877–1915	Deeds—Commissioners
A	1857–1899	Guardian Bonds
U	1857–1899	Guardian Bonds
A	1879–1926	Inventory Books and Appraisals
U	1879–1926	Inventory Books and Appraisements
A	1858–1872	Marriage Bonds
U	1858–1913	Marriage Bonds
A	1878–1913	Marriage Bonds
U	1858–1968	Marriage Index—Brides and Grooms
U	1873–1909	Marriage Register
A	1878–1909	Marriage Register
A	1873–1909	Marriage Register and Bonds
A	1896–1898	Marriage Register and Bonds
A	1858–1969	Marriage Register Index
A	1909–1984	Minute Books—Mt. Vernon (IN from 1930)
U	1815–1895	Misc. Records—Depositions, Deeds, Wills, etc.
A	1873–1917	Order Books
U	1873–1917	Order Books

A	1873–1902	Order Books—Circuit Court
U	1873–1902	Order Books—Circuit Court
H	1893–1918	School Records—Books
A	1939–1980	Suit Index Off Docket—Circuit Court
A	1875–1939	Suit Index—Circuit Court
H	1811–1892	Tax Book
A	1811–1892	Tax Book (EX 1818, 1823, 1832, 1836, 1868, 1876–78)
H	1852–1878	Vital Statistics (SY)
A	1855–1924	Will Books
U	1873–1924	Will Books
A	1873–1969	Will Index
U	1873–1969	Will Index

ROWAN COUNTY

Morehead 40351
606-784-5212

Public Library
129 Trumbo Street
Morehead 40351
606-784-7137

Historical Society
c/o Public Library
Morehead 40351

Rowan was formed in 1856 from Fleming and Morgan counties. On 21 March 1864 there was courthouse fire that destroyed some records. There was a second fire in the 1890s that destroyed many old records of the county.

A	1958–1985	Agreements and Contracts for City of Morehead
A	1910–1970	Articles of Incorporation
A	1889–1979	Criminal Order Books—Circuit Court (IN)
U	1880–1907	Deed Books
A	1880–1976	Deed Books
U	1880–1930	Deed Index
A	1880–1976	Deed Index
A	1939–1984	Deeds and Easements—City Property of Morehead
A	1880–1914	Deeds—Commissioners
U	1880–1914	Deeds—Commissioners
U	1881–1912	Marriage Bonds
H	1882–1912	Marriage Register
A	1882–1912	Marriage Register
U	1882–1912	Marriage Register
A	1964–1972	Mineral Lease Books
A	1912–1984	Minute Books—City Council of Morehead
A	1977–1985	Minutes—Zoning Board of Morehead
U	1878–1906	Misc. Records—Depositions, Deeds, Wills
A	1955–1972	Misc. Lease Books
A	1932–1971	Misc. Record Book—County Clerk
A	1965–1969	Mortgage Books

A	1880–1903	Order Books
U	1880–1903	Order Books
U	1880–1903	Order Books—Circuit Court
A	1880–1979	Order Books—Circuit Court (IN)
A	1980–1985	Orders—Executive of Morehead
A	1952–1983	Ordinance Book—City Council of Morehead
A	1951–1983	Payroll Registers of Morehead
A	1940–1972	Power of Attorney Book
A	1856–1892	Tax Book (EX 1876–78)
H	1856–1892	Tax Book (EX 1876–78)
A	1919–1985	Veterans Discharge Book (IN)
H	1856–1906	Vital Statistics (SY)
H	1853–1947	Will Books
U	1853–1947	Will Books
A	1853–1971	Will Books

RUSSELL COUNTY

Jamestown 42629
502-343-2125

Public Library	Historical Society
Box 246	P.O. Box 246
N. Main Street	Jamestown 42629
Jamestown 42629	
502-343-3545	

This county was formed in 1826 from Adair, Cumberland, and Wayne counties. In 1976 there was a courthouse disaster, but no old records were destroyed.

A	1830–1907	Administrator Bonds
U	1830–1907	Administrator Bonds
A	1826–1938	Civil Case Files Index
A	1826–1977	Civil Case Files Index
A	1830–1938	Criminal Case Files Index
A	1876–1977	Criminal Order Books (IN)
U	1826–1903	Deed Books
A	1826–1985	Deed Books
U	1825–1948	Deed Index
A	1825–1957	Deed Index
A	1875–1909	Deeds—Commissioners
U	1875–1909	Deeds—Commissioners
U	1830–1852	Executor Bonds
A	1830–1852	Executor Bonds
U	1830–1909	Guardian Bonds
A	1830–1909	Guardian Bonds
A	1879–1901	Inventory Books

U	1879-1901	Inventory Books
U	1861-1901	Marriage Bonds and Certificates
U	1826-1860	Marriage Records
A	1826-1875	Marriage Register
A	1875-1901	Marriage Register and Bonds
A	1867-1984	Minute Books—Jamestown
A	1826-1901	Order Books
U	1826-1901	Order Books
A	1826-1977	Order Books—Circuit Court (IN from 1846)
A	1826-1896	Stray Book
U	1826-1896	Stray Book
A	1826-1892	Tax Book (EX 1830, 1832, 1834, 1876-78)
H	1826-1892	Tax Book (EX 1876-79, 1886)
H	1852-1904	Vital Statistics (SY)
A	1826-1955	Will Books
H	1826-1955	Will Books
U	1826-1955	Will Books

SCOTT COUNTY

Georgetown 40324
502-863-0284

Public Library	Genealogical Society	Historical Society
East Main Street	c/o Public Library	306 Clinton Street
Georgetown 40324	230 East Main Street	Georgetown 40324
502-863-3566	Georgetown 40324	
	502-863-3566	

Scott County was formed in 1792 from Woodford County. George Town, as it was originally known, was established in December of 1790. On 9 August 1837 and again in 1876, there were courthouse disasters that resulted in loss of records.

A	1856-1891	Administrator Bonds (IN from 1882)
A	1887-1944	Appointments and Resignations—Georgetown
A	1902-1906	Births, Deaths—Board of Health—Georgetown
A	1797-1835	Burned Records Recordings
A	1888-1930	Cash Book—Georgetown
A	1952-1969	Cash Disbursement Ledger—Georgetown
A	1876-1894	Church Records—Mt. Olivet Baptist
A	1837-1953	Civil Case Files Index
A	1880-1922	Contracts and Agreements—Georgetown
A	1880-1951	Criminal Case Files Index
A	1898-1970	Criminal Order Books (IN)
A	1783-1986	Deed Books (IN)
U	1783-1865	Deed Books
H	1817-1866	Deed Books (IN)

A	1807–1866	Deed Index
U	1807–1866	Deed Index
A	1837–1903	Executor Bonds (IN from 1867)
A	1837–1881	Guardian Bonds (IN from 1867)
A	1875–1896	Judgments by Default Book (IN)
A	1874–1892	Judgments by Default–Court of Common Pleas
A	1863–1904	Judgments of Circuit Court by Default (IN)
A	1855–1914	Judgments of Circuit Court of Lower Courts (IN)
A	1879–1887	Land Sold for Taxes Book (IN from 1883)
A	1850–1850	Legal Instruments–Samples
A	1901–1943	License Records–Georgetown
A	1875–1890	Magistrate and Constable Bond Book (IN)
H	1837–1883	Marriage Records (IN)
U	1837–1883	Marriage Records of Reuben Lee (black minister)
A	1837–1883	Marriage Register
A	1867–1918	Marriage Register–Blacks (IN)
A	1898–1930	Marriage Register–County Judges (PIN)
A	1886–1905	Marriage Register of Ministers (IN)
A	1872–1982	Minute Books–Georgetown (PIN)
A	1902–1914	Minute Books–Board of Health–Georgetown
U	1808–1848	Misc. Records–Depositions, Deeds, Wills
A	1984–1985	Mortgage Books
A	1842–1888	Mortgage Books (IN)
A	1812–1880	Newspapers–Georgetown Papers (SI)
A	1816–1816	Newspapers–*Georgetown Patriot*
A	1887–1907	Newspapers–*Georgetown Times*
A	1881–1886	Newspapers–*Georgetown Weekly Times*
H	1814–1946	Newspapers (SA)
A	1877–1879	Occupational Fee Collection–Georgetown (IN)
A	1921–1946	Occupational Fee Collection–Georgetown (IN)
A	1920–1945	Occupational License Register–Georgetown
U	1792–1867	Order Books (IN)
A	1792–1888	Order Books (IN)
H	1792–1867	Order Books (IN)
A	1793–1958	Order Books–Circuit Court (IN from 1833)
A	1874–1889	Order Books–Court of Common Pleas (IN)
H	1795–1865	Order Books–Circuit Court (IN from 1833)
U	1795–1865	Order Books–Circuit Court (most vols.)
A	1837–1918	Order Index–Circuit Court
A	1837–1918	Order Index–Circuit Court
A	1880–1950	Ordinances–Petitions and Papers–Georgetown
U	1875–1875	Poll Books
A	1875–1875	Poll Books–Constitution Convention
A	1877–1890	Probate Records–Inventory Books, Sales, etc. (IN)
A	1797–1824	Records of Chancery Cases (burned) (IN)
A	1815–1835	Records of Circuit Court (burned) (IN)
A	1840–1849	Register of Road Surveyors

A	1874-1892	Suit Index—Court of Common Pleas
A	1947-1967	Tax Book
A	1794-1830	Tax Book (EX 1798, 1802-04, 1813, 1818, 1824)
A	1831-1956	Tax Book (EX 1832, 1834, 1886)
A	1894-1926	Tax Book—Georgetown
A	1927-1933	Tax Book—Georgetown
A	1934-1969	Tax Book—Georgetown
A	1880-1959	Tax Delinquents—Georgetown—Black and White
A	1899-1922	Treasurer Settlements—Georgetown
H	1852-1879	Vital Statistics (SY)
A	1792-1924	Will Books
U	1792-1865	Will Books
H	1792-1865	Will Books (IN)
A	1796-1913	Will Index
U	1792-1912	Will Index (vols. A-U)

SHELBY COUNTY

Shelbyville 40065
502-633-4410

Public Library	Historical Society
309 Eighth Street	Box 318B
Shelbyville 40065	R.R. 2
502-633-3803	Shelbyville 40065

Shelby County was formed in 1792 from Jefferson County. Courthouses were built in 1793, 1796, 1814, 1847, and the current one was built in 1912.

A	1816-1854	Administrator Bonds
U	1816-1854	Administrator Bonds
H	1882-1934	Cemetery Records—Account Books
H	1819-1900	Church Records
A	1792-1866	Deed Books
U	1792-1866	Deed Books
U	1792-1878	Deed Index
A	1793-1867	Deed Index
U	1816-1854	Executor Bonds
A	1816-1854	Executor Bonds
A	1798-1859	Guardian Bonds
U	1834-1854	Guardian Bonds
U	1798-1859	Guardian Lists
A	1795-1805	Marriage Bonds
A	1800-1865	Marriage Bonds
H	1914-1916	Marriage Bonds and Certificates
A	1797-1869	Marriage Bonds and Licenses
U	1833-1869	Marriage Bonds and Licenses
U	1792-1833	Marriage Bonds—Loose

A	1792-1799	Marriage Bonds—Loose
H	1792-1848	Marriage Books and Bonds
U	1834-1865	Marriage Licenses—Loose
U	1792-1865	Marriage Records (misc. and not in order)
U	1797-1869	Marriages
U	1797-1835	Ministers Returns
H	1878-1917	Newspapers (SA)
A	1804-1868	Order Books
U	1804-1868	Order Books
H	1821-1831	Order Books
A	1904-1971	School Records—Lincoln Institute of Kentucky
A	1792-1830	Tax Book (EX 1793, 1798, 1810)
H	1792-1875	Tax Book (EX 1838-39)
A	1835-1892	Tax Book (EX 1838-39, 1876-78)
H	1852-1878	Vital Statistics (SY)
A	1792-1866	Will Books
U	1792-1866	Will Books
H	1792-1911	Will Books
H	1792-1913	Will Index
A	1792-1913	Will Index
U	1792-1913	Will Index

SIMPSON COUNTY

Franklin 42134
502-586-8161

Goodnight Memorial Public Library	Historical Society
203 S. Main Street	1936 Macedonia Road
Franklin 42134	Franklin 42134
502-586-8397	

Simpson was formed in 1819 from Allen, Logan, and Warren counties. On 16 May 1882 there was a courthouse fire in which most of its records were destroyed. Circuit court records were saved. However, deeds, notes, mortgages, marriages, and other county court records burned.

A	1937-1974	Administrators and Executors Settlements
H	1882-1995	Appraisements
H	1821-1922	Church Records—Baptist
A	1827-1858	Civil Case Files
A	1856-1918	Commonwealth Cases—Circuit Court
H	1882-1904	Deed Books
A	1882-1985	Deed Books
A	1882-1978	Deed Books Index
A	1822-1860	Deed Books—Circuit Court
A	1882-1981	Deed Books—Commissioners (UNIN)
H	1892-1956	Deed Books—Commissioners

H	1882–1938	Deed Index
A	1978–1981	Deed Index
H	1882–1926	Guardian Settlements
A	1882–1926	Guardian Settlements
A	1829–1873	Land Records
A	1861–1918	Lands Sold under Execution—Circuit Court
A	1964–1964	Leases—Oil and Gas
A	1882–1979	Marriage Bonds
A	1882–1890	Marriage Bonds—Black
A	1902–1913	Marriage Bonds—Black
A	1918–1931	Marriage Bonds—Black
H	1888–1922	Marriage Bonds
A	1882–1930	Marriage Licenses and Bonds (some black) (IN)
A	1913–1914	Marriage Licenses and Bonds—Black
A	1918–1923	Marriage Licenses and Bonds—Black
H	1889–1922	Marriage Records (IN)
A	1862–1862	Minutes—Circuit Court
A	1928–1974	Mortgage Books
A	1882–1978	Mortgage Index
H	1916–1939	Newspapers (SA)
A	1819–1904	Order Book—Circuit Court
H	1882–1908	Order Books
A	1882–1974	Order Books
A	?–?	Order Books—Circuit Court—Judges' Executions
A	1859–1912	Order Books—Circuit Court Index
A	1816–1912	Order Books—Circuit Court
H	1846–1911	Order Books—Circuit Court (IN)
A	1972–1980	Order Books—District Court (IN)
A	1893–1981	Order Books—Fiscal Court (IN 1915–48)
A	1948–1962	Plat Book
H	1868–1909	School Records—Franklin Female College
A	1974–1977	Settlement and Estate Book (IN)
H	1960–1962	Settlements
A	1882–1926	Settlements and Sales
H	1819–1875	Tax Book (EX 1832, 1834, 1836)
A	1819–1892	Tax Book (EX 1832, 1834, 1836, 1852–54, 1876–78)
H	1852–1907	Vital Statistics (SY)
H	1827–1880	Warrants and Misc. Land Records (IN)
A	1882–1981	Will Books (IN)
H	1882–1962	Will Books (IN)

SPENCER COUNTY

Taylorsville 40071
502-477-8121

Public Library	Historical Society
412 Railroad Street	Little Mount Road
Taylorsville 40071	Taylorsville 40071
502-477-8137	

This county was formed in 1824 from Bullitt, Nelson, and Shelby counties. Taylorsville was originally known as Belgrade and Spencerville before it became the county seat. There was a courthouse fire on 25 January 1865. There was another fire in 1914, but records were saved.

A	1877–1950	Commissioners Division of Land (UNIN)
U	1824–1905	Deed Books
A	1824–1979	Deed Books
H	1824–1904	Deed Books (IN)
A	1824–1979	Deed Index
H	1824–1938	Deed Index
U	1824–1938	Deed Index
A	1969–1979	Easements—Water Right of Way (IN)
A	1950–1979	Encumbrance Books
A	1824–1918	Guardian Books
U	1824–1920	Guardian Index
H	1824–1920	Guardians (IN)
H	1827–1910	Marriage Bonds
U	1827–1912	Marriage Bonds
A	1827–1912	Marriage Bonds (PIN)
A	1824–1856	Marriage Bonds, Licenses, and Certificates
H	1824–1852	Marriage Licenses and Certificates
A	1824–1852	Marriage Licenses
U	1824–1852	Marriage Licenses and Certificates
U	1824–1911	Marriage Licenses and Certificates (UNIN)
H	1825–1911	Marriage Records, Licenses, and Certificates
A	1824–1931	Marriage Register
U	1824–1931	Marriage Register
H	1852–1923	Marriage Register
U	1891–1931	Marriage Register
A	1979–1979	Mortgage Book
A	1890–1979	Mortgage Book (UNIN)
A	1890–1979	Mortgage Index
A	1824–1908	Order Books
H	1824–1908	Order Books
U	1824–1908	Order Books
A	1917–1917	School Records—Normandy School
A	1925–1979	Settlements (UNIN)

A	1824–1862	Tax Book (EX 1832, 1836, 1838–39)
H	1824–1875	Tax Book (EX 1832, 1836, 1839, 1863–64)
A	1865–1892	Tax Book (EX 1874, 1876–78)
A	1971–1979	Taxes—Delinquent (UNIN)
H	1852–1894	Vital Statistics (SY)
A	1824–1911	Will Books
H	1824–1911	Will Books
U	1824–1911	Will Books
H	1824–1918	Will Index
A	1824–1918	Will Index
U	1824–1918	Will Index
A	1828–1978	Will Index
A	1824–1925	Will and Inventory Books (UNIN)

TAYLOR COUNTY

Campbellsville 42718
502-465-6677

Public Library
205 N. Columbia Avenue
Campbellsville 42718
502-465-2562

Historical Society
P.O. Box 14
Campbellsville 42718

This county was formed in 1848 from Green County. On 25 December 1864 there was a courthouse fire that destroyed some of its records. After the fire, a small one-story brick building was used to house the county clerk's office.

A	1850–1890	Administrator Bonds (IN)
H	1802–1967	Church Records—Presbyterian, Baptist
A	1848–1984	Deed Books
A	1848–1981	Deed Index
A	1872–1885	Deeds—Commissioners (IN)
A	1848–1864	Executor and Administrator Lists
A	1848–1887	Executor Bonds (IN from 1853)
A	1848–1887	Guardian Bonds (IN from 1855)
A	1848–1909	Guardian Lists (arranged chronologically)
A	1848–1888	Inventory, Appraisements, and Sales Books (IN)
A	1866–1918	Marriage Bonds—Black (IN)
A	1848–1916	Marriage Bonds (IN)
A	1866–1875	Marriage Declarations—Freedmens (IN)
A	1848–1879	Marriage Registers
A	1848–1885	Mortgage Book
A	1848–1885	Mortgage Index
A	1848–1888	Order Books (IN)
A	1848–1886	Order Books—Circuit Court (IN)
A	1870–1893	Settlements (IN)
H	1849–1874	Tax Book

A	1849–1892	Tax Book (EX 1875–78)
H	1852–1904	Vital Statistics (SY)
H	1848–1924	Will Books
A	1848–1924	Will Books (IN)

TODD COUNTY

Elkton 42220
502-265-2363

Public Library
P.O. Box 670
On-the-Square
Elkton 42220
502-265-9071

Historical Society
Box 155
Elkton 42220

The county was formed in 1820 from Christian and Logan counties. The Todd County courthouse was completed by 1836 and was one of the oldest in Kentucky. The current courthouse was built in 1975–76.

A	1852–1893	Administrator Bonds (IN EX 1860–70)
A	1820–1878	Deed Books
U	1820–1878	Deed Books
A	1820–1892	Deed Index
U	1820–1892	Deed Index
A	1874–1930	Division of Lands (IN)
A	1902–1927	Election Minutes (UNIN)
A	1839–1887	Execution Books (IN)
A	1851–1907	Executor Bonds (IN)
A	1865–1941	Executors and Administrators Lists (IN from 1872)
A	1860–1886	Guardian Bonds
U	1860–1886	Guardian Bonds
A	1862–1887	Guardian Lists (IN)
A	1866–1930	Guardians Reports (IN)
A	1820–1888	Indenture of Apprenticeship Books (IN)
A	1825–1854	Land Entry Book (some from Tennessee) (UNIN)
A	1834–1849	Land Possessions Book (UNIN)
A	1838–1852	Land Warrants (UNIN)
A	1857–1897	Marriage Bonds
U	1857–1897	Marriage Bonds
A	1914–1918	Marriage Bonds—Black (UNIN)
A	1866–1872	Marriage Bonds—Black Freedmen (IN)
A	1872–1894	Marriage Bonds (IN)
A	1914–1918	Marriage Bonds (UNIN)
A	1845–1875	Marriage Certificates and other Records (UNIN)
A	1908–1915	Marriage Consents
A	1866–1884	Marriage Declarations—Blacks (IN)
A	1820–1964	Marriage Index

U	1820–1964	Marriage Index
A	1820–1870	Marriage Register
U	1820–1878	Marriage Register
A	1875–1921	Ministers Bonds
A	1854–1879	Minute Books
A	1877–1893	Notary Bonds (IN)
A	1822–1891	Order Books (PIN)
U	1822–1877	Order Books
A	1820–1823	Papers—County founding Todd County (UNIN)
A	1857–1903	Processioners Report (UNIN)
A	1863–1889	Road Order Books
A	1870–1882	Settlements with Guardians (IN)
A	1820–1927	Stray Book (UNIN)
U	1821–1833	Survey Book
A	1821–1837	Survey Book
A	1821–1930	Surveyor Books (PIN)
A	1823–1844	Surveys by Order of Court (UNIN)
A	1893–1901	Tavern Keepers Bonds (IN)
H	1820–1875	Tax Book
A	1820–1892	Tax Book (EX 1831–32, 1836, 1876–78)
H	1851–1907	Vital Statistics (SY)
H	1820–1915	Will Books
U	1820–1915	Will Books
A	1820–1985	Will Books (IN)

TRIGG COUNTY

Cadiz 42211
502-522-6661

Public Library	Historical Society	Historical and Preservation
244 Main Street	Rt. 2	Society
Cadiz 42211	274 Dyers Hill Road	Box 1008
502-522-6301	Cadiz 42211	Cadiz 42211

Trigg was formed in 1820 from Caldwell and Christian counties. There were courthouse fires on these dates: 13 December 1864, 13 January 1892, and 29 November 1920. There were record losses. The sixth and present courthouse was completed in 1923 after two years of conducting business at offices scattered throughout the town.

A	1842–1952	Church Records
U	1805–1963	Church Records—Baptist, Christian
A	1842–1952	Church Records—Baptist, Methodist, Christian
A	1882–1978	Civil Case Files—Plaintiff Index
A	1872–1978	Civil Case Files Index—Defendants
U	1820–1866	Deed Books
A	1820–1974	Deed Books

U	1820–1887	Deed Index
A	1820–1982	Deed Index
A	1872–1920	Injunction Bonds—Circuit Court
A	1872–1915	Injunction Bonds—Circuit Court
A	1857–1867	Marriage Bonds (IN)
U	1820–1867	Marriage Bonds
A	1820–1857	Marriage Register (IN)
U	1820–1866	Order Books
A	1820–1866	Order Books (IN)
A	1912–1941	Pension Applications–Confederate
U	1872–1912	Records—Circuit Court
H	1820–1875	Tax Book
A	1820–1911	Tax Book (EX 1876–78, 1900)
H	1852–1907	Vital Statistics (SY)
H	1820–1868	Will Books
U	1820–1868	Will Books
A	1820–1868	Will Books (IN)

TRIMBLE COUNTY

Bedford 40006
502-255-7174

Public Library
Box 249
Main Street
Bedford 40006
502-255-7362

Historical Society
P.O. Box 53
Bedford 40006

The county was formed in 1837 from Gallatin, Henry, and Oldham counties. Trimble County was in a key location during the flow of immigrants into Kentucky on flatboats settling along the Ohio River. A 1952 fire nearly demolished the courthouse and destroyed some records.

A	1838–1977	Civil Case Files—Circuit Court Index
A	1874–1977	Criminal Order Books (IN)
U	1837–1902	Deed Books
A	1837–1987	Deed Books
A	1837–1965	Deed Index
U	1837–1965	Deed Index
U	1871–1907	Inventory Books and Sales Books
A	1871–1907	Inventory Books and Sales Books
A	1863–1987	Marriage Bonds (IN)
H	1837–1877	Marriage Bonds and Other Records
U	1863–1913	Marriage Bonds Book
A	1866–1911	Marriage Books—Black (IN from 1873)
A	1872–1890	Marriage Certificate Book (IN)
A	1837–1910	Marriage Records

U	1837–1911	Marriage Records
U	1863–1918	Marriage Register
A	1863–1959	Marriage Register (IN)
H	1837–1863	Order Books
U	1837–1902	Order Books
A	1837–1902	Order Books (IN from 1850)
A	1846–1978	Order Books—Circuit Court (IN)
A	1907–1922	School Census
U	1907–1922	School Census
H	1837–1875	Tax Book
A	1837–1892	Tax Book (EX 1838–39, 1873, 1876–78, 1882, 1891)
H	1852–1894	Vital Statistics (SY)
H	1837–1965	Will Books
U	1837–1965	Will Books
A	1837–1985	Will Books (IN)

UNION COUNTY

Morganfield 42437
502-389-1334

Public Library
126 S. Morgan Street
Morganfield 42437
502-389-1696

Union Historical Society
213 W. O'Bannion
Morganfield 42437

Union county was formed in 1811 from Henderson County. The county's third and current courthouse was completed in 1872.

U	1848–1919	Administrator Bonds
A	1848–1918	Administrator Bonds (IN)
U	1864–1914	Appraisements and Settlements
U	1864–1968	Appraisements and Settlements Index
A	1788–1871	Case Fragments—Circuit Court
U	1818–1904	Church Records—Sacred Heart Baptismals, etc.
U	1811–1911	Deed Books
A	1811–1984	Deed Books
A	1800–1950	Deed Index
A	1848–1919	Executor Bonds (IN from 1853)
U	1848–1919	Executor Bonds
A	1853–1918	Guardian Bonds (PIN)
U	1848–1918	Guardian Bonds
A	1837–1854	Land Fees—Vacant
U	1783–1872	Land Grants
A	1981–1985	Marriage Bonds
A	1850–1965	Marriage Bonds (IN)
H	1853–1914	Marriage Bonds
U	1853–1914	Marriage Bonds

H	1833–1903	Marriage Bonds and Licenses
U	1811–1911	Marriage Bonds, Licenses, and Certificates
H	1850–1865	Marriage Index—Brides and Grooms
U	1853–1964	Marriage Index—Brides and Grooms
A	1811–1911	Marriage Records
H	1851–1875	Marriage Register
U	1851–1875	Marriage Register
A	1863–1875	Marriage Register
A	1851–1867	Marriage Returns
A	1983–1984	Mineral Lease Books
U	1823–1913	Order Books
A	1823–1913	Order Books (PIN from 1836–79)
A	1864–1918	Settlements
U	1864–1918	Settlements
H	1811–1875	Tax Book
A	1811–1892	Tax Book (EX 1813–14, 1832, 1845–47, 1876–78)
H	1852–1878	Vital Statistics (SY)
U	1811–1922	Will Books
H	1811–1922	Will Books (IN)
A	1811–1922	Will Books (IN)
U	1811–1922	Will Index

WARREN COUNTY

Bowling Green 42101
502-842-9416

Public Library	South Kentucky	Historical Society	Western Kentucky
1225 State Street	Genealogical Society	333 Hillwood	University
Bowling Green 42101	P.O. Box 1905	Bowling Green 42101	Folklore, Folklife, and
502-781-4882	Bowling Green 42101		Oral History Archives
			Bowling Green 42101
			502-745-3951, ext. 53

Warren was formed in 1797 from Logan County. In 1864 there was a courthouse fire that destroyed some records. The current courthouse was built in 1867/68 and restored in 1958.

U	1800–1860	Administrator Bonds
U	1800–1850	Appointments and Suits
A	1830–1866	Apprentice Bonds
U	1800–1860	Apprentice Bonds and Records
U	1800–1850	Building Petitions
A	1797–1802	Cases Index—Quarter Sessions
U	?–?	Cemetery Records
H	1798–1871	Circuit Court Record Index
H	1803–1865	Circuit Court Records
A	1965–1977	Civil Case Files—Plaintiff Index

A	1953–1965	Civil Case Files Index
A	1953–1961	Civil Case Files–Circuit Court
A	1971–1977	Civil Order Books (IN)
A	1800–1850	County Officers Appointments
U	1800–1850	Court Records
A	1954–1966	Criminal Case Files Index
A	1971–1977	Criminal Order Books (IN)
U	1797–1841	Deed Books
A	1797–1876	Deed Books
U	1800–1860	Deed Books
A	1947–1974	Deed Books
U	1800–1820	Deed Books (scattered)
U	1797–1880	Deed Index
A	1797–1923	Deed Index
A	1947–1971	Deed Index
A	1821–1861	Deeds and Misc. Papers
U	1799–1812	Early Fines
U	1796–1860	Equities and Marriages
A	1798–1871	Equity Case Files Index
A	1796–1860	Equity Judgments and Misc. Papers
A	1807–1914	Equity Suits Off Docket Index
A	1898–1916	Equity Suits–Circuit Court
A	1800–1860	Estate Settlements
U	?–?	Family Group Sheets
U	1797–1890	Genealogy–Cox, Cooney, and Other Families
A	1844–1878	Guardian Bonds
U	1844–1878	Guardian Bonds
U	1796–1860	Justice of Peace
A	1796–1860	Justice of Peace
U	1800–1820	Land Entries
A	1800–1850	Land Entries
U	1839–1851	Land Entries
A	1801–1807	Land Office Records–Vacant Land
U	1797–1880	Marriage Bonds
U	1851–1876	Marriage Bonds
U	1851–1900	Marriage Bonds and Licenses
U	1797–1880	Marriage Consents
A	1797–1935	Marriage Index
U	1797–1935	Marriage Index
A	1800–1860	Marriage Licenses and Certificates
A	1797–1876	Marriage Records
U	1800–1860	Marriage Records
A	1797–1851	Marriage Records (includes bride list)
A	1812–1912	Marriage Records (SY)
U	1797–1869	Marriage Register
U	1797–1880	Marriage Returns
A	1797–1880	Marriage Returns

U	1779–1830	Marriage Returns (SY)
U	1796–1880	Marriages, Wills, and Deeds
U	1797–1850	Mill Sites
U	1824–1832	Minute Books
A	1869–190?	Minute Books–Council (Bowling Green)
A	1803–1865	Minute/Order Books–Circuit Court
A	?–1860	Misc. Papers–Estate Papers, Roads, Fines
A	1797–1866	Misc. Records–Wills, Deeds, etc.
H	1853–1934	Newspapers (SA)
A	1901–1901	Newspapers–*Times Journal* (8 July only)
A	1801–1877	Order Books
U	1801–1877	Order Books
A	1859–1861	Order Books–Circuit Court
U	1803–1861	Order Books–Circuit Court
A	1894–1918	Order Books–Police Court–Brandenburg (IN)
U	1798–1835	Partitions
A	1796–1855	Probate Loose Papers and Wills
U	1800–1850	Road Returns
A	1796–1860	Road, Justice of Peace, Mill Sites, etc.
U	1813–1854	Roads and Bridges Building
U	1796–1860	Roads of Warren County
U	1800–1860	Settlements of Estates
U	1798–1830	Stray Notices
H	1790–?	Suits
A	1797–1802	Suits–Quarter Session Court
H	1881–1881	Tax Book
H	1797–1828	Tax Book (EX 1798, 1810, 1814, 1827)
A	1797–1840	Tax Book (EX 1798, 1810, 1814, 1827, 1832)
H	1833–1875	Tax Book (EX 1832, part of 1839, 1841)
A	1842–1892	Tax Book (EX 1876, 1879)
A	1908–1911	Tax Book–Brandenburg
A	1869–?	Town Council Minute Books
H	1852–1907	Vital Statistics (SY)
A	1799–1889	Will Books
U	1799–1889	Will Books
U	1797–1963	Will Index
A	1797–1963	Will Index
A	1821–1862	Will Index and Abstracts–DAR
U	1796–1855	Wills (and some deeds)
U	1800–1820	Wills (scattered)
A	1796–1880	Wills, Deeds, and Marriages

WASHINGTON COUNTY

Springfield 40069
606-336-3471

Public Library	Genealogical Society
210 E. Main Street	210 E. Main Street
Springfield 40069	Springfield 40069
606-336-7655	

Washington County was formed in 1792 from Nelson County. The courthouse was completed by 1816 and is the oldest Kentucky courthouse still in use. The first courthouse, built in 1794, was burned in 1795. The second one, built in 1797, burned in the spring of 1814, but the clerk's brick office was spared.

A	1793–1926	Case Files Index–Circuit Court
H	?–?	Cemetery Records
U	1792–1911	Deed Books
A	1792–1978	Deed Books
H	1792–?	Deed Books
H	1792–1860	Deed Index
A	1792–1905	Deed Index
U	1792–1905	Deed Index
A	?–?	Deed Index–Unrecorded Deeds (no dates)
U	1833–1851	Deeds–Commissioners (IN)
H	1833–1851	Deeds–Commissioners
U	1877–1960	Deeds–Commissioners (IN)
A	1833–1960	Deeds–Commissioners (IN)
A	1840–1850	Deeds–Unrecorded (1840s and 1850s)
A	1896–1961	Encumbrances (IN)
A	1919–1924	Lease Book
A	1959–1959	Lease Book (IN)
A	1961–1961	Maps–Washington County
A	1870–1942	Marriage Bonds (PIN)
U	1845–1849	Marriage Bonds
H	1870–1923	Marriage Bonds
H	1899–1960	Marriage Bonds
U	1858–1913	Marriage Bonds (EX 1894–98)
U	1931–1944	Marriage Bonds–Black
H	1821–1852	Marriage Licenses
A	1792–1855	Marriage Records
U	1822–1852	Marriage Records
A	1792–1826	Marriage Records Index
U	1792–1826	Marriage Records Index
A	1792–1858	Marriage Records (IN)
A	1830–1870	Marriage Register
A	1792–1826	Marriage Register (IN)
A	1878–1914	Marriage Register (IN)

U	1792-1826	Marriage Returns
U	1852-1914	Marriage Returns
U	1877-1958	Mechanic's Liens (IN)
A	1877-1958	Mechanic's Liens (IN)
U	1893-1959	Medical Register
U	1806-1825	Minute Books—Circuit Court
H	1806-1825	Minute Books—Circuit Court
U	1820-1826	Misc. Records—Depositions, Deeds, Wills
U	1905-1913	Mortgage Book
A	1905-1961	Mortgage Book
U	1960-1961	Mortgage Book (IN)
A	1905-1927	Mortgage Index
U	1905-1927	Mortgage Index
H	1936-1940	Newspapers (SA)
U	1959-1960	Oil and Gas Leases
U	1919-1924	Oil and Gas Leases (IN)
H	1792-1914	Order Books
U	1792-1961	Order Books (IN)
A	1792-1961	Order Books (IN)
U	1902-1923	Order Books—Fiscal Court (IN)
A	1902-1919	Order Books—Fiscal Court (IN)
U	1922-1959	Orders for Juveniles and Index
A	1797-1903	Processioners Books
U	1779-1913	Processioners Books
U	1896-1961	Real Estate (IN)
H	1793-1873	Suit Index
U	1793-1959	Suit Index
H	1879-1881	Tax Book
H	1792-1875	Tax Book (EX 1793, 1798, 1818, 1819, 1931-32, 1836)
A	1792-1963	Tax Book (EX 1810, 1818, 1831-32, 1836, 1876-78)
H	1946-1960	Veterans Discharges
U	1919-1946	Veterans Records
U	1944-1960	Veterans Records (IN)
H	1852-1878	Vital Statistics (SY)
A	1792-1858	Will Abstracts—DAR
A	1792-1919	Will Books
H	1792-1918	Will Books (IN)
U	1792-1922	Will Books (PIN)

WAYNE COUNTY

Monticello 42633
606-348-5721

Public Library
159 S. Main Street
Monticello 42633
606-348-8565

Historical Society
P.O. Box 320
Monticello 42633

Wayne County was formed in 1801 from Cumberland and Pulaski counties. The county has had six courthouses over the years, and the fourth was destroyed by fire in 1898.

U	1884–1908	Administrator Bonds
A	1884–1908	Administrator Bonds (IN)
U	1816–1907	Appraisements and Inventory Books
U	1800–1901	Deed Books
A	1800–1901	Deed Books
A	1800–1960	Deed Index
U	1800–1960	Deed Index
U	1876–1909	Deeds—Commissioners
A	1877–1909	Deeds—Commissioners (IN)
A	1853–1904	Guardian Bonds (IN)
U	1853–1904	Guardian Bonds
A	1875–1905	Guardian Settlements
U	1875–1905	Guardian Settlements
A	1816–1907	Inventory Books, Appraisements, and Sales Books (PIN)
A	1801–1807	Land Office Records—Vacant Land
A	1801–1813	Marriage Bonds
U	1801–1900	Marriage Bonds
A	1853–1900	Marriage Bonds (IN)
U	1801–1969	Marriage Bonds Index
A	1801–1969	Marriage Licenses Index
A	1832–1848	Marriage Register
U	1801–1902	Order Books
A	1801–1902	Order Books (PIN)
A	1877–1878	Sheriffs Bonds (missing)
A	1801–1892	Tax Book (EX 1818, 1831–32, 1847, 1876–78, 1885, 1887)
H	1801–1881	Tax Book (EX 1876–78, 1880)
H	1852–1878	Vital Statistics (SY)
U	1801–1909	Will Books
A	1801–1909	Will Books (PIN)

WEBSTER COUNTY

Dixon 42409
502-639-5063

Public Library
300 East Leiper Street
Dixon 42409
502-639-9171

Historical and Genealogical Society
Webster County Library
300 E. Leiper Street
Dixon 42409
502-639-9171

Webster County was formed in 1860 from Henderson, Hopkins, and Union counties. Courthouses were built after formation of the county in 1860 and in 1939-40.

U	1860-1909	Administrator Bonds
A	1860-1909	Administrator Bonds (IN EX 1871-79)
A	1860-1979	Civil Case Files Index
A	1916-1978	Criminal Case File Index
A	1861-1902	Criminal Order Books (IN)
A	1860-1912	Deed Books
U	1860-1912	Deed Books
A	1983-1985	Deed Books
U	1860-1957	Deed Index
A	1860-1981	Deed Index
U	1884-1910	Deeds of Partition
A	1887-1900	Deeds of Partition
A	1877-1910	Deeds—Commissioners
U	1877-1910	Deeds—Commissioners (IN)
A	1877-1941	Deeds—Commissioners Index
A	1860-1904	Guardian Bonds (IN)
U	1860-1904	Guardian Bonds
A	1867-1904	Guardian Settlements (IN from 1892)
U	1867-1904	Guardian Settlements
U	1860-1962	Marriage Bonds Index
A	1860-1912	Marriage License and Bonds (IN)
A	1860-1960	Marriage License and Bond Index
U	1860-1900	Marriage Licenses
U	1860-1912	Marriage Licenses and Bonds
A	1860-1900	Marriage Licenses and Certificates
U	1863-1911	Order Books
A	1860-1911	Order Books (PIN)
A	1865-1901	Order Books—Circuit Court (IN)
U	1867-1901	Order Books—Circuit Court
U	1861-1902	Order Books—Circuit Court—Commonwealth Orders
A	1867-1871	Order Books—Common Pleas Court (IN)
H	1861-1875	Tax Book
H	1879-1881	Tax Book
A	1861-1892	Tax Book (EX 1876-78, 1886)

H	1874–1877	Vital Statistics (SY)
H	1860–1916	Will Books
U	1860–1916	Will Books
A	1860–1923	Will Books (IN)

WHITLEY COUNTY

Williamsburg 40769
606-549-0416

Public Library	Genealogical Society
285 S. Third Street	P.O. Box 353
Williamsburg 40769	Corbin 40701
606-549-0818	

Whitley was formed in 1818 from Knox County. Williamsburg was originally known as Whitley Court House. In 1930 there was a courthouse disaster that resulted in some record loss.

U	1867–1911	Administrator and Executor Bonds
A	1870–1878	Administrator and Executor List
A	1867–1911	Administrator Bonds (IN)
A	1860–1908	Case Files Index
A	1860–1927	Case Files Off Docket Index
A	1895–1922	Civil Case Files—Equity—Plaintiff Index
A	1880–1887	Commissioners Land Sale (IN)
A	1904–1916	Commissioners Reports (IN)
U	1818–1829	Court Book
A	1896–1907	Criminal Order Books (IN)
A	1902–1912	Declarations of Intention Book (IN)
U	1818–1911	Deed Books
A	1818–1943	Deed Books
A	1827–1934	Deed Index
U	1818–1934	Deed Index (to vol. 130)
A	1818–1907	Deed Index—Grantees
A	1852–1852	Docket of the Circuit Court
A	1844–1901	Execution Book (PIN)
A	1872–1906	Executor Bonds (IN)
A	1867–1912	Guardian Bonds (IN)
U	1867–1919	Guardian Bonds
A	1890–1919	Guardian Reports Book (IN)
A	1853–1894	Judgment Book—Circuit Court (IN EX 1883–94)
A	1867–1877	Judgments by Default Book—Circuit Court (IN)
A	1860–1912	Marriage Bonds (IN from 1867)
U	1860–1912	Marriage Licenses, Bonds, and Records
A	1820–1829	Minute Books—Circuit Court
U	?–?	Misc. Records—Depositions, Deeds, Wills, etc.
A	1908–1912	Naturalization Petitions

A	1818–1868	Order Books
U	1818–1868	Order Books
A	1888–1892	Order Books—Common Pleas Court (PIN)
A	1818–1907	Order Books—Circuit Court (PIN)
A	1878–1909	Orders de Idiota Inquirendo
A	1892–1918	Pauper Idiot List
A	1839–1851	Stud Horse Fee List
A	1818–1903	Survey Book
A	1818–1887	Survey Book Index
H	1819–1875	Tax Book
H	1879–1879	Tax Book
A	1819–1892	Tax Book (EX 1832, 1834, 1876–78, 1884, 1889)
H	1852–1904	Vital Statistics (SY)
H	1818–1963	Will Books
U	1818–1967	Will Books
A	1818–1968	Will Books (IN from 1853)

WOLFE COUNTY

Campton 41301
606-668-3515

Public Library
P.O. Box 10
Main Street
Campton 41301
606-668-6571

The county was formed in 1860 from Breathitt, Morgan, Owsley, and Powell counties. A courthouse was destroyed by an 1886 fire along with important early records. The next frame courthouse was also destroyed by fire in 1913.

A	1887–1978	Deed Books
A	1982–1984	Deed Books
A	1963–1982	Deed Index
A	1887–1934	Deeds—Commissioners
A	1913–1984	Marriage Books (IN)
A	1958–1984	Minute Books—Campton
A	1966–1984	Mortgage Index
A	1885–1917	Newspapers—*Hazel Green Herald*
H	1890–1890	Tax Book
H	1861–1875	Tax Book (EX 1863–64, 1890)
A	1861–1892	Tax Book (EX 1863–64, 1876–78)
H	1861–1903	Vital Statistics (SY)

WOODFORD COUNTY

Versailles 40383
606-873-3421

Logan Helm-Woodford Library
115 N. Main Street
Versailles 40383
606-873-5191

Historical Society
121 Rose Hill
Versailles 40381

    Woodford was formed in 1789 from Fayette County and was the first county to have its present boundaries set. Versailles is an old Kentucky town and was originally known to the pioneers as Falling Spring because of the large stream that ran from a cavern. There was a fire on 11 October 1965 at the courthouse that resulted in loss of records. However, old records were saved.

U	1818–1868	Administrator Bonds
A	1818–1868	Administrator Bonds (IN from 1856)
H	1802–1868	Administrator Execution Bonds
U	1802–1855	Administrators and Executor Bonds
H	1885–1890	Business Records
A	1840–1845	Business Records—Day Book
A	1933–1977	Case Files Index—Circuit Court
H	1890–1977	Cemetery Records—Midway Cemetery
H	1850–1988	Cemetery Records—Versailles Burial Book (IN)
H	1850–1988	Cemetery Records—Versailles Cemetery Lot Books
H	1879–1980	Church Records—Christian
A	1969–1974	Criminal Order Books (IN)
A	1939–1977	Criminal Order Books (PIN)
H	1789–1870	Deed Books
A	1789–1985	Deed Books (PIN)
U	1789–1870	Deed Books (IN)
A	1789–1870	Deed Index
A	1802–1856	Executor Bonds
H	?–?	Genealogy—Various Families
A	1818–1874	Guardian Bonds (IN from 1856)
H	1818–1874	Guardian Bonds
U	1818–1874	Guardian Bonds
A	1856–1863	Guardians List
A	1789–1879	Marriage Bonds (IN)
U	1789–1879	Marriage Bonds
U	1789–1860	Marriage Bonds and Licenses
H	1789–1878	Marriage Bonds and Licenses
H	1860–1879	Marriage Books
A	1866–1970	Marriage Books—Blacks (IN)
A	1849–1986	Marriage Books (IN)
A	1789–1878	Marriage Records
U	1789–1872	Marriage Records (EX 1844–48)

A	1789–1872	Marriage Returns
H	1789–1872	Marriages—Misc. Records
A	1880–1985	Minute Books—City Clerk of Versailles (PIN)
A	1811–1861	Minute/Order Books (PIN)
U	1806–1866	Misc. Records—Depositions, Deeds, Wills
A	1877–1897	Newspapers—*Bluegrass Clipper* (SI)
H	1824–1978	Newspapers (SA)
U	1789–1867	Order Books
A	1789–1867	Order Books (PIN)
A	1937–1977	Order Books—Circuit Court (PIN)
H	1894–1934	School Board Minute Books
H	1887–1909	School Census
A	1841–1852	Stud Book
A	1790–1844	Survey Book (IN)
H	1790–1875	Tax Book
A	1790–1840	Tax Book (EX 1798, 1818, 1831–32, 1839)
A	1843–1892	Tax Book (EX 1876–78)
H	1861–1878	Vital Statistics (SY)
A	1788–1851	Will Abstracts—DAR
H	1789–1870	Will Books
U	1789–1870	Will Books
A	1789–1984	Will Books (IN)
H	1789–1960	Will Index
U	1789–1868	Will Index

KENTUCKY STATEWIDE RECORDS

The following inventory lists records available for more than one Kentucky county. A majority are statewide series records. However, not all counties will necessarily have records in the series.

A	1811–1814	Affidavits for Slave Passports to Mississippi
A	1947–1970	Apprenticeship File Cards
A	1820–1850	Bank of Commonwealth of Kentucky
A	1907–1910	Birth Records
U	1907–1910	Birth Records (some marriages and deaths)
H	1890–1911	Birth Records—Certificates—Delayed
A	1891–1977	Birth Records—Index by Child
A	1912–1977	Birth Records—Index by Mother
A	1874–1874	Birth Records—Register of Birth
A	1876–1876	Birth Records—Register of Birth
A	1877–1877	Birth Records—Register of Birth
A	1878–1878	Birth Records—Register of Birth
H	1866–1870	Black Records—Bureau of Refugees and Freedmen
A	1807–1845	Business Records—Old Bank of Kentucky Records
U	1780–1914	Case Papers—Kentucky County
A	1899–1980	Cases—Court of Appeals (case number)

A	1976–1980	Cases–New Court of Appeals
A	1850–1880	Census–Agriculture (by county)
A	1860–1950	Census–Agriculture (statistics only)
A	1940–1940	Census–Business
A	1930–1930	Census–Distribution
A	1890–1890	Census–Housing
A	1940–1960	Census–Housing
A	1920–1930	Census–Irrigation and Drainage
A	1850–1880	Census–Manufacturing
A	1850–1880	Census–Manufacturing (by county)
A	1810–1940	Census–Manufacturing (statistics only)
A	1880–1940	Census–Mineral Industries
A	1900–1930	Census–Mines and Quarries
A	1850–1880	Census–Mortality
A	1880–1890	Census–Transportation
A	1840–1840	Census–Veterans and Pensioners
A	1850–1940	Census–Vital Statistics (statistics only)
A	1864–1952	Court of Appeals Index
A	1874–1874	Death Records
A	1876–1878	Death Records
U	1905–1910	Death Records (some births and marriages)
A	1963–1977	Death Records (IN for Kentucky)
A	1905–1910	Deaths
U	1874–1878	Deaths (EX 1875)
A	1796–1845	Deed Index (some Virginia Supreme Court Deeds)
A	1780–1835	Deed Books–Kentucky Court of Appeals (IN)
U	1783–1839	Deeds List in Office of the General Court
H	1783–1789	Deeds–Supreme Court
H	1838–1909	Deeds–Supreme Court
A	1796–1806	Delinquent Lands Record
A	1800–1900	Draper Manuscripts–Kentucky Collection
K	1800–1900	Draper Manuscripts–Kentucky Collection
U	1800–1900	Draper Manuscripts–Kentucky Collection
A	1782–1817	Entries and Deeds–Fayette Entries
U	1782–1817	Entries and Deeds–Fayette Entries
U	1779–1792	Entries and Deeds–Lincoln Entries
A	1799–1792	Entries and Deeds–Lincoln Entries
A	1910–1910	Enumeration Districts of Kentucky
H	?–?	Genealogy–Barton Collection
A	1792–1983	Governors Papers
U	1793–1856	Grants and Index
U	?–?	Grants South of Green River Surveys
U	1797–1866	Grants South of Green River (IN)
U	1825–1924	Grants South of Walker's Line (IN)
U	1822–1900	Grants West of Tennessee River
U	1820–1858	Grants West of Tennessee River Index
U	1836–1956	Grants in County Court Orders

A	1835-1956	Grants—County Court Orders
A	1836-1956	Grants—County Court Orders
A	?-?	Grants—Old Kentucky
A	1793-1856	Grants—Old Kentucky Index
A	1797-1866	Grants—South of Green River
A	1797-1866	Grants—South of Green River
A	1825-1924	Grants—South of Walker's Line
A	1825-1923	Grants—South of Walker's Line Index
A	1803-1853	Grants—Tellico
A	1782-1792	Grants—Virginia
U	1782-1792	Grants—Virginia
A	?-?	Grants—Virginia Land Grants (IN)
A	1822-1900	Grants—West of Tennessee River
A	1820-1858	Grants—West of Tennessee River Index
A	1796-1796	Green River Settlers
A	1799-1807	Green River Settlers Records of Payments
A	1854-1913	Land Forfeited to the State (Resident)
U	1782-1792	Land Grants Surveys and Index—Virginia
U	1782-1924	Land Grants by Jillson
A	1782-1924	Land Grants—Kentucky—Jillson's Index
A	1782-1792	Land Grants—Virginia Index
A	1795-1806	Land Office—Actual Settlers
U	1795-1806	Land Office—Actual Settlers
A	1884-1891	Land Office—Cash Receipts
U	1884-1891	Land Office—Cash Receipts
A	1857-1857	Land Office—Cross Index
U	1857-1857	Land Office—Cross Index
A	1794-1817	Land Office—Fee Book
U	1794-1817	Land Office—Fee Book
U	1796-1816	Land Office—Grantees
U	1796-1806	Land Office—Grants
A	1796-1816	Land Office—Grants (SY)
A	1825-1837	Land Office—Head Right Book
U	1825-1837	Land Office—Head Right Book
A	1796-1867	Land Office—Land Payments
U	1796-1867	Land Office—Land Payments
A	1796-1809	Land Office—Ledger
U	1796-1809	Land Office—Ledger
A	1796-1820	Land Office—Non-Resident Land Sales (SY)
U	1796-1819	Land Office—Non-Resident Land Sales (SY)
A	1805-1845	Land Office—Surveys (EX 1813-34)
U	1805-1812	Land Office—Surveys
U	1835-1845	Land Office—Surveys
A	1827-1837	Land Office—Warrants, Forfeited Lands
U	1827-1837	Land Office—Warrants
U	1796-1806	Land Records—Delinquent Lands
A	1796-1806	Land Records—Green River Settlers (grants)

U	?–?	Land Records—Green River Settlers Records
U	1792–1843	Land Records—Non-Resident Land
A	1791–1816	Land Records—Non-Resident Land
U	1792–1818	Land Records—Non-Resident Land Sold for Taxes (SY)
A	1792–1818	Land Records—Non-Resident Land Sold for Taxes
U	1799–1814	Land Records—Payments by Green River Settlers
U	1796–1796	Land Records—Records of Green River Settlers
U	1833–1868	Land Records—Resident Land Sold for Taxes
U	1865–1913	Land Records—Resident Lands Forfeited
U	1854–1865	Land Records—Resident Lands Forfeited (IN)
U	?–?	Land Records—Treasurer's—Green River
U	1801–1807	Land Records—Vacant Lands
H	?–?	Land Records—Warrants and Plats (Virginia)
A	1816–1873	Land Warrants and Grants
U	1816–1873	Land Warrants and Grants
A	1833–1868	Lands Sold for Taxes (resident) (SY)
U	1906–1914	Marriage Records (and some births and deaths)
A	1876–1876	Marriages
U	1876–1878	Marriages
A	1877–1878	Marriages
A	1906–1914	Marriages
U	1779–1784	May's Entries (IN)
A	1779–1784	May's Entries (Jefferson Entries)
A	1861–1862	Military Board Record Book
U	1861–1862	Military Board Record Book
A	1784–1797	Military Entries
U	1784–1797	Military Entries
A	1861–1866	Military Records—Adjutant General Report Index
A	1840–1840	Military Records—Census of Pensioners
H	?–?	Military Records—Civil War—Adjutant General
H	?–?	Military Records—Civil War—Confederate Vols.
H	?–?	Military Records—Civil War—Union Regiments
A	1861–1865	Military Records—Confederate Confined Deaths
A	1865–1867	Military Records—Confederate Amnesty Appls.
A	1902–1917	Military Records—Confederate Home Records
H	1913–1922	Military Records—Confederate Pension Claims
A	?–?	Military Records—Confederate Pensions
A	1861–1866	Military Records—Union and Confederate Index
A	?–?	Military Records—Revolutionary War Records Index
A	1796–1808	Military Records—Indian War Index to Order
A	1784–1811	Military Records—Kentucky Volunteers
A	1861–1864	Military Records—Louisville Prison Register
U	1878–1913	Military Records—National Guard Roster
H	1812–1816	Military Records—Officers War of 1812 Roster
A	1796–1808	Military Records—Order Book—Gen. Wilkinson
H	1902–1933	Military Records—Pee Wee Confederate Home
H	1812–1812	Military Records—Pension Index for War of 1812

H	?-?	Military Records—Revolutionary Burials
H	?-?	Military Records—Revolutionary War Soldiers in Kentucky —DAR
H	?-?	Military Records—Revolutionary War—DAR (Indiana and Kentucky)
A	?-?	Military Records—Revolutionary War (IN)
H	?-?	Military Records—Spanish American—Adjutant General
H	?-?	Military Records—Spanish American—Veterans Index
H	?-?	Military Records—Spanish American—Volunteer Officers
H	?-?	Military Records—WWI Veterans Army and Navy
H	?-?	Military Records—WWI Veterans Graves
A	1782-1793	Military Warrants
U	1782-1797	Military Warrants
A	1877-1887	National Guard Roster
H	1736-1780	Newspapers—*Virginia Gazette* (2 vol. IN)
A	1930-1960	Occupation Records—Retired Registered Architects
A	1962-1967	Occupational Records—Board of Auctioneers Applications
A	1780-1971	Postmasters Appointments for Kentucky
A	1848-1983	Prison and Corrections Records (restricted)
U	1874-1878	Register of Births
A	1798-1859	Register of Warrants
A	1848-1950	Registers of Prisoners
A	1893-1953	School Records—Kentucky State University—Black
U	1869-1889	School Records—Matriculates Record Book
U	1871-1901	School Records—School of Pharmacy
U	?-?	Survey County Court Orders
U	?-?	Survey South Green River Index
U	?-?	Survey Warrants for Headrights
U	?-?	Surveys, Grants, and Land Warrants
A	?-?	Surveys—Kentucky Land Warrants and Grants
A	?-?	Surveys—Old Kentucky Grants
U	?-?	Surveys—Old Kentucky Grants
U	?-?	Surveys—South Green River Grants
A	?-?	Surveys—South of Green River Grants
U	?-?	Surveys—South of Walker's Line
A	?-?	Surveys—South of Walker's Line Grants
A	?-?	Surveys—Tellico
A	?-?	Surveys—Warrants for Headright Grants
A	1796-1823	Tax Book—Resident
A	1862-1866	Tax Book—IRS (by county for 1862, 1864, 1866)
U	1796-1823	Tax Lists—Resident
U	1879-1892	Tax Lists by County (all counties)
U	1893-1911	Tax Lists by County (scattered counties)
U	1803-1853	Tellico Grants and Surveys
U	1785-1789	Treasurer's Fee Book
U	1805-1806	Treasurer's Fee Book

U	1813–1814	Treasurer's Fee Book
U	1821–1854	Treasurer's Fee Book (SY)
A	1785–1847	Treasurer's Fee Book (SY)
U	1808–1834	Treasurer's Receipts—Vacant Lands
A	1808–1834	Treasurer's Receipts—Vacant Lands
U	1794–1869	Treasurer's Reports (SY)
A	1794–1869	Treasurer's Reports (SY)
U	1798–1859	Truants—Register of Truants
U	1852–1861	Vital Statistics
A	1911–1986	Vital Statistics Index on Microfiche
H	1911–1986	Vital Statistics Index on Microfiche
A	1852–1910	Vital Statistics (1852–61, 1874–78, 1893, 1900–08)
H	1852–1910	Vital Statistics (1852–61, 1874–78, 1893, 1900–08)
A	1912–1977	Vital Statistics Index—Birth by Child
A	1912–1977	Vital Statistics Index—Birth by Mother
A	1963–1977	Vital Statistics—Death Index
A	1827–1849	Warrants for Headright Grants
U	1827–1849	Warrants for Headright Grants

APPENDIX 1

BIBLIOGRAPHY AND REFERENCES CITED

Adkinson, Kandie. 1990. "The Kentucky Land Grant System." *The Circuit Rider.* Saddlebag Notes Technical Leaflet. 13, no. 3 (May–June). This succinct explanation of Kentucky's land grant system is an excellent work to help a genealogist learn how to search the often confusing land grant records effectively and interpret findings.

Antoniak, Eleanor, indexer. 1983. *Kentucky Marriage Records.* Baltimore, Md.: Genealogical Publishing Company. This indexed volume contains a list of all marriages published in the *Register of the Kentucky Historical Society.* Not all counties are represented in this list, but some of the oldest counties are included in whole or in part. Years covered in general are for the period 1781 to 1854.

Ardery, Philip. 1987. "Barton Stone and The Drama of Cane Ridge." *The Register of the Kentucky Historical Society* 85:308–21.

Ardery, Mrs. W. B. 1977. *Kentucky Records.* Vol. 1. Lexington, Ky.: D.A.R. This volume contains scattered records including early wills and marriages, old Bible records, and tombstone inscriptions from Barren, Bath, Bourbon, Clark, Daviess, Fayette, Harrison, Jessamine, Lincoln, Madison, Mason, Montgomery, Nelson, Nicholas, Ohio, Scott, and Shelby counties.

——. 1979. *Kentucky Records.* Vol. 2. Lexington, Ky.: D.A.R. This volume contains scattered records from Fayette, Jefferson, Lincoln, Bath, Bourbon, Bracken, Clark, Fleming, Harrison, Hardin, Jessamine, Mason, Madison, Montgomery, Nicholas, Oldham, Scott, Woodford, and Warren counties.

Barbour, J., and John D. Carroll. 1894. *The Kentucky Statutes: Containing All General Laws Including Those Passed at Session of 1894.* Louisville, Ky.: Courier-Journal Job Printing Company.

Boatner, Mark M. 1959. *The Civil War Dictionary.* New York: McKay Company.

Brookes-Smith, Joan, comp. 1976. *Master Index: Virginia Surveys and Grants, 1774–1791.* Frankfort, Ky.: Kentucky Historical Society.

Bullock, Edward I., and William Johnson. 1873. *The General Statutes of the Commonwealth of Kentucky.* Frankfort, Ky.: Kentucky Yeoman Office.

Butler, Mann. 1971. *Valley of the Ohio.* Frankfort, Ky.: Kentucky Historical Society.

Carpenter, John W. 1988. *Kentucky Courthouses.* London, Ky.: the author.

Censer, Jane T. 1981. "Smiling Through Her Tears: Antebellum Southern Women and Divorce." *American Journal of Legal History* 25:24–47.

Clark, Thomas. 1960. *History of Kentucky.* Lexington, Ky.: John Bradford Press.

Clift, G. Glenn. 1964. *Notes on Kentucky Veterans of the War of 1812.* Anchorage, Ky.: Borderland Books.

——. 1966. *Second Census of Kentucky, 1800.* Baltimore, Md.: Genealogical Publishing Company. This listing is a much needed replacement for the lost 1800 federal census. The work is a compilation of tax enumerations of the 42 counties existing in Kentucky in 1800.

——. 1977. *Kentucky Obituaries, 1787–1854.* Baltimore, Md.: Genealogical Publishing Company. Obituaries excerpted and reprinted from the *Register of the Kentucky Historical Society*, vols. 39–41, 1941–43.

——. 1978. *Kentucky Marriages, 1797–1865.* Baltimore, Md.: Genealogical Publishing Company. This index of marriages was reprinted from the *Register of the Kentucky Historical Society* volumes from 1938 to 1940. The notices were taken from the Lexington library's 1787–1865 newspaper files. The counties covered include those of central Kentucky (Fayette, Mercer, Clark, Nelson, Jefferson, Franklin) and other counties.

Coleman, J. Winston. 1949. *Bibliography of Kentucky History.* Lexington, Ky.: University of Kentucky Press. A dated, annotated bibliography of Kentuckiana that lists some 3,400 monographic works.

——. 1968. *Historic Kentucky.* Lexington, Ky.: Henry Clay Press.

——. 1971. *Kentucky: A Pictoral History.* Lexington, Ky.:University of Kentucky Press.

——. 1979. *Sketches of Kentucky's Past.* Lexington, Ky.: Winburn Press.

Collins, Richard. 1976. *History of Kentucky.* 1874. Reprint. Berea, Ky.: Kentucky Imprints.

Conrad, John. 1988. "Marriage in Virginia and Kentucky." *Bluegrass Roots,* vol. 15, pp. 104-111.

Cook, Michael L., comp. 1979. *Index to Report of the Adjutant General of the State of Kentucky. Confederate Kentucky Volunteers. Vol. 1: Infantry Regiments.* Hartford, Ky.: Cook-McDowell Publications. Index by page number of Kentucky volunteers listed in the adjutant general's report.

——. 1985. *Kentucky Court of Appeals Deed Books.* Vols. I-IV. Evansville, Ind.: Cook Publications. This four-volume set of deeds was recorded in 1796 but dates as early as 1775. Later deeds involve Indiana and Missouri territories. The four volumes cover 1796 to 1835. Supreme Court records from 1783 to 1792 are also included in volume IV.

——. 1986. *Kentucky Index of Biographical Sketches in State, Regional and County Histories.* Evansville, Ind.: Cook Publications. This volume indexed some of the biographical books published in Kentucky from the 1870s to the 1910s. It is not an every-name index—only an index to the subjects of the biography. Copies of the references can be obtained from the publisher.

——. 1988a. *Jefferson County, Kentucky Records.* Vol. 5. Evansville, Ind.: Cook Publications. Deed books 1-7 for period 1783 to 1806 are included. Covers what is now Nelson, Shelby, and Bullitt counties.

——. 1988b. *Virginia Supreme Court, District of Kentucky Order Books 1783-1792.* Evansville, Ind.: Cook Publications. This independent court was formed for the district of Kentucky due to the distance from the regular Virginia Supreme Court in 1783. It continued until 1792 when Kentucky became a state. The court heard cases involving minor offenses as well as criminal cases, estates, guardianship matters, and other suits. This was the only court to hear land dispute cases between settlers. Decisions are given in detail. Over 14,000 names are indexed.

Cook, Michael L., and Bettie C. Cook. 1977. *Breckinridge County Records Vols. 1-5.* Evansville, Ind.: Cook Publications. These volumes contain the following: minute book, 1803-23; slave importation declaration book; deed books, 1800-10; the 1880 census; reconstructed marriages, 1800-81; and other records.

———. 1986. *Ohio County Records*. Vol. 1. Evansville, Ind.: Cook Publications. Contains marriage records dating from 1799 to 1880 and county court deed records for 1799-1809.

———. 1986-87. *Fayette County Records*. Vols. 1-5. Evansville, Ind.: Cook Publications. Volume 1 includes circuit court records A-H, 1797-1825. Volume 2 contains deed books of the district and circuit court covering 1803-07. The third volume contains marriage bonds from 1796 to 1850. The fourth volume has 1803-12 court orders. Volume 5 includes Fayette County will books dating from 1793 to 1824 and guardian bonds from 1803 to 1816. Also includes some re-recordings of the records lost in the 1803 fire. Every-name index.

———. 1987. *Fincastle and Kentucky County Virginia*. Vol. 1. Evansville, Ind.: Cook Publications. This book gives the history of the two Virginia counties that became Kentucky for the years 1772 to 1780. Includes all known existing records for these counties and the Virginia legislative acts pertaining to Kentucky statehood. This volume also contains records that did not appear in the *Annals of Southwest Virginia* published in 1929 by Lewis Summers. Every-name index.

———. 1988a. *Lincoln County Records*. Vol. 2. Evansville, Ind.: Cook Publications. This book includes the county court orders from 1781 to 1791 when Lincoln included Mercer and Madison counties.

———. 1988b. *Mercer County Records*. Vol. 2. Evansville, Ind.: Cook Publications. Includes marriage records from 1786 to 1835.

Cook, Michael L., and Glenda Trapp. 1985. *Kentucky Genealogical Index*. Vol. I. Utica, Ky.: McDowell Publications. An every-name index to the following genealogical publications: *Kentucky Ancestors*, 1965-80; *Eastern Kentuckian*, 1965-80; *Kentucky Genealogist*, 1950-80; *Kentucky Pioneer and Genealogical Records*, 1979-80; *Bluegrass Roots*, 1974-80.

Cotterill, R. S. 1917. *History of Pioneer Kentucky*. Cincinnati, Ohio: Johnson and Hardin.

Cox, Clayton. 1980. *Early Kentucky Records*. Prestonsburg, Ky.: State-Wide Press. Excerpts from the published pages of *The East Kentuckian*, a genealogical journal, are collected in this book. Indexed.

Daughters of the American Revolution, comps. 1962a. *Kentucky Bible Records*. Lexington, Ky.: the compilers. Indexed. Multivolume.

———, comps. 1962b. *Kentucky Cemetery Records*. Lexington, Ky.: Daughters of the American Revolution. Multivolume reference.

Davis, Clara, ed. 1958. *Revolutionary Ancestors of Kentucky Daughters of the American Revolution.* Frankfort, Ky.: Daughters of the American Revolution, Kentucky Society.

Deitz, Robert E., ed. 1976. *Travels Through Kentucky History.* Louisville, Ky.: Fetter Printing Company.

Dilts, Bryan Lee. 1984. *1890 Kentucky Census Index of Civil War Veterans or Their Widows.* Salt Lake City, Utah: Index Publishing. Gives the name, county, and page number in the census of the veterans and/or their widows as they appear in the 1890 census. Well-documented book.

Duff, Jeffrey Michael. 1976. *Inventory of Records of the Bank of Kentucky, 1806–1835.* Frankfort, Ky.: Archives Branch, Division of Archives and Records Management.

Duff, Jeffrey Michael. 1980. *Inventory of Kentucky Birth, Marriage, and Death Records: 1852–1910.* Frankfort, Ky.: Archives Branch, Division of Archives and Records Management. This county-by-county inventory of assessors lists gives the availablility of birth records for 1852 to 1910, marriages for 1852 to 1910, and deaths for the period 1852 to 1910.

Dyche, Russell. 1946. "Sesquicentennial of the Wilderness Road." *The Register of the Kentucky State Historical Society* 44:81–5.

Eakle, Arlene, and Johni Cerny, eds. 1984. *The Source: A Guidebook of American Genealogy.* Salt Lake City, Utah: Ancestry.

Eckenrode, H. J. 1978. *List of Colonial Soldiers of Virginia.* Baltimore, Md.: Genealogical Publishing Company. The book is a compilation of a number of sources including Hening's Statutes, manuscripts, and published county histories, that give names of colonial soldiers.

Felldin, Jeanne Robey, and Gloria Kay Vandiver Inman, comps. 1981. *Index to the 1820 Census of Kentucky.* Baltimore, Md.: Genealogical Publishing Company.

Felty, Harold G. 1987. "Marriage Practices on Frontier Varied." *Bluegrass Roots* 14:54.

Field, Thomas. 1961. *A Guide to Kentucky Place Names.* Lexington, Ky.: University of Kentucky, Geological Survey. This index of Kentucky place names contains references to small towns and villages that may not always appear on maps. Small neighborhoods, creeks, schools, and even family cemeteries are included.

Finger, John R. 1984. "Witness to Expansion: Bishop Francis Asbury on the Trans-Appalachian Frontier." *The Register of the Kentucky Historical Society* 82:334–57.

Filson Club. 1988. *Early Kentucky Settlers: The Records of Jefferson County, Kentucky.* Baltimore, Md.: Genealogical Publishing Company. Records reprinted in this volume are minute books from 1781 to 1785, will books from 1784 to 1833, bond and power of attorney books from 1783 to 1798, and the division book covering 1797 to 1832. Indexed.

Ford, Thomas R. 1982. "Kentucky in the 1880s." *Kentucky Review* 3, no. 2.

———.. 1981. "Kentucky in the 1880s." Unpublished paper.

Fothergill, Augusta, and John M. Naugle. 1978. *Virginia Tax Payers, 1782–87.* Baltimore, Md.: Genealogical Publishing Company. Kentucky taxpayers prior to the state's formation are listed in this volume along with the county of residence and assessment.

Fowler, Ila. 1935. "Revolutionary Soldiers and Their Land Grants in the Tradewater River Country of Western Kentucky." *Register of the Kentucky Historical Society* 33:160–64.

———, comp. 1967. *Kentucky Pioneers and Their Descendants.* Baltimore, Md.: Genealogical Publishing Company. This book contains scattered church, marriage, deed, cemetery, and tax records for a few counties. The best coverage is for Mason. Some records from Bracken, Caldwell, Christian, Fleming, and Hopkins are also included. Indexed.

Fugate, Betty Kelly. 1989. *The 1989–90 Directory of Kentucky Historical Organizations and Speakers Bureau and Kentucky Publications Survey.* Frankfort, Ky.: Kentucky Historical Society. The directory gives information on more than 300 heritage and historical organizations by county. The second section is a list of speakers who are available for presentations along with information on their areas of expertise and fees. The third section of the book is a listing of Kentucky publications, their prices, and availability information. The listing included as section three may be obtained free of charge with a self-addressed stamped envelope from the Kentucky Historical Society.

Garr, Elisabeth Headley. 1972. *The History of Kentucky Courthouses: An Illustrated Story of Courthouses and County Historical Data.* Lexington, Ky.: National Society of the Colonial Dames of America in Kentucky. Pioneering work gives a brief narrative of each county courthouse including architecture and historical background.

Green, Karen Mauer. 1983. *The Kentucky Gazette, 1787–1800*. Baltimore, Md.: Gateway Press.

———. 1985. *The Kentucky Gazette, 1801–1820*. Baltimore, Md.: Gateway Press.

Green, Thomas Marshall. 1889. *Historic Families of Kentucky*. Cincinnati, Ohio: R. Clarke.

Hammon, Neal O. 1986. "Settlers, Land Jobbers, and Outlyers: A Quantitative Analysis of Land Acquisition on the Kentucky Frontier." *The Register of the Kentucky Historical Society* 84:241–62.

Harney, Brian D. 1985. *Index to Bluegrass Roots 1973-1984*. Utica, Ky.: McDowell Publications. This index is an every-name index to *Bluegrass Roots*. The citation gives the date, volume, and page number of the issue that contains the referenced ancestor.

———. 1987. "What Computers Can Do For You!" *Circuit Rider* 9:5.

Harrison, Richard L. 1984. "Locating and Using Church Records." *Bluegrass Roots* 11:42–55.

Hathaway, Beverley West. 1974. *Kentucky Genealogical Records*. West Jordan, Utah: Allstates Research. Kentucky records along with a brief history of the state that is oriented to an understanding of genealogy are covered in this reference.

Hearn, William. 1973. *Kentucky County Courthouses (Statistical Report)*. Unpublished manuscript.

Henderson, Dorothy, ed. 1977. *Kentucky Treasure Trails*. Nashville, Tenn.: Favorite Recipes Press. This book, billed as a historical and cultural travel guide, is actually a little more. For each county, there is a brief history and basic county information. In addition, there are also listings of festivals and other events, memorials and museums, historical markers, historical homes, cemeteries, and other points of interest.

Hening, William. 1823. *The Statutes at Large*. Richmond, Va.: Samuel Pleasants.

Hilliard, Edward H. 1960. "When Kentucky had Two Courts of Appeal." *The Filson Club Quarterly* 34:228–36.

Humphreys, Charles. 1822. *A Compendium of the Common Law in Force in Kentucky*. Lexington, Ky.: William Gibbes Hunt.

Ireland, Robert M. 1972. *The County Courts in Antebellum Kentucky*. Lexington, Ky.: University of Kentucky Press.

Jackson, Ronald V., et al. 1977. *Index to Kentucky Wills to 1851*. Bountiful, Utah: Accelerated Indexing Service. Kentucky testators from all counties through 1850 are included. The county book and page number are given. Not included in the index, however, are other probate records such as settlements, sales, and appraisals.

Jillson, Willard Rouse. 1934. *Pioneer Kentucky: An Outline of Its Exploration and Settlement, Its Early Cartography and Primitive Geography, Coupled with a Brief Presentation of the Principal Trails, Traces, Forts, Stations, Springs, Licks, Fords and Ferries Used Prior to the Year 1800*. Frankfort, Ky.: State Journal Company.

———. 1950. *A Bibliography of Kentucky County, Virginia, 1776-1780*. Frankfort, Ky.: Roberts Printing Company. Includes annotations.

———. 1971. *The Kentucky Land Grants: A Systematic Index to All of the Land Grants Recorded in the State Land Office at Frankfort, Kentucky, 1782-1924*. Baltimore, Md.: Genealogical Publishing Company.

———. 1978. *Old Kentucky Entries and Deeds: A Complete Index to All of the Earliest Land Entries, Military Warrants, Deeds and Wills of the Commonwealth of Kentucky*. Baltimore, Md.: Genealogy Publishing Company.

Kentucky Court of Justice, Administrative Office of the Courts. 1985-86. *Annual Report*. Frankfort, Ky.: Administrative Office of the Courts, Commonwealth of Kentucky.

Kentucky Department for Libraries and Archives. 1988. *Directory of Kentucky's Libraries and Archives*. Frankfort, Ky.: Division of Field Services, Kentucky Department for Libraries and Archives. Contains information on archives, special collections, and institutional, academic, public, and school libraries. Library information in chapter 8 is taken from the latest version of this directory.

Kentucky Division of Archives and Records Management. 1986. *The Guide to Kentucky Archival and Manuscript Repositories*. Frankfort, Ky.: Public Records Division. This guide gives an overview of the general holdings of libraries in the state by individual library.

Kentucky Genealogical Society. 1980s. *Kentucky Family Archives*. Frankfort, Ky: the society. This publication is currently a five-volume work that contains family group sheets submitted by society members.

Kentucky Heritage Commission. 1971. *Survey of Historic Sites in Kentucky*. Frankfort, Ky.: the commision.

Kentucky Historical Society. n.d. *Supplemental files to the Microfilm Catalog*. N.p.

——. n.d. *Surveys and Grants Not Issued*. Frankfort, Ky.: the society. This unpublished computer list is available from the society for a small fee.

——. 1921. "Locations and Water Courses." *The Register of the Kentucky Historical Society* 19:314-21. List of the locations and water courses mentioned in the certificate book of the Virginia Land Commission.

——. [1923] 1981. *Certificate Book of the Virginia Land Commission of 1779-80.* Reprint. Easley, S.C.: Southern Historical Press. Index of certificates used to prove claims by early settlers. The commission held sittings at St. Asaph's (Stanford), Harrodsburg, Bryant's Station, Boonesborough, and Falls of the Ohio. This land court's proceedings are explained in a book by Samuel M. Wilson also available at the Kentucky Historical Society library. See also the 1921 issue of the *Register* for locations and water courses listed in this book.

——. 1975. *Index for Old Kentucky Surveys & Grants*. Frankfort, Ky.: the society. Also includes Tellico surveys and grants.

——. 1978. *Microfilm Catalog*. Vol. 3, *Excerpted Manuscripts and Pertinent Genealogical Source Material—Adair to Johnson*. Frankfort, Ky.: the society. The above two volumes list some of the microfilmed records available for purchase from the Kentucky Historical Society library. These records are not neccessarily in the holdings of the society. The lists are quite dated, many more films are available currently than are listed.

——. 1980. *Warrants Used in Virginia & Old Kentucky Surveys*. Frankfort, Ky.: the society. This work references the warrants actually located and their appropriate survey numbers.

——. 1982. *Microfilm Catalog*. Vol. 4, *Excerpted Manuscripts and Pertinent Genealogical Source Material—Kenton to Menifee*. Frankfort, Ky.: the society.

——. 1984. *Early Kentucky Tax Records*. Baltimore, Md.: Genealogical Publishing Company. This consolidated list of tax records dates from 1788 to 1801 for various counties in Kentucky. Provides a supplement to the 1790 and 1800 reconstructed census lists. Indexed.

——. 1988-89. *County Resources Available in the Historical Society Library*. Frankfort, Ky.: the society. The society has compiled all genealogical sources in their library by county. These are available for purchase from the society.

Kentucky Public Works Administration. n.d. *Kentucky Records Survey*. Mimeograph copy.

Kentucky Public Works Project. 1937. *Kentucky Historical Records Survey*. N.p. Inventories of the various counties including Anderson, Fayette, Laurel.

Kincaid, Robert L. 1947. *The Wilderness Road*. New York: Bobbs Merrill Company.

King, J. Estelle Stewart. 1969. *Abstract of Early Kentucky Wills and Inventories*. Baltimore, Md.: Genealogical Publishing Company. Abstracts copies of original wills and inventories from as early as the 1790s to the mid-1800s from thirty-six of Kentucky's 120 counties are included. Indexed.

Klotter, James C., ed. 1981. *Genealogies of Kentucky Families*. Baltimore, Md.: Genealogical Publishing Company. These volumes contain all the family history articles published in the *Register* between 1903 and 1965 when genealogical contributions were discontinued. Every Bible record and genealogical fragment known to have been published in the *Register* has also been included. Indexed.

Kozee, William Carlos. 1957. *Pioneer Families of Eastern and Southeastern Kentucky*. Huntington, W. Va.: Standard Printing and Publishing Company.

Loughborough, Preston S. 1842. *A Digest of the Statute Laws of Kentucky of a Public and Permanent Nature Passed since 1834*. Frankfort, Ky.: Albert G. Hodges.

Littell, William. 1809. *The Statute Law of Kentucky*. Frankfort, Ky.: William Hunter.

Littell, William, and Jacob Swigert. 1822. *A Digest of the Statute Law of Kentucky: Being a Collection of All the Acts of the General Assembly of a Public and Permanent Nature*. Frankfort, Ky.: Kendall and Russell.

McAdams, Ednah (Wilson). 1967. *Kentucky Pioneer and Court Records: Abstracts of Early Wills, Deeds, and Marriages*. Baltimore, Md.: Genealogical Publishing Company.

Morehead, C. S., and Mason Brown. 1834. *A Digest of the Statute Laws of Kentucky*. Frankfort, Ky.: Albert G. Hodges. Statutes of the government from the commencement of the government to the session ending 1834.

National Register of Historical Places. n.d. *Historic Places in Kentucky*. Washington, D.C. This six-volume microfiche lists sites on the National Historic Register. Available in the Kentucky archives research room.

O'Brien, Michael Joseph. 1916. *Irish Pioneers in Kentucky*: Louisville, Ky.: the author. A series of articles published in the *Gaelic American*.

Place, Walter. 1983. "The Governors' Papers." *Bluegrass Roots* 10:52–54.

Pritchard, James M. 1989. Personal correspondence, 14 September. Archivist, Kentucky Department for Libraries and Archives.

Puetz, C. J. n.d. *Kentucky County Maps.* N.p. County highway maps for all of Kentucky's 120 counties are included in this large (16-by-11) book. Wildlife parks, highways, churches, creeks, and cemeteries are marked.

Purvis, Thomas L. 1982. "The Ethnic Descent of Kentucky's Early Population, 1790-1820." *The Register of the Kentucky Historical Society* 80:253-66.

Quissenberry, Anderson C. [1896] 1974. *Revolutionary Soldiers in Kentucky.* Reprint. Baltimore, Md.: Genealogical Publishing Company. These records were excerpted from the *Yearbook, Kentucky Society, Sons of the American Revolution.*

Rennick, Robert M. 1984. *Kentucky Place Names.* Lexington, Ky.: University of Kentucky Press. Contains descriptions and brief histories of 100,000 place names including towns as well as geographic features.

Robertson, James Rood. 1981. *Petitions of the Early Inhabitants of Kentucky.* Easley, S.C.: Southern Historical Press. Contains the petitions and index to signers of early petitions to Virginia by Kentuckians. Name index.

Rone, Wendell H., Sr. 1965. *An Historical Atlas of Kentucky and Her Counties.* Mayfield, Ky.: Mayfield Printing Company. This invaluable book is available for purchase at the Kentucky Historical Society gift shop. Traces development of Kentucky's counties from prior to statehood to modern times.

Sanderlin, John B. 1987. "Ethnic Origins of Early Kentucky Land Grantees." *The Register of the Kentucky Historical Society* 85:103-10.

Schweitzer, George Keene. 1981. *Kentucky Genealogical Research.* Knoxville, Tenn.: the author.

Sears, Richard. 1989. "Working Like A Slave: Views of Slavery and the Status of Women in Antebellum Kentucky." *The Register of the Kentucky Historical Society* 87:1-19.

Secretary of War Report. 1959. *Kentucky Pension Roll of 1835.* Baltimore, Md.: Southern Book Company. This index lists pensioners who served in the Revolution along with the soldier's rank, amount of allowance, description of service, and date on pension roll.

Shammas, Carole. 1987a. "English Inheritance Law and Its Transfer to the Colonnies." *American Journal of Legal History* 31:145-63.

——. 1987b. *Inheritance in America from Colonial Times to the Present.* New Brunswick, N.J.: Rutgers University Press.

Simpson, Alicia, comp. 1978. *Inventory of Confederate Pension Applications, Commonwealth of Kentucky*. Rev. ed. Frankfort, Ky.: Archives Branch, Division of Archives and Records Management, Department of Library and Archives.

Speed, Thomas. 1886. *The Wilderness Road*. Louisville, Ky.: The Filson Club, Publication No. 2.

Speth, Linda E., and Alison D. Hirsch. 1983. *Women, Family, and Community in Colonial America: Two Perspectives*. New York: Haworth Press.

Sprague, Stuart. 1984a. "Pitfalls, Treasures, and Boobytraps: A Historian Views Local History." *Circuit Rider* 3-5.

Sprague, Stuart. 1984b. "Newspaper Files Useful in History and Genealogy." *Bluegrass Roots* 11:5-8.

Stanton, Richard H. 1867. *The Revised Statutes of Kentucky. Approved and Adopted by the General Assembly 1851 and 1852*. Cincinnati, Ohio: Robert Clarke & Company, 2 vols.

Sutherland, James F. 1986. *Early Kentucky Householders, 1787-1811*. Baltimore, Md.: Genealogical Publishing Company. This book is an index of the tax lists of Lincoln County containing more than 34,000 entries. Great care has been taken to ensure that variant spellings have been considered and can be found. Householder data includes the person's name, date of list, book, and page of the original tax roll. See also Sutherland's *Kentucky Landholders*, also published by Genealogical Publishing Company. Data available on diskette from James Sutherland, 306 Newbury Drive, Monroeville, Pennsylvania 15146.

Taylor, Philip Fall. 1967. *A Calendar of the Warrants for Land in Kentucky, Granted for Service in the French and Indian War*. Baltimore, Md.: Genealogical Publishing Company.

Teague, Barbara, ed. 1986. *Guide to Kentucky Archival and Manuscript Collections*. Vol. 1. Frankfort, Ky.: Public Records Division, Department of Libraries and Archives.

Thompson, Milton. 1985. "Kentucky Tax Lists." *Bluegrass Roots* 12:96.

Trimble, Jeanne, comp. 1987. *Guide to Selected Manuscripts Housed in Special Collections and Archives of Margaret I. King Library*. Lexington, Ky.: University of Kentucky.

Wade, Richard C. 1959. *The Urban Frontier*. Chicago: University of Chicago Press.

Wagstaff, Ann T., comp. 1980. *Index to the 1810 Census of Kentucky*. Baltimore, Md.: Genealogical Publishing Company.

Weaks, Mabel C. 1979. *Calendar of the Kentucky Papers of the Draper Collection of Manuscripts*. Vol. II. Hartford, Ky.: Cook and McDowell Publications.

Wilder, Minnie S., indexer. 1969. *War of 1812 Report of the Adjutant General of the State of Kentucky Soldiers of the War of 1812*. Baltimore, Md.: Genealogical Publishing Company.

Wilson, Samuel M. 1967. *Catalogue of Revolutionary Soldiers and Sailors of the Commonwealth of Virginia to Whom Land Bounty Warrants Were Granted*. Baltimore, Md.: Genealogical Publishing Company. Reprinted from the *Yearbook of the Society, Sons of the American Revolution in the Commonwealth of Kentucky, 1894–1913*.

APPENDIX 2

KENTUCKY COUNTY BOUNDARY MAPS

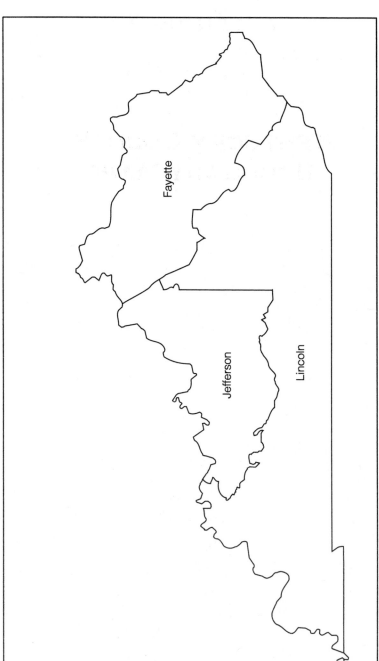

Kentucky County Map 1780 (O'Malley 1987, 42)

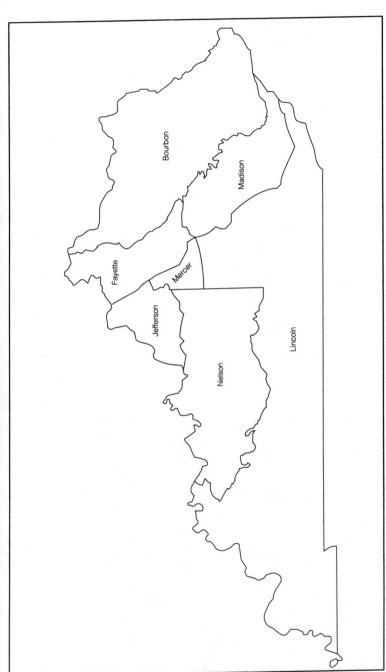

Kentucky County Map 1785–86 (O'Malley 1987, 42)

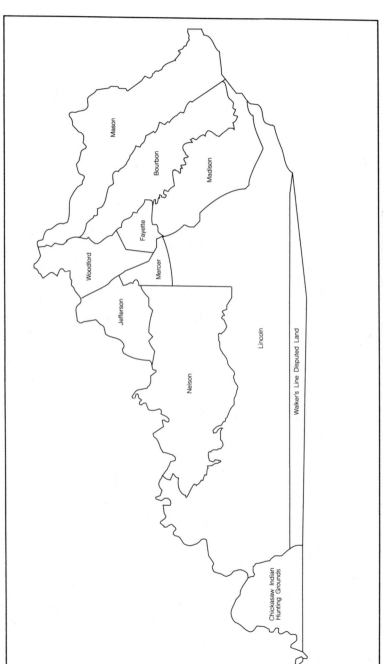

Kentucky County Map 1792 (*Bluegrass Roots* 1978, 30)

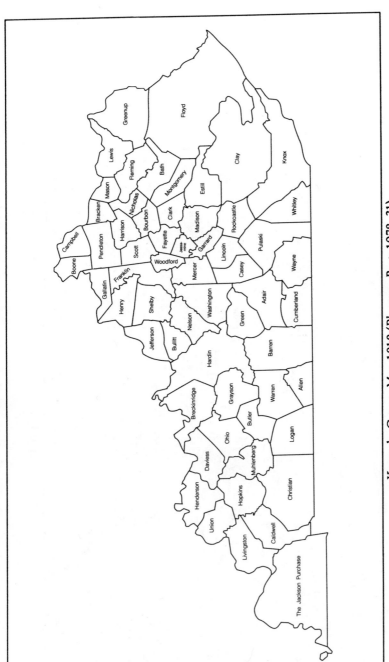

Kentucky County Map 1818 (*Bluegrass Roots* 1978, 31)

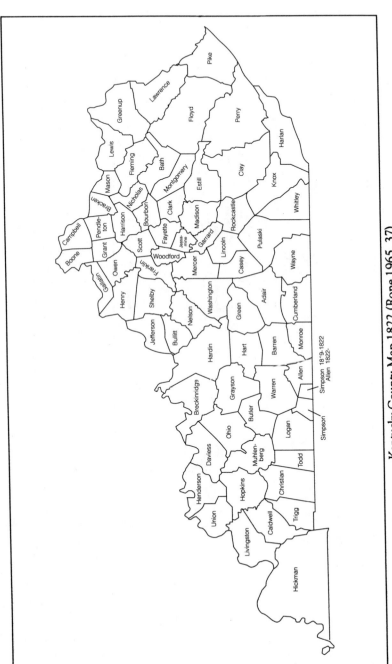

Kentucky County Map 1822 (Rone 1965, 37)

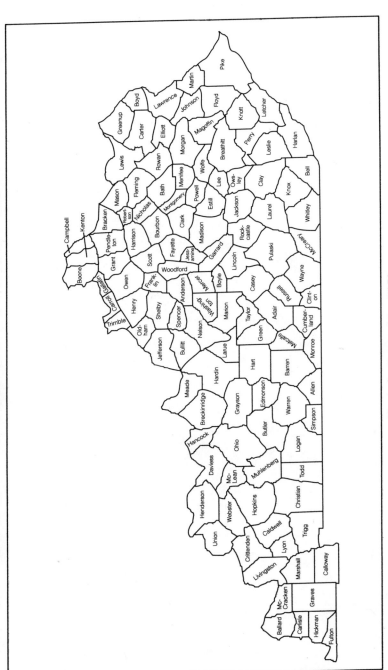

Kentucky County Map 1972–

APPENDIX 3

STATEWIDE JOURNALS, MAGAZINES, AND OTHER KENTUCKY PUBLICATION SOURCES

KENTUCKY JOURNALS

Appalachian Heritage, Box 623, Hindman, Kentucky 41822. A regional quarterly magazine housed at the James Still Building on the Hindman Settlement School campus.

Back Home in Kentucky, Cockrel Corporation, Route 9, Box 10, Bowling Green, Kentucky 42101. *Back Home in Kentucky* is a history and Kentuckiana magazine that contains articles of interest about Kentucky.

Bluegrass Roots. A quarterly published by the Kentucky Genealogical Society, P.O. Box 153, Frankfort, Kentucky 40602.

The Circuit Rider. A publication of the Historical Confederation of Kentucky, P.O. Box H, Frankfort, Kentucky 40602. The confederation publication is a very helpful newsletter with announcements of events and articles discussing issues of importance to Kentucky heritage.

Journal of Kentucky Studies, Department of History, Northern Kentucky University, Highland Heights, Kentucky 41076. Begun in 1984, this journal provides a forum for articles in history, literary criticism, critical essays, local history, oral histories, as well as short fiction and poetry.

Kentucky Ancestors. A quarterly (begun in 1965) of the Kentucky Historical Society, Box H, Frankfort, Kentucky 40602. Membership in the society includes a subscription to *Kentucky Ancestors, The Register of the Kentucky Historical Society,* and a bimonthly newsletter.

Kentucky Folklore Record. The University of Kentucky special collections library and Kentucky Historical Society have these volumes, which were published from 1955 to 1986.

Kentucky Review. Published by the University of Kentucky Library Associates, this journal contains articles of Kentucky's literature, culture, and history. Special emphasis is given to library holdings, acquisitions, and other activities.

The Mountain Empire Genealogical Quarterly, P.O. Box 628, Pound, Virginia 24279. This magazine covers counties in eastern Kentucky, western North Carolina, eastern Tennessee, southwestern Virginia, and southern West Virginia. The *Empire* contains original records as well as family group sheets, queries, photographs, and recollections of pioneers. Back issues are available from 1982.

The Register of the Kentucky Historical Society, Box H, Frankfort, Kentucky 40601. Order by joining the society. Begun in 1903, the *Register* now focuses on historical articles. Early publications contain a great deal of genealogical information.

OTHER KENTUCKY SOURCES

Publishers who specialize in Kentucky publications or have a Kentucky collection are listed below.

Appalachian Heritage Society, Inc., Box 623, Hindman, Kentucky 41882. Publishes *Appalachian Heritage,* a regional quarterly magazine that explores appalachian culture, history, folklore, education, and crafts.

Cabin Trails Heritage Distributors, 417 Shelby Street, Frankfort, Kentucky 40601. Contact: Donna Stark Thompson. Cabin Trails serves as a distributor for Kentucky publications for a number of counties. At the present time, these counties include Trimble, Woodford, Scott, Franklin, and Estill. The publications index wills, censuses, vital statistics, etc.

Cook Publications, 3316 Wimberg Avenue, Evansville, Indiana 47712. Cook Publications is publishing one of the most extensive Kentucky records series yet attempted. Their books are well indexed and provide access to many early Kentucky records that were previously difficult to access. See appendix 1 under Cook for a description of some of their Kentucky volumes.

Iberian Publishing Company, 548 Cedar Creek Drive, Athens, Georgia 30605-3408. This company publishes the *Virginiana Library Catalog*, which contains many Virginia resources that are helpful to tracking early Kentuckians.

Kentucky Heritage Commission, Frankfort, Kentucky. The commission conducts surveys of historical sites by county and publishes inventories of county historical sites. See appendix 5 for its county publications.

Kentucky Images, 527 S. Upper Street, Lexington, Kentucky 40508. Contact: Mr. Robert Powell. This publishing house handles a variety of Kentucky publications and was formerly the source of the *Kentucky Images Magazine*, which contained articles about history and folklife. The company now focuses on high quality prints and other Kentucky related publications.

Kentucky Oral History Commission, Box H, Frankfort, Kentucky 40601. The commission archives and supports the collection of oral histories of prominent Kentuckians, including political leaders as well as ordinary citizens. Their tapes are held by the historical society and the archives.

McDowell Publications, 11129 Pleasant Ridge Road, Utica, Kentucky 41375. McDowell publishes a number of Kentucky sources including *Kentucky Genealogical Sources*, which lists libraries and societies, and prints the *Kentucky Pioneer Quarterly*.

Simmons Historical Publications, Box 66, Melber, Kentucky 42069. The list of publications for Simmons seems to indicate a specialization in western Kentucky counties, but there are also publications from Virginia, North Carolina, and Tennessee.

The Ancestor Detective, Ancestor Publishers, Box 682, Arvada, Colorado 80001. This company publishes a number of bibliographies of Kentucky counties, which vary in price and coverage. Some county bibliographies are 63 pages long; others are only two pages.

Ye Olde Genealogie Shoppe, Box 39128, Indianapolis, Indiana 46239. Ye Olde Genealogie Shoppe has a collection of forms and genealogical aids, and it has recently compiled a listing of "Kentucky Books In Print" costing $14 including postage.

APPENDIX 4

AFRICAN-AMERICAN
BIBLIOGRAPHY FOR KENTUCKY

Although not a great deal has been published on black Kentuckians exclusively, below is a listing of known Kentucky publications to date. Also included are basic references for learning about African-American history and family history.

Amico, Colette, and Shirley Burton. 1989. "Freedmen's Bureau Records as a Family Resource at the National Archives." *Federation of Genealogial Societies Forum* 1, no. 3 (Fall): 8-10.

Blassingame, John W. 1979. *The Slave Community: Plantation Life in the Antebellum South.* New York: Oxford University Press.

Blockson, Charles L. 1977. *Black Genealogy.* Englewood Cliffs, N.J.: Prentice Hall.

Brown, Richard C. 1989. "The Free Blacks of Boyle County, Kentucky, 1850-1860." *The Register of the Kentucky Historical Society* 87:426-38.

Coleman, J. Winston. 1940. *Slavery Times in Kentucky.* Chapel Hill, N.C.: University of North Carolina Press.

Donald, Henderson H. 1952. *The Negro Freedman: Life Conditions of the American Negro in the Early Years After Emancipation.* New York: H. Schuman.

Dunningan, Alice A. 1982. *The Fascinating Story of Black Kentuckians: Their Heritage and Tradition.* Washington, D.C.: Association for Study of Afro-American Life and History. History of blacks and famous blacks in Kentucky. Contains some genealogical information on a few of the subjects of the author's biographies. Ms. Dunningham has also written an autobiography entitled *A Black Woman's Experience: From Schoolhouse to White House.* It includes a short account of her parents and grandparents.

Gara, Larry. 1967. *The Liberty Line: The Legend of the Underground Railroad.* Lexington, Ky.: University of Kentucky Press.

Garrison, Gwendolyn. 1985. *Black Marriage Records of Fayette County, Kentucky, 1866-1876.* Lexington, Ky.: Kentucky Tree Search.

Gutman, Herbert G. 1976. *The Black Family in Slavery and Freedom, 1750-1925.* New York: Pantheon Books.

Harrison, Lowell. 1978. *The Antislavery Movement In Kentucky.* Lexington, Ky.: University of Kentucky.

Henri, Florette. 1975. *Black Migration, 1900-1920.* New York: Doubleday Anchor Press.

Howard, Victor. 1983. *Black Liberation in Kentucky. Emancipation and Freedom 1862-1884.* Lexington, Ky.: University Press of Kentucky. History of black participation in the Civil War. No genealogical information.

Johnson, William Decker. [1897] 1973. *Biographical Sketches of Prominent Negro Men and Women of Kentucky.* Reprint. New York.

Kellogg, John. 1982. "The Formation of Black Residential Areas in Lexington, Kentucky." *The Journal of Southern History* 48, no. 1:21-52.

Linder, Bill R. 1981. *Black Genealogy: Basic Steps to Research.* Technical Leaflet #135. Nashville, Tenn.: American Asssociation for State and Local History.

Lucas, Marion B. 1989. "Camp Nelson, Kentucky during the Civil War: Cradle of Liberty or Refugee Death Camp?" *Filson Club History Quarterly* 63, no. 4:439-52.

McDougal, Ivan. 1918. *Slavery in Kentucky: 1792-1865.* Lancaster, Ky.: New Era Printing.

Montell, William Lynwood. 1970. *The Saga of Coe Ridge.* Knoxville, Tenn.: University of Tennessee Press. This history of a black town in Monroe County, Kentucky, is based on interviews with the inhabitants. It includes a short genealogy of both the black and white branches of the Coe family.

National Archives and Records Service. 1969. *Registers of Signatures of Depositors in Branches of the Freedmen's Savings and Trust Company, 1865-1874.* Washington, D.C.: National Archives and Records Service. Microcopy M816.

——. 1984. *Black Studies: A Select Catalog of National Archives Microfilm Publications.* Washington, D.C.: National Archives Trust Fund Board.

Newman, Deborah L. 1973. *Lists of Free Black Heads of Families in the First Census of the United States, 1790.* Washington, D.C.: National Archives and Record Services.

O'Malley, Nancy, and Emily Parker. 1990. "A Documentary Review of the Rose Street Extension Project Area, Lexington, Kentucky." In *Archaeological Report 228.* Lexington, Ky.: University of Kentucky Program for Cultural Resource Assessment. This archaelogical report gives a history of a post-Civil War black neighborhood in Lexington called Kinkeadtown. Gives good insight into the everyday life of blacks during this time period. Contains a few oral history interviews.

Parrish, C. H., ed. 1915. *Golden Jubilee of the General Association of Colored Baptists in Kentucky.* Louisville, Ky.: Mayes Printing Company.

Peters, Norman R. 1987. "Free Black Residents of Logan County, Kentucky, 1850." *Kentucky Ancestors.* 23:178-83.

Porter, Kenneth W. 1971. *The Negro on the American Frontier.* New York: Arno Press.

Puckett, Newbell N., and Murray Heller. 1975. *Black Names in America: Origins and Usage.* Boston: G. K. Hall and Company.

Rawick, George P., ed. 1972. *The American Slave: A Composite Autobiography* Westport, Conn.: Greenwood Publishing Company.

Robinson, Lottie Offett. 1983. *The Bond-Washington Story: The Education of Black People, Elizabethtown, Kentucky.* Elizabethtown, Ky.: Bond Washington School.

Sears, Richard. 1987. "John G. Fee, Camp Nelson, and Kentucky Blacks, 1864-1865." *The Register of the Kentucky Historical Society* 85:29-45.

——. 1989. "Working Like a Slave: Views of Slavery and the Status of Women in Antebellum Kentucky." *The Register of the Kentucky Historical Society* 87:1-19.

Smith, Leslie S. 1979. *A Black History Around Muhlenberg County, Kentucky.* Evansville, Ind.: Unigraphic.

Streets, David H. 1986. *Slave Genealogy: A Research Guide with Case Studies.* Bowie, Md.: Heritage Books. Three case studies are included that use Wayne County, Kentucky records.

Sue, Jacqueline Annette. 1983. *Black Seeds in the Blue Grass.* Corte Madera, Calif.: Khedcanron Press.

Thomas, Herbert A., Jr. 1973. "Victims of Circumstance: Negroes in a Southern Town, 1865–1880." *Register of the Kentucky Historical Society* 71, no. 3:253–71.

Timberlake, C. L. 1973. "The Early Struggle for Education of the Blacks in the Commonwealth of Kentucky." *Register of the Kentucky Historical Society* 71, no. 3:253–71.

Tippie, Gwendolyn, comp. 1980a. *Afro-American Births of Adair thru Bath County, Kentucky, 1852–1862.* The author. Available at the University of Kentucky special collections library.

———, comp. 1980b. *Afro-American Deaths of Adair thru Boyle County, Kentucky, 1852-1862.* The author. Available at the University of Kentucky special collections library.

Vanderpool, Montgomery. 1985. *Colored Marriage Bonds, Logan County, Kentucky to 1900.* Russellville, Ky.: the author.

Walker, Juliet E. K. 1983. *Free Frank: A Black Pioneer on the Antebellum Frontier.* Lexington, Ky.: University of Kentucky Press.

Wax, Darold D. 1983. "Robert Ball Anderson, A Kentucky Slave, 1843–1864." *The Register of the Kentucky Historical Society* 81:255–73.

Webb, Ross A. 1986. "The Past Is Never Dead, It's Not Even Past: Benjamin P. Runkle and the Freedmen's Bureau in Kentucky, 1866–1870." *The Register of the Kentucky Historical Society* 84:343–60.

Witcher, Curt Bryan. 1989. *Bibliography of Sources for Black Family History in the Allen County Public Library Genealogy Department.* Unpublished manuscript. Contains a state-by-state bibliography of black history sources available in one of the largest city genealogy libraries in the country.

Woodson, Carter G. 1925. *Free Negro Heads of Families in the United States Census of 1830.* Association for the Study of Negro Life and History.

Wright, George C. 1985. *Life Behind a Veil: Blacks in Louisville, Kentucky 1865-1930.* Baton Rouge: Louisiana State University Press. A well-researched and documented book of black life in Louisville from the end of the Civil War until 1930.

———. 1990a. *Racial Violence in Kentucky, 1865–1940: Lynchings, Mob Rule, and "Legal Lynchings."* Baton Rouge: Louisiana State University Press.

———. 1990b. "The Forced Removal of Afro-Americans from Rural Kentucky." *Reflections* 1, no. 1.

APPENDIX 5

FOLKLORE AND SOCIAL HISTORY BIBLIOGRAPHY

One of the pleasures of genealogy is learning about the times and events that influenced our ancestors. Genealogy without knowledge of how our ancestors lived, what they believed, and how they thought, would be empty indeed. Kentucky is fortunate to have many resources that explore its social history. Two examples are the state's fine oral history project administered by the Kentucky Oral History Commission and the University of Kentucky's historical archives of family papers and letters.

In addition, there are many published sources whose subject is Kentucky and its people. Below is a listing of books and novels that give insight into the lives of early Kentucky and Virginia families. This listing has been compiled based on works that are well written and readily available either in print or in libraries. It is not by any means complete.

Special thanks to Ms. Julie Wiley who reviewed early drafts of this bibliography and added to it.

Andrews, Charles M. *Colonial Folkways.* New Haven, Conn.: Yale University Press, 1919. This book chronicles American life in the reign of the Georges. The chapters cover the land and the people, colonial houses, everyday needs, occupations, diversions, travel, habits, and religion. Arnow, Harriett Simpson. *The Kentucky Trace.* New York: Alfred Knopf, 1974. This novel, from the author of *The Dollmaker* and *Hunter's Horn* is about Kentuckians during the Revolutionary War period. The setting is in the Cumberlands as are Arnow's two other social histories: *The Flowering of the Cumberland* and *Seedtime on the Cumberland. The Flowering of the Cumberland* discusses everyday life in the Tennessee/Kentucky area from ca. 1780. *Seedtime on the Cumberland* is a story of how men from the southern colonies lived and took care of providing for their physical needs such as food, clothing, shelter, and the struggle to hold the land.

Bird, Robert Montgomery. *Nick of the Woods or The Jibbenainosay.* Edited by Curtis Dahl. New Haven, Conn.: College and University Press Publishers, 1967. One of the most popular and widely read novels about the western frontier is *Nick of the Woods.* This reprint of the original 1837 book is set on the Kentucky frontier. The novel is noted for its extraordinarily vivid and realistic picture of ordinary life in Kentucky in the latter part of the eighteenth century.

Brownstone, Douglass L. *A Field Guide to America's History.* New York: Facts on File, 1984. Brownstone gives information to help you read the environment and make a family history come alive. The book tells how to uncover ruins of old mills or factories, to date houses, and to locate bridges or old inns. It is a good reference and gives many clues in preparation for that visit to the old Kentucky homestead.

Clark, Thomas D. *Frontier America.* New York: Scribner and Sons, 1969. Dr. Clark's classic textbook on the frontier is essentially a history of Kentucky; it also contains information on the nature of the frontier society.

Clark, Thomas D. *The Rampaging Frontier.* Bloomington, Ind.: University Press, 1964. This book discusses the "manner and humors of pioneer days." Dr. Clark has published many books dealing with Kentucky history. The time period covers generally from 1775 to 1850. See also *Kentucky: Land of Contrasts.*

Coleman, J. Winston, Jr. *Sketches of Kentucky's Past.* Lexington, Ky.: Winburn Press, 1979. Thirty-five short essays that cover events in Kentucky's history from the Revolutionary War to the present. Most of this book is historical in nature, but there are many references to everyday life in Kentucky. Coleman also published many other books of interest such as *Slavery Times in Kentucky.*

Deetz, James. *In Small Things Forgotten: The Archaeology of Early American Life.* Garden City, N.Y.: Anchor Books, 1977. This slim volume gives a scholarly but lively view of the methods of historical archaeology. The concept that beneath your feet may lie the remnants of your ancestors' lives is quite fascinating.

Drake, Daniel. *Pioneer Life in Kentucky 1785–1800.* Edited by Emmet F. Horine. New York: Schuman, 1948. The classic work of early pioneer Kentucky as told by Drake through a series of letters to his children. Edited with notes and a biographical sketch by his son, Charles D. Drake.

Earle, Alice Morse. *Home Life in Colonial Days*. Stockbridge, Mass.: Berkshire Traveller Press, 1974. Morse wrote this work in 1898. She has published other works of everyday life in colonial America, but this is her best. The book vividly describes such topics as lighting of the homes, preparation of meals, dress, industries, leisure pursuits, and customs of the colonists.

Eckert, Allan. *The Frontiersmen*. New York: Little Brown and Company, 1967. This is one of Eckert's remarkable historical presentations. Eckert reconstructs true stories of the western frontier from the viewpoint of both the settlers and the Indians. The work is based on meticulous research of primary sources such as the Draper manuscripts. This volume directly covers Kentucky and centers around the life of Simon Kenton.

Egerton, John. *Generations: An American Family*. New York: Simon and Schuster, 1983. This family history gives the family biography and social history of Burnam and Addie Ledford via oral history by many family members.

Giles, Janice Holt. *The Kentuckians*. Boston: Houghton Mifflin Company, 1953. This novel is about the people who first migrated through the Cumberland Gap and established homes in the wilderness during the Revolutionary War. Giles used the journals of early Kentuckians and has tried to tell their story in an authentic manner. Only three of the central characteristics are fictional. The rest of the book, including the historical events, are authentic.

Hawke, David Freeman. *Everyday Life in Early America*. New York: Harper Row, 1988. One of a series of books on the subject of everyday life, this volume focuses on the very early American settlers. Among the fascinating topics covered are the manners, morals, customs, beliefs, and behaviors of the first Americans as they made their home in a strange new world.

Klotter, James. *The Breckinridges of Kentucky: 1760-1981*. Lexington, Ky.: University of Kentucky Press, 1986. This fine work combines the narrative of a family history with the insights of the new social history.

Larkin, Jack. *The Reshaping of Everyday Life: 1790-1840*. New York: Harper Row, 1988. The social history of the daily lives of Americans in the first 50 years of the new republic is told in this book, often in their own words. Contains many Kentucky, Ohio, and Pennsylvania references.

Lebsock, Suzanne. *The Free Women of Petersburg: Status and Culture in a Southern Town, 1784-1860*. New York: W. W. Norton and Company, 1984. Dr. Lebsock uses letters, diaries, and official records to study the women of Petersburg, Virginia. Her exploration of their lives, behaviors, attitudes, and beliefs demonstrates the impact of the social world upon individual lives.

McVey, Frances J., and Robert Berry Jewell. *Uncle Will of Wildwood: Nineteenth-Century Life in the Bluegrass*. Lexington, Ky.: University Press of Kentucky, 1974. This memoir of the nineteenth-century bluegrass tells the story of Uncle Will who owned a large farm near Harrodsburg. The book was written by a brother and sister team based on their memories of their maternal great uncle.

Merrill, Boynton, Jr. *Jefferson's Nephews: A Frontier Tragedy*. New York: Avon Books, 1976. This narrative chronicles the life of an aristocratic Virginia family who moves to western Kentucky in 1807. This well-documented book is also well written. The author gives an especially memorable description of the earthquake of 1811. The book contains an excellent and extensive bibliography.

Moore, Arthur. *The Frontier Mind: A Cultural Analysis of Kentucky Frontiersmen*. Lexington, Ky.: University of Kentucky Press, 1957. While not a social history per se, Moore analyzes why people came to Kentucky and how Kentucky was perceived by would-be immigrants. As a result, he explores motivations for coming to the Kentucky "paradise."

Miller, John C. *The First Frontier: Life in Colonial America*. New York: Dell Publishing, 1976. This work recreates the everyday experiences of the earliest generations of Americans through the use of original letters, public documents, diary entries, and comments of travelers. The first Americans from Massachusetts to Virginia speak in their own voices in this well-documented and well-written book.

Mitchell, John Hanson. *Ceremonial Time: Fifteen Thousand Years on One Square Mile*. Garden City, N.Y.: Anchor Press/Doubleday, 1984. The events in this book take place thirty-five miles west of Boston. The author traces the history of a one square mile plot of land from prehistory to the present day.

Raine, James W. *The Land of Saddlebags*. Detroit, Mich.: Singing Tree Press/Book Tower, 1969. This 1924 study of the mountain people of Appalachia is by a former head of the Department of English at Berea College. Covers Appalachian's heritage, habits, occupations, religion, and pastimes.

Roberts, Elizabeth Madox. *The Great Meadow*. New York: Viking Press, 1930. This novel recounts the trek of the American pioneer toward the wilderness in the 1770s. The story centers around a young married couple from Virginia who settle in Kentucky. The author presents a good picture of everyday frontier life.

Sutherland, Daniel E. *The Expansion of Everyday Life: 1860–1876*. New York: Harper & Row, 1989. Sutherland outlines the content and structure of the personal lives of millions of ordinary Americans during a period of rapid culture change through diaries, letters, and the popular press. The era of the Civil War, the reconstruction, western movement boosted by the first intercontinental railroad, and migration from the farms to the urban areas is described in this lively book.

Thom, James Alexander. *Follow the River.* New York: Random House, 1981. The novel is based on the true ordeal of Mary Draper Ingles who was captured in 1755 by Shawnee Indians while living in Virginia. She was taken to Big Bone Lick in present-day Boone County, Kentucky. The novel focuses on her captivity and her travels back home by following the Ohio River. Thom has published other historical books that are excellent, such as *Long Knife* and *From Sea to Shining Sea*, which is about George Rogers Clark.

Van Every, Dale. *Forth to the Wilderness.* New York: William Morrow and Company, 1962. This history gives a detailed picture of colonial Americans who fought for, and conquered, the Appalachian mountain barrier, gateway to the western frontier. The book covers the period 1754 to 1774.

Wade, Richard C. *The Urban Frontier: Pioneer Life in Early Pittsburgh, Cincinnati, Lexington, Louisville, and St. Louis.* Chicago: University of Chicago Press, 1959. The development of the important pioneer river cities of the Ohio Valley is recounted in this fascinating book. The development of each city during the period of 1790 to 1815, including the economic base and the development of urban services, is discussed in the first section of the book. The author discusses the 1815–30 period, including the Depression and changing social structures of the cities in the second section. The book is a scholarly work based on primary documents and is must reading for understanding urban ancestors.

Waller, Altina L. *Feud: Hatfields, McCoys, and Social Change in Appalachia.* Chapel Hill, N.C.: University of North Carolina Press, 1988. This social history covers the period of 1860 to 1900.

Wamsley, James S. *Idols, Victims, Pioneers: Virginia's Women from 1607.* Richmond, Va.: Virginia State Chamber of Commerce, 1976. The role women played in settling the Virginia frontier, from the London Company period, 1607 through 1624, to the nineteenth century.

APPENDIX 6

COUNTY HISTORIC SITES SURVEYS

The information provided below is the most current available from the Kentucky Heritage Council. However, prices may have increased and some publications may no longer be in print.

STATEWIDE

Kentucky Heritage Commission. 1971. *Survey of Historic Sites in Kentucky.* Frankfort, Kentucky.

BALLARD

1978. *Survey of Historic Sites in Kentucky: Ballard County.* $7.50. Order from Kentucky Heritage Council, 12th Floor, Capital Plaza Tower, Frankfort, Kentucky 40601.

BOONE

Survey of Historic Sites: Boone County. $5. Order from Boone County Extension Service, Box 218, Burlington, Kentucky 41005.

BOURBON

Langsam, Walter, and William G. Johnson. 1985. *Historic Architecture of Bourbon County, Kentucky.* Order from Historic Paris-Bourbon County, Inc., Ms. Susan Hinkle, 1500 Cane Ridge Road, Paris, Kentucky 40361.

BOYD

Chappell, Edward. 1978. *A Historic Preservation Plan for Ashland, Kentucky*. Order from City of Ashland, Planning and Community Development, 17th and Greenup Avenue, Ashland, Kentucky 41101.

CHRISTIAN

Gibbs, Kenneth, and Carolyn Torma. 1982. *Hopkinsville and Christian County Historic Sites*. $5. Order from Hopkinsville Pride, Inc., 1904 South Main, Hopkinsville, Kentucky 42240.

CLARK

Torma, Carolyn, et al. 1979. *Survey of Historic Sites in Kentucky: Clark County*. Order from James Kirby, president, Clark County Historical Society, 122 Bellmont, Winchester, Kentucky 40391.

FLEMING

1978. *Survey of Historic Sites in Kentucky: Fleming County*. $9. Order from Kentucky Heritage Council, 12th Floor Capital Plaza Tower, Frankfort, Kentucky 40601.

GARRARD

Ballard, Patricia, and Helen Powell. 1987. *Historic Sites of Lancaster and Garrard County, Kentucky*. 1987. Order from Lancaster Women's Club, Box 647, Lancaster, Kentucky 40444.

GREEN

Historic Architecture of Green County, Kentucky. Order from Green County Historical Society, Box 376, Greensburg, Kentucky 42743.

HARDIN

Order from Tim Asher, 14 Public Square, Elizabethtown, Kentucky 42701.

HENDERSON

Merrill, Boynton, Jr. 1985. *Old Henderson Homes*. Order from Historic Henderson Publishing Council, Henderson County Public Library, Henderson, Kentucky 42420.

JEFFERSON

Jones, Elizabeth, and Mary Jean Kinsman. 1981. *Survey of Historic Sites in Kentucky: Jefferson County.* $7.50. Order from Jefferson Company Historic Preservation, 100 Fiscal Court Building, Louisville, Kentucky 40202.

JESSAMINE

1979. *Survey of Historic Sites in Kentucky: Jessamine County.* $7.50. Order from Jessamine County Historical Society, 102 Richmond Avenue, Nicholasville, Kentucky 40356.

JOHNSON

1985. *Historic Sites of Paintsville and Johnson County, Kentucky.* Order from Johnson County Historical Society, Box 788, Paintsville, Kentucky 41240.

McCRACKEN

Wells, Camille. 1981. *Architecture of Paducah and McCracken County.* $7. Order from Paducah County Growth, Inc., Box 2632, Paducah, Kentucky 42001.

MADISON

Kubiak, Lavina H. 1988. *Madison County Rediscovered: Selected Historic Architecture.* Order from Madison County Historical Society, 204 Lancaster Avenue, Richmond, Kentucky 40475.

MERCER

Powell, Helen. 1988. *Historic Sites of Harrodsburg and Mercer County, Kentucky.* Order from Harrodsburg Landmark Association, Box 362, Harrodsburg, Kentucky 40330.

PULASKI

Torma, Carolyn, et al. 1985. *Architecture and Historic Sites of Pulaski County.* Order from Wayne Eastman, president, Pulaski Heritage, Inc., Box 683, Somerset, Kentucky 42501.

SCOTT

1981. *A History of Scott County As Told by Selected Buildings.* $32.50. Order from Ann Bevins, 1175 Lexington Pike, Georgetown, Kentucky 40324.

WARREN

1984. *Architecture of Warren County, Kentucky 1790-1940.* Order from Landmark Association of Bowling Green, 914 1/2 State Street, Box 1812, Bowling Green, Kentucky 42101-1812.

INDEX

Roseann Reinemuth Hogan was born in Mannheim, Germany, to an Irish-American father and a German mother. She holds a B.S., M.A., and Ph.D. in sociology. She was raised in the Cincinnati/Northern Kentucky area and has been researching her family since 1978. Her special interests include early Kentucky oral histories, women's histories, and social history.

Dr. Hogan is married to Dennis Haggard. They are the parents of one son, Derek.